YALE SOUTHEAST ASIA STUDIES, 4

Editorial Committee

Harry J. Benda
Harold C. Conklin
Karl J. Pelzer
Robert O. Tilman

Library of Congress catalog card number: 77–81435
SBN 300–01156–3
Designed by Helen Frisk Buzyna,
set in Garamond type,
and printed in the United States of America by
The Carl Purington Rollins Printing-Office
of the Yale University Press, New Haven, Connecticut.
Distributed in Great Britain, Europe, Asia, and
Africa by Yale University Press Ltd., London; in
Canada by McGill-Queen's University Press, Montreal; and
in Mexico by Centro Interamericano de Libros
Académicos, Mexico City.

The Politics of Reform
In Thailand: Education in the

Reign of King Chulalongkorn

by David K. Wyatt

New Haven and London, Yale University Pr

To
Alene

Preface

The reign of King Chulalongkorn (1868-1910) is generally accepted as the period during which Thailand, by astute leadership and timely modernization, built its foundations as a modern nation. During this forty-two year period, Thailand's rulers actively set about transforming every facet of national life. They entered into a creative process of national development at a time when the impact of the West was at its greatest, yet maintained their national identity as Thai.

Thailand's modernization and political survival have come to be represented as products of the fortuitous historical circumstances that allowed her to balance against each other the French and British threats to her independence and of the ability of her absolute, but Westernized, monarch to force the introduction of Western institutions and techniques suggested by his numerous foreign advisers.[1] Such an interpretation of this important period in Thai history fails to explain what happened and merely describes; and for lack of adequate historical materials, the most crucial domestic factors in this process have been left undescribed. Thailand's response to the West was a creative one which flowed painfully but naturally out of Thai history, society, and culture to transform the old Kingdom of Siam into a new and modern Thai nation. The central problem

1. See, for example, D. G. E. Hall, *A History of South-East Asia* (2d ed. London, 1964), chs. 36–37; and John F. Cady, *Southeast Asia: Its Historical Development* (New York, 1964), ch. 21.

in dealing with the reign of King Chulalongkorn is, first, to add to the description of the challenge and the response some indication of the conditions that governed the perception of the challenge and the formulation of the response, and second, to see this dynamic and creative process within the context of Thai history.

Eighty years ago, in the midst of this period, the editor of the *Bangkok Times* deplored the fact that "We know nothing about [the Siamese] except in the vaguest possible way, through a distorting myth and fable."[2] The passage of time has done little to dispel that cloud. Thailand has not been without its historians, Siamese and foreign, but they have been far too few, the bulk of their energies has been expended on the earlier periods of Thai history, and the work of Siamese historians far too often has remained untranslated. Ample materials exist for the serious study of most of the long span of Thai history,[3] but the work of Vella, Skinner, and Ingram has hardly begun to exhaust their potentialities.[4] Thus a fair, detailed, and comprehensive study of Thai modernization probably cannot be expected in this generation: the subject is too vast, the materials are too numerous, and the time required for their digestion is too great to allow for a quick answer to this complex problem. The Thailand of 1910 was very different from that of 1851. Its transformation was accomplished at an exorbitant cost in mental and physical energy, which to some degree touched everyone in the kingdom. The reign of Chulalongkorn brought administrative, judicial, and financial reform; the development of modern communications; the first stirrings of political development; the growth of social services; and great economic

2. "Siamese Historians: A Want," *Bangkok Times,* 17 Mar. 1888.
3. See David K. Wyatt and Constance M. Wilson, "Thai Historical Materials in Bangkok," *Journal of Asian Studies,* 25 (Nov. 1965), 105–118.
4. Walter F. Vella, *The Impact of the West on Government in Thailand* (Berkeley and Los Angeles, 1955), and *Siam Under Rama III* (Locust Valley, N.Y., 1957); G. William Skinner, *Chinese Society in Thailand* (Ithaca, N.Y., 1957); and James C. Ingram, *Economic Change in Thailand Since 1850* (Stanford, 1955).

development. It was also a period of intense conflict and controversy, and of serious danger to the nation. The present work is an attempt to begin to understand this momentous period through an examination of one small facet of Thailand's modernization: the development of modern education.

This study is not intended as a history of education in Thailand, for others have adequately covered that subject.[5] What is attempted here is both more broadly and more narrowly conceived. First, this study is concerned with only one period in Thai educational history, the period during which the Thai made the transition from their own centuries-old educational practices to a Western educational system. It is concerned only with government educational efforts and almost exclusively with education for boys. Second, this study is more broadly defined in its attempt to relate this transition to the context within which it occurred, taking into account the political, economic, and sociocultural factors that conditioned the course of Thai history in this critical period.

Underlying this research has been the assumption that some light may be shed on the totality of the reign of King Chulalongkorn by the detailed examination of one aspect of its development. The validity of this assumption has in large measure been confirmed in the course of some years' work. In dealing with the problems of educational reform, Thailand's rulers faced the same basic political and economic constraints, although perhaps to a lesser degree, that they encountered in pressing for administrative, financial, and judicial reforms. Educational matters called forth from them serious examinations of a deeper nature: they were forced to ask and answer the question of what sort of nation and society they wished to build; a question that at least implicitly was an essential part of every discussion of educational policy. They came to realize

5. See M. L. Manich Jumsai, *Compulsory Education in Thailand* (Paris, 1955); and the theses on Thai education by Ambhorn Meesook, Boonsom Arawarop, Swat Sukonterangsi, and Tasniya Isarasena, details of which are given in the Bibliography.

that education was a prerequisite for, or at least a concomitant of, political, economic, and social development. Finally, it seems that, in connection with educational questions more often than with others, Thailand's rulers were forced to a consideration of the nature of modernization as the confrontation of Thailand and the West, a situation in which the commerce in ideas and techniques had to be regulated both by the Thai understanding of the West and by their understanding of themselves.

The process of educational reform ran parallel to similar changes in other facets of national life, and it shared in common with them the unmistakable direction of the king, who intermittently reached into the process to prod it along, ever faster. Ideally, this study should have been placed fully into the context of these wider developments. Although an attempt has been made to do so at those points in time when it seemed most necessary (particularly in Chapters 2 and 4), these excursions into political life and administrative and financial developments are sketchy, based upon materials even more fragmentary than those bearing upon early educational development. The author would hope, above all else, to succeed in enticing others to pick up the threads he has left dangling.

Acknowledgments

The completion of this book has taken an embarrassingly long time, and the number of people and institutions who have assisted me has grown correspondingly. To my teachers at Cornell University, for whom it originally was written as a doctoral dissertation, I owe an everlasting debt for their patient assistance, advice, encouragement, and inspiration, particularly to Knight Biggerstaff, Lauriston Sharp, and O. W. Wolters. It is a great pleasure for me to acknowledge the assistance and friendship of many in Bangkok who helped to make my stay and research there in 1962–63 both productive and pleasant. Among them, I must single out Dhanit Yupho, Director-General of the Fine Arts Department; Tri Amatyakul, then Head of the Literature and History Division of the Fine Arts Department; Thawat Sumawong, Head of the National Archives; Čharat Kamphlasiri, Head of the Documents Section; and Praphat Trinarong, Head of the National Diary Section in the National Archives; Sa-nguan Ankhong of the National Library; Bunčhüa Ongkhapradit of the Teachers' Institute Library; J. J. Boeles, Director of the Siam Society Research Center; and Chucheep Thiarabongse Boyle, Librarian of the Siam Society Research Center. To Kachorn Sukhabanij I am especially grateful for his patient friendship and encouragement.

Many colleagues and friends were generous with their advice and encouragement, particularly A. Thomas Kirsch, John Smail, William R. Roff, and Thamsook Numnonda. This project could neither have been begun nor completed without the generous financial assistance of the Foreign Area Training Fellowship Program, the Southeast Asia Program of Cornell University, and the London-Cornell Project for East and South-East Asian Studies, to all of which I owe a deep debt of gratitude.

To my wife, Alene Wilson Wyatt, go my loving thanks for tolerating this rival so graciously, for so long.

David K. Wyatt

London
27 April 1968

Contents

TABLES

Illustrations

Notes and Abbreviations

TRANSCRIPTION

Throughout this study, the "General System of Phonetic Transcription of Thai Characters into Roman" has been employed, as set forth in the supplement to *Phraya* Anuman Rajadhon, *The Nature and Development of the Thai Language* (2d ed. Bangkok, Fine Arts Dept., 1963), pp. 32–36. There are two exceptions. First, *ü* has been used in place of *u'*. Second, in the case of personal names and titles I have wherever possible followed the known preferences of the individuals concerned, as with King Chulalongkorn (and not Čhulalongkǫn), who himself signed his letters "Chulalongkorn" in the early years of his reign. I have followed Thai practice in referring to individuals by their personal names and in making no distinction between the singular and plural of Thai words; thus, "a *monthon*" and "two *monthon.*" I have also maintained the Pali spellings of such well-known terms as *Sangha* (monkhood) and *Vinaya* (discipline), in preference to their phonetic Thai equivalents.

CHRONOLOGY

Three chronological systems were found in use in the materials for this study. The earliest was the *Čhunlasakkarat* (Č.s.)

or Lesser Era of the Burmese ($+638$ = A.D.). It was superseded in the late 1880s by the Bangkok Era, *Rattanakosinsok*
(R.S. $+$ 1781 = A.D.), which in turn gave way to the Buddhist
Era, *Phutthasakkarat* (B.E. — 543 = A.D.), in 1911. The traditional Thai luni-solar calendar began the year in April, in
the fifth or sixth month of the lunar calendar, and until 1940
the official Thai year ran from 1 April to 31 March. Accordingly, in converting all dates to the Gregorian calendar, I have
had to use such cumbrous forms as "1888/89" to convey the
exact equivalent of "R.S. 107."

ABBREVIATIONS

Documents	Thailand, Fine Arts Dept., eds., *Phrabqromma-rachowat phrabat somdet phra čhunlačhqmklao čhaoyuhua phraratchathan phračhaolukyathoe phraratchaprarop nai phrabat somdet ... waduai rüang kasian ayu kap samnao krasae phrabqrom-maratcha-ongkan phraratchabanyat phraratcha-damrat phraratchahatlekha lae prakat kansüksa nai samai phrabat somdet ...* Bangkok, 1966.
DUSCB	United States, Consulate, Thailand, *Despatches from United States Consuls in Bangkok, 1856–1906,* 11 Reels of microfilm, Washington, D.C., 1959.
FO	United Kingdom, Public Record Office, Foreign Office Series.
JSS	*Journal of the Siam Society,* Bangkok, 1904–.
NA	National Archives Division, Fine Arts Depart-ment, Ministry of Education, Bangkok. See Bib-liography for explanation of system used in citing documents.
PKPS	Sathian Laiyalak et al., comps., *Prachum kotmai pračham sok,* 69 vols. Bangkok, 1935–53.
PSSR	Kings Chulalongkorn and Vajiravudh, *Phrarat-*

chahatlekha song sang ratchakan nai ratchakan thi 5 lae 6 kap rüang prakǫp, Bangkok, 1964.

RKB *Ratchakitčhanubeksa,* Bangkok, 1858, 1874–79, 1888–.

SWA *Siam Weekly Advertiser, Bangkok,* 1869–86.

1

Early Education and Thai Society

Underlying and permeating the modern educational system introduced in Thailand in the reign of King Chulalongkorn was a complex of educational patterns deeply embedded in traditional Thai culture. Over more than seven centuries these patterns had served the corporate and personal ends of the society and its members and had facilitated the creation and perpetuation of a distinctive Siamese civilization. Profoundly characteristic of this old system of education was its organic relationship with Thai culture as a whole and with the historical development of the Kingdom of Siam. Thai education systematically evolved to meet changing political and cultural situations, and it both responded to pressures for change and creatively shaped their issue. The structure and content of Thai education maintained a continuity with the past, while ingesting and integrating the products of foreign arts and sciences.

SUKHOTHAI

The first major Thai kingdom was founded at the town of Sukhothai, on the northern edge of the great Central Plain of the Čhaophraya River system, in the first quarter of the thirteenth century. The political and cultural foundations of Sukhothai established by its great rulers, from King Ram Khamhaeng at the end of the thirteenth century to King Lü Thai at the middle of the fourteenth, served as models and examples to be perpetuated and elaborated upon by later Thai kingdoms further to the south at Ayudhya and Bangkok. By examining the interrelationships between religion, statecraft and education in the Kingdom of Sukhothai, one can gain an appreciation of the threads of continuity and the discontinuities, the elements of stability and diversity, in Thai education and cultural life from the thirteenth century to the nineteenth and can thereby enlighten the study of the great changes that King Chulalongkorn introduced.

The foundation of the Kingdom of Sukhothai around A.D. 1219 occurred, at least in part, within the context of a more general political revolution against the earlier Indianized empires of mainland Southeast Asia, and specifically against the Khmer empire of Angkor, so distinguished over the previous four centuries for the brilliance with which it built upon the cultural and political models of classical Indian civilization. Sukhothai, as an outlying province of the Angkorian empire in the twelfth century, probably was dominated politically and culturally by men educated in the classical Indian tradition and representative of Angkorian society: the nobles, Brahmans, merchants, astrologers, and physicians recalled in a later inscription.[1] The position of such men in Sukhothai society may have been temporarily eclipsed in the early years of independence, an era of Thai reaction against all that recalled an earlier period of Khmer domination,[2] when they were displaced from the inscriptions by Thai warriors and learned Buddhist monks, and the civilization for which they stood, essentially Hinduistic in tenor, was replaced by a blend of Theravada Buddhism and the primeval animism of the Thai.

Certainly from at least the reign of Ram Khamhaeng, Bud-

1. G. Coedès, ed. and tr., *Recueil des inscriptions du Siam, première partié: Inscriptions de Sukhodaya* (Bangkok, 1924), p. 77.

2. G. Coedès, "L'art siamois de l'époque de Sukhodaya (XIIIe–XIVe siècles): circonstances de son éclosion," *Arts asiatiques*, *I*, no. 4 (1954), 281–302.

dhism was the dominant force in the intellectual life of Sukhothai. All the inscriptions of Sukhothai are essentially Buddhist
in nature and extol the merits of its kings in Buddhist terms of
piety, conformity to the Law, patronage of the *Sangha,* and the
defense and propagation of the faith. The revival of classical
Indian learning, however, was necessary in terms both of Sukhothai's inheritance from its predecessor states in central Indochina and of the quintessentially Indian character of Buddhism,
which is as much a total intellectual system as a religious faith
and ethical system. Gradually, the balance was restored, and
Sukhothai came to terms with the heritage of India. A syncretic
cosmological foundation for the political and moral universe
was constructed of Buddhist and Hindu elements, and the
representatives of Indian learning regained much of their earlier
prominence. The growth and development of scholarship was
nourished by efforts that had been made to domesticate Hindu
traditions in the Buddhist Mōn country of Lower Burma. Indian
legal thought, exemplified in the *Dharmaśāstra* of Manu, was
introduced through the medium of Mōn versions which already
had been so transmuted as to permit their application in Buddhist Southeast Asian societies in which castes did not exist and
in which women enjoyed a position unthinkable in India.[3] It
was likewise from the Mōn that King Lü Thai probably obtained the classical Buddhist texts upon which he based his
Traibhūmikathā, the cosmological and ethical work that he
composed in 1345.[4] It was the same king who had at his court
Brahmans and other men to teach him the Vedas and classical

3. Committee for the Publication of Historical, Cultural, and Archeological Records, comps., *Prachum sila čharuk, phak thi 3* (Bangkok, 1965),
pp. 25–38 (inscription XXXVIII, face A, lines 22, 33, 39; face B, lines 1,
24, 32). On the role of the Mōn in modifying the *Dharmaśāstra,* see R.
Lingat, "L'Influence indoue dans l'ancien droit siamois," Etudes de sociologie
et d'ethnologie juridiques, Faculte de Droit de Paris, *Conferences* (1936),
pp. 1–29, and "Evolution of the Conception of Law in Burma and Siam,"
JSS, 38, pt. 1 (1950), 9–31.
4. G. Coedès, "The Traibhūmikathā: Buddhist Cosmology and Treaty
on Ethics," *East and West,* 7 (1957), 349–52.

Indian treatises on the arts and sciences.[5] By the middle of the fourteenth century Sukhothai had been drawn into the intellectual and religious traditions of mainland Southeast Asia, in all their variety; and while Buddhism enjoyed a preeminent position in the life of the state, Sukhothai maintained a continuity with the great traditions that so distinguished the "Indianized states" of Southeast Asia.

Given this intellectual continuity between Khmer Sukhothai and the kingdom of King Lü Thai, it remains to be explained how the classical Indian arts and sciences might have been perpetuated. There are at least four alternative answers to this question. First, while the Brahmans, astrologers, and physicians may have lost their primacy with the advent of Thai rule, there is little reason to suppose that they disappeared altogether from the kingdom, particularly as the state's epigraphy continued to refer to the sorts of knowledge with which they were associated. Second, it seems even more likely that Buddhism, in addition to its religious impact, brought with it from Burma and Ceylon (and from the early states of peninsular Siam) many elements of the traditional Indian arts and sciences which were specifically Buddhist neither in origin nor in later orientation or association: they were simply integral elements of Indian civilization.[6] Third, it may well be that the exponents of Indian learning in an earlier, Khmer day were in Thai Sukhothai absorbed into the Buddhist monasteries, to which they were attracted by the new religion, its learned monks, and a contemplative atmosphere.[7] Finally, the early Thai chronicles indicate that the Khmer or Môn city of Lopburi may have served as a center for both Buddhist and classical Indian studies, to which

5. Coedès, *Recueil,* pp. 98–99.

6. Cf. Than Tun, "Religion in Burma, A.D. 1000–1300," *Journal of the Burma Research Society, 42* (1959), 48–49; and Mabel Haynes Bode, *The Pali Literature of Burma* (London, 1909), pp. 20–21, 102–109.

7. In this connection the case of Shin Arahan of Burma is instructive. The son of a Brahman of Thaton in the Môn country, he brought Hinayana Buddhism to the Kingdom of Pagān in 1056. G. Coedès, *Les États hindouisés d'Indochine et d'Indonésie* (3d ed. Paris, 1964), pp. 274–75.

young men were attracted from north Thailand,[8] and undoubtedly there were other such centers.

Whether or not the Brahmanical personnel or books were brought into the Buddhist monasteries, there are ample historical grounds to characterize Buddhist education in general as broadly founded in the great traditions of Indian civilization. Buddhist monastic life in India and Ceylon incorporated much of the secular learning of the Vedic Age. Although Buddhist education might be called "but a phase of the ancient Hindu or Brahminical system of education,"[9] it seems to have moved at an early date into social channels which had not theretofore been its province. To Ceylon, and later to Burma and Indochina, it brought not only a new moral and religious system but also the accumulated wisdom of Indian civilization. Its monks were adept in grammar and the fine arts, law and medicine, arithmetic and astronomy. In Siam, as in Ceylon, "Buddhist monasteries became centres of learning and culture, and bhikkhus had to master all subjects that had to be taught to everyone from prince down to peasant."[10]

The pattern of discipleship found in Indian and Sinhalese Buddhism seems in Southeast Asia to have been embodied in a basic educational practice: the sending of young boys to the monasteries to learn reading and writing and the basic principles of their religion. Thus learning to read and write was a religious act. It began with religious ceremonies on an auspicious day; reading began with Pali invocations calling upon the name of the Buddha; and both teachers and books were

8. Phra Phutthaphukam and Phra Phutthayuan *(Munlasatsana* [Bangkok, 1939], pp. 225–26) pictured Lopburi as a Buddhist center where young men went to study with learned monks; and Phraya Prachakit Korachak *(Phongsawadan yonok* [Bangkok, 1961], p. 270) states that Phraya Ngam Müang of Phayao studied the arts and sciences in Lopburi with a monk who had taught Ram Khamhaeng.

9. Radha Kumud Mookerji, *Ancient Indian Education* (London, 1947), p. 374.

10. Walpola Rahula, *History of Buddhism in Ceylon: The Anuradhapura Period, 3rd Century BC–10th century AC* (Colombo, 1956), pp. 161, 162–65, 292.

6 POLITICS OF REFORM IN THAILAND

treated in the same respectful manner otherwise reserved for objects of religious veneration and for royalty. The boys and young men who went to the monasteries to study were there introduced to the governing principles of life in society. However, because Buddhist monasteries in old Siam were as much the repositories of the secular attainments of Indian civilization as of a specifically Buddhist religious tradition, at least some monasteries in Sukhothai Siam must have functioned as the academies and universities of their day, like the medieval Buddhist university of Nālandā in India[11] or the old church universities of Europe.

In thirteenth- and fourteenth-century Sukhothai the basic patterns of Thai education were set and the unity of religion, statecraft, and education was directed towards common moral ends. The ideals of Buddhist kingship set a standard for the conduct of state affairs and required royal patronage of Buddhist scholarship; and at least formal support for the practice of the Brahmanical cults was required by political and intellectual necessity. The monkhood required for its own preservation a relatively high degree of scholarship and wide distribution of literacy. The secular interest of the state in absorbing peoples of other languages and its tolerant attitude toward remnants of the Hindu religion necessitated the development of a Thai script which could make tonal Thai sensible to speakers of nontonal Môn-Khmer tongues and allow for the expression of Sanskrit and Pali concepts.[12] Finally, the secular and semimagical interests of the society demanded that there be institutional arrangements to provide for the perpetuation of expertise in such essential fields as astronomy and medicine. Together these factors made possible and called forth a set of educational patterns which was, at least in theory, universal, religious in

11. A. L. Basham, *The Wonder that was India* (New York, 1959), pp. 164–65.
12. J. Burnay and G. Coedès, "The Origins of the Sukhodaya Script," *JSS, 21,* pt. 2 (1927); reprinted in *The Siam Society Fiftieth Anniversary Commemorative Publication, 1* (Bangkok, 1954), 199–202.

tone but competent over wide areas of secular learning for those in need of such instruction, and bent to the ends of the society, defined in the widest political and religious terms.

SEVENTEENTH-CENTURY AYUDHYA

The "Indianization" of the Kingdom of Ayudhya may be considered the end product of that process which had begun in Sukhothai in the thirteenth and fourteenth centuries; and there is reason to believe that, had Sukhothai's independent existence been prolonged a century or two, it would have become as "Indianized" as Ayudhya later was. Likewise, it seems likely that by 1350, when Ayudhya was established as a kingdom, it also had developed the same or analogous symptoms of Indianization as were evident in its rival to the north.[13] By the middle of the seventeenth century, Ayudhya bore all the marks of the classical Indian state, primarily through traditions and institutions inherited from its predecessors in the lower Čhaophraya Valley, the Môn and Khmer. The increasing Indianization of Ayudhya did not, however, diminish the role or importance of Buddhism in the life of the country. On the contrary, Buddhism, which flourished during the Ayudhya period, acted as a check upon the influence of Hinduism. The explanation for their mutual growth and elaboration must be sought in terms of the roles these two systems played in the state and in Thai society. The Brahmanical elements provided the kingship with the majestic aura of mystery and a legitimate place in the cosmic order, which, in easily understandable physical terms, buttressed the ·authority it needed to rule over a varied and widely scattered population. Buddhism, in its modifications of an essentially Brahmanical cosmology, directed the moral authority of the

13. These developments may be traced through the first century of Ayudhya's history in the more detailed versions of the Royal Chronicles, e.g. *Phraratchaphongsawadan krung si ayutthaya chabap phra phonnarat wat phrachetuphon* (Bangkok, 1962).

kingship toward ends that were in harmony with the ethical tenets of Buddhism. The Brahmanical concept of the *Devarāja*, the king as god, was modified to make the king the embodiment of the Law, while the reign of Buddhist moral principles ensured that he should be measured against the Law.[14] The effect of this transformation was to strengthen the checks which, in the Khmer empire, Brahmans had attempted to exercise against despotic excesses of absolute rule.[15]

The kings of Ayudhya had all the trappings and symbols of an Indian kingdom, yet Ayudhya was not an Indian kingdom but a Thai one. While many of the Indian elements were present in form, the feeling and spirit of the kingdom were quite different. This was not a result of the incomplete assimilation of the classical system, although the classical system was not completely present (e.g. the caste system was absent). It was as if the Thai had installed the Brahmanical elements how and where they wanted them, for ends that they themselves set and defined within limits imposed by their own cultural, religious, and political predispositions. Just as Thai craftsmen paid careful attention to the classical traditions of Buddhist iconography, yet produced wholly unique images of the Buddha, so the kings of old Siam established all the classical patterns of state and kingship—for example, the cosmological orientation of the kingdom and the strict formal differentiation of official functions—and yet these patterns were so woven into the fabric of the state and society that they did little to interfere with indigenous modes of social behavior.[16]

14. See Prince Dhani Nivat, "The Old Siamese Conception of the Monarchy," *JSS, 36,* pt. 2 (1947), 91–106; reprinted in *The Siam Society Fiftieth Anniversary Commemorative Publication, 2* (Bangkok, 1954), 160–75.

15. H. G. Quaritch Wales, *Ancient Siamese Government and Administration* (London, 1934), pp. 16–17.

16. One of the best examples of the persistence of such behavior is the way in which bureaucratic specialization and the civil-military distinction broke down in the seventeenth and eighteenth centuries. See Wales, *Ancient Siamese Government,* pp. 86–87; and King Chulalongkorn, *Phra-*

Seventeenth-century visitors to Siam described a vigorous and flourishing Buddhism. Their accounts spoke in tones of incredulity of the wealth lavished on the countless monasteries of Ayudhya. The laws of the time indicate that formal measures long had been taken to encourage monastic education and scholarship, for ranks and positions were given to the most learned of the monks[17] and government-supervised ecclesiastical examinations were introduced during the reign of King Narai (1657–88).[18] A Dutch visitor reported that there were about 20,000 "ecclesiastics" in Ayudhya and more than four times that number in the whole kingdom. "The most learned," he wrote, "become priests, and from these priests the chiefs of the temples are chosen, who are held in high honour by the people."[19] The monastic hierarchy, constituted largely on the basis of scholastic attainments, was appointed and supported by the king through a system of royal patronage extended to designated royal monasteries;[20] but the monkhood as a whole depended upon and enjoyed the support of "the common people, who furnish them with food and other necessities."[21]

A highly developed institutional structure, religious and secular, with its bureaucracy, its specialists in the classical arts and sciences, and its establishment of learning centered around the court and the capital, rested upon a solid educational base

ratchadamrat nai phrabat somdet phra chunlachomklao chaoyuhua song thalaeng phraborommarachathibai kaekhai kanpokkhrong phaendin (Bangkok, 1927), pp. 1–12.

17. The "Royal Ordinance on the Provincial and Military Hierarchy" of 1454 (?) *(Kotmai tra sam duang, 1* [Bangkok, 1962], 315) distinguished between monks and novices according to whether or not they were "thoroughly cognizant of the Dhamma."

18. Simon de la Loubere, *A New Historical Relation of the Kingdom of Siam* (London, 1693), p. 115.

19. "Translation of Jeremias van Vliet's Description of the Kingdom of Siam," tr. L. F. van Ravenswaay, *JSS,* 7, pt. 1 (1910), 76–77.

20. By the end of the Ayudhya period there were forty-seven royal monasteries in the capital. Thailand, Fine Arts Dept., eds., *Khamhaikan chao krung kao* (Bangkok, 1964), pp. 214–16.

21. "Van Vliet's Description," pp. 76–77.

which was succinctly described by Joost Schouten, who visited Siam in the 1630s:

> Till their fifth or sixth year the children are allowed to run about the house; then they are sent to the priests to learn to write and read and to acquire other useful arts. Those who serve the priests in public worship [novices] go very seldom home. When they can read and write properly they are sent to learn a trade or to take up some other employment. Frequently, however, the cleverest of them are allowed to pursue their studies, on account of the greater talent which they display. Instruction secular as well as religious is given solely by the priests, till they are qualified to fill public positions and offices. They then discard their yellow robes, but many intelligent and talented pupils remain in the monasteries, in order to become Heads of temples and schools, or Priests.[22]

Several things in this description are striking. First, the practice of sending boys to the monasteries to be instructed is reported by almost all the Europeans who visited Siam in this period and later, and generally they write as though this was a universal practice, applied to all male children. Whether or not all male children actually were able to avail themselves of such educational opportunities, or whether they were equally available throughout the kingdom is difficult to judge.[23] It does appear, however, that there was little by way of a prescribed course of

22. Joost Schouten, *Siam 250 Years Ago: A Description of the Kingdom of Siam, Written in 1636* (Bangkok, 1889), p. 15. "Van Vliet's Description," pp. 87–88, is virtually identical. Loubere *(New Historical Relation,* pp. 87–88) states that monastery education began at seven or eight years of age.

23. Although the "Law on Slavery" *(Kotmai tra sam duang,* 2 [Bangkok, 1962] 285–343) makes no mention of education, it would be reasonable to assume that the children of slaves, children of the poorest classes in the capital, and many rural children were unable to gain access to education. On the other hand, extreme poverty might force a family literally to give a child to a monk to rear and care for, in which case the child might obtain excellent instruction. One such late case was Čhaophraya

study, and that of the boys who began their studies at the age of five or six years, few remained in school beyond puberty, when they underwent the tonsure ceremony and were admitted into the Buddhist novitiate, which most soon left to join their families in the fields.

When a boy began his studies at the local monastery, he typically was presented to a particular monk, perhaps a family member or one with whom his family had some association, and he was expected to serve that monk respectfully.[24] If he lived at home while engaged in his studies, his responsibilities to his teacher were minimal, consisting only in respecting and honoring his teacher and serving him during the day. Most boys, however, lived within the monastery compound and were known as *luksit* or *sitwat*.[25] They had to act as servants for their teachers, helping them with their alms bowls on their morning rounds, assisting in the preparation and serving of meals and in other housekeeping chores such as fetching water, preparing betel, sweeping the floors and grounds, washing pots and utensils, and so forth. During their stay in the monastery, the boys were bound by what could be an elaborate code of regulations which laid particular stress on enforcing respect for their teachers and for learning, and on complete obedience as

---

Yommarat (Pan Sukhum), who became Minister of Local Government late in the reign of King Chulalongkorn. Chulalongkorn, *Samnao phraratchahatlekha suan phra-ong phrabat somdet phra čhunlačhọmklao čhaoyuhua thüng čhaophraya yommarat* (Bangkok, 1939), p. xxiii.

24. For the part of this chapter dealing with traditional education I have relied heavily upon Luang Prasoet Aksọnnit, "Borannasüksa," in Luang Prasoet Aksọnnit and Phraya Si Sunthọn Wohan, *Borannasüksa lae withi sọn nangsü thai* (Bangkok, 1959), pp. 1–73. Luang Prasoet's article was first published in the literary journal *Wachirayan*, 5, nos. 4–5 (1896/97). The author obtained his information from an elderly monk who related to him his own educational experience in the early years of the nineteenth century.

25. *Luksit* (Thai *luk*, "child," + Pali *sissa*, "pupil") might be applied to any child in a student or disciple relationship, while *sitwat* (*sissa* + Thai *wat*, "monastery"), literally "monastery pupil," would apply to him specifically in the context of monastery education.

well as on good manners. Infringement of these regulations generally brought on corporal punishment.[26]

It was the responsibility of the parents of the boy to clothe him and to contribute liberally to the alms bowl of his teacher. On the monk himself fell the burden of caring for the boys committed to his charge, numbering, perhaps, between one and twelve. He was primarily responsible for seeing that they were taught to read and write, and perhaps to figure, and that they were instructed in the principles of Buddhism. He also was responsible to some extent for their physical welfare, for their health and safety. He might counsel his charges, help them out of scrapes, and, if appropriate and feasible, arrange for their higher studies elsewhere or for their ordination as novices or monks. But most of all the monk was teacher, *ačhan* (Sanskrit, *ācāriya)*, and to him would be due unfailing homage and respect throughout the lives of his pupils.

The monasteries *(wat)* to which these boys went for their education were distributed very widely over the kingdom, having been built as acts of merit by a community or its leading members and, particularly in the area around the capital, by the king. The function of these monasteries was primarily religious, but "religious" in its broadest sense. They served as the focus of the religious life of the community, to be sure; but they also engaged in other activities which in a modern context would be considered secular, in much the same way as the medieval Church in Europe did, although never with the same degree of temporal power. The Thai monastery was the center of all learning and art, of medicine and astronomy, law and philosophy, sculpture and science; but all these were ancillary attributes of the monkhood: all were taught by monks, in build-

---

26. Luang Prasoet, "Borannasüksa," pp. 46–48. Mrs. S. G. McFarland ("The Schools of Siam," in Mary Backus, ed., *Siam and Laos as Seen by Our American Missionaries* [Philadelphia, 1884], p. 209) reports that corporal punishment was felt to be such an integral part of education that parents would think their son poorly taught if he were not frequently "birched."

ings constructed for and devoted to religious exercises and the monastic life.

In most monasteries boys were instructed in the *sala wat,* an open wood structure without walls which also was used for the most common religious exercises, the chanting of the sacred scriptures. In larger, more extensive monasteries, the chanting hall *(hǫ suatmon),* the monks' dining hall *(hǫ chan),* the hall for Pali instruction *(sala kan parian),* the monks' cells *(kudi),* or the *vihara* might be used during those portions of the day when they were free. Into these buildings after the morning meal the pupils and their teachers would stroll, seating themselves on mats on the floor, perhaps in small groups scattered about the hall, with their slates and palm-leaf books resting on small bamboo tripods before them. After a short ceremony of prostration before their teacher and their books, the boys would begin by reciting aloud what they had been assigned to memorize the previous day, each boy his own assignment, all at once; their shrill voices, floating in a tumultuous din out of the open building and over its immediate neighborhood, joined with the lower rumbling tones of the teacher-monks, who themselves had passages to memorize. Now and again a boy would stop, have a new passage written on his slate, recopy it, recite it, and memorize it. Occasionally a boy would find that he had finished a particular section and would then be examined by his teacher. Now and then a boy would be caught in an infringement of the rules—dropping his slate, stepping over a book, throwing his chalk pencil, quarreling with his neighbor—and would be given three, five, or ten strokes with the stick his teacher kept for this purpose. And then the din would resume, and the monks and boys again would bend over their slates and books and intone the ancient Pali texts or the various combinations of vowels and consonants.[27]

The most essential characteristic of this system was that, like Thai society, it was open and relatively loosely structured. Boys

27. On the daily life of the monastery, see also Jean Baptiste Pallegoix, *Description du royaume thai ou siam* (2 vols., Paris, 1854), 2, 30–32.

might enter upon their studies at any age, on any Thursday of the year,[28] and they might remain in the monastery for a few weeks or months or for a lifetime. They could enter and leave at any time. The course of studies they followed was geared to this fact. It was relatively informal, having no fixed classes or grades, but rather a series of a great many short steps through which each boy passed at his own speed, in as short a time as one day or as long as several months. This was most characteristic of the elementary stage of education, which was most widespread.

Traditional monastery education was a relatively simple matter, consisting of little more than introducing youths to the workings of the Thai writing system. This system serves almost perfectly to express the sounds of spoken Thai by means of an alphabet. Once learned, it can express in a correct or nearly correct spelling any Thai word, including its tone.[29] Thus, once the boys had learned the twenty-six vowels and forty-four consonants, the mechanics of representing tones by means of different classes of consonants and various tone markers, and a few basic exceptions to the general rules of spelling, they were functionally literate.[30] They would be able to read and write, however slowly, a passage of ordinary prose. This limited proficiency could be attained in a short time, perhaps six months or a year, during which the pupils also were given some grounding in the principal tenets of Buddhism. At the onset of the rainy season, a boy might leave the monastery to help his family in the fields and never return to school; or he might enter the novitiate for a short time and then reenter the secular world; or

28. Thursday was traditionally Teachers' Day and is still the day on which schools open in Thailand.

29. Words of Pali or Sanskrit origin generally have maintained their orthodox spellings in Thai, but they are relatively uncommon in ordinary speech and were even more uncommon in the seventeenth century than they are today.

30. For an excellent general description of the Thai language and its writing system, see Phraya Anuman Rajadhon, *The Nature and Development of the Thai Language* (Bangkok, 1963).

he might continue his studies. If he stayed in the monastery, or returned after a short spell in the fields, he would be given further practice in reading, and, if there happened to be a competent monk in the monastery, usually a specialist, he would be given instruction in mathematics, at a rudimentary level. With such training he would have minimal qualifications for a minor position in government and, if his parents were well situated or his teacher particularly influential, might actually secure a position as a minor clerk in the establishment of a lesser official.

Ordination as a novice marked the passage to a second stage of education, in which the fundamentals were put to work in the pursuit of more specialized knowledge. For all boys it served to mark religious attainment, in the same way that ordination as a monk does today, and for most boys it was the terminal point of their formal education.[31] Princes and the sons of nobles might have received their elementary education at home, from retainers in the palace or the noble's household, but they too entered the novitiate to make what was in effect their profession of faith, the most meritorious act a male could perform. After a few months of religious instruction and the acquisition of a smattering of specialized knowledge[32] they left the monastery and entered upon the vocational phase of their education.

This third stage in the pattern of traditional education, the

31. Prince Damrong Rajanubhab to Prince Naris, 8 Dec. 1938, in Prince Naritsaranuwattiwong and Prince Damrong Rajanubhab, *San somdet* (26 vols. Bangkok, 1961), *14*, 100–05. Prince Damrong explained that children were sent into the monastery primarily for religious instruction, for which literacy was a tool, and that when their belief was "awakened" they were ordained as novices for a short time and then returned to secular life. Ordination as a novice was considered basic to a man's growth to maturity, and ordination as a monk was only for those who intended to spend their entire lives in the monkhood. "The custom of two ordinations, as novice *and* as monk," he wrote, "is modern, and dates from the end of the Ayudhya period" (p. 102). The older pattern still persists in North Thailand.

32. When in the novitiate in the fall of 1875, Prince Damrong chose from among a number of options the study of the *Vedamantra*, the casting of spells and the characteristics of various types of Buddhist amulets. Prince Damrong Rajanubhab, *Khwamsongčham* (Bangkok, 1963), pp. 196–97.

period extending from puberty to manhood, during which young men were prepared specifically for their vocations, was appropriately varied and diffuse to meet the requirements of the individual. In the vast majority of cases this was a period during which fathers passed on to their sons their knowledge of wet-rice agriculture and village life. Similarly, the sons of provincial and capital craftsmen were initiated into both the formal and informal aspects of their crafts and began serving their apprenticeships, seated by their fathers during the working day. The sons of government officers likewise began to attend upon their fathers at their place of work and, if they were of sufficiently high status, entered the Royal Pages' Corps to be exposed to the workings of government and the eyes of the king, hoping to be singled out for promising careers. It is this third educational phase that reveals most clearly the limits of social mobility in traditional Siam. Although others rightly have stressed the surprising degree of social mobility that existed in old Siam, such mobility was in fact exceptional, and was confined to the narrow channels of personal allegiances and to such special institutions as the monkhood,[33] the crafts, and the professions. Within each segment of society, and especially within the government service and the monkhood, mobility could be and often was quite striking; but rare indeed was the case of the farmer's son becoming a high government official. For the most part, the third stage in the educational process was vocational and not academic, for the scope for social advancement by academic qualification was limited. There was, however, one significant exception which held occasionally in the case of the monkhood, among those who elected to remain in the monkhood. These young men thereby were afforded an opportunity for higher academic study and a slender chance for influence and perhaps a government appointment. Needless to say, such opportunities must have been much more readily available in the capital and the royal monasteries than elsewhere.

33. See David K. Wyatt, "Khana song pen khrüang yok thana khün nai sangkhom thai boran," *Sinlapakon*, 10: 1 (May 1966), 41–52.

Those who remained in the monastery had a number of alternatives open to them. They might study Pali and the scriptures in preparation for a religious life and career. Most who remained must have chosen such a course; but the amount of Pali they might learn and the length of time they might have persisted in such studies must have varied widely. Some who studied Pali all their lives and undertook detailed study of the *Tripitaka* became learned monks and later abbots of important monasteries. Others might have specialized in particular portions of the texts and later have taught others. Still others may have become "professors" of Pali in the monasteries. There were also monks who taught what Schouten referred to as "other useful arts." Some of these arts were religious and Buddhist: iconography, the orthography of the Khmer script used in religious writings, and probably some of the religious decorative arts. Other subjects in which there were experts and specialists who taught in the monastery included history, astronomy, astrology, medicine, mathematics, grammar, and literature, and probably law.[34] Students might also learn the composition of verse and perhaps also such practical subjects as the forms used in government correspondence and accounting. Instruction in these subjects was probably confined, however, to monasteries in the capital and the larger towns, where it might be offered as an option to any pupil, lay or religious, luksit, novice, or monk who had the requisite background. If a pupil was interested in studying medicine, for example, and there was no specialist in the particular monastery in which he lived, his teacher might send him to another monastery, per-

34. See Luang Prasoet, "Borannasüksa," p. 31, for a list of some of the textbooks used in the nineteenth century, a list probably not very different from any that could have been compiled in the seventeenth or eighteenth centuries. The list of books used in Burma, mentioned in inscriptions of 1442 (Bode, *Pali Literature,* pp. 102–109), probably was typical also of Thailand. Adolf Bastian, who visited Bangkok in 1863, reported that at Wat Kanlayannamit he met a monk who was an alchemist and possessed a textbook on alchemy attributed to an author of the Sukhothai period. Adolf Bastian, *Reisen in Siam im Jahre 1863* (Jena, 1867), p. 127.

18   POLITICS OF REFORM IN THAILAND

haps at a great distance and even in the capital, to be instructed.
To the great monasteries of Ayudhya came laymen and monks
from all over the kingdom seeking higher knowledge. It is
likely that the court did not hesitate to draw from these monasteries the specialists it required in the fields of medicine, astrology, law, and literature, thereby benefiting from the basic instruction given to youths by admitting some of them into the
bureaucracy.

The traditional Thai educational system thus consisted of
more than simple instruction in reading, writing, and religion
offered indiscriminately to all males. These elements assuredly
were at the very basis of the system, but they did not exist alone.
Just as Sukhothai and Ayudhya had been domesticated into
the classical Indian traditions of their predecessors on the Indo-
chinese peninsula, so were Thai educational practices open to
these elements. This is not surprising. The important fact is
that the educational traditions of classical India were modified
to serve the secular and religious ends of Thai society. Because
of the openness of the religious career and its virtual univers-
ality, and because of the relatively great social and economic
mobility in traditional Thai society, learning and scholarship
never became the exclusive preserve of a single class, caste, or
order. While the highest positions in the monkhood may have
been reserved for those of royal or noble descent—and this is by
no means certain—men of families of no distinction were able
to obtain highly specialized educations and attain relatively
high ecclesiastical or secular positions.[35] The educational system
of the Ayudhya period blended diverse elements to the service

35. To cite but one example: the chief of the king's astrologers in the
reign of King Narai, known only by his title, Phra Horathibǫdi, was a
native of the Sukhothai-Phitchit region in the North who came to Ayudhya
to finish his studies and became a court official. He is thought to have been
one of the teachers of Narai when the latter was a young prince. He was
the author of a textbook used in monastery instruction, the Čhindamani, of
a treatise on verification, and of one version of the chronicles of Auydhya.
See Dhanit Yupho, "Banthük rüang nangsü čhindamani," in Thailand,
Fine Arts Dept., eds., Čhindamani lem 1–2 (Bangkok, 1961), pp. 146–54.

of the society: providing avenues of mobility for specialists, expressing the highest ideals of a universalistic Buddhism, and perpetuating the classical arts and sciences as well as a growing body of indigenous cultural and intellectual products.

In order to accomplish these ends, the educational system assumed some of the attributes of Buddhist Thai society. Just as Buddhist merit-making is an individual pursuit, and just as one's secular fate was forever uncertain and subject to sudden strokes of good or ill fortune, the essence of both being unstructured progress hither and thither, up and down a hierarchy of merit and status, the educational system was relatively unstructured, individualized, and basically the same for all men though capable of extremely wide variation. Kings, princes, nobles, merchants, and common peasants entered and left the same system at a wide variety of points. They shared the common bonds of a universal language and a universal religion, but each sought to make his merit and assure his future salvation in his individual way.[36]

To gauge the effects of these traditional patterns of Thai education would require a great deal more information than we possess about old Thai society and its education. Nonetheless, it is possible and desirable to postulate tentatively their potential intellectual and social consequences. It is apparent that the rational, logical structure of the cosmos was imparted to young men to a high degree. The moral and physical order of the world were securely defined, to regulate not only life in general but also the social conduct and economic activity of the individual. Whether as a farmer, a craftsman, an official, or the king himself, the individual was aware of and heeded both abstract principles and concrete prescriptions which were

36. For the basic view of Thai society implied in these paragraphs I am greatly indebted to A. Thomas Kirsch, whose unpublished doctoral dissertation, "Phu Thai Religious Syncretism: A Case Study of Thai Religion and Society" (Harvard University, 1967), does not begin to exhaust the insights he has shared with me in conversation and correspondence. See also Lucien M. Hanks, Jr., "Merit and Power in the Thai Social Order," *American Anthropologist,* 64 (Dec. 1962), 1247–61.

directly relevant to the conduct of his daily life. The farmer, for example, was acutely conscious of the significance of astronomical phenomena for the prospects of his rice crop, and if the calendar indicated that he should expect late rains, he would postpone the planting of his crop.[37] The craftsman, artist, or professional man was aware of the abstract principles and concrete prescriptions governing the practice of his art or science, whether it was sculpture, poetry, architecture, elephantry, medicine, or boxing. Whether in the monastery, the workshop and office, or informally in the community, it was the function of the educational system to provide the rational grounding in principles and prescriptions that he required. Any craft, art, or science was susceptible to study, and almost all, save the kingship itself, were open to the study of anyone who could gain admission to a teacher.

The ultimate significance of the rationality and susceptibility to study of social activity lies, however, not so much in the fact of its rationality as in popular and personal attitudes toward that rationality and toward the body of principle and prescription inherited largely from Indian tradition. Given the distinctively Thai products of this rational tradition, and given the heavily practical orientation of much traditional education, however much it was loaded with formalistic deduction, one can only conclude that the general attitude of the society toward this intellectual tradition was reserved and pragmatic. Principles were not to be maintained at the expense of socially conditioned definitions of beauty, propriety, or utility. One can see this in the application of Indian legal principles, particularly in the *Dharmaśāstra;* one can see it in Thai art and literature, and again in the general tenor of Thai social life, which was much less rigidly prescriptive, frequently more ribald, and more aesthetically pleasant to the Thai than classical Indian society. One would expect that this reserved attitude toward Indian

37. See Tiao Maha Oupahat Phetsarath, "The Laotian Calendar," in Rene de Berval, ed., *Kingdom of Laos* (Saigon, 1959), pp. 122–23; and Khlọi Songbandit, *Patithin 250 pi* (Bangkok, 1954), pp. 14–23.

rationalism both stemmed from and made possible rapid change in Thai society.

It is difficult to assess the changes that occurred in Thai educational practices between the fourteenth and seventeenth centuries, as the evidence, especially for the earlier period, is so meager. The evidence for increasing Indianization seems sufficiently clear, as also for an increase in specialization and for the institutionalization of education and religion. Educational change between 1350 and 1650 might be characterized generally as elaboration on basic themes and patterns which were present at the beginning of the period.

In the latter half of the seventeenth century a new factor was introduced. The Portuguese had begun to visit Ayudhya shortly before their capture of Malacca in 1511, but Western visitors were comparatively rare until the seventeenth century, when the Dutch, English, and French competed for trade and power in the kingdom. In the 1670s and 80s there followed a period of international rivalry during which King Narai attempted to overthrow the commercial position the Dutch enjoyed in the kingdom by encouraging closer relations with the French, and the great increase in Western power and influence resulted in the introduction of new ideas and new material goods.[38]

The political impact of this period was, if anything, negative on both sides. However, one legacy of the period was an intellectual one. During this brief period, French missionaries had established a school at Ayudhya. Prince Damrong Rajanubhab suggests that "King Narai probably felt that he had to match their accomplishments in promoting education, and therefore had Phra Horathibọdi, his Court Astrologer, an accomplished savant of renown, write a new textbook for teaching Thai, perhaps for use in instruction or for the information of the foreign diplomats."[39] To this textbook, the *Čhindamani (Gems*

38. For a good survey of this period, see E. W. Hutchinson, *Adventurers in Siam in the Seventeenth Century* (London, 1940).

39. Quoted in Dhanit Yupho, "Banthük," pp. 149–50.

of Thought),[40] must go some of the credit for the improvement in educational standards which took place during this century, as evidenced by the improvements in style, orthography, and spelling in documents of the period, as well as for its great influence upon the development of Thai literature.[41] The *Čhindamani* is in many ways typical of Indian textbooks and treatises. Its approach to its subject is wholly through rules and categories which are laid down as fundamentals. After an introductory section filled with lists of words derived from Pali and Sanskrit, followed by lists of homonyms, there is a dedicatory passage or invocation, and then the principles of the Thai writing system are stated and applications of their application are cited. This is followed by a lengthy discussion of the various types of verse forms. The book abounds in such statements as "Once you know this, you can become a clerk and enjoy an easy life" (literally "you will eat easily").[42] One might doubt whether all who used it were so fortunate or even whether many boys managed to work through the entire book, but it served countless Siamese boys for the next two centuries.

Much of what characterized the intellectual vitality of the court of King Narai, however, was developed and came forth not so much from foreign contact, although this may have been an important factor, as from the interest in and patronage extended to learning and accomplishment by the court, as in so many of the major courts of the world in that day, from France to India, China, and Siam. Like the Bourbons and the Moghuls, the Ayudhya dynasty reached the peak of its flowering in the seventeenth century. The kingdom had fully donned the classical forms and found that it could live and move com-

40. See ibid., pp. 123–28, and G. B. McFarland, *Thai-English Dictionary* (Stanford, 1944), p. 251, for an explanation of the definition of this title.

41. Dhanit Yupho, "Banthük," pp. 146–57; Dhanit Yupho, *Somdet phra narai maharat lae nakprat ratchakawi nai ratchasamai* (Bangkok, 1956), pp. 15–17; and P. Schweisguth, *Étude sur la litterature siamoise* (Paris, 1951), pp. 106–107.

42. Fine Arts Dept., *Čhindamani,* p. 27.

fortably within them. Narai's empire was vast, but administered by a well-ordered bureaucracy it was peaceful and prosperous. The needs of the state were met not only by prosperity, which provided the means to sustain the life of the court, but also by an educational system which supplied the bureaucracy with men adequate for its increasingly paper-bound tasks, the monk-hood with scholarly men who reflected credit not only on the Buddhist establishment but also on its patron, the court with its poets, astrologers, physicians, and artisans, and the society as a whole with men attuned to a culture of Indian origin but of a distinctively Thai expression. The kingdom had assimilated successfully the diverse traditions within which it found itself and had creatively fused them together into a living culture which was its own.

THE BANGKOK PERIOD

The capture and sack of Ayudhya by invading Burmese armies in 1767 brought an end to the old Ayudhyan civiliza-tion. Its successor kingdom, established first at Thonburi and then, in 1782, at Bangkok, could never entirely resurrect the glory that had been Ayudhya. The damage had been too great; and the beginnings of Western influence with its new ideas and techniques and the political threats it posed were soon to divert the work of reconstruction into a new course.

When the task of reconstructing Ayudhya's civilization was taken up by King Rama I (1782–1809), old court officials had to be called upon to impart their memories of the way things had been and the few remaining documents were pored over for what they could reveal of what had constituted proper Thai court life under the old regime. One would suspect that, while many of the new ruling class had seen or participated in the ceremonies and institutions of old Ayudhya, few were really steeped in them. The aberrations of the reign of King Taksin (1767–82) must further have confused the memory of a glorious past and provided ample evidence that only an orthodox, traditional government could expect to win the widespread support and steady allegiance required for its stability, security, and prosperity.

One of the first acts of Rama I on becoming king was to begin issuing a series of regulations aimed at restoring discipline and orthodoxy to the Buddhist monkhood.[43] Six years later, in 1788, he convoked a great Council of the Sangha to undertake the compilation of a new edition of the *Tripitaka,* an action that brought orthodox standards to bear upon the monasteries while at the same time bringing great merit to the name of the king as patron and defender of Buddhism. In addition, Rama I revived the patronage traditionally extended to the royal monasteries and to the instruction and examination of the monkhood. Rama I also undertook several other important works of reconstruction. His best known is the great legal revision that culminated in the completion of the "Laws of the Three Seals" in 1805, which gave the kingdom a single, consistent code of laws which could serve as a sure guide for the kingdom's jurists. He also found it necessary to reconstruct all the developed, involved ceremonial that had surrounded the kingship in Ayudhya times. In reviving these patterns, Rama I always had proclamations read out at ceremonies to explain their nature and implications to those who were not familiar with them. Finally, the king devoted considerable energy and talent to the revival of Thai literature and the performing arts. From the king's own pen are said to have come new versions of the Thai *Ramayana,* the *Ramakian,* and of the classical *Dalang, Inao,* and *Unarut.* His Minister of the Treasury, Čhaophraya Phrakhlang (Hon), was a lavish patron of literature, with a taste for translations from Chinese and other foreign languages, and was an accomplished poet himself.[44] Others at court showed great talent in

43. "Kot phra song," 1782–1801, in *Kotmai tra sam duang, 4,* 164–228.

44. One can see in the Chinese elements of the literature of the early Bangkok period some evidence of a process of Sinicization then taking place

the writing of verse, drama, and history. The literary products of the First Reign of the Bangkok period are remarkable by any standard, but they are doubly so for having been produced in an age of warfare and reconstruction.[45]

What was the nature of this work of reconstruction accomplished by King Rama I? How essential was the cultural revival to the general work of restabilization of a country torn by war and internal strife? Scholars have hardly begun to utilize the sources that might make possible definite answers to such questions, so that tentative answers can be posited only in terms of fragmentary sources and of what they reveal of the temper of the times and the nature of the possibilities open to the founders of the Čhakri dynasty. It would appear that King Rama I and his brother were faced with the task of restoring focus and momentum to a society shaken by turmoil. They themselves could constitute a focus for military and civil administration only as rulers defined in the manner that the traditions of the society demanded—only by reviving the elevated position of the kingship and surrounding it with the aura and majesty of Indian kingship as translated long ago into the Thai context. They could capture the allegiance and good will of the critically important institution of the Sangha only by respecting, supporting, and defending it and promoting its

---

in some areas of Thai intellectual life. Chinese literature enjoyed considerable popularity in the First and subsequent reigns, notably in the Fourth and Fifth, when under the patronage of Čhaophraya Si Suriyawong no fewer than nineteen of the Chinese historical romances were translated and published (Natthawutthi Sutthisongkhram, *Somdet čhaophraya bǫrommaha si suriyawong* [Bangkok, 1961], pp. 179–84). The same influence is apparent in Thai architecture and the decorative arts during the same period. It is tempting to see this "Sinicization" as a prelude to later "Westernization," and it may well be that this is an important aspect of the changes of the nineteenth century. Until further research has been done into the history of the eighteenth and early nineteenth centuries, however, it would be premature to make a judgment on the significance of "Sinicization."

45. See Prince Dhani Nivat, "The Reconstruction of Rama I of the Chakri Dynasty," *JSS, 43*, pt. 1 (1955), 21–48.

strength. They could make the court the center of national artistic and intellectual life only by evincing interest in, and extending patronage to, cultural and intellectual pursuits. King Taksin may have perceived these necessities, but he failed to heed them, and the men who seized his throne in 1782 must have known how and why Taksin had failed. Rama I went on, in his reign of twenty-seven years, to succeed in a spectacular fashion, not only because he was aware of these requirements and fulfilled them, but also because he was such an extraordinarily gifted man: soldier, governor, diplomat, king, poet, dramatist, Buddhist layman, and politician. Yet behind all this, one cannot help but feel that Rama I must have considered himself a usurper and upstart, a parvenu, a man who had become king simply because he was the only man who could fulfill that function properly. And it may just be that this personal feeling of his is what gave him and his successors their special sensitivity to necessity and the pragmatism and shrewdness that so characterized the Thai rulers of the nineteenth century.

The reign of King Rama III (1824–51) was to some extent a continuation of the reconstruction of the earlier portion of the Bangkok period; but it was also a period during which the West began, very slowly, to make its influence felt in Thai life. As a whole, his reign presents the curious picture of a great flourishing of Thai traditional culture, on the one hand, and, on the other, the modifying of that tradition by foreign elements.[46] During the Third Reign many of the Thai arts received their last full expression in traditional form. This was a period of prodigious literary endeavor, but it is significant that much of this was undertaken outside official circles. The greatest poet of the period, Sunthǫn Phu, who had been a favorite during the Second Reign, was in virtual exile from the capital during the Third Reign. The king, himself a poet of some merit, confined his interest to religious and historical

46. For an excellent survey of this reign, see Walter F. Vella, *Siam Under Rama III.*

literature and discouraged secular literature and the traditional dramatic arts. The old artistic forms survived and produced a while longer only on the momentum of the earlier portion of the century. There is something about the artistic production of this period that seems to presage its own impending end. The influence of foreign literature and models increased greatly during the reign, through the medium of translations from Chinese, Môn, and Pali; and one might view the inscriptions of Wat Phra Chetuphon, with their expressed purpose of preserving for posterity the traditional arts and sciences, and the strange stone Chinese sailing vessel of Wat Yannawa as recognitions that old Siam was approaching its end.[47] And these expressions certainly must have found reinforcement in the events imperiling China and Burma in these years.

In the perspective of later years it is not the many pious works of Rama III that seem significant for the period, but rather the contacts of many highly placed Thai with Westerners and the reforms which the prince-priest Mongkut led within the Buddhist Sangha. Excluded from the succession to the throne in 1824, Mongkut remained in the monkhood and took up the serious study of Pali and the religious texts. Finding the practices of Thai Buddhism considerably at variance with the classical Theravada canon, he took the daring step of breaking with Thai Buddhist traditions and borrowing the dress and disciplinary forms of the Môn sect.[48] Mongkut's founding of the Thammayut reform sect has a modernist as well as a classicist aspect. In his later contact with Protestant and Catholic Christian missionaries, Mongkut engaged in serious dialogue on the merits of their respective religions. Tutored by the missionaries in English and Western Science he came to apply his newfound knowledge and a critical mind to the consideration

47. Ibid., ch. IV; Prince Dhani Nivat, "The Inscriptions of Wat Phra Jetubon," *JSS*, 25, pt. 2 (1933), 143–70; and Prince Damrong Rajanubhab's preface to *Prachum čharük wat phra chetuphon* (1st ed. Bangkok, 1929), 1, esp. i–ii.

48. Čhaophraya Thiphakǫrawong, *Phraratchaphongsawadan krung rattanakosin ratchakan thi 3 ... thi 4* (Bangkok, 1963), p. 365.

of his own religion. He was exceedingly well educated in his own culture and religion, so that out of his contacts with the missionaries came a creative response: a Buddhism that was no longer simply a national tradition but rather a universal religion, which could compete with Christianity for the allegiance of intellectual Thai minds on very favorable terms.[49]

One of the noteworthy aspects of Thai intercourse with the West during the Third Reign was the fact that the missionaries and other visitors, unlike those in China, made a distinct impression on the ruling classes of Siam. This impression, however, was selective, perhaps much more so than the missionaries desired. Prince Mongkut gained from them fluency in English and a broad acquaintance with Western science, particularly astronomy and physics; Prince Wongsathirat Sanit, his younger brother and head of the Department of the Royal Physicians, studied Western medicine. Another brother, later known as Phra Pin Klao, "second king," in Mongkut's reign, used his acquaintance with the missionaries and merchants to study Western military science and English. In addition, several members of the bureaucratic nobility studied English and science with them; these included Somdet Chaophraya Si Suriyawong (Chuang Bunnag), who became the chief of Mongkut's ministers of state and regent in the early years of Chulalongkorn's reign; and *nai* Mot Amatyakul, later director of the Royal Mint, among others.[50] What is particularly striking about these associations is the caliber of the men who engaged in them and the type of knowledge that attracted them. These were men of high position, men well educated in the traditions of Thai culture, men who continually showed their loyalty to tradi-

49. Alexander B. Griswold, *King Mongkut of Siam* (New York, 1961), pp. 13–26; Abbot Low Moffat, *Mongkut, the King of Siam* (Ithaca, N.Y., 1961), pp. 11–22; Vella, *Rama III*, pp. 38–42; and Robert Lingat, "La Vie religieuse du roi Mongkut," *JSS*, 20, pt. 2 (1926), 129–48.

50. Prince Damrong Rajanubhab, "Athibai rüang ratchathut thai pai yurop," in *Prachum phongsawadan*, pt. 29, new ed. 7 (Bangkok, 1964), 337–45. See also D. K. Wyatt, "Family Politics in Nineteenth Century Thailand," *Journal of Southeast Asian History*, 9 (Sept. 1968), 208–28.

tional customs, manners, practices, and ideas. All of them showed their devotion to Thai Buddhism in the accustomed manner. All of them were heavily involved in the politics of the day and were, in Sir John Bowring's word, "patriots." None had necessary cause to desert his background or traditions, for all had much to lose and little to gain. Yet all of them were sufficiently intrigued and perhaps sufficiently uncertain of the adequacy of their traditions and knowledge to deal effectively with new conditions to seek out the missionaries, to learn from them, and in some instances to employ their new knowledge in modifying traditional patterns, whether by adding new techniques to medical treatment, disproving the court astrologers, printing codes of law, building foreign-style ships for government trading, or founding a new Buddhist sect.

It would be incorrect to say that the men of Mongkut's generation were, in opening their minds to the West, unsure of themselves. On the contrary, these men were and had to be highly self-confident. The distinguishing features of their intellectual quest, whether undertaken for novelty or enlightenment, were the attitudes they displayed toward the traditional abstract rules and concrete prescriptions, their fundamental belief that the world was susceptible to rational inquiry, and their willingness to entertain the truth of other ideas if these proved more true or more useful than those they previously had held. Even Rama III himself, who certainly is not known for his radicalism, became excited by the idea of vaccination against smallpox.[51] As for the extent to which their education predisposed them toward such attitudes and approaches, one might say that it inclined them more toward pragmatic rationalism than toward any specific system of thought and ideas. It would appear that Thai culture, rather than formal aspects of Thai education, produced such men. It was the culture, in its historical context of change and flux, that called forth from the society the education it required. Education may have intro-

51. H. C. Highet, "Smallpox, Vaccination and the New Vaccination Law in Siam," *JSS,* 9, pt. 1 (1914), 17–18.

duced ideas, but it was the culture that religiously, socially, and economically determined the values these ideas could be accorded. By the Third Reign, changing historical circumstances and the recent experience of innovation had begun to elicit a creative response from a new generation.[52]

It is clear that, far from being "typical of traditional Siam,"[53] this period was one of transition. The group of princes and nobles who sipped at the well of Western culture did not, during most of this period, sense any great urgency in their thirst. They partook for taste and novelty and pleasure. Only the king, who had remained aloof from such contacts, seems to have seen their significance at the time. On his deathbed in February 1851, he sent for Phraya Si Suriyawong and said to him,

> I personally think that for whoever is chief of the king's ministers, there will be no more wars with Vietnam and Burma. We will have them only with the West. Take care, and do not lose any opportunity to them. Anything which they propose should be held up to close scrutiny before acceptance; and do not blindly believe in them.[54]

Thus the West made its first impression on the Thai at a time when the political threat it posed was not yet fully appreciated, and the effects of these early contacts were limited to the superficial attainments of a few self-confident and liberal-minded men of secure position. It was these men, the next generation of Thai rulers, who once exposed were forced to open their doors to the West and were caught in a flood of ideas and challenges to the old Siam they represented.

To King Mongkut (1851–68), who ascended the throne in 1851 as the fourth of his line, fell the task of meeting Western demands for open commercial intercourse. The treaties signed

---

52. For a brilliant examination of the relationship between historical experience and cultural attitudes, see Charles Archaimbault, "Religious Structures in Laos," *JSS, 52,* pt. 1 (1964), 57–74.

53. Vella, *Rama III,* p. vii.

54. Thiphakọrawong, *Phraratchaphongsawadan ratchakan 3–4,* p. 366.

with the major Western powers were the result, accomplished
not without thinly veiled threats on the part of the European
powers[55] and considerable efforts on the part of the king and
his ministers to overcome domestic resistance. Thailand's rulers
correctly perceived the dangers that faced their country and
acted accordingly. The pattern of settlement set forth in the
British treaty of 1855 was primarily political. The economic
sacrifices required of the Thai were viewed by them as means to
a political end, the maintenance of Siam's independence. Although the Thai very quickly came to find new economic opportunities in the treaty arrangement, their understanding of the
possible economic consequences of the treaties was most imperfect. With the very rapid expansion of foreign intercourse a
wave of change swept over Bangkok. The fiscal arrangements
designed as an alternative to the taxes abolished by treaty
worked well, and the revenues of the country steadily increased.[56] The country entered upon a period of increasing
prosperity that was not to abate for decades. The primary factor in this economic development was foreign trade, which
brought increasing numbers of foreign ships to Bangkok each
year, and with them a growing community of resident foreigners which included the representatives of foreign governments,
businessmen, and missionaries. The face of Bangkok was
changed considerably. Roads were constructed and canals were
dug. A police force and a customs house were provided for the
safety and convenience of foreigners. Printing presses were set
up and utilized by the government, the monkhood, the missionaries, and a growing commercial press. The city entered
upon a period of building and of bustling commercial and governmental activity.

Very little by way of institutional reform, however, was accomplished during the reign of King Mongkut. The political
patterns of kingship and bureaucracy remained much as they

55. Natthawutthi, *Somdet čhaophraya,* pp. 327–28.
56. See Wira Wimoniti, *Historical Patterns of Tax Administration in
Thailand* (Bangkok, 1961), p. 74.

had been for a century, tempered to some degree perhaps by the easy-going, benevolent monarch. King Mongkut had little desire to change Siam in a fundamental manner, and he probably did not have the power to do so, as his position vis-à-vis his chief ministers was so weak. His primary concern was to maintain the independence of his kingdom in the face of Western pressures which were overwhelming his neighbors. Surely the most lasting impression Mongkut left on his country was that of his mind and outlook. He was a man of wide-ranging interests, curious and logical. He was stubborn enough to be forthright when he knew and humble enough to find out what he did not know. He was willing to make changes when he could see their necessity; but he was cautious enough to try to prepare the way for change rather than force its pace. He was a practical, no-nonsense, realistic king who did what he had to do; but he was sufficiently the prophet to attempt to prepare his sons for a different world which soon would come. This new world, however, arrived much sooner for him than he expected, with his sudden death in 1868.

Over this broad expanse of more than six hundred years from the foundation of the kingdom of Sukhothai to the death of King Mongkut there are three major features that should be especially noted and emphasized in the context of cultural innovation and educational development. All three concern the role of education in Thai society.

First, there are ample indications that by the reign of King Ram Khamhaeng the Thai had adopted what was essentially an Indian mode of education, modified to suit Buddhist conditions and the more open society characteristic of Theravada Southeast Asia, and also to accommodate the broader aspects of Indian culture which had preceded Theravada Buddhism into Southeast Asia. By the seventeenth century these relatively universal and widespread patterns of education had reached their traditional Thai forms. It was by means of this educational system, and because of it, that the vernacular culture of Thailand flourished and developed along richly diverse lines and gave the

nation a splendid literary heritage which was diffused throughout the society.[57]

Second, with respect to the content of traditional education,
although we have noted that the system was pervaded by Indian
principles and ideas, we need again to distinguish between the
forms and the life that went on within them. While it may be
argued that analytical Indian thought was successfully trans-
planted to old Siam, it would appear at least as important that
the Thai seem to have taken more readily to the forms and
tendencies indicated than to the solutions and prescriptions
specified by classical Indian thought. This distinction is significant, for it alone provides for and assists in explaining the
manner in which the Thai were able to maintain their distinctive
value system. The Thai appear to have succeeded in extracting
the best of two worlds in their six-century exposure to Indian
civilization: they appropriated to themselves much of classical
Indian tradition, but in doing so they maintained their own
identity. By the middle of the nineteenth century it was their
own cherished values—independence, survival, and personal
and communal mobility—which permitted and even encouraged them to turn, at least in part, from one rational explanation
of the world to another, maintaining all the while their Indian-
derived propensity for an analytical, rational expression of
order to serve as a framework on which new ideas could be
hung.

Third, one will note in the preceding account the close interrelationships which bound education, religion, and cultural and
political life in a complex whole, in which changes of any basic
order had wide repercussions. It took more than Buddhism as a
religion to bring the Thai out of the semi-tribal conditions in
which many of their cousins lived and remained. The increasing
political and cultural responsibilities of the Sukhothai monarchy

57. See E. H. S. Simmonds, "Thai Narrative Poetry: Palace and Provincial Texts of an Episode from 'Khun Chang Khun Phaen'," *Asia Major*,
n.s. 10 (1964), 279–99, for an example of the diffusion of court literature
through the countryside.

brought with them an increased respect for and interest in the broader, Indian-based culture which had been and was becoming implanted in the states of Southeast Asia, and to some extent this was reinforced by similar adjustments which Buddhism already had made in response to similar circumstances in Ceylon, Burma, and the Môn country. In the Ayudhya period these two strains of religious orthodoxy and the Indian classical tradition became fused with indigenous creativity into what we know as traditional Thai culture, which was challenged very briefly but not without effect in the reign of King Narai. It was not until the first half of the nineteenth century, however, that this culture began to meet the full measure of the Western challenge to its integrity.

The most significant thing about the response to the Western challenge is that it was met not with weakness but with strength, in a direct confrontation in the minds of men of influence, who exhibited an unusual degree of flexibility and pragmatism. Perhaps such attributes and attitudes were not so new to Siam's rulers: one is tempted to attribute to Ram Khamhaeng, Lü Thai, Narai, and Rama I a measure of the same. None of them, from Ram Khamhaeng to Mongkut, struggled against the realities of their day; and they provided King Chulalongkorn with a noble example to follow in his confrontation with the West in the last third of the nineteenth century.

2
Politics and Reform, 1868–1880

At midnight on the night of 18–19 October 1868 a council composed of leading members of the royal family and the nobility met to decide upon a successor to King Mongkut. Without dissension or discussion they elected to succeed the late king his eldest surviving son, Prince Chulalongkorn. They also chose a new "second king" *(uparāja),* and appointed the chief among Mongkut's ministers, Čhaophraya Si Suriyawong (Chuang Bunnag), to act as regent during the remaining five years of the young king's minority.[1] Thus began the forty-two-year reign of Chulalongkorn, with a boy-king only fifteen years old and seriously ill of the same disease that had just felled his father. The circumstances with which the reign began could hardly have been less auspicious. It was the young king's fate to have to effect the fundamental changes his father had avoided; yet in the early years of the reign his power to do so was even more restricted than King's Mongkut's had been. These were years of fundamental importance in the history of the reign and in one way or another they were to color all that followed.

1. There are several accounts of the proceedings of that evening, all of considerable importance. These include: Čhaophraya Thiphakǫrawong, *Phraratchaphongsawadan ratchakan 3–4,* pp. 837–39; Prince Damrong Rajanubhab, *Phraratchaphongsawadan krung rattanakosin ratchakan thi 5* (Bangkok, 1951), pp. 19–30; Čhaophraya Mahintharasakthamrong, *Čhotmaihet rüang phrabat somdet phra čhǫmklao čhaoyuhua song prachuan* (Bangkok, 1947), pp. 27–30; and Thailand, Fine Arts Dept., eds., *Čhotmaihet phraratchakit raiwan ph.s. 2411* (Bangkok, 1965), esp. pp. 26–28.

KING CHULALONGKORN

Chulalongkorn was born in the Royal Palace on 20 September 1853, the eldest surviving son born to King Mongkut by a queen, and thus in a favored position to succeed his father. From an early age he was his father's favorite, and accompanied him on trips to the provinces and attended him during royal audiences. His boyhood was spent in almost total immersion in affairs of state, and his education was directed toward his ultimate succession to the throne.

Chulalongkorn's education followed the traditional patterns established for princes in the early years of the Ayudhya period. Before the age of six years he was sent to learn to read and write under his cousin, Princess Wọrasetsuda (1828–1907), a daughter of Rama III, who had a great literary reputation and a thorough acquaintance with the customs of the royal family.[2] He went on to study other subjects which at that time were thought appropriate to the education of princes, including Pali. He was trained in the use of firearms, in wrestling and fencing, and was taught horsemanship by his father and elephantry by his uncle. During this whole period, King Mongkut took special pains to teach him the elements of statecraft, royal customs, and history. This part of Chulalongkorn's education had a plainly traditional character and was similar to that training which had produced the warrior kings of the past. Times had changed, however, and the king who had battled the Burmese and Vietnamese was not necessarily the sort of king who could deal successfully with the problems of relations with the West. Mongkut unmistakably realized this and, in his private tutoring of his young son in the principles of statecraft, imparted to him something of the optimistic outlook and conciliatory approach that so impressed Sir John Bowring in 1855.

2. Prince Damrong Rajanubhab et al., *Phraratchaprawat phrabat somdet phra čhunlačhọmklao čhaoyuhua müa kọn sawoei rat* (Bangkok, 1961), p. 10. On Princess Wọrasetsuda, see Prince Sommot Amọraphan, comp., *Rüang chaloem phrayot čhaonai* (Bangkok, 1929), *1*, 255–57.

Mongkut was not slow in bringing into his palace the influences of Western culture to which he himself had been exposed by the American missionaries. In the first year of his reign he invited the women of the American missions to tutor the women of the palace so that they might be able to converse with him in English.[3] In 1859, when his sons began to reach the appropriate ages, he sought an English teacher for them and asked an American medical missionary, Dr. Samuel House, to organize instruction within the palace.[4] Dr. House declining the position, it remained unfilled until the well-known Mrs. Anna Leonowens was hired in 1862. Mrs. Leonowens' instructions from the king were to "do your best endeavorment upon us and our children" for "knowledge of English language, science, and literature."[5] Prince Chulalongkorn, then scarcely ten years old, was one of her pupils and impressed her with his personal warmth, his serious nature, and the way in which he threw himself into his studies and was excited by them.[6] Chulalongkorn studied with Mrs. Leonowens from 1862 until he underwent the tonsure ceremony *(sokan)* marking puberty and was ordained a Buddhist novice in 1866. When he left the monastery and went to live in Suankulap Palace, in a rear compound of the Grand Palace, he continued his studies with Mrs. Leonowens, until she left Bangkok in 1867, and then with Dr. Chandler, an American missionary, until the end of his father's reign.[7]

After his period in the monastery in 1866, Chulalongkorn's practical education was made more rigorous. He was constantly in attendance upon his father during the royal audiences at which public business was transacted, and he stayed by his

3. G. H. Feltus, *Samuel Reynolds House of Siam* (New York, 1924), pp. 109–11, 128–30; and *Siam Repository*, 2 (1870), 133–34, and 4 (1872), 264.

4. Feltus, p. 159.

5. Anna H. Leonowens, *Siam and the Siamese: Six Years' Recollections of an English Governess at the Siamese Court* (Philadelphia, 1897), p. vi.

6. Ibid., pp. 155–56.

7. Ibid., p. 166; and Damrong et al., *Phraratchaprawat*, pp. 21–22.

father's side at the multitude of ceremonies that filled the year. On occasion, when Mongk·it was deliberating public affairs, even in the middle of the night, Chulalongkorn was sent for and employed as a sounding board for his father's opinions or asked for his own opinions. Sometimes he was sent to discuss affairs with Čhaophraya Si Suriyawong, Mongkut's chief minister, and he made frequent morning visits to the latter's home on the opposite bank of the river which divides Bangkok from Thonburi. He thus was no stranger to politics and administration when called upon to succeed his father, although his education was far from complete.[8]

In assessing the character of Chulalongkorn's education, it is difficult to distinguish between the traditional and modern elements. On the one hand, the general pattern of his education was dictated by the traditional practices of the royal family, and the modern elements were subordinated to them. Thus his regular formal classes with Mrs. Leonowens were broken off at puberty, when he could no longer mix with the women of the palace, and much of his time thereafter was taken up with the "vocational" training directed by his father. Even the content of his education was overwhelmingly traditional in nature, including such subjects as elephantry and fencing. On the one hand, his five-year experience with Mrs. Leonowens must have affected him strongly, giving him more than simply his facility with the English language, for he came almost daily into contact with another culture in the person of a stubborn and opinionated, Western, Christian woman. On balance, it would appear that the determining influence in young Chulalongkorn's education was his father, who was himself a blend of these two elements. King Mongkut was exceedingly well versed in traditional Thai culture and well acquainted with Western culture. He was perhaps the leading Thai Buddhist scholar of his day and far more universally minded than most Thai of his generation. Chulalongkorn's later writings suggest that his own Western education served primarily to reinforce the universalism of

8. Damrong et al., *Phraratchaprawat*, pp. 35–37.

his father's outlook. From his father he inherited a practical and conciliatory approach to governmental affairs, domestic and foreign, and perhaps also a certain naïveté or optimism about their final issue. In comparison with his father, however, he began much earlier in life to face the necessity of reconciling the traditional and modern elements in his thought; and the pains his father suffered in trying to do so must have been of considerable help to him.

King Mongkut intended to continue his tutoring of Chulalongkorn until the latter had come of age in 1873 and then retire from active political life to a new palace he waś having constructed outside the walls of the Grand Palace, there to act as adviser to his son who would become king.[9] But death cut short his plans, and Chulalongkorn was thrust upon the throne still a boy, his education incomplete.

One of the major tasks of the regency was to prepare the young king for the full assumption of his duties. To this end, after Chulalongkorn's first coronation in November 1868, the major officials of the government drew up a daily schedule for the conduct of state business and the activities of the king, designed so as to preserve a degree of decentralization in the government and to accustom the king to the business of governing.[10] The most prominent aspect of this schedule was the extent to which it provided for a constant flow of information to the king by means of a steady succession of reports and audiences spaced through the day. Based on the royal routines of earlier reigns and traceable to the Code of Manu, it set a pattern for the whole forty-two years of the reign, and gave Chulalongkorn from the beginning an intimate acquaintance with the remotest details of government which never left him. By virtue of this practical training he would throughout his reign be as concerned with such simple details as the style of lettering to be

9. Damrong, *Khwamsongčham*, pp. 108–109.

10. Ibid., pp. 122–23; and Damrong, *Rüang phrarachanukit* (Bangkok, 1946), pp. 18–28, which treats his schedule in greater detail. Extremely interesting as well is an extended, almost sermon-like, "moral in-

used in a public inscription as with the general outlines of state policy, and equally at home with both.

Another important part of the king's education was the traveling he did during the regency period. King Mongkut often thought he might like to visit Singapore, but made no plans for such a trip until shortly before he died, when, while observing a solar eclipse in South Siam in the company of a number of foreign dignitaries, he was invited by Sir Harry Ord, governor of Singapore, to come and visit him, possibly in March 1869. But a month later Mongkut died, and it fell to Chulalongkorn to make the voyage his father had missed. Shortly after his coronation, when the British consul, (Sir) Thomas Knox, asked Chaophraya Si Suriyawong what plans he had for preparing the king for the full assumption of his duties, the regent replied that he was considering having the king travel to observe British administration in Singapore and that of the Dutch on Java.[11] In due course the arrangements were made, and in March 1871 the king and his party left Bangkok.

This trip, which lasted thirty-seven days, included stays of nine days in Singapore, five days in Batavia, and three days in Semarang. In the king's entourage were several of his younger brothers, the Minister of Foreign Affairs, the Minister for the Southern and Western Provinces (the *kalahom*), and numerous other officials. In the brief time available to him, the king was able to see many of the more obvious accomplishments of Western colonial administration: post offices, jails, hospitals, schools, telegraph offices, fire stations, lighthouses, botanical gardens and museums, theaters, shops and stores, orphanages, railways, and factories. He was entertained in grand style by the governments of the two colonies at dinners, banquets, receptions,

---

struction *(owat)"* offered the young king by Chaophraya Thiphakɔrawong (Kham Bunnag), who was then retiring as Foreign Minister. See Damrong, *Phraratchaphongsawadan ratchakan 5*, pp. 295–312.

11. Damrong, *Khwamsongčham*, pp. 163–64.

parties, and "entertainments." These must have made some impression on the nineteen-year-old king.[12]

After this first trip, Chulalongkorn expressed to friends his strong desire to visit Europe while he still had sufficient free time before assuming the full responsibilities of the throne. The regent, however, would not consent to such a trip, and agreed only on a visit to India as a compromise. The royal party left Bangkok in December 1871 and returned in March, having visited Singapore, Malacca, Penang, Moulmein, Rangoon, Calcutta, Delhi, Agra, Lucknow, Cawnpore, Bombay, and Benares.

Associated with these trips were a number of changes at Court, made primarily on the young king's initiative. In preparation for the first voyage, the members of the entourage had to become accustomed to Western styles of dress and coiffure, and from this period can be dated the decline of the traditional brush-style haircut of both men and women. Western forms of etiquette began to be applied more frequently at court, the royal audiences, and at the dinner table. The king and regent had no desire to appear in Singapore and Batavia as barbarians.[13]

On returning from the first voyage, Chulalongkorn initiated further changes so that, as Prince Damrong put it, the trip would not appear to have been undertaken only for pleasure.[14] One palace building was newly arranged for royal audiences with chairs and tables, a step in part preparatory to the abolition of the practice of prostration before the king which came a few years later. The king continued the program of municipal improvements begun by his father, constructing more streets and modern shops, and he began to change traditional patterns of education.[15] But the most notable reforms of the period were

12. Bangkok, National Library comp., *Čhotmaihet sadet praphat tang prathet nai ratchakan thi 5* (Bangkok, 1917).

13. Damrong, *Khwamsongčham*, pp. 165–68. These reforms were chronicled in the traditional style by the court astrologers: Čhamün Kongsin (Run), "Čhotmaihet hon," *Prachum phongsawadan*, pt. 8, new ed. 4 (Bangkok, 1964), 132–33.

14. Damrong, *Khwamsongčham*, p. 171.

15. Ibid., pp. 171, 174. The educational innovations are treated below in Chapter 3.

distinctly more momentous and brought Chulalongkorn fully
into the arena of political conflict.

POLITICS AND THE THRONE

The course of modernization throughout the reign of King
Chulalongkorn, but especially during its first decade, was
heavily determined by considerations of domestic politics, and
only to a lesser degree by foreign pressures and influences. Very
little is yet known of the background of domestic politics in the
reign of King Mongkut, but there is every indication that the
reign was not nearly as internally peaceful, nor the throne as
absolutely powerful, as has conventionally come to be believed.[16] Certainly the politics of the regency period at the
beginning of Chulalongkorn's reign had roots that extended
back in time to the Fourth and even the Third Reign; but it
must suffice here to begin where the evidence is clear.

Chulalongkorn's own memories of his accession to the throne
were far from pleasant. Writing to advise his son some years
later, he recalled that, without close friends or powerful pro-
tectors, he had been dominated by the regent and the men of his
father's generation. He was then "like a headless person, my
body propped up as a puppet king. . . . And there were enemies
whose intentions were openly bared around me, both within
and without, in the capital and abroad."[17] And the worst was
yet to come.

The initial political alignment of the reign was evident at the
meeting that elected Chulalongkorn king. A young boy, whose
health and survival were in question, was elevated to the throne
after his nomination by the most powerful of Mongkut's ministers, Čhaophraya Si Suriyawong. This minister was himself

16. Neon Snidvongs, "The Development of Siamese Relations with
Britain and France in the Reign of Maha Mongkut, 1851–1868" (Ph.D.
diss., University of London, 1961), passim.

17. King Chulalongkorn, *Phrabǫrommarachowat nai ratchakan thi 5*
(Bangkok, 1960), pp. 20–21.

appointed to act as regent for the young king, and he secured the appointment of the "second king," Chulalongkorn's cousin, over the objections of at least one member of the royal family, who justly argued that the appointment of the "second king" was by right the prerogative of the monarch alone.[18] With a boy on the throne, and with the appointment as his heir-apparent of a man who otherwise could not have expected that right, Suriyawong's authority as the "real ruler" of Siam was assured.[19]

Given absolute powers over all affairs of state, including the power of life and death, Suriyawong could act as king. Although there can be some legitimate doubt as to whether or not he abused these powers, particularly in filling state offices with his friends and family and in financial manipulations of dubious character, he at least made no overt move to follow the example of his sixteenth-century namesake and seize the throne for himself. He made an attempt to rule by consultation, and he moved quickly and effectively to quell the problems of domestic order that accompanied the succession, while at the same time continuing the conciliatory open-door policy in foreign affairs which he had carried out so successfully in the previous reign.[20]

Some, however, were not so certain as to the regent's intentions. Either out of loyalty to the young king, or acting within the framework of political rivalries developed over a longer period, a group of high government officials friendly to the king joined in a conspiracy to depose the regent and place the young king fully on the throne in the event that the regent should entertain more ambitious ideas.[21] They found, however, no occasion for action.

By 1872 or 1873, as Chulalongkorn's second coronation as king in his own right approached (it finally took place on 16

18. See sources cited in n. 1, this chapter. On the office of "second king," see Wales, *Ancient Siamese Government,* pp. 26–32.

19. Frank Vincent, Jr., *The Land of the White Elephant* (London, 1873), pp. 157–58.

20. Damrong, *Phraratchaphongsawadan ratchakan 5,* pp. 353–428, and *Khwamsongčham,* pp. 126–34.

21. "Death of Ex-Phya Kasap Mote," *Bangkok Times,* 27 Aug. 1896.

November 1873), the political divisions at Court were clearly established, and a contemporary observed that there were "three political parties in Siam, now known as 'Young Siam,' 'Conservative Siam,' and 'Old Siam.' "[22] These parties, or, more properly, factions, may have corresponded with the parties of the king, the regent, and the old nobles.

Unquestionably it was the king's party that represented "Young Siam." Composed of many younger members of the royal family, those officials who had joined together to defend the king against Suriyawong, and some younger officials who identified themselves with the king either because of their favorable attitudes toward Western civilization and ideas or out of long-standing political rivalries with the predominant cliques, this faction was united by two common denominators: youth and a degree of reforming zeal. Their youth requires no explanation, but their reforming zeal does. It stemmed from the fact that these were, for the most part, men (or boys) of the *second* Westernized generation.[23] Most of their fathers were men who had sipped at the well of Western culture without great thirst, while their sons drank deeply. Most of them had at least partially Western educations, particularly those members of the royal family who had studied with Mrs. Leonowens or Dr. Chandler, and many of them came from families that continued to maintain close relations with the American missionaries. While none of them, including especially the king, was *deraciné,* for all had every reason to maintain their roots in all that they considered fine in traditional Thai culture, all of them were sufficiently detached from the status quo to be able to contemplate radical change—political, institutional, and intellectual. Their commitment to change went beyond a view of Western ideas and techniques as means to ends. They had internalized

22. "Phya Krasap," *Siam Repository,* 5 (1873), 451. See also W. H. Senn van Basel, *Schetsen uit Siam* (Amsterdam, 1880), pp. 118–19.

23. On the generation as an historical concept, see José Ortega y Gasset, *Man and Crisis* (New York, 1962).

and made their own those values in Western culture which could be construed as elaborations and refinements of indigenous Thai values. This group's strength lay in its educated skills, its ideas, and its moral and intellectual conviction. Its weakness lay in its disregard for political reality and its lack of a secure political base in the executive offices of government.

The work of "Young Siam" gathered momentum only slowly, but its members were sufficiently strong by 1873 to be taking the lead in urging reforms of a radical nature. They began to issue their own newspaper, *Darunowat,* which published considerable foreign news and much comment on and discussion of reforms that they felt needed to be undertaken in Siam.[24] They formed a "Young Siam Society," of which Chulalongkorn's full brother, Prince Phanurangsi, was president.[25] And they were given new administrative and political responsibilities which challenged the old order and other established factions.

It was the regent, Čhaophraya Si Suriyawong, who, from the beginning of the reign until well after the period of the regency ended, had the most secure political position. This was a position founded on ability and experience, power, and wealth, all of which had been increasing steadily since the Second Reign. Based first on the office of *phrakhlang,* or Minister of the Treasury and Foreign Affairs, and then on the *kalahom,* this was the bureaucratic fief of the Bunnag family, who firmly controlled half of the six ministries, the southern, western, and coastal provinces, and much of the central financial organization of the

24. *Darunowat* was published from July 1874 to June 1875 by one of the king's younger brothers, Prince Phrom Wǫranurak. It was succeeded by the *Nangsü 'Court' khao ratchakan* (Sept. 1875–Sept. 1876), published within the palace walls by eleven of the king's younger brothers, one of whom, Prince Phanurangsi, republished the entire run of this newspaper in two volumes on the occasion of his birthday in 1923. On these newspapers, see Kachorn Sukhabanij, *Kao raek khǫng nangsüphim nai prathet thai* (Bangkok, 1965), pp. 27–53.

25. See a letter from Chulalongkorn to the "Young Siam Society," 10 Feb. 1875, printed in Natthawutthi, *Somdet čhaophraya,* pp. 785–86.

state. This faction aided, and probably engineered, Mongkut's accession to the throne, and the heir to the family's fortunes, Suriyawong, was nominated by Mongkut as the only possible regent for Chulalongkorn. By the time the regency was well established, Suriyawong's son was kalahom (Čhaophraya Surawong Waiyawat, Wǫn Bunnag); his brother, Čhaophraya Phanuwong Mahakosathibǫdi (Thuam Bunnag), was phrakhlang; his nephew, Phraya Ahanbǫrirak (Nut Bun-Long), was Minister of Lands *(krom na);* and his youngest brother, Phraya Phatsakǫrawong (Phǫn Bunnag), was the king's English-language secretary. Together with numerous sons and nephews scattered throughout the administration, Suriyawong could count on at least the tacit support of the majority of government officials, who could recognize and respect his position and real power.[26]

One might identify this group of officials around the regent as the party of "Conservative Siam" which Samuel Smith mentioned. If Smith used the term in the conventional manner, to denote a political position of resistance to abrupt or drastic change, favorable to the maintenance of the status quo and permitting only essential modifications in it, then it serves quite adequately to define this group. It is essential to note, however, that the determining factor in defining the composition of "Conservative Siam" was not an ideological framework but rather a pragmatic pattern. This faction had, over the course of time and as a result of a multitude of practical actions, worked its way into a position that was defined in terms of its experience, its interests, and its ideas. It tended to be older, well entrenched in positions of power and influence, and not unfavorable to some aspects of Westernization. Breaking with tradition, the Bunnags had taken great risks in working for the accommodation with the West embodied in the treaties of the fifties and

26. For a genealogy of the Bunnag family at this period, see Thailand, Fine Arts Dept., comp., *Lamdap rachinikun bang chang* (3d rev. ed. Bangkok, 1958), pp. 9–47. On the regency generally, see Dhanit Yupho, *Somdet čhaophraya bǫrommaha si suriyawong müa pen phusamretratchakan phaendin* (Bangkok, 1968).

sixties, and by the seventies they were in a splendid position to consolidate their gains. They tended to view Western ideas and techniques as means to ends that still were firmly determined in a traditional Thai context, on a practical rather than an ideal level.

Čhaophraya Si Suriyawong himself exemplified this position very well. In the Third Reign he had been one of the first Thai to undertake the construction of Western-type sailing vessels, which he used in his own as well as in government commercial ventures. He was an important figure in the accession of King Mongkut and instrumental in concluding the Bowring Treaty with Great Britain in 1855. As Mongkut's kalahom and "prime minister" he played a vital role in all the events of the Fourth Reign. He enjoyed cordial relations with many individual Europeans. But fundamentally he was still a man of the old order. He used Western methods when they seemed appropriate to achieve his own ends, which included the pursuit of personal power, wealth, and status, and the maintenance of the old Siam which he knew, rather than for abstract, ideal ends. He had no quarrel with the old order, for he, better than anyone else, could manipulate it and be successful in it.

Another major political figure was the "second king," Krom Phraratchawangbǫwǫn Wichaichan, the eldest son of Phra Pin Klao, who ruled as Mongkut's coequal at the beginning of the Fourth Reign and had been a true "second king." There are ample grounds for identifying Prince Wichaichan and his following with the regent's party, for he owed his position to Suriyawong's insistence on his appointment in the face of contrary precedent. Chulalongkorn was convinced that his cousin had been appointed in the expectation that Chulalongkorn would die of the illness from which he was suffering at the time of his accession, thereby bringing the "second king" to the throne and assuring the regent's continued influence over the throne.[27]

27. King to Prince Maha Mala, 31 Dec. 1874; and King to Prince Pawaret Wariyalongkǫn, 7 March 1876, printed in Natthawutthi, *Somdet čhaophraya*, pp. 721–25, 838.

In one sense, Prince Wichaichan must have found himself in a dilemma. Like the young men of "Young Siam," he was of the second Westernized generation and, indeed, like his father before him, he was more Westernized than most of the men who surrounded the king. On the other hand, he was pushed toward the regent's party by the logic of his position. Judging from the history of the previous four reigns, in each of which there had been serious collisions between the king and the "second king,"[28] the two offices were inherently antagonistic, and they became increasingly so with the relative rise in the position of the "second king" during the Fourth Reign, when Mongkut initially insisted upon making Phra Pin Klao virtually his equal. Prince Wichaichan appears to have wished to maintain the position of power and influence that his father had enjoyed, but he could do so only by gaining the support of the regent and his party, as such an enhancement of his powers could only come at the expense of the king.

It would be difficult to see in the "second king" a representative of "Old Siam." He and his party only once, and very briefly, took up a political position independent of the regent's faction. One would have to seek "Old Siam" among the masses of the capital bureaucracy, those older and lesser officials whose families had created small niches for themselves in the ministries and departments of government and who feared their loss in the event of any change. Many of them may have made their living by petty exactions from their dues of office which financial reforms would threaten. Many were caught between the rationalizing policies of the king's party and growing Bunnag encroachment upon their positions. Their reaction probably was a simple wish to be left alone, undisturbed by anyone, and not to be drawn into the games of higher stakes which the major actors were playing. It is only among this group—at whom the epithet "ancient heads" undoubtedly was directed by the king[29]—that

28. Chulalongkorn, *Phrabqrommarachowat*, pp. 3–16.
29. Kachorn, *Kao raek*, p. 35.

any substantial amount of xenophobic anti-Western sentiment might have been found.

Certainly much of the antagonism that separated the three major parties must have flowed from generational differences and the vast disparities in experience each had known. The "ancient heads" of Suriyawong's generation were all active in public life by the middle of the Third Reign, in an old Bangkok but little frequented by Singapore traders. Prince Wichaichan was among the eldest of the sons of this generation and grew up in the early years of Mongkut's reign, at the very time when rapid change first began to transform the life and concerns of the city. Chulalongkorn and his brothers were of the age of the regent's grandchildren and Wichaichan's children, and they had never known a Siam without an omnipresent West as threat and example. By each group the West was differently perceived in memory and in portent. It must be of some significance that one generation—that of Wichaichan—was lost in the transition from Mongkut to Chulalongkorn, from the court of a grandfather to the court of a boy, when in the eighties ministerial posts passed from the hands of the regent's generation to those of Chulalongkorn's young brothers and friends. But more important is the fact that common to each of the three major factions was some degree of Westernization, expressed in the use of Western methods and techniques, the application of Western ideas to the correction of Thai weaknesses, or the extent to which imitation and emulation could be carried. Thus the political struggles these groups fought were partly over objects expressed in Western terms (reform and modernization) and partly over objects expressed in traditional Thai terms (the nature of political power and the identity of those who would wield it); but the struggles always revolved around problems of timing and degree, and not around the fundamental commitment the nation's rulers had made to conciliation and accommodation of the West. That decision had been made. The three major parties, however, disagreed violently in their assessments of the present dangers of their nation's situation and of the necessity for reform and its urgency. As Chulalongkorn's second coronation approached, the battle became more intense.

REFORM, CRISIS, AND RETREAT

Toward the end of the regency period, King Chulalongkorn initiated a series of limited but not inconsequential reforms. As their implications and the tenor of the young king's reforming propensities became clear, these reforms provoked one of the most serious political crises in modern Thai history, which left a scar to caution the king for all the years of his reign.

The initial legislation of King Chulalongkorn's reign was, generally, a continuation of the program of King Mongkut, although at a stepped-up pace. These laws included a decree regulating the conditions of debt slavery and making it easier for a debt slave to be redeemed, a decree liberalizing the ancient law governing witnesses in litigation, a decree establishing new procedures for speeding criminal and civil cases through the courts in Bangkok, decrees calling for the keeping of more accurate and less easily falsified records of taxation, land ownership, and litigation, and a decree regulating the sale of opium and strengthening the opium monopoly.[30] In addition, at his coronation in November 1873, Chulalongkorn announced his celebrated decree abolishing prostration in the royal presence.[31] These were important laws, consistent with the enlightened principles of the day. They were promulgated under the authority of the regent and drawn up with the common consent and advice of the most important state officials. They were not, however, basic laws which in themselves could affect the fiber of the kingdom or challenge the power, authority, position, or wealth of the "pillars of the state," the chief ministers of the kingdom and the political factions they led or joined. They were

30. *PKPS,* vol. 8, which contains laws for the years 1868–71.
31. *PKPS, 8,* 114. For a translation of parts of this decree, which emphasized the king's desire to emulate "civilized" standards, see Detchard Vongkomolshet, "The Administrative, Judicial, and Financial Reforms of

the sorts of laws which, even when unpopular, demanded at least lip service from all, particularly when they were cast in orthodox, traditional religious and moral terms.

The decrees that followed Chulalongkorn's coronation as king in his own right, however, brought political conflict into the open. The most important of these attempted to effect reforms in slavery, the judiciary, finance, and the political process.

The first steps toward the abolition of slavery had been taken early in the regency period, but these touched only debt slavery. On 21 August 1874, however, the king, with the advice and consent of his government, issued a new decree requiring that all children born into slavery beginning in the year 1868/69 should be freed upon attaining the age of twenty-one years.[32] The preface to this law stated that it was the king's policy to reconsider the laws and customs of the country with a view to their effect on the progress of the nation and the justice of its institutions, and to abolish those practices and laws that did not meet these tests. The preface did, however, recognize the necessity for gradual reform. The most noxious feature of the traditional laws on slavery, dating back to the very beginning of the Ayudhya period, was that they considered as slaves those who, through no fault of their own, were born into the condition of slavery, visiting, so to speak, the sins of the parents on their children. It was particularly to remove this feature that this decree was promulgated.[33] In a later decree, the king expressed his hope and intention that slaves so freed might engage in paid labor and buy their parents' freedom, and that the increasing use of wage labor would work to the diminution of slavery.[34] To the degree to which the nobles had their capital invested in such captive labor, to that extent was the reform of

---

King Chulalongkorn, 1868–1910" (M.A. thesis, Cornell University, 1958), pp. 54–55; and *SWA*, 29 Nov. 1873.

32. "Phraratchabanyat phikat krasian ayu luk that luk thai," *PKPS, 8,* 197–207.

33. Ibid., pp. 198–99.

34. "Prakat krasian ayu luk that luk thai," *PKPS, 8,* 219–21.

slavery an attack upon their wealth and position. Although it is
impossible to assess the proportion of the population so affected,
slaveholding undoubtedly was common, and many nobles must
have viewed the king's action with some alarm.

In 1874, the king also attempted to alleviate some of the
most flagrant abuses in the judicial system. A special court was
established directly responsible to the king in order to clear the
backlog of cases pending in the courts of the major ministries,
in the *krom nakhǫnban* (Capital) *mahatthai* (North), *kalahom*
(South), and *krom tha* (Coastal) jurisdictions.[35] This action constituted a threat to the established judicial order (or disorder),
by which each of four ministries, with responsibilities for omni-
competent administration in defined geographical areas, had
its own courts of law. More immediately, however, this decree
undermined the economic status of many individuals in each of
the ministries concerned, since all officials engaged in judicial
work derived a substantial proportion of their income from
court and legal fees. The new court instituted new procedures
and court rules to attempt to reduce opportunities for corrup-
tion and marked a further advance on the procedural reforms
of the regency period. The challenge this reform posed to established interests could not have been ignored.[36]

Similarly far-reaching reforms were initiated in the financial
administration. Financial reforms were a common feature of
each reign of the Bangkok period, occasioned partly by the
Burney and Bowring treaties but primarily by the personal
nature of much of the revenue system, by which revenues frequently were apportioned to individuals rather than to offices.
Chulalongkorn's moves toward financial reform partook of
some of these common features, but also introduced new, abstract considerations of impartiality, economic viability, and
modernity.

35. "Phraratchabanyat samrap tralakan san rap sang" 14 July, 1874,
PKPS, 8, 162.
36. These judicial measures later were modified to accommodate established interests, in the aftermath of the Front Palace Incident described
below. See a decree of 10 Mar. 1875, in *PKPS, 8,* 257.

During the early years of the regency period minor reforms had been effected to standardize taxation rates and to reduce opportunities for peculation. The most significant reform, however, came near the end of the regency period with the promulgation of the "Royal Ordinance for the Finance Office *(hǫ ratsadakǫnphiphat)*" on 4 June 1873.[37] Chulalongkorn was himself heavily committed to this reform. He was aware of the fact that whatever progressive reforms he might accomplish would depend for their success upon the provision of adequate revenues, and the traditional organization of state finances would not suffice to raise them.[38] He had, moreover, a special impetus to reform in the fact that state finances, which normally were in balance, ran 8,000,000 *baht* in debt during the five years of the regency period. Many revenues that formerly had been paid into the national treasury or the privy purse had been diverted into the pockets of the regent and other high government officials, and the incomes of some members of the royal family were so reduced that they were forced, according to the king, to scurry around Bangkok to dun their official debtors.[39]

With the aid of the king's elderly uncle, Prince Čhaofa Mahamala, then Minister of Finance, the new Finance Office was established to centralize the collection of revenues from the various tax farms and ministries in a single office, to provide for uniform accounting procedures, to safeguard against embezzlement and bribery, to provide for the public auction of tax farms, and to space the revenues over the twelve months of the year. The king personally supervised the task of auditing

37. "Phraratchabanyat samrap hǫ ratsadakǫnphiphat," *PKPS, 8,* 83–99. A summary of this law is given by Wira, *Historical Patterns,* pp. 112–14; and there is a full translation in *Siam Repository,* 6 (1874), 183–89.

38. Prince Damrong Rajanubhab, "Phraprawat somdet phračhao bǫrommawongthoe kromphraya thewawong waroprakan," in Damrong et al., *Phraratchaprawat,* pp. 112–13; and Detchard, "Reforms," pp. 180–87.

39. Chulalongkorn to Prince Wachirayan, 28 Oct. 1903, printed in King Chulalongkorn and Prince Wachirayan Warorot, *Phraratchahatlekha phrabat somdet phra čhunlačhǫmklao čhaoyuhua song mi paima kap somdet phra maha samanačhao kromphraya wachirayan warorot* (Bangkok, 1929), pp. 224–28.

the accounts of the various ministries, assisted by three of his younger brothers, the princes Devawongse, Sommot, and Naret, in what became known as the Royal Audit Office in 1874.[40] With the assistance of the Privy Council and the Council of State, the king's control over state finances was further extended with an announcement in 1874 that the ministries and departments of government thenceforth would be required to budget their expenditures in consultation with the Finance Office and obtain permission for any unusual expenditures.[41] These reforms had the effect of bringing about a 50 percent increase in state revenues in two years and relieved the financial pressures which might otherwise have tended to inhibit reform.[42]

Finally, in a decree of 8 May 1874, the king moved to transform the political system. It had long been his desire, he stated, to work for the improvement of Siam, and his travels abroad had shown him forms and practices that might profitably be put to use in Siam. Success in reform, however, could come only through the joint efforts of the king and others. In order that a wider spectrum of advice and experience might be brought to bear on this work, he announced the inauguration of two advisory councils. One, the Council of State, was to be composed of twenty senior government officials and members of the royal family and was to act as the official adviser of the government at a subministerial or ministerial level. Matters of importance, when decided upon by the council, still had to gain the sanction of the ministers of state, although the king could override the council or the ministers. This body was most frequently concerned with the drafting of new laws. A second body, the Privy Council, was composed of younger officials and members of the royal family. Its primary function was to serve

40. Damrong, "Phraprawat thewawong," p. 113; Phraya Si Wǫrawong, *Phraprawat phračhaobǫrommawongthoe kromphra sommot amǫraphan* (Bangkok, 1916), p. 5; and Detchard, pp. 185–87.

41. "Wa duai čhatkan phraklang thang puang" 22 June 1874, *PKPS*, 8, 139–43. This decree later was formalized in law on 14 Apr. 1875, *PKPS, 9,* 16–92.

42. See Wira, *Historical Patterns,* pp. 112–14, tables VI and VIII.

as the "eyes and ears" of the king, to point out abuses and recommend corrective measures. It was given powers to investigate matters of common concern and had the powers of a court in this respect. It enjoyed the privilege of direct access to the king, either in public audience or, if permitted by the king, privately. The activities of its members were, on the whole, directed by the king, and their recommendations were subject to the approval of the Council of State and the king.[43]

Each of these reforms aroused some opposition and controversy, and each of the major decrees had to be followed by supplementary expressions and explanations of the king's intentions in promoting these reforms. Thus, two months after the decree providing for the freeing of all children born into slavery after 1868, an announcement was published emphasizing the gradual nature of this reform and the king's restraint in not following the advice of those who would abolish slavery outright. In this decree, the king also stated that he would like to abolish gambling, which was the cause of so much debt slavery, but that he was prevented from doing so by the government's financial dependence on the revenues from gambling taxes, which amounted to 880,000 baht each year. He further expressed his expectation that slavery eventually would die of its own accord as the use of wage labor increased.[44] Slavery did not, however, become a major political issue, primarily because it was attacked in a combination of traditional and modern moral terms which could not seriously be opposed, and because it was handled in a conciliatory and purposeful manner.

On the issues of financial reform and the inauguration of

43. See *PKPS,* vol. 8, for the series of nine decrees establishing the councils. Note that English terms were used for the councils and their members: "Khaonsin ǫp satet" for Council of State, "Priwi khaonsin" for Privy Council, and "khaonsinlǫ" for "councillor." For good summary descriptions of the councils, see Detchard, pp. 63–73; and Prachoom Chomchai, ed. and tr., *Chulalongkorn the Great: A Volume of Readings Edited and Translated from Thai Texts* (Tokyo, 1965), pp. 31–43.

44. "Prakat krasian ayu luk that luk thai" 18 Oct. 1874, *PKPS, 8,* 216–21.

the advisory councils, however, the factions collided. That they
did so was mainly the fault of the young king—an error of
his youth and political inexperience. Both these innovations
had their roots in Chulalongkorn's personally troubled and
unhappy experience during the regency, in his fears for his
own and his dynasty's safety, and in what must have been his
rage at the financial indignities he and his family had to face.
The councils, and particularly the Privy Council, were a cal-
culated attack upon the old order and the regent's group,
and most members of the latter refused to serve on them.[45]
These councils were patterned very obviously on Western models, even to the procedural details that governed their meetings
and the titles that designated their officers, as well as the names
given to the councils themselves, all of which were direct tran-
scriptions from English. The Privy Council was packed with the
king's favorites, including men from the antiregent conspiracy,
and their speeches in the council appeared extremely radical
to most officials in the capital. Finally, the regent's group
feared, perhaps justifiably, that the special oath required of
councillors might be used against them if they swore it. Their
fears seemed confirmed, when, in October 1874, the Minister
of Lands, Phraya Ahanborirak (Nut Phlangkun), a member
of the Privy Council and nephew of Suriyawong, was charged
with violating his oath by engaging in official peculation and
was dismissed from his high position.[46] With the establishment

45. The ex-regent was followed by his son, the *Kalahom* Čhaophraya
Surawong Waiyawat (Wǫn Bunnag), who pleaded overwork and ill health
in asking to be excused from service on the Privy Council. Suriyawong,
who initially had agreed to the establishing of the councils, objected to the
oath required of Privy Councillors, arguing that such rigorous oaths never
before had been required of state officers, according to Natthawutthi,
Somdet čhaophraya, pp. 640–79.

46. Natthawutthi, *Somdet čhaophraya*, pp. 680–89. The decree announcing his dismissal is given in *PKPS, 8,* 222. Chulalongkorn directly
blamed Phraya Ahan for the financial troubles of the regency period, at least
as far as the Privy Purse was concerned. When Mongkut had been in financial difficulties at the beginning of his reign, Phraya Ahan's father, Čhaophraya Phonlathep (Long Bun-Long), had granted the king an annual sti-

of the councils, Chulalongkorn's party and "Young Siam" began to consolidate a position of power and challenge the old order.

The reforms and their advocates were attacked together. In an announcement apparently published early in 1875, the king took up the defense of the councils, pointing out that their financial reforms were necessary, and were, after all, only the efforts of a government attempting to collect the revenues rightly due to it and to control its expenditures so as to use these funds as wisely as possible. The king emphasized that the only people who would suffer from these reforms were those who had dishonestly been robbing the country of its revenues. The livelihood and prosperity of everyone, he argued, depended on government expenditures for police and military protection and facilities for transportation, and further economic progress would require heavy investment in roads, canals, telegraphs, railroads, and rapid water transport. For all these reasons, it was necessary that the government collect all funds due it and that expenditures be controlled, and the councils were only doing their duty in promoting financial reform.[47]

The most serious expression of opposition came in the "Front Palace Incident," which extended from December 1874 to February 1875, when the country came close to the point of political collapse and direct foreign intervention. Friction between the king and "second king," colloquially termed the "Front Palace," was common in the Bangkok period; but in the Fifth Reign there were more than the usual incentives to

pend of 160,000 baht in gratitude for his appointment as head of the *Krom na*. When Phraya Ahan, his son, succeeded him on his death in 1869, the sum instead was sent to his uncle the regent, in gratitude for *his* appointment, thereby reducing the Privy Purse by half. Chulalongkorn to Wachirayan, 28 Oct. 1903, printed in Chulalongkorn and Wachirayan, *Phraratchahatlekha song mi paima,* pp. 224–28. See also Salao Lekharuchi, *Piyamaharat čhulalongkǫn* (Bangkok, 1961), p. 136; and Sa-nguan Leksakun, *Rüang ngan patirup nai ratchakan thi 5* (Bangkok, 1954), p. 108.

47. "Wa duai prüksa čhatkan nai khaonsin ǫp satet, khü thiprüksa ratchakan phaendin," n.d., *PKPS, 8,* 271–75.

58   POLITICS OF REFORM IN THAILAND

conflict. Prince Wichaichan's appointment had been forced
upon the king, and the regent used him as a counterpoise to the
power of the king. Chulalongkorn appears to have viewed
Wichaichan's attempts to claim a status equal to that of Phra
Pin Klao as a challenge to the power and authority of the
absolute monarchy. Together with simple personal rivalry, all
these matters were issues in their relationship. The mutual dis-
trust of the two men and their parties was heightened in the
period following the end of the regency in 1873. The establishment of the advisory councils gave the king a wider base of
support, extending through and beyond the ministries, which
were headed by the regent's men; the financial and judicial
reforms of 1873–74 gave the king additional economic strength
and judicial initiative and posed a direct challenge to the regent's party. Meanwhile, the "second king" suffered the diminution of the power of his strongest supporter, Suriyawong, while
he saw at the same time a marked improvement in the health
and the economic and political fortunes of the king.[48]

The sparks that touched off the conflict were struck by the
king's young secretary, Phraya Phatsakɔrawong (Phɔn Bunnag), who had broken with the older members of his family
to lend leadership to "Young Siam." In an article in *Darunowat*
he took to task the members of the regent's party for their
failure to serve on the new councils and publicly stated that
his allegiance was to the ruling dynasty and to the royal succession through the ruling monarch's sons, implicity denying
the validity of the "second king's" position.[49] He apparently

48. Chulalongkorn to Wachirayan, 28 Oct. 1903, printed in Chula-
longkorn and Wachirayan, p. 228; and Chulalongkorn to Phraya Narin
Ratchaseni (Phum Sichaiyan), 25 Jan. 1875, printed in Natthawutthi,
Somdet čhaophraya, pp. 766–69.

49. Phatsakɔrawong's authorship of this article is convincingly argued
by Kachorn, *Kao raek*, p. 35, and his case is strengthened by two letters
the King wrote to Phraya Mahamontri (Am Ammaranon) on 24 and 26
December 1874, reprinted in Natthawutthi Sutthisongkhram, *Somdet
phra nang rüa lom* (Bangkok, 1960), pp. 175–78. Phatsakɔrawong, a major
figure in this book, is treated in greater detail in Chapter 6 below.

made a speech to the same effect in the Privy Council, of which he was a leading member, in November or early December 1874.[50] In response, the "second king," Wichaichan, began to smuggle large bodies of troops into his palace by night, where they were reported to be drilling while the rest of Bangkok slept.[51] At the same time he moved to rally support behind him. The ex-regent quietly removed himself from the capital, but Wichaichan expected support from the British consul, (Sir) Thomas George Knox, then temporarily absent in Europe, who was a close personal friend, a former drillmaster of Phra Pin Klao's troops, and married to a Thai woman formerly in the service of the Front Palace.[52]

On the night of 28–29 December 1874, a fire was set near the gunpowder warehouse within the walls of the Grand Palace, and the "second king's" troops, fully armed, sought entrance to the Grand Palace offering their assistance in putting out the fire. They were refused admission. The fire was quenched by

50. Chulalongkorn to Narin Ratchaseni, 25 Jan. 1875, printed in Natthawutthi, *Somdet čhaophraya*, pp. 766–69.

51. See the king's letters of 27–28 December, printed in Natthawutthi, *Somdet čhaophraya*, pp. 692–702. I have been given to understand that some years ago, when workmen were preparing the foundations for the central auditorium of Thammasat University, on ground formerly within the walls of the Front Palace, they unearthed a large cache of arms and ammunition dating from the nineteenth century, and probably from this period.

52. According to the king's spies in the Front Palace, Mrs. Knox, with her husband's and Suriyawong's blessings, was trying to marry her daughter Caroline to the "second king," assuming that Chulalongkorn's health would fail, bringing the prince to the throne and her daughter to great power as his chief queen. She and her husband reportedly told others that in this manner their daughter would become queen and their grandson king. Chulalongkorn took these reports very seriously in 1876. Chulalongkorn to Prince Pawaret, 7 Mar. 1876, printed in Natthawutthi, *Somdet čhaophraya*, pp. 835–41. The American consul was just as convinced of Knox's and his staff's complicity in the "second king's" political ambitions: see F. W. Partridge (U.S. Consul) to W. Hunter (Second Asst. Secy. of State), 4 Mar. 1875, no. 143; Partridge to Hunter, 25 May 1875, no. 146; and David B. Sickels (U.S. Consul), to Charles Payson (Third Asst. Secy. of State), 30 May 1879, no. 107; all in *DUSCB*, reels V–VI.

the palace guard, and the king moved quickly to strengthen the palace defenses, putting his men on round-the-clock duty. The ex-regent hurriedly was called in from Ratburi and undertook to find a solution to the crisis, whereupon the "second king" fled the Front Palace and took up residence in the British consulate on 2 January 1875. During the next two months the king and his ministers sought to effect a compromise, but the "second king" resisted, having been assured by the acting British consul that British aid in the form of a gunboat was on the way from Hong Kong. Finally, in mid-February, the governor of Singapore, Sir Andrew Clarke, came to Bangkok at Chulalongkorn's invitation and, by treating the incident as a purely domestic quarrel within the Thai royal family and refusing to intervene, ended all Wichaichan's hopes for British aid. Chulalongkorn effectively rallied the support of his ministers to buttress his resistance to some of the Second King's demands, in particular the demand that any agreement should be guaranteed by the British and French consuls. The solution gave the king the restoration of domestic peace and the reduction of the armed forces of the "second king" to a maximum of 200 men, while the "second king" was granted a larger proportion of the state revenues. Finally, and most importantly, Siam avoided succumbing to the drastic measures proposed by the foreign consuls to solve the crisis—the partition of the country into three parcels to be ruled by the king, Prince Wichaichan, and the ex-regent[53] —and he forestalled the extension of direct foreign interference in domestic Thai politics.[54]

53. See Natthawutthi, *Somdet čhaophraya*, pp. 793–94.

54. The story of this episode has never been told in full. The only substantial account of it was written by one of the participants, Sir Andrew Clarke, "My First Visit to Siam," *Contemporary Review, 81* (1902), 221–30. It is briefly and inaccurately alluded to in R. J. Minney, *Fanny and the Regent of Siam* (London, 1962), pp. 24–27, 36; and there is a passing reference to it in Pensri (Suvanij) Duke, *Les Relations entre la France et la Thaïlande (Siam) au XIXᵉ siècle* (Bangkok, 1962), p. 79. It has hardly been mentioned in Thai accounts of the period until recently. The account above is derived almost entirely from Natthawutthi Sutthisongkhram's

While this episode issued in a favorable conclusion to a dangerous domestic and international challenge, it had serious consequences for the cause of reform and modernization. In the early years of the reign, King Chulalongkorn had tended to be naïve and optimistic as to what he might accomplish with the power of the throne, and he seriously underestimated the divisive forces within the country. He had assumed a modicum of national unity and the general benevolence of the Western powers, but while he had mustered a show of patriotic unity in the face of foreign demands in 1875, he was able to do so only at the expense of his program of radical domestic reform. He barely survived this storm and could not risk another. Thus he had to strive both to maintain the political detente established at that time and to live with it. His own party of young reformers, most prominent among whom were his younger brothers, had to be asked to restrain their reforming zeal.[55] And the king himself had to face the fact of his uncertain tenure upon the throne, and began, as his father had before him, to buy property abroad for use in the event that abdication and exile became necessary.[56] Whatever youthful idealism he may have had vanished in those two months in 1875, and it was to be ten years before he regained it.

Thus began Chulalongkorn's reign, with a young and insecure king at the head of a small party of reform-minded young men, opposed by more powerful elements which neither shared its ideas nor were satisfied to follow the increasingly

---

monumental biography of Suriyawong, *Somdet čhaophraya*, pp. 690–819, 1863–88. He includes more than one hundred letters written by the king during the course of the incident. More supporting documents are presented by the same author in *Somdet phra nang rüa lom*, pp. 29–65, 172–85. These are usefully supplemented by the British diplomatic records in the Public Record Office, FO 69, vol. 62, and by the dispatches of the American consul in *DUSCB*, reels V–VI.

55. Chulalongkorn to Prince Phanurangsi, 28 Feb. 1875, printed in Natthawutthi, *Somdet čhaophraya*, pp. 786–88.

56. Chulalongkorn to Prince Čhaofa Maha Mala, 27 Aug. 1876, printed in Natthawutthi, *Somdet čhaophraya*, pp. 849–58, esp. pp. 856–57.

strong lead of the king. The reign did begin in a burst of reform, but it would be well to note the ambiguous nature of
some of these measures, particularly those introducing financial
reorganization and the advisory councils, which were much
more politically and personally than idealistically motivated.
In the end, it was clear by 1875 that domestic politics took
precedence over abstract considerations in governing the course
of events. Chulalongkorn's recognition of this fact may have
been brought about in an unnecessarily painful fashion, but
the king nonetheless deserves credit for assessing the situation
accurately and shaping his subsequent policies accordingly in
the remainder of the decade. Here he proved himself as adept
as his father in bowing to necessity and making the most of
time, which ultimately would work in his favor.

3
Educational Beginnings, 1870–1880

Together with the other reforms of the early years of the reign, one of "Young Siam's" interests was the introduction of Western-style education. Building and elaborating on long-established themes, practices, and patterns, the king and his party began almost immediately to attempt to provide for the young men of their class the benefits they had themselves gained from informal tutelage in the Fourth Reign, by establishing regular, Western-style schools teaching Thai and English within the walls of the Grand Palace. Within a few years they had in hand a program for extending at least the rudiments of such secular, Western education throughout the kingdom. Both the Palace program and its national extension, however, failed in the aftermath of the Front Palace Incident of 1875. The account that follows is an attempt both to describe the background and course of these modest innovations and to explore the relationship between their failure and the political circumstances of the period already examined in the previous chapter.

THE FIRST SCHOOLS, 1870–1875

The education of princes and nobles around the middle of the nineteenth century still lay very much in traditional patterns, despite occasional instances of Western-language or scientific instruction. Young men were expected to gain a minimal competence in reading and writing, an exposure to Pali and the principles of their religion, and a systematic vocational training in the profession of their class, the business of governing. All of them acquired this education, to a greater or lesser degree, as Chulalongkorn had, in the same sequence and at the same ages. It was the exceptional boy who continued his studies beyond the elementary stage in the arts and sciences, for most boys, particularly in the developing Siam of the nineteenth century, found ample opportunities for satisfying employment in the growing government bureaucracy. Well into the reign of King Chulalongkorn, a thorough training in reading and writing was not considered necessary for boys of the upper classes, for they would always have clerks to conduct their correspondence.[1] These patterns showed signs of change in the Third Reign, when men, particularly of the nobility, began to seek instruction in foreign languages and sciences from the American missionaries. Those who were the ardent students of Western culture in the Third Reign—Prince Mongkut, Prince Čhuthamani, who later became Phra Pin Klao, "second king" in the Fourth Reign, Nai Mot Amatyakul, who later established the Government Mint, and Čhaophraya Si Suriyawong, later kalahom in the Fourth Reign and regent in the Fifth—were in the course of the Fourth Reign to promote the instruction of others in English, especially but not exclusively their own sons. It was these men who were the first to send Thai students abroad,[2] and it was their sons who were to consider offering to others, in a more systematic manner in Bangkok, the opportunities for modern education which they had so imperfectly been afforded.

1. Damrong, *Khwamsongčham*, pp. 9–11; and Damrong, "Rüang prawat khọng čhaophraya phatsakọrawong," in Čhaophraya Phatsakọrawong, *Khamklọn khọng čhaophraya phatsakọrawong* (Bangkok, 1922), p. iii. See also Prince Damrong's "Laksana kansüksa khọng čhaonai tae boran," in Damrong, *Prachum phraniphon bettalet* (Bangkok, 1961), pp. 117–20.

2. On early Thai students abroad, see Ratchawọrin, pseud., "Nakrian thai nai tangprathet khon raek," *Chao krung, 12* (Jan. 1963), 35–39.

King Chulalongkorn, who had himself had extensive English instruction in his youth, had decided to establish regular, modern-style schools in Thailand even before his first trip abroad.[3] His idea was, strictly speaking, not a new one. There were ample precedents for his action in the tradition of royal patronage for ecclesiastical education, which dated far back in the Ayudhya period. According to Prince Damrong,[4] such instruction had been offered within the palace walls by King Song Tham early in the seventeenth century, and it was revived by King Rama I, the teachers being government officials, *ratchabandit* (Royal pundits). Rama III is said to have enlarged upon this tradition by establishing a school for the teaching of Thai when he was still a prince in 1820.[5] There is little evidence that this school continued long, and in all likelihood it was merged with the palace ecclesiastical school. The more cogent precedent would appear to have been the one set by Mongkut in hiring Mrs. Leonowens, in his efforts to hire Dr. House, and in his later engagement of Dr. Chandler for the instruction of his sons. However small these beginnings, they did mark the first steps toward the provision of formal secular education to groups of children. It was left to Chulalongkorn to enlarge and formalize the groups and modernize the syllabus.

The palace Thai school had its origins in a situation common to the beginning of every reign. Anticipating the sorts of personal changes a new king would make in the administration of the kingdom, highly placed families would present their sons at court for service in the Corps of Royal Pages, with the hope that they would be noticed by the king and chosen for government positions. More than a thousand such young men,

3. The erroneous impression one receives from most accounts is that the first schools followed these trips abroad.

4. "Prawat wat mahathat," in Bangkok, Wat Mahathat, *Anusǫn 25 phutthasattawat wat mahathat yuwaratcharangsarit* (Bangkok, 1957), pp. 51–52.

5. Ibid., p. 53; and Čhaophraya Thiphakǫrawong and Prince Damrong Rajanubhab, *Phraratchaphongsawadan krung rattanakosin ratchakan thi 1 ... thi 2* (Bangkok, 1962), p. 621, n. 1.

more than could be accommodated in the Corps of Royal Pages, poured into the palace at the beginning of Chulalongkorn's reign. The king chose from among them those with personal ties to him and formed them into a Western-style military unit, meeting on a very irregular basis, beginning early in 1869. By 1870 the group was flourishing, its numbers swelled by the addition of the king's brothers and cousins, and the king decided to have them trained in other than military subjects. For this purpose a school was established in the Royal Pages' Corps late in 1870.[6]

Some six months after returning from his first visit abroad in 1871, the king, seeing the progress the school had made, issued a decree inviting others to enter it.[7] Most prominent in this decree are the values that it expressed, couched in conventional terms. Literacy and knowledge of the "customs and practices of government" were held up as desirable goals and as means to the dual ends of service to the king and what in the Thai context constituted "liberal education," knowledge of the "sciences and manners." Thus, on this level, the decree can be seen to announce the conferral of royal patronage on these educational activities in pursuance of traditional ends. A departure from tradition in this decree, however, was the complete absence of any reference to the traditional association of education with Buddhism and religious values. But was this really a significant departure? It is also conceivable that the decree could be viewed as a traditionally valid extension of the royal powers of cultural patronage, not totally unlike the patronage that previous kings had extended to literature and drama, in their sponsoring of such poets as Sunthǫn Phu or the dramatic

6. Damrong, *Khwamsongčham*, pp. 160–61; Prince Phanurangsi Sawangwong, *Tamnan thahan mahatlek* (Bangkok, 1953), pp. 1–8; and Čhaophraya Surasakmontri, *Prawatkan khǫng čhaophraya surasakmontri* (Bangkok, 1961), *1*, 16–27. Surasak states (p. 25) that it was at the request of his father, Phraya Surasakmontri (Saeng Saeng-Xuto), that the school was founded.

7. "Prakat rüang rongrian," 30 Nov. 1871, *PKPS, 8,* 81–82, and in *Documents,* pp. 2–3.

troupes of the Second Reign. Nonetheless, the forms this patronage took, in the founding of a regular, classroom-type school and in the substitution of common instruction for individual instruction, cannot but have been construed as the borrowing of a Western form in the service of traditional values.

One other phrase in the decree is puzzling: the assertion that "once they have acquired a literate education, goodness, beauty and prosperity will be with them to the end of their days." This may be interpreted in one of two ways. First, it could be viewed as a vague and naïve expression of the traditional religious values ascribed to education, growing out of the belief that the purpose of education is to further one's religious progress toward enlightenment. On the other hand, a cynical reading of the decree would interpret this phrase as a veiled recruiting message, calling upon volunteers to join the king's cause and party and promising them tangible benefits if they heeded it. Because the education promised by the decree was to be offered in the Corps of Royal Pages, the single most important recruiting ground for both the king's personal service and government service in general, this interpretation cannot be ignored, particularly in the political context of the beginnings of the Fifth Reign.

Finally, one can discern in this decree the germ of an idea of great significance in the history of modern education in Thailand: the implied assertion that, in order for certain qualitative standards of government service to be maintained, it was desirable that these same standards be promoted through the educational system under royal patronage. At this time, however, the full implications of this assumption were not drawn out, and they were suggested here only in a somewhat tentative form. It was only much later that the consequences of this line of thought began to be realized.

The administration of and instruction in the school were placed in the hands of several of the king's personal retainers in the Department of the Royal Scribes *(krom phra alak)*, the most notable among whom was Luang San Prasoet (later

Phraya Si Sunthǫn Wohan, Nǫi Ačhanyangkun).[8] Chosen as the first teacher and later as headmaster of the school, he was to play a continually important role in Thai education until his death in 1891.

For classroom use in the palace school, Phraya Si Sunthǫn Wohan compiled a series of textbooks known collectively by the title of the first, *Munlabot banphakit* (Sanskrit, *mulapada parvakicca*, "First Steps toward the Performance of Obligatory Duties"). These were presented in 1871 to the king, who ordered them printed at the Royal Press in an edition of 2000 copies, to "serve as textbooks for the instruction of youths in Thai, for the increase of their knowledge, that they might become proficient in the use of the alphabet and the tone markers, correctly, expertly, clearly, and widely, and for the future benefit of the government."[9] Unlike the seventeenth-century *Čhindamani,* which was much more of the nature of a treatise on the principles of the Thai language and the rules governing poetical composition, the *Munlabot* series was very much oriented to actual classroom instruction. While the *Čhindamani* used examples only illustratively, in exposition and explanation of its theory and rules, the emphasis of the *Munlabot* series (which was four times the length of its predecessor) was overwhelmingly on drills designed to inculcate the rules, which were very briefly stated. In addition, the *Munlabot* series did not attempt to introduce students to the rigors of Thai poetical composition. Thus the difference between the books was simply that the *Čhindamani* was an old, Indian-style literary treatise, similar to traditional treatises on Pali and Sanskrit composition, while the *Munlabot* series was simply a textbook. In assuming this latter

8. Phraya Si Sunthǫn Wohan (Nǫi) was one of a large number of monks who had been acquainted with King Mongkut in the Third Reign, and who left the monkhood to enter the palace service during the Fourth Reign. There is a biography of Phraya Si Sunthǫn by his son, Luang Mahasitthiwohan, in Thailand, Fine Arts Dept. comp., *Phasa thai khǫng phraya si sunthǫn wohan* (Bangkok, 1961), 2, 1–26.

9. King Chulalongkorn's preface to the first edition, reprinted in the Fine Arts Dept. edition (Bangkok, 1963), pp. 1–2.

function, the *Munlabot* series fulfilled what must have been a long-standing need in Thai education which had only imperfectly been served since the end of the eighteenth century by the reader *Pathom k ka* ("First A B C"), of unknown authorship, a textbook of much less coherence and completeness which became popular early in the nineteenth century and was finally published at Dr. Bradley's press in Bangkok in the Fourth Reign.[10] Phraya Si Sunthǫn Wohan, who had spent most of his life in the monastery, teaching and studying, was well aware of the needs of both teachers and students for a simple but accurate and comprehensive textbook, and he filled this need with the *Munlabot* series. He broke with the Indian treatise style and method, with its highly logical and systematic exposition of the principles governing bodies of knowledge, and instead concentrated on the practice of reading and writing. In doing so, he contributed one more step to the reorientation of Thai cultural traditions in a new rational framework which was not as rigidly deductive and a priori as it had at least formally been in the past.

Once established, in a large building just inside the main gate of the Grand Palace, the school very quickly took hold and grew and for some years alone shouldered the burden of providing a basic, practical Thai education in the "three r's" for young princes and the sons of noblemen, a minimum curriculum which, it was hoped, would make them better crown servants. Thus from the very beginning of modern-style education in Thailand, the school was made a part of the process by which young men were transformed into government officials, and it was attached securely to previously existing insti-

10. Dan Beach Bradley, ed., *Nangsü prathom k ka čhaek luk aksǫn lae čhindamuni kap prathom mala lae pathanukrom: Elementary Tables & Lessons in the Siamese Language* (8th ed. Bangkok, 1875). There are a number of early textbooks of similar nature, all relatively short in length, and all dating from the mid-nineteenth century. They have been collected by the Fine Arts Department in a single volume, *Prathom k ka, prathom k ka hat an, pathom mala, aksǫranitti: baeprian nangsü thai, chabap hǫsamut haeng chat* (Bangkok, 1963).

tutions, the Royal Scribes' department and the Corps of Royal Pages.[11]

In addition to the Thai school, Chulalongkorn had hoped to establish an English school in the palace as well, when he returned from Singapore in 1871, but no teacher could be found for the boys and the project had to be postponed. In order not to delay the boys' education, a group of fourteen of the king's cousins were selected and entered in the Raffles Institution in Singapore when the king passed through there on his way to India early in 1872.[12]

Shortly after the king's return from India, an English school was finally established in a building next to that occupied by the palace vernacular school. An Englishman, Francis George Patterson, who had come to Bangkok to visit a relative in the Siamese service, was engaged as a teacher on a three-year contract, to offer instruction in reading, writing, and speaking English and French, and in mathematics. The student body consisted of two distinct groups. The brothers of the king were commanded to attend and were instructed in the morning, while in the afternoon boys came to the school from the Royal Pages' Bodyguard Regiment.

The school flourished for a brief period in 1872. Although Patterson knew no Siamese at the beginning, lively communication in the classroom was established with the aid of Pallegoix's dictionary and McFarland's grammar and with the assistance of boys who had studied with Mrs. Leonowens or at the Raffles Institution in Singapore. Although the progress of studies must have been slow under such conditions, the boys were able to answer simple questions put to them in English by visitors within six months after the founding of the school.[13] Patterson, who had had several years of teaching experience in his father's

11. For glimpses of this school in operation, see *Siam Repository*, 5 (1873), 114; 6 (1874), 18, 284–85.

12. Damrong, *Khwamsongčham*, pp. 172–73; and Bangkok, National Library, *Čhotmaihet sadet tang prathet*, pp. 57–61. All these boys were princes of the rank of *mǫm čhao*.

13. "Siamese Schools," *Siam Repository*, 5 (1873), 114.

school on Jersey, ran the school on English lines, both in organization and discipline, which could not but have appeared strange to pupils who were accustomed to much more informal schooling.

The school opened with nearly fifty pupils, but departures for government service, the Buddhist novitiate, other service, and studies, as well as simple dropouts, rapidly reduced the number of pupils by half in the first six months. By 1873 only five princes, brothers of the king, remained in the school, and in 1874 there were only three. Patterson was on the verge of packing up and leaving for home when his remaining pupils begged him to continue for the duration of his contract and petitioned the king for use of smaller quarters;[14] Patterson was thus persuaded to remain on into mid-1875.

By any normal standards this school would have to be judged a failure for its high attrition rate. As a teacher, however, Patterson's influence should not be dismissed, for the students who remained in his school were to be the outstanding leaders of their generation: Prince Devawongse, Minister of Foreign Affairs for thirty-seven years; Prince Damrong Rajanubhab, Minister of Education for seven years and Minister of Interior for twenty-three; Prince Phanurangsi Sawangwong, for many years Minister of War; and Prince Wachirayan Warorot, later Supreme Patriarch of the Buddhist Order. All these men were close advisers of the king, all were fluent in English, and all were men of an unmistakably new generation.

During the last months of the school's existence, Prince Damrong was Patterson's only formal pupil, but during this period Patterson also assumed the task of tutoring the young king in English twice each week. Damrong, who spent most of his days with Patterson—visiting other Europeans, walking about the city, talking and reading—accompanied Patterson during his sessions with the king. From these meetings, which lasted for only a short time, came the king's increased facility in English, and, most importantly, the beginning of the close

14. Damrong, "Phraprawat thewawong," p. 110.

collaboration between King Chulalongkorn and Prince Damrong which is such a prominent feature of Siam's modernization.
Chulalongkorn was later to tell Prince Damrong that it was
during these tutoring sessions that he first recognized his younger brother's character and ability.[15]

Patterson's contract expired in mid-1875, and he returned to
Europe. Some of his pupils continued their studies independently, but formal English instruction for the upper classes ceased
completely for three years. Although the king undoubtedly
was concerned for the higher education of the royal family and
the sons of high government officials, too much else was occur-
ring to divert both his and his generation's attention to allow
much scope to this concern.

The English school died a natural death with the departure
of its teacher, while Phraya Si Sunthọn's Palace Thai school
continued on quietly, unnoticed in the documents of the day.
For these two schools, the events of 1875 made little difference,
perhaps because neither seemed sufficiently important to those
who might have opposed or supported them at the time. To
those who so strongly opposed Chulalongkorn's other innovations, these two schools could have appeared as little more than
simple conveniences of which the king had availed himself.
Nothing about Phraya Si Sunthọn seemed very radical, and,
too, most young men must have continued to find good official
positions without attending his school. As for Patterson's school,
it could not have been perceived as anything very different from
Mongkut's employing Mrs. Leonowens and Dr. Chandler, and
it did not suffer from the additional disadvantage, in the view of
conventional Thai, of missionary associations.

It is likely that the king regretted the failure of the English
school to take hold and grow. At the same time, his goals
were considerably lowered by the sobering experience of 1875

15. Damrong, *Khwamsongčham*, pp. 185, 190. This account of the
Palace English school is based primarily upon Damrong, *Khwamsongčham*,
pp. 172, 179–90; and *Siam Repository*, 4 (1872), 399; 5 (1873), 114; 6
(1874), 18, 56, 284–85.

and the realization that reform would be a long, slow process. He could have felt that he had begun the epochal work which he may only dimly have viewed before him, but he was certainly far from completing it.

AT REDUCED TEMPO, 1875–1880

Between 1875 and about 1885 the course of reform was very much slowed. While some reforms and innovations continued to be promoted, they did not in any fundamental manner affect the distribution of political power or the foundations of the old order. Some alterations were made in legal procedures, and some changes occurred in Bangkok life. Police and fire departments were established, and Bangkok was connected to the wider world by telegraph lines. But for a period of about ten years, Chulalongkorn made no attempt to challenge his established political rivals or to effect far-reaching changes in Thai society.

During the period 1875–80, two attempts were made to achieve further educational modernization. The first was the most ambitious. Just four months after the solution of the Front Palace crisis, a decree was published in the government gazette calling for the extension of public primary education under royal patronage to all the royal monasteries.[16] This decree set forth the perception of the condition of Thai education and the proposed solutions for it which were to govern Thai educational policy for more than twenty years.

In the decree, Chulalongkorn expressed real concern for the quality of Thai education. He was well aware that its informal nature and the personal bonds between teacher and pupil and the pupil's family could work at times to the detriment of educational standards. Without explicitly stating his criticisms, he called into question the abilities of the monks and the methods and textbooks they were using. These defects, he felt, were

16. "Prot klao čha hai mi ačhan sǫn nangsü thai lae sǫn lek thukthuk phra-aram," *RKB*, 2 (1875–76), 111–12, and in *Documents*, pp. 11–14.

injurious to Buddhism, for they deprived a portion of the monkhood and the general population of the means by which higher
standards of Buddhist understanding might be attained, and,
concomitantly, provided the state with but a poor standard
of literacy.

One can only speculate as to the origins of this perception.
One might expect of Chulalongkorn something of his father's
impatience with imperfect standards of usage and spelling in
government correspondence,[17] and this was indeed a frequent
complaint of Chulalongkorn as king. One might also expect
of him some measure of his father's concern for the standards
of Buddhist scholarship, and the same demand that royal
patronage be productive of results.[18] Finally, it is a distinct possibility that, as Narai had before him, King Chulalongkorn had
compared the existing Thai educational system with that displayed in Siam by the Christian missionaries, and with that he
had seen in Singapore and India, and had found the Thai system wanting. There is no doubt that he was familiar with the
educational work of the missionaries, and it seems clear that he
preferred that Thai children seek their education elsewhere, if
possible.

The concept and organization of education proposed in this
decree were perfectly in keeping with traditional practices of
royal patronage for Buddhism. The traditions of maintaining
a class of monasteries as royal monasteries, of disbursing special
stipends to learned monks within them, and of holding ecclesiastical examinations were well established.[19] What is of particular interest in the decree, however, is that it brought new
secular emphasis into what had been almost exclusively a re-

17. See, for example, King Mongkut, *Prachum prakat ratchakan thi 4*
(4 vols. Bangkok, 1960–61), decrees no. 9, 11, 14, 15, 20, 35, 41, 179,
and 311.

18. "Prakat lai nangsü phra song samanen," 19 Nov. 1876, *PKPS, 9*
159–60.

19. Damrong, "Prawat wat mahathat," pp. 51–53; and Mongkut,
Prachum prakat, decree no. 33.

ligious activity. Literacy, according to the decree, was of value
not only for Buddhist scholarship but also for the government
service and for personal advancement. The instruction called
for in the decree was exclusively secular, as were the examinations which were to be sponsored by the king. The textbooks
on which studies were to be based were the *Munlabot* series of
Phraya Si Sunthǫn Wohan, books of an essentially secular
nature. Finally, these studies were such as could be provided
in the royal monasteries even with lay teachers, who would then
be paid salaries by the king in the same manner as the monks
were remunerated for religious instruction. These factors taken
together indicate a very real shift in educational policy, characterized by the beginnings of government concern for public
literacy for secular ends, while at the same time promoting the
continued use of traditional religious institutions to attain those
ends. This was, of course, made easier by the lack of clear
distinctions between the religious and the secular, but the beginnings of distinctions can be seen in this decree.

The most curious thing about this decree of 1875 is that
it seems to have had absolutely no effect at the time it was
issued. Contemporary sources make no mention of any regular
teaching having been established in the royal monasteries;
they report on no distribution of textbooks and no public examinations. The decree seems to have died completely, to be
resurrected only many years later. One can only speculate on
the reasons for its apparent failure to bring about any educational development. While it is likely that a few monks began
to make use of the government textbooks, no significant leadership arose, either within the monkhood or in the government,
to promote the educational activities called for in the decree.
One might suspect that it failed to gain the support of the
sexagenarian Supreme Patriarch, Prince Pawaret Wariyalongkǫn, and that it lacked a strong patron among the higher officials of government, who were either disinterested or too deeply
involved in the political intrigues of the day to work actively
to promote it. This explanation seems particularly valid in view

of the fact that when an essentially identical decree was issued nine years later, backed by influential people in government, it succeeded almost immediately.[20]

Thus, in spite of its constructive yet inherently conservative nature, the 1875 decree on public monastery education added little or no impetus to the pace of reform. It reflected novel ideas but, without patrons, it failed as action.

The next step in Siam's educational development did not come until more than two years later, with the reintroduction of government support for English education. Samuel G. McFarland, an American missionary who had been working in Phetburi and who had established a school there, wrote to the king in October 1877 to suggest that Americans might endow "a college at Bangkok for the education of Siamese youth, similar to Robert College in Constantinople."[21] Coming to Bangkok on a visit in November of that year, he was sought out by the king's private secretary, Phraya Phatsakọrawong (Phọn Bunnak) and was informed that the king desired to establish such a school and would like to have McFarland direct it. After some months, McFarland agreed to abandon his missionary labors and submitted a proposal to the king.[22]

20. See Chapter 5. It should be noted that the director of the *krom thammakan*, Phra Wutthikanbọdi (M.R.W. Khli Suthat na Ayudhya), under whose name the 1875 decree was issued, appears to have been unpopular with some elements of the Sangha at this time. *Darunowat*, 3 7 8 1236 (4 Aug. 1875). He later served as Minister of Public Instruction, 1902–1911.

21. Text is given in *SWA*, 16 May 1878.

22. L. [sic] G. McFarland to Mr. Torry, n.d., printed in U.S. Dept. of Interior, Bureau of Education, *Progress of Western Education in China and Siam* (Washington, D.C., 1880), p. 13. On McFarland and his school, see the present author's "Samuel McFarland and Early Educational Modernization in Thailand, 1877–1895," *Felicitation Volumes of Southeast-Asian Studies Presented to His Highness Prince Dhaninivat* (Bangkok, 1965), *1*, 1–16. The American consul, David B. Sickels, reported that McFarland's appointment as "Superintendent of Education" was strongly opposed by Knox, the British consul-general, who went so far as to import his own candidate for the post. Sickels to Hunter, 19 July 1878, no. 92; and Sickels to Payson, 30 Oct. 1879, no. 120; both in *DUSCB*, reel VI.

In July 1878, McFarland's plan was presented to the king. At the suggestion of Phraya Phatsakǫrawong, the government agreed to grant McFarland an annual salary of 6400 baht over a five-year term, and to provide 9600 baht annually for the expenses of the school. The old Nantha-Utthayan Palace, generally known as Suan Anand, was refurbished and put at the school's disposal. The school was set up as a combination boarding and day school, teaching in both English and Siamese. According to the king's diary, on the advice of Phraya Phatsakǫrawong, "only training in reading and writing and handwriting sufficient for clerks" was to be taught, and "the teaching of Christianity will be strictly prohibited." The school might also offer such instruction in mathematics and the arts and sciences as might be "useful to the country."[23]

Rather than be made an organ of government, the school was put under a governing committee whose members included Phraya Phatsakǫrawong, Phraya Aphairannarit (Wet), Čhaomün Waiwǫranat (Čhoem Saeng-Xuto), Phraya Si Sunthǫn Wohan, and Phraya Owatwǫrakit (Kaen), teachers at the Palace Thai school, and several of the king's brothers, including Princes Čhakkraphat, Phitchit Prichakan, and Sommot Amǫraphan. It was with this committee that Dr. McFarland signed his contract in October 1878, with the understanding that he would be given a free hand in all academic matters.[24]

The school opened on 2 January 1879 and admitted in its first year one hundred royal and noble pupils, of whom half were awarded full scholarships for tuition and board by the school committee. They were taught by four Thai and three American teachers, including Dr. McFarland and, later, his

23. King Chulalongkorn, *Čhotmaihet phraratchakit raiwan,* 7 (Bangkok, 1934), 164–66.

24. Ibid.; Surasakmontri, *Prawatkan, 1,* 159; and Bertha Blount McFarland, *McFarland of Siam* (New York, 1958), pp. 48–49. Documents concerning the hiring of Dr. McFarland and the founding and early history of this school, formerly kept in the National Museum, were lost in a disastrous fire in 1960.

son George Bradley McFarland and John Eakin.[25] It is likely that many of the boys already had begun their studies in the Thai school within the Grand Palace walls.[26] The first year of studies at the school was concluded with examinations, said to be the first such examinations held in Thailand, on 19 December 1879, presided over by Prince Phitchit and Phraya Si Sunthǫn. The results of the examinations greatly pleased contemporary observers, and the school subsequently was advertised as offering a better education than could be obtained abroad, primarily because its American teachers all were proficient in Thai.[27]

The founding of Suan Anand gave the king two schools under his direct patronage, one administered through the Department of the Royal Scribes and the other through a committee composed of some of his personal retainers, friends, and younger brothers. The two schools complemented each other, as Suan Anand could offer either an alternative to or a continuation of the studies of the palace Siamese school, which was still flourishing in 1880.[28] Together these two schools were, however, the sole substantial accomplishments of a decade of thought and considerable activity in the field of education. Surely they must have been viewed with some disappointment by those who had hoped for more.

AFTER A DECADE

Over the first decade of Chulalongkorn's reign there were numerous indications of the king's interest in educational reform—in the early interest he had taken in the founding of a

25. *Chotmaihet sayam samai* (4 Nov. 1885), pp. 83–84; and Paul A. Eakin, *The Eakin Family in Thailand* (Bangkok, 1955), pp. 11–14.

26. Chulalongkorn, *Chotmaihet phraratchakit raiwan*, 7, 164–66.

27. *Chotmaihet sayam samai* (4 Nov. 1885), pp. 83–84.

28. McFarland to Torry, n.d., in U.S. Dept. of Interior, *Western Education*, p. 13.

Thai school, in his personal activity on behalf of the founding of the first English school, in the abortive decree of 1875, and in the high hopes with which Dr. McFarland was called in to run the Suan Anand school. There is also every reason to expect that his party, and particularly his brothers, was at least as vitally interested in modern education as in foreign newspapers, American history, constitutional government and liberal views of the kingship, and Western manners and customs. But what was the exact nature and strength of their commitment to modern education, and why did this commitment fail of execution?

One need not look far to see that their efforts, if they did not completely fail, did not measure up even to the minimal standards that had been set. The first English school had but a brief existence, and the second (McFarland's) took on only a semigovernmental character. The Thai school of Phraya Si Sunthọn Wohan continued on through the period and into the eighties, but it was of a special character, buried rather out of sight and serving specialized needs, virtually a special school for the Department of Royal Scribes. Finally, potentially the most ambitious act of the period, the 1875 decree, seems to have had no effect whatsover. The vast majority of young men entering government service continued to be educated in the same manner as their grandfathers and fathers had been before them, and with but one or two exceptions monastery education for the lay public underwent no changes whatsoever, save in those monasteries in Bangkok where printed textbooks began to be used. Even in the latter case, one would expect that for the most part this change consisted of no more than the substitution of the printed *Pathom k ka* for the manuscript version of the same primer.[29]

29. Two monasteries that seem to have been exceptions to the general pattern of stasis in this period were Wat Niwetthammaprawat, which was the chapel royal at the king's Summer Palace at Bang Pa-in near Ayudhya, and Wat Anongkharam in Thonburi. As to the question of the use of printed textbooks, this subject is discussed at length in Chapter 8.

All three goals—education for the improvement of the civil service and the ruling classes, education for religious enlightenment, and education for its own sake—had been frustrated to some degree; but was this a result of a failure in the commitment of Chulalongkorn and his party to these values, or was it a failure resulting from contemporary conditions? Can the relative failure of educational innovation during this early period be attributed to the same causes that contributed to the more dangerous failures of political and financial reform?

The value that Chulalongkorn and his party ascribed to education is understandable, given their own educational backgrounds. Chulalongkorn and his brothers all were exposed to Western-style instruction by Western teachers, and one must assume that the psychological and cultural impact of this instruction was not substantially less powerful than its curricular content, which imparted to these young men considerable facility in the English language, Western mathematics, sciences, history, geography, and Western manners and customs. Had these young men come to such education poorly grounded in their own culture, society, and intellectual traditions, they might have been regarded as what became known (pejoratively) in such a context in India as "Wogs"—"Westernized Oriental Gentlemen"—and indeed many contemporary observers seem to have thought of them as such. A reading of Chulalongkorn's letters, from any period in his reign, will belie such a characterization. To these young men, the attraction of "traditional" Thai culture was exceptionally strong, not only because it was theirs but also because in a great many ways it was good and it served them well. Thus they were faced increasingly with a crucial dilemma. They began by thinking that they could choose between Western and Thai values when the occasion for decision arose on specific issues; only later did they find, especially after 1875, that they were not free to choose, no matter how urgently the situation might in their eyes demand a choice.

The initial choices that Chulalongkorn and his party made, in favor of Western dress and manners and Western-style

schools for Thai and English instruction in the palace, in favor
of the abolition of prostration in the royal presence and the
abolition of slavery, were relatively easy, and they were followed
by no immediately unfavorable consequences. These choices
must have been satisfying to those who made and implemented
them. They satisfied new standards of propriety or othodox
Buddhist ethics or simple personal preferences developed out
of past education and experience. Chulalongkorn could be
praised by Westerners for his liberal, enlightened, Western
outlook on precisely those points that most irritated foreign
visitors to Bangkok. But the same observers severely questioned
Chulalongkorn's sincerity when he disappointed them on similar issues throughout the latter years of the reign. In doing so,
they misjudged both his commitment to some Western values
and the place these values held in the minds of "Young Siam."

Chulalongkorn was firmly committed to an Enlightenment
view of material and moral progress. He shared with his nineteenth-century contemporaries a belief in legal and social justice, which he could relate, however, to orthodox Buddhist moral
thought. Similarly, he conceived of his royal power as being
held in trust and shared by his ministers. He believed strongly
that it was the function of government to serve the people it
ruled, to advance their welfare and promote commonly shared
moral values. In strengthening his resolution to further the
practice of these values, Chulalongkorn drew support from
several factors. In the first place, his education, both traditional
and Western, inculcated these values in mutually reinforcing
Western and orthodox traditional terms, thanks both to Mrs.
Leonowens and to his father. To an important extent these
two sides of his education were complementary in mutually
stimulating the growth of strongly held and enduring commitments to such values. On another level, Chulalongkorn found
considerable personal and social pressure urging him to put
these ideals into practice, partly from "Young Siam" but even
more strongly from those who influenced both them and him—
certain members of the European community in Bangkok and

especially the European colonial rulers of neighboring states, whom he wished to treat him as an equal.

The overriding value, however, to which all others had to be related, was the survival of an independent Thailand and its survival as *Thai*. One can assume this value in Chulalongkorn as king, but it is also important to see it in Chulalongkorn as an individual Thai. In the political sphere, its primacy was essential in an age when Thailand's neighbors were falling, one by one or piece by piece, under foreign rule; but it was given an additional dimension in the context of domestic politics by Chulalongkorn's assessment that his own preservation on the throne was a necessary precondition to its fulfillment. Had he any doubts the Front Palace Incident would have convinced him of this.

Prior to the Front Palace Incident of 1875, Chulalongkorn proceeded with innovation and reform as if the validity of his modern ideas was sufficient cause to put them into practice and embody them in modern institutions, laws, and actions. He felt that such reforms as the advisory councils and financial reorganization, compatible as they were with both Western standards and Buddhist morality, would work simply because they were right and because in his view they promoted the attainment of a goal shared by all Thai, the preservation of national independence. With the tragedy of 1875 Chulalongkorn discovered that the rightness of an idea was no guarantee of its efficacy; that, at least in the short run, men, and not ideas, would make history. The Western benevolence he felt he deserved and on which he counted nearly failed him, the Western institutions and techniques he had imported had failed to produce the results he had hoped for, and the Thai institutions in which he had kept his faith proved only as strong or as weak as the men who ran them.

With these realizations came a new policy and a new attitude toward politics and reform, which applied as well to education as to anything else. It was perceived most accurately by the American consul, David B. Sickels, in 1880:

The party of progress, "Young Siam," appreciate the value of the old adage, "the more haste the less speed," and their policy is to move slowly and gradually, temporizing rather than raising bitter issues, abiding their time, until its efflux shall have removed the more acrid and influential members of the old conservative party and left the field clear for the introduction of more modern and more enlightened ideas.

The King is young; the contemporaries and counsellors of his father are old. He has all the advantages on his side and can afford to wait.[30]

Thus, in the decade after 1875, King Chulalongkorn restrained his reforming efforts. The few innovations he introduced were in areas where his authority was unchallenged and they were administered by trusted friends and relatives, prominent among whom were his younger brothers. For the time being, ideas had to be held in abeyance until men were ready for them.

30. Sickels to Payson, 18 Mar. 1880, printed in U.S. Dept. of Interior, *Western Education*, pp. 12–13.

4
Transitional Politics, 1880–1897

Early in the 1880s one could begin to discern a change in the political climate of Siam. This was not a sudden change, for Thai and foreigners alike continued to find fault with old Siam and to express the same hopes that changes would be effected to bring a new and modern Siam into being. By the middle of the decade, however, no one could doubt that the country was moving forward again, for the change in the character of political leadership was unmistakable. The king regained the control over affairs that he had enjoyed so briefly in the year after his second coronation, and the party of "Conservative Siam" was weakened by the loss of its most influential spokesmen. Under new conditions, reform could begin to regain its lost momentum. Extensively using his younger brothers, who during a quiet decade had been groomed for new roles in government, Chulalongkorn began around 1885 to start again the processes of innovation, thereby setting in motion a transition, a transfer of power, which was not to be completed until 1897.

THE DECLINE OF OLD SIAM

The decline of the old order was epitomized in the last days of the ex-regent, Somdet Čhaophraya Bǫrommaha Si Suriyawong. He had reached the height of his power in the post-regency period with the Front Palace Incident in 1875, and by taking advantage of an unfortunate episode in 1878–79 which brought about the disgrace of some of the king's most prominent supporters[1] he maintained a position of leadership from which he could exert a negative check upon innovation and reform.[2] By the beginning of 1880, however, his health was failing, and he spent an increasing proportion of his time in the western province of Ratburi. He finally died on 19 January 1883 at the age of seventy-four.[3]

The ex-regent was not the only major political figure to pass from the scene at this time. All seven of the traditional ministries changed hands betwen 1876 and 1888.[4] The Bunnag triumvirate, consisting of the ex-regent, his eldest son the kalahom, Čhaophraya Surawong, and his brother the phrakhlang, Čhaophraya Phanuwong, all left office within the short space of five years. Finally, the "second king," Prince Wichaichan, died in August 1885, having spent the last decade of his forty-seven years in relative political peace. The retirement of the old guard could not but have affected deeply the distribution of political power in the kingdom.[5]

Another factor that affected the character of Thai political life in the 1880s was the alienation of many younger officials

1. In 1879, one of the king's close friends and supporters, Phra Pricha Konlakan (Sam-ang Amatyakul), on marrying Fanny Knox, daughter of the British consul, was charged and convicted of insulting the king, embezzlement, and murder, and was executed. This episode is chronicled somewhat fancifully in R. J. Minney, *Fanny and the Regent of Siam*.

2. "Political Policy," *SWA*, 17 Mar. 1883.

3. *SWA*, 27 Jan. 1883.

4. Considering Foreign Affairs and Finance as separate ministries, which they had been since 1873.

5. The dates of the retirements or deaths of the six ministers are: Čhaophraya Yommarat (Choei Yamaphai, Capital), died 1876; Čhaophraya Thammathikǫranathibǫdi (Lamang Sonthirat, Palace), died 1882; Čhaophraya Phonlathep (Bunrǫt Kanlayannamit, Lands), transferred to Interior 1886; Čhaophraya Phanuwong (Thuam Bunnag, Foreign Affairs), retired 1885; Prince Čhaofa Maha Mala (Interior and Treasury), died 1886; and Čhaophraya Surawong (Wǫn Bunnag, *kalahom*), retired 1888.

from the old order. A few of these young men had been educated abroad, and many more entered the Corps of Royal Pages as their fathers had; but the corps they entered was very different from that of previous generations, suffused with a new spirit of innovation and a sense of national loyalty which went far beyond that of the past. By virtue of such experience these young men found their ties to the old order loosened, and many were drawn into what has been termed the party of Young Siam. These new ties were sufficiently strong in some cases to divide father and son, enabling the king to win to his side even some of the sons and younger brothers of the ex-regent. Given the decline of the older generation and the leadership of the increasingly confident king, the party of Young Siam found its influence expanding rapidly by the middle of the decade.

An equally important element in the rise of Young Siam was the growth to maturity of many of the king's younger brothers, upon whom he increasingly came to rely in the administration of the state. Chulalongkorn had assumed the father's role in the upbringing of these young men, arranging for their education in schools which he established and testing their abilities in his personal service in the Royal Pages' Corps and its military wing, as well as in some of the government agencies under his direct control, such as the Royal Secretariat, the Audit Office, and the departments of the Palace Ministry. Those who showed insufficient ability and devotion to duty were relegated to minor positions and sinecures,[6] while those who proved themselves moved rapidly to positions of great responsibility, where as a group they performed well. Between 1875 and 1889, fifteen of the king's brothers were elevated to *krom* rank, marking their passage to positions of responsibility after thorough testing in lesser positions. By 1885, four of the king's brothers were acting

6. See Prince Damrong's preface to M.Č. Wibun Sawatwong, *Khwam-songčham* (Bangkok, 1942), pp. i-iv. Prince Phuttharet, the first of Chulalongkorn's brothers to attain ministerial rank as Minister of the Capital in 1876, also was the first to be dismissed for lack of ability, in 1886. King Chulalongkorn, *Čhotmaihet phraratchakit raiwan, 22,* 30.

as ministers of state,[7] while others were being trained to assume ministerial positions and still others held important religious, civil, and military positions below ministerial rank.[8] This group of princes was to supply the country with some of its ablest leaders during a critical period in Thai history.

Chulalongkorn's use of his brothers in the highest state positions during the latter half of his reign might be termed nepotistic, but such a term has little meaning in the context of traditional and transitional Thai politics. Such a system had its roots in the limitations of traditional patterns of education, in which the only vocational training offered was that exemplified in the passing of a craft or profession from father to son. This was no less true for the arts of statecraft than for carpentry or medicine. But there were also additional incentives to follow such practices at this particular time. In the early decades of the Chakri Dynasty, a small group had freshly established its own vested interests and divisions of labor within the kingdom with respect to political power, and the natural growth of the leading families, including the royal family, did not put much pressure on the available bureaucratic positions until the Fourth and Fifth Reigns. By then, such families as the Bunnags numbered their descendants in the hundreds, the fourth Bunnag generation

7. Prince Phuttharet as Minister of the Capital (1876), Prince Pračhak Sinlapakhom as Minister of the Palace (1882), Prince Devawongse as Foreign Minister (1885), and Prince Čhakkraphat as acting Minister of Finance (1885).

8. In 1883, a year for which we have a complete listing, Chulalongkorn's brothers were distributed through the government as follows (all are princes): Phuttharet and Pračhak were Cabinet ministers; Čhaturon, Naret, Phitchit, Adit, and Phuttharet were members of the Privy Council; Sirithat, Devawongse, Sommot, Saowaphang, Sonabandit, and Naris were in the Royal Secretariat; Čhaturon, Čhakkraphat, Devawongse, and Wǫnwannakǫn were in the Audit Office; Phanurangsi headed the Palace Guard; Damrong headed the Royal Pages' Bodyguard Corps, of which Sonabandit, Adit, Narit, and Chumphǫn were officers; Phrom Wǫranurak directed the Royal Printing Office; Phanurangsi headed the Post and Telegraph Department; and several courts of law were under the direction of Phitchit. See Thailand, Post and Telegraph Dept., comp., *Sarabanchi suan thi 1* (Bangkok, 1883).

alone numbering 394 children.[9] The growth of the royal family was just as dramatic. In simplest terms, the ruling classes were growing at a rate considerably faster than that of the general population, owing to the greater prevalence of polygamy among them, and the pressure on the available government positions, which were still relatively limited until the 1890s, increased proportionately. The departments traditionally held to be suitable for the employment of royal princes, such as the Royal Pages' Corps and the Department of the Royal Elephants, not only were insufficient in number but were also of such a character as to be unattractive to this new generation. These departments were being superseded in power and prestige by such modern offices as the Customs Service and the Posts and Telegraph Department. Chulalongkorn had a remarkably talented group of brothers with whom he was well acquainted and whose talents were well known to him, and it was natural that he should place them in positions where their educational superiority and developed abilities could be utilized to the best advantage of the country, particularly in the new government departments which required such qualities.

The alternative to employing his brothers in critical positions of responsibility would have been for the king to turn to the more progressive elements of the old nobility. There are clear indications that Chulalongkorn followed his father's lead in attempting to do so, looking particularly to members of the Amatyakul family and some others who did not feel their positions or prospects to be threatened by the strong hold the Bunnags had over the traditional bureaucracy. Such men as these were active in the Privy Council, and were among the few who had appreciated the king's call for reform. This party and the king's faith in them, however, were severely crippled by the disgrace and exclusion from public life of the Amatyakuls following the

9. Thailand, Fine Arts Dept., comp., *Lamdap rachinikum bang chang* (Bangkok, 1958), pp. 9–47. The fourth generation of the Bunnag family here is defined to include the children of the ex-regent and of his brothers and sisters.

Phra Pricha case in 1879.[10] Without them, the king could turn only to his brothers, who shared his sympathies and were trained to assume responsibility.

During the decade 1875–85, the king appears to have restricted both his own and others' propensities for reform to the limited areas of government under his personal control. Thus Prince Devawongse acted as the king's foreign-language secretary until he was able to move over to the Foreign Office; Prince Sommot prepared for later duties as Royal Secretary and Keeper of the Privy Purse by work in the Royal Secretariat and the Audit Office; and Prince Damrong was prepared for a military career in the Royal Pages' Bodyguard Regiment. It was as if the zeal and youthful vigor of these intelligent young men had been bottled up for a decade when in the mid-eighties they left the palace and began to apply their energies to the building of a new Siam.

POLITICAL DEVELOPMENT, 1885–1892

With the turnover in administrative and political leadership in the mid-eighties, political change was inevitable: an older generation was rapidly yielding to a new one. Their modern ideas and ambitions would of themselves have stimulated change. The political evolution that they started, however, received a dramatic impetus in 1887.

Prince Svasti Sobhon (Sawat), the only one of King Chulalongkorn's brothers to receive a university education abroad, completed his legal studies at Oxford and returned to Bangkok on 16 April 1886. Nine months later, on 8 January 1887, he joined two of his brothers with whom he had become well ac-

10. On the Amatyakul family, see Sickels to Payson, 20 Dec. 1879, *DUSCB*, reel VI; and the biography of Phraya Aphirak Ratcha-utthayan (Chalaem Amatyakul), in Bangkok, National Library, *Chotmaihet sadet tang prathet* (Bangkok, 1917), p. (11). The documents on the case are in Natthawutthi, *Somdet chaophraya*, vol. 2; FO 69, vol. 70; and *DUSCB*, reel VI.

quainted when they were attached to the Siamese Embassy in London, Prince Bidyalabh (Phitthayalap) and Prince Naret, a cousin, Prince Pritsadang Chumsai, and seven other junior officials who had traveled abroad, in addressing a petition to the king, asking that a constitutional monarchy be established in Siam.[11] This document, sixty pages long, criticized the excessive centralization of political authority, the lack of ministerial responsibility, and the anachronism of absolute kingship, and suggested that only a more broadly based political structure could successfully resist the imperialist West.

The king's reply to this treasonable challenge to his traditional authority took the form of a written argument addressed to the petitioners,[12] in which he disclaimed any personal responsibility for the nature of the kingdom's political system and for the weakness of the throne vis-à-vis the bureaucracy, which had gained such an unusually strong position during the early years of his reign. He explained that the increase in his own executive powers in the interval since the death of the ex-regent had limited the amount of attention he could devote to legislative affairs. The king agreed with the petitioners' criticisms of the existing state of affairs, but he doubted whether the borrowing of Western political and administrative institutions would solve his difficulties until such time as sufficient educated men were available to assume such executive and legislative responsibilities. Two fundamental reforms were required before any political progress would be possible: the bureaucracy would have to assume more responsibility for the efficient performance of its proper functions, and men would have to be found to undertake the monumental task of legislative reform, which

11. The documents relating to this incident were utilized by Prince Chula Chakrabongse, *Lords of Life* (New York, 1960), pp. 261–63, and *Čhao chiwit* (2d Thai ed. Bangkok, 1962), pp. 548–54. They have now been published in Thailand, Fine Arts Dept., comp., *Čhaonai lae kharatchakan krap bangkhom thun khwamhen čhat kanplianplaeng ratchakan phaendin r.s. 103* (Bangkok, 1967), pp. 1–60.

12. Thailand, Fine Arts Dept., comp., *Čhaonai lae kharatchakan,* pp. 53–60.

was necessary to effect permanent institutional improvements. To the petitioners the king expressed his determination to achieve these objects, and he asked them for their continued advice and participation.

Only a few months after this incident the king sent Prince Devawongse, who was then, at twenty-nine years of age, the foreign minister and *Wunderkind* of the government, as his personal representative to attend the celebrations marking Queen Victoria's fiftieth year on the throne. He was instructed to investigate European systems of governmental organization and administration and to pay special attention to the criteria used in distributing the functions of government among the various ministries and departments. Prince Devawongse traveled through Europe and returned home by way of the United States and Japan. On his arrival in Bangkok he submitted to the king a report and draft "constitution," recommending the founding of a cabinet (Council of Ministers, *senabọdi sapha)* of twelve ministries, in which the seven old ministries would be continued but reorganized on functional lines, and five new functionally defined ministries added: Justice, Army, Public Instruction, Public Works, and Privy Seal. The heads of all twelve were to be accorded equal, full ministerial rank, and the two old offices of "supreme minister" *(akkhọramahasenabọdi),* the traditional prerogatives of the ministers of the North and South (mahatthai and kalahom), were to be abolished.[13]

At a special meeting convened on 8 March 1888, the king introduced to those selected for positions in the new Cabinet his scheme for the reorganization of the government, by delivering a lengthy speech in which he examined the weakness, inconsistency, and inadequacy of the old system of government and

13. Damrong, "Phraprawat thewawong," p. 128; and Prince Damrong Rajanubhab and Phraya Ratchasena, *Thetsaphiban* (Bangkok, 1960), p. 4. There are excerpts of this draft "constitution" in Prayut Sitthiphan, *Phaendin phra phutthachao luang* (Bangkok, 1958), pp. 249–71. On all essential points it confirmed the existing prerogatives of the king.

explained the reforms he was about to undertake.[14] He showed, however, considerable wisdom and political sagacity in presenting the new scheme, in the way in which he distributed functions among the ministries, in the regard he showed to senior officials and established ways of doing things, in the gradual manner by which he proposed to introduce the new order, and in his choice of men to fill the new positions.

The plan as adopted by the king called for maintaining the provincial administrations of the ministry of the North (mahatthai), which governed the northern and eastern provinces, and the ministry of the South (kalahom), which was responsible for the provinces of the west and south, although both logically should have been returned to their original functional character as defined in the fifteenth century, with the kalahom taking charge of all military affairs and the mahatthai of all provincial administration. The men in charge of these two offices, however, Čhaophraya Rattanathibet (Phum Sichaiyan, kalahom) and Čhaophraya Rattanabọdin (Bunrọt Kanlayannamit), both were elderly men of considerable power, influence, and experience. Any attempt to juggle their prerogatives would have jeopardized the reform program, so their ministries were simply bypassed for the time being. Because military reform was urgent, however, a separate Ministry of the Army was created, headed by the king's full brother, Prince Phanurangsi, who had been head of the Palace Guard *(krom lọm phraratchawang)* and the Post and Telegraph Department.

Reorganization preparatory to the major reforms was undertaken almost immediately, although the new ministries were not

14. Evidence of this meeting comes from two letters in private hands in Bangkok: Devawongse to Damrong, 7 Mar. 1888; and King to Devawongse, same date, R.648/49, copy. These clearly indicate that the king's "Speech Explaining the Changes in the Government" was delivered not in 1892, as has been commonly believed (see, e.g., Prince Dhani Nivat, "The Reign of King Chulalongkorn," *Cahiers d'histoire mondiale, 2* [1954], p. 456), but rather in 1888. Those attending the meeting included the princes Devawongse (Minister of Foreign Affairs), Naret and Svasti (Capital), Pračhak (Palace), Damrong (Army), Sommot (Royal Secretariat), Wọrawan (later Narathip, Finance), and čhaophrayas Rattanabọdin *(Mahatthai)* and Phonlathep (later Rattanathibet, *Kalahom).*

accorded full status until four years later, in 1892. Prince Damrong Rajanubhab, for example, who had been directing schools
and the Royal Museum from his office in the Royal Pages'
Bodyguard Regiment, was moved over to become assistant to
Prince Phanurangsi in the new Department of the Army, which
was slated to become a ministry; and at the same time the Education Department, which he continued to direct, was given an
independent civil status. In the following year, 1889, the organization of the future Ministry of Public Instruction was completed by adding the two old departments of religious affairs
(krom thammakan and *krom sangkhakan)* and the hospitals
(krom phayaban) and museum *(krom phiphitthaphan)* departments to the Education Department, forming the Department
of Public Instruction.[15] Other departments were regrouped
into ministries in much the same manner during these years.

   In 1888, the king chose the princes who were to head the
new ministries, and began their training by having them attend meetings of the Council of Ministers, while he himself
presided. The young princes brought the affairs of their departments and proto-ministries to the chamber and discussed them
with the others, while the king and the old ministers retained
their former authority.[16] In the course of the next four years,
departments were shifted and regrouped under one ministry or
another, and men prepared to take full responsibility for their
operations. Thus the transition to cabinet, collective government proceeded over a period of four years during which the
king prepared to devolve some of his responsibilities upon the
men of his own generation.

---

15. Damrong and Ratchasena, *Thetsaphiban*, pp. 3–4.
   16. Ibid., p. 5. The Cabinet of 1889 included the men noted in note 14
above, with the following changes: Prince Naret as Minister of the
Capital; Prince Čhakkraphong as Minister of Finance (Prince Narathip
acting in his illness); Phraya Phatsakǫrawong as Minister of Agriculture;
Prince Phanurangsi as Minister of the Army; Prince Svasti as Minister of
Justice; Prince Damrong as Minister of Public Instruction; Prince Naris as
Minister of Public Works; and Prince Sommot as Minister of the Privy
Seal.

CABINET GOVERNMENT ON TRIAL, 1892–1897

On 1 April 1892 a new era in Thai government began with the formal inauguration of a cabinet government, responsible to and named by the king. To this group of twelve men, nine of whom were King Chulalongkorn's brothers, a large proportion of the royal administrative power and policy-making was formally delegated, subject to royal approval for all their individual and corporate acts. This was indeed a step in the direction of the democratization urged some six years earlier by Prince Svasti, Prince Naret, and Prince Bidyalabh, all of whom sat in the Cabinet; but this organ was by no means a representative one. In many ways it functioned as the old Council of Ministers had done, with a group of semi-autonomous bureaucratic heads acting as arms of the royal authority. The Cabinet differed from its precedessors, however, in three essentials. First, the division of responsibilities among the ministries, at least in the early stages, was made primarily on functional lines, and an attempt was made to do away with the old omnibus concept of the ministry, which had tended to heighten the autonomy of each ministry and make each independent of the royal authority. This had been possible as long as each ministry could collect taxes, administer provinces, and decide litigation within defined geographical units. Second, this was a Cabinet chosen entirely by the king, staffed by men whom he could trust. Its composition reflected a drastic shift in power away from the old noble families, preeminently the Bunnag family, and to the royal family and the king. For reasons which already have been outlined, the king must have felt this shift to be a necessary one. The fact that the Cabinet was primarily a royal cabinet meant, however, that the royal authority lost much of the social cushion that formerly lay between it and the general public. This exposure of the power of the throne and the royal family may have been risky, but it certainly lent additional strength to immediate efforts at reform and modernization. For better or for worse, the acts of the government from 1892 onward clearly were the actions of the *king's* government. Finally, the effects of functional specialization of the ministries and of the Cabinet's composition made coordination of action and policy the chief object of government at this level. Siam's efforts to modernize clearly had reached the point where such coordination was necessary, as the tasks of government were so monumental and the resources of the state still very limited. It was assumed at the time that this new form of government would be able more effectively to marshal the resources of the nation in pursuit of improved domestic strength, efficiency, and welfare, the better to be able to resist the ever increasing Western pressures of the age of high imperialism.[17] In the face of a foreign crisis of major proportions, however, frustrated by the stubborn persistence of traditional governmental and personal political patterns, these hopes soon were disappointed.

The best contemporary description of these first years of the 1892 government and its operation has been left by (Sir) Henry Norman, who visited Bangkok for a short period in 1893.[18] According to Norman, the 1892 Cabinet proved to be not a deliberative and administrative body which could forge a common policy of internal modernization and united resistance to Western pressures, but rather a battleground for personal, intrafamily "cabals and recriminations."[19] King Chulalongkorn made the mistake of removing from the government his firm hand, his own ready grasp of administrative detail, and his single-minded devotion to what he considered the national interest, when he handed the day-to-day affairs of state over to his brothers in 1892. By the time the crisis in Franco-Siamese

17. See the king's decree establishing the new system, in *PSSR*, pp. 249–54.

18. Sir Henry Norman, *The Peoples and Politics of the Far East* (New York, 1895), esp. pp. 411–14, 435–40, 451–53, and 486. Norman's remarks about the king (p. 438) are wild exaggerations, but he had good informants on domestic politics, mainly Europeans in the Thai government service. I use his material with some reservations, but find it frequently borne out by scattered Thai documentation (note n. 22 below).

19. Ibid., p. 451.

relations came to a head in 1893, the Cabinet was in a state of constant chaos, totally unable to cope with the realities of the crisis; it was only by taking defense and foreign affairs out of the hands of the Cabinet that Siam survived and was able to come to a settlement with the French, at considerable cost to the kingdom. King Chulalongkorn then collapsed in remorse, his health broken and his heart saddened with the overwhelming sorrow he felt at Siam's great territorial losses and the personal failure of his own carefully prepared government. It was even rumored that he was contemplating suicide. For the next twelve months the wheels of government almost completely ceased to turn.[20]

One crisis that directly affected the future of the Ministry of Public Instruction and serves admirably to illustrate the instability of this new system occurred early in 1892, a few months before the Cabinet was formally inaugurated. While the minister-designate, Prince Damrong, was in Europe, his transfer to the Ministry of Interior was decided upon, leaving vacant his post in the Ministry of Public Instruction. At about the same time, the commander of the army, Phraya Surasakmontri (Choem Saeng-Xuto), presented to the Cabinet a request for a budgetary appropriation for modern equipment and uniforms for the army. The Acting Minister of Finance, Prince Narathip Praphanphong, a poet and dramatist of some note, would not consent to the request, explaining that "Nowadays the whole world has stopped using weapons of war and has taken to the pen instead." When the rest of the Cabinet refused to support his case, Surasak resigned his position, and asked that he be

20. Norman circulated the suicide rumor in "Urgency in Siam," *Contemporary Review*, 64 (1893), 745. In *Peoples and Politics*, pp. 451–53, Norman indicates that Chulalongkorn's withdrawal from state affairs and the breakdown in his health began in 1892. The Cabinet attendance records, however, show that he attended and presided over meetings throughout that year. These records lapse completely early in 1893. NA, 5 Q, 21/2. For Chulalaongkorn's postcrisis collapse, see James Mosel, "A Poetic Translation from the Siamese: Prince Damrong's Reply in Verse to Rama V," *JSS, 47*, pt. 1 (1959), 103–11.

allowed to retire. But King Chulalongkorn, anxious to retain the services of a loyal and able man, asked the Cabinet to find a new position for him. They hit upon the solution of moving the Minister of Agriculture to the Ministry of Public Instruction, giving Surasak the Agriculture post. So out of a Cabinet squabble—not his last—Phraya Phatsakọrawong came into the Ministry of Public Instruction as Prince Damrong made that fateful transfer to the Ministry of Interior which was to make his reputation.[21]

Prince Narathip soon received his due from those who resented his overly firm grip on the nation's purse strings. Early in 1893, the Cabinet and king ordered an investigation of the Ministry of Finance and an audit of its accounts, which was carried out by princes Phanurangsi, Naris, Devawongse, Damrong, and Svasti, at the conclusion of which Prince Narathip was dismissed and replaced by Prince Naris.[22]

Toward the mid-1890s, it began to be apparent that the new political order inaugurated in 1892 would not in and of itself generate the new Siam which had been its object. The first few years of the new regime brought the king to a realization similar to that he had experienced in 1875. Out of the king's perplexity, as events showed the weaknesses of his political strategy, came the beginnings of movement toward change, innovation, and reform, and the rise of a new generation of leaders very different in outlook and attitude from those who had preceded them. Around 1895 this change was first noticeable and by 1897 it was fully evident.

There are many things Chulalongkorn was not, as amply attested by a growing number of Western critics at the end of the century; but he was certainly his own and his country's severest critic—perhaps not least because he, more than anyone else, was aware both of the full force of the problems his coun-

21. Surasak, *Prawatkan, 4,* 265.

22. Phraya Anuman Rajadhon, "Phraprawat phrawọrawongthoe phra-ong čhao phrọmphong athirat," in *Tamnan sunlakakọn* (Bangkok, 1939), p. ii. See also Norman, *Peoples and Politics,* p. 436.

try had to meet and the slender resources it could bring to bear upon them. His 1888 speech on the foundation of cabinet government was a scathing indictment of the old order, and it set the tone for a good deal of his subsequent private correspondence and public pronouncements.[23] Most certainly he again became aware by 1895 that administrative reforms and new ideas alone were not enough to bring into being the new Siam he demanded as the price of national survival. Strong, capable men were needed. The 1893 crisis had shown him as much, for the Cabinet collectively had failed to respond effectively, and the king's own despair at this failure had thrown him into a state of mental and physical collapse from which he did not recover fully until well into 1894.

This is not to say that the new system failed completely, for there were a number of bright spots in the work of individual ministries and ministers. The best known of these is the reorganization of provincial administration undertaken by Prince Damrong in the Ministry of Interior. This work began to move forward with great speed in 1894, after the transfer to the Ministry of Interior of the southern and western provinces from the *kalahom* on the death of Čhaophraya Rattanathibet (Phum Sichaiyan) in that year.[24] Similar constructive work was being accomplished by other brothers of the king, especially by Prince Devawongse in the Ministry of Foreign Affairs, Prince Naret in the Ministry of Local Government (Capital), and Prince Naris, who was the "jack-of-all-trades" of the period, serving in the ministries of Public Works, Finance, and War.[25] However, the

23. King Chulalongkorn, *Phraratchadamrat song thalaeng phrabǫrommarachathibai kaekhai kanpokkhrǫng phaendin* (Bangkok, 1927).

24. On the work of Prince Damrong in the Minister of Interior, see Damrong and Ratchasena, *Thetsaphiban;* and the more complete account of Čhakkrit Nǫranittiphadungkan, *Somdet phračhaobǫrommawongthoe kromphraya damrong rachanuphap kap krasuang mahatthai* (Bangkok, 1963). A dissertation on this subject, based on the Thai National Archives, has been completed by Tej Bunnag, at St. Antony's College, University of Oxford.

25. See the biography of Prince Naris by his daughter, M.Č.Y. Duangčhit Čhittraphong, "Phraprawat somdet čhaofa kromphraya naritsaranu-

achievements of individuals did not add up to the success of the new system of administration. Other ministries did not fare nearly as well, and the Cabinet as a deliberative body simply did not function in the manner in which similar bodies functioned in the West. During the king's incapacity in 1893–94, public business came to a standstill, owing to the inability of individuals in the Cabinet to set aside their personal feuds for the sake of the public interest. In addition, the ministers could agree among themselves neither as to what the national interest indeed was, nor on the means of promoting that interest. Without the firm leadership of the king, they could as a body reach no decisions on matters of state. Thus they went on, juggling and haggling, each trying to obtain as large a share of the national budget for his personal ministerial empire as he could without giving much thought to the priorities the national interest demanded.[26]

It was only around 1895 that order began to be restored. As the king's health returned, one of his first acts, perhaps at the instigation of his Belgian Adviser-General, Rolin-Jacquemyns, was to revive the advisory councils of the early years of the reign, this time in the form of a Legislative Council, the main task of which was to oversee the general overhaul of the kingdom's legal system.[27] This council set in motion the process of legal

wattiwong," *Čhantharakasem*, no. 51 (Mar.-Apr. 1963), pp. 4–20; of Prince Devawongse by Damrong, "Phraprawat thewawong"; and of Naret in Prince Bidyalabh, *Samnao rai-ngan phračhaobǫrommawongthoe kromphra naret wǫrarit sadet prathet amerika ph.s. 2427* (Bangkok, 1926), pp. (5)–(15).

26. See Norman, *Peoples and Politics*, p. 451; and Surasak, *Prawatkan*, vol. 4. The budget figures for these years, reproduced in Appendix B, show an extraordinary fluctuation from year to year.

27. See Chulalongkorn's speech on the occasion of the inauguration of this council *(Ratthamontri sapha)*, 24 Jan. 1895, in King Chulalongkorn, *Phraratchadamrat nai phrabat somdet phra čhunlačhǫmklao čhaoyuhua (tangtae ph.s 2417 thüng ph.s. 2453)* (Bangkok, 1915), pp. 94–99; and the text of the decree regulating its acts, dated 10 Jan. 1895, in Prachoom Chomchai, *Chulalongkorn the Great*, pp. 44–48, where it is incorrectly identified as a law regulating the Cabinet.

reform which underlay much administrative reform and eventually was to make possible the abolition of extraterritoriality. The Legislative Council, however, could be effective only over a longer period of time. Of more immediate importance was governmental reorganization aimed at minimizing its weaknesses and maximizing its strengths. Its strength, such as it was, lay in the great ability of certain individuals and could not be attributed to any value inherent in the imported institutions. This being so, there was only one course open to the king: to rely temporarily on the best of the men he had, while working in the long run toward raising up good new men. In 1896, eight of the twelve ministries changed hands. The general effect of the changes was to take the most favored and able of the king's brothers out of lesser positions and to put them into the most important ministries. Thus Prince Naris moved from the kalahom to the Army, Prince Bidyalabh moved from the Privy Seal to act in two ministries, Palace and Public Works, Prince Mahis took over both Finance and Agriculture, and Prince Rabi, the first of the king's son to achieve ministerial rank, took over as Minister of Justice. The only ministers who retained their positions were Prince Damrong (Interior), Prince Devawongse (Foreign Affairs), Prince Naret (Local Government), and Čhaophraya Phatsakǫrawong (Public Instruction).

The problems with which the country had to cope at this time were too serious to be left to men of the old order or to the imperfect workings of borrowed political institutions. The army had to be brought to a reasonable degree of modern efficiency for protection against both external enemies and internal disorder; finances had to be put in order to support the other reforms of government; the legal system had to be brought into line with Western standards of justice in order to end the system of extraterritoriality which so seriously compromised Siam's sovereignty; provincial administration had to be reformed, both to strengthen central control over troublesome provinces and tributary states and to improve the ability of the government to tap the resources of the provinces; higher standards of law and order and better transportation facilities had to be achieved if foreign commerce was not to be dangerously disturbed; and an effort had to be made to remove practices and customs which at times were viewed by Westerners as "barbarous." Given a free hand and sufficient funds by their fellow ministers and the king, the best of Chulalongkorn's brothers could work toward the fulfillment of these objectives almost on their own. It was during this period, between about 1894 and 1897, that they began to make substantial progress toward meeting these vital requirements of survival and modernization.

By the time of the king's first visit to Europe in 1897 the political transition begun more than a decade earlier had been completed. There is a rhythm to this period very similar to that of the decade of the seventies. It began full of great promise and high expectations as the generation of Chulalongkorn and his brothers stepped into their inheritance, and plans grew to reality as long-nurtured Western political and administrative ideas and techniques took shape in new institutions, formalized in the cabinet government of 1892. There followed a three-year period of collapse as what can be described only as the ingrained habits of traditional politics and the bitter fraternal rivalries common in any polygamous society broke through the veneer of Westernized institutions and brought the kingdom to a state of paralysis such as had not been seen since 1875. The king, as in 1875, seems to have profited, if reluctantly, from the experience, and he set about salvaging from the wreckage those elements of order and progress, while seeking to isolate and neutralize the effects of some of his more willful and disruptive brothers. Through 1896 he reorganized his government and was sufficiently satisfied with it to entrust the kingdom to it during a nine-month absence abroad. The transition, the transfer of power from one generation to another, from the generation of Suriyawong to Chulalongkorn and his brothers and friends, was at last complete. Neither the individuals involved nor the institutions they established and attempted to run survived without damage, but they did survive.

5

Prince Damrong and the Education Department, 1880–1892

Prince Damrong Rajanubhab unquestionably was one of the most outstanding men of Chulalongkorn's generation. Born to King Mongkut in 1862 by the daughter of a prominent noble-man, he served his elder half-brother, King Chulalongkorn, and his nephew, King Vajiravudh, in a succession of vital posi-tions. He is best known for his work as Minister of Interior from 1892 to 1915, during which time he created the system of pro-vincial administration which, more effectively and rapidly than any other innovation of the period, made a reality of Thai nationhood. During these years, as well as in the three decades of active retirement that followed, he took up scholarship with the same great intelligence and energy that his administrative work displayed so brilliantly and left his country an immense legacy of historical and literary scholarship which stands as a permanent monument to his name.

Less well remembered, though equally deserving of attention, is Prince Damrong's early career as educator and first director of the Education Department, between 1880 and 1892. It was he who revived the dying educational reforms of the previous decade, first in founding specialized schools for the sons of princes and nobles, and then in taking up again the 1875 pro-posals for mass primary education. He consolidated the reforms, first under an Education Department in 1885 and then in the proto-Ministry of Public Instruction, serving as head of both. In his labors, after the abortive starts of the 1870s, came the real beginnings of modern education in Thailand.

SUANKULAP SCHOOL

In many ways it was natural that it should have been Prince Damrong, of all Chulalongkorn's brothers, who led this process of educational reform. Of all his generation in the palace, his education had been the longest and most thoroughly Western. He was the only one of Francis Patterson's pupils to carry his studies through the entire three years of the Palace English School, where he gained not only a formidable command of English but also a thorough acquaintance with the ways of Westerners. During the last year of Patterson's stay in Bangkok, Damrong had his teacher virtually to himself, accompanying him on social visits in the foreign community and enjoying long discussions with him on a wide variety of topics. For an exceptionally talented and intelligent boy like the young prince, this could not but have been a heady experience and he obviously made the most of it.[1]

Out of this period, which brought Damrong into increasing contact with the king,[2] came Damrong's first government appointment as an officer in the Royal Pages' Bodyguard Regiment, of which he became commander in 1880 at the age of eighteen. By this date, after five years in the department, Damrong had developed a concern for the effectiveness of the institution of the Royal Pages as an avenue through which young men could pass between boyhood and careers, where they were supposed to acquire sufficient general knowledge and acquaintance with government procedures to prepare them for their public lives, and where they might come into contact with the king and his court, so that their abilities might be measured and suitable jobs found for them. Although the Pages' Department had begun the reign auspiciously, attracting large numbers of royal and noble youths to its schools and service, its status by 1880 had declined with the prestige of the throne and the alternative attractions which an expanding bureaucracy could

1. Damrong, *Khwamsongcham*, pp. 184–85.
2. See above, pp. 71–72.

provide. Damrong found, on taking charge of the regiment, that young princes and nobles were not being attracted to his department but instead were rushing through brief periods of service as pages at court between their novitiates and government positions. They arrived at these junior positions with an inadequate education and with little knowledge of bureaucratic practices and procedures. To remedy this situation Damrong proposed to establish a school in his department that could provide all the advantages of the traditional system as well as the higher standard of education which government service increasingly required. His proposal met with the approval of the king and a promise of his full support, and the school began instruction in September 1881 with a headmaster, Phraya Owatwǫrakit (Kaen Owatsan), who was a teaching veteran of the earlier schools of Phraya Si Sunthǫn and Dr. McFarland.[3]

The school began with only ten pupils, almost all of whom were of royal blood, of the ranks of *mǫm čhao* and *mǫm ratchawong*. They lived at the school and, put under regular military discipline, they were given uniforms and military salaries and began their daily schedule with drill. Their academic studies centered, as they had in the earlier schools, on the six volumes of the *Munlabot* series of Phraya Si Sunthǫn Wohan, and the boys were directed toward military careers although they remained free to enter civilian pursuits.

The school quickly prospered and flourished, and it attracted large numbers of boys from the royal and official families. Within a year of its founding Prince Damrong was faced with a crucial decision as to its future. The number of places in the Royal Pages' Bodyguard Regiment was limited and, if the school were to continue to prepare boys for that service, further admis-

3. Prince Damrong Rajanubhab, *Tamnan suankulap* (Bangkok, 1963), pp. 26–27; McFarland, *McFarland of Siam,* p. 57; and *Prawat phraya owatwǫrakit (kaen)* (Bangkok, 1907). Damrong himself assisted in the teaching, in developing the syllabus, and in drawing up the examinations. M. Č. Phunphitsamai Diskul, "Somdet phrachaobǫrommawongthoe kromphraya damrong rachanuphap," *Čhantharakasem,* no. 46 (May–June, 1962), p. 9.

sions into the school would have to be restricted. If, on the other hand, Damrong were to follow the inclinations of his students and make the school a general training school for the bureaucracy, the curriculum and organization of the school would have to be altered considerably. He took these alternatives to the king, who unhesitatingly chose the latter, justifying his choice on the ground that the country was more in need of intelligent, educated young men for the civil service than for the army.[4]

In speaking to students and guests on the occasion of the school's annual prize-giving day in 1885, the king summarized his intentions in founding and supporting the school. He admitted that a major object of his concern was the junior members of the royal family, the grandsons and great-grandsons of kings, who without connections among the nobility were severely handicapped by lack of experience and training in competing with the sons of nobles for government positions. "I intend," he stated, "that this school shall be a means of preserving their position, that they might not be ignored as [junior members of the royal family] have been in the past." The king appealed to members of the royal family to send their children to the school for instruction, exhorted them to ignore its military associations with the Royal Pages' Bodyguard Regiment, and promised that its graduates would be free to choose their adult careers.[5]

There is more than one element worthy of note in this informal statement of Chulalongkorn's thinking in 1885. Immediately obvious is his concern for the prestige and power of the royal family, but what is more important is the sense of change he communicates and his determination to ride its crest. While it is true that personal considerations lay behind his desire to assert his power in the years immediately following the death of the ex-regent, it might also be well to bear in mind the political departures the king was taking in the

4. Damrong, *Tamnan suankulap*, pp. 27–28.
5. Chulalongkorn, *Phraratchadamrat 2417–2453*, pp. 36–38; also in *Documents*, pp. 18–22.

administration of the kingdom. His brothers were beginning, for the first time in the Bangkok period, to hold substantive positions of state, making realities of their departmental (krom) titles, which so often in the past had denoted mere sinecures. Chulalongkorn intended that his sons and grandsons should continue this practice, by virtue not of birth alone but also because they would be the ablest and best-trained men in the kingdom. He may have exhibited in his speech fears about the reappearance of the sort of situation he had experienced in the early years of his reign, when the traditional politics of the Bangkok period reached what may have been their logical conclusion, but he apparently was concerned equally for the political position of the throne and the royal family in a modern period just dawning.

A corollary of this changing political aspect was the changing character of public administration. Chulalongkorn's reference to the lack of opportunities open to junior members of the royal family reflected the traditional practices of vocational education in government circles, particularly at higher levels, by which government positions were handed down from father to son (or son-in-law). Such practices made it difficult for mǫm čhao and mǫm ratchawong to enter the administrative departments except by marriage into the established official families. Chulalongkorn's advocacy of modern education for the royal family was not only a reaction to this official exclusivity, but also a presentiment of a new Siam, in which increasing weight would be given to knowledge and ability in filling government positions. By the early 1880s, the king, with the support of his growing band of followers, was increasingly able to demand the rationalization of governmental procedures and organization in a formal, functionally specialized structure. This new system required men of a higher standard of education than the old order could provide. The evolution of Suankulap School into a preparatory school for the bureaucracy gave the junior members of the royal family an ideal stepping-stone to effective positions in the new administrative system which was then just beginning to take shape.

It was on such principles as these that Prince Damrong's school was reorganized in 1882. Given more spacious accommodation in the old Suankulap ("Rose Garden") Palace at the rear of the Grand Palace enclosure, the palace which Chulalongkorn had occupied before coming to the throne, the school then had room to grow and develop. The development of Suankulap School is interesting in itself, for it was first government school to take root in the institutional structure of the country; but it is even more important because it served as the experimental model upon which much of the country's subsequent educational development was based.

In line with the new civil character of the school, Prince Damrong eliminated military discipline and training in the lower grades of the school, reserving entrance into the Royal Pages' Bodyguard Regiment to the advanced students and providing that military training in the upper grades be made optional. It thus became possible to receive a purely civilian education in the school. Shortly thereafter, he lowered the age of admission, so that the education of the pupils could be relatively more complete when they left Suankulap for government positions.[6] The curriculum of the school was divided into two standards. An elementary course was offered which stayed well within the pattern established by the palace school, using the six readers of the *Munlabot* series. Standard II, which was not added to the curriculum until about 1882, was more specifically oriented to the needs of the bureaucracy. Entering this standard with a good grasp of reading, writing, and spelling, students were introduced to the formal handwriting required in official correspondence and were taught to take dictation, to write précis of letters, to compose letters and reports in accept-

6. Damrong, *Tamnan suankulap,* p. 28; and Prince Damrong Rajanubhab and W. G. Johnson, *Prawat sangkhep haeng kansüksa khong prathet sayam* (Bangkok, 1920), pp. 8–9.

able government style, and to perform simple mathematical operations.[7]

One of the major problems faced by Prince Damrong in the early years was that the school fulfilled too well its function of preparing young men for the bureaucracy. The demand for clerks in the expanding agencies of government was so heavy that many boys left school after completing only half of the first standard. As a result, these boys were entering government service half-literate and ill-trained in government practices and procedures, and the opportunities the school provided for a substantial education were being neglected by many. Prince Damrong called upon Phraya Si Sunthǫn Wohan, by then over sixty years of age and retired from active teaching, and Phraya Owatwǫrakit, headmaster of the school, for their advice on how best to deal with the situation. The two officials, both former monks, recommended that the system of ecclesiastical examinations be copied in this civil context. This would provide a means whereby the educational attainments of the pupils might be measured, and their diplomas from the school would signify the result to their prospective employers. In addition, the school and the ministries could specify the standards that entering employees would have to meet, so that students might be encouraged to remain at the school until they could meet these standards. Their proposals were approved, and the examination system went into operation in 1884.[8]

When McFarland's Suan Anand School was established in 1878, it was expected that it would provide English instruction for the young princes and nobility, as successor to the earlier palace school of Patterson. For a number of reasons—the relatively remote location of Suan Anand and the hesitation felt

7. Damrong, *Tamnan suankulap*, pp. 31–32.
8. Damrong and Johnson, *Prawat sangkhep*, pp. 9–10. To enhance the prestige of the examinations, the king appointed to the examining committee men of high scholastic reputation, including princes Sommot, Damrong, and Saowaphang, Phraya Phatsakǫrawong (Phǫn Bunnag), and Phraya Si Sunthǫn Wohan (Nǫi).

by many parents at sending their children, particularly young princes, to a school run by a Christian (ex-) missionary—it very soon became apparent that these young men would not go to Suan Anand for their English instruction.[9] Since the king was determined that English education should be available for them, Suankulap began to teach English late in 1881. A "Calcutta Brahman," Baboo Ramsamy Pultar, was attached to Prince Damrong's department, and soon was teaching "quite a number of the King's sons, some of the King's brothers, and many children of princes and nobles."[10] Baboo Ramsamy, it would appear, was not all that Prince Damrong desired in an English teacher. Damrong offered his post to John Eakin of Suan Anand School in 1884 but he declined it, objecting to Suankulap's undemocratic admissions policy,[11] and it was not until 1885 that an English clergyman, the Reverend J. Wastie Green, was found to replace him.[12]

It appears that the English department of Suankulap School remained separate from the general Thai department from the beginning. At least four of Chulalongkorn's sons began their education in this English section, being transferred to the Thai section only for the last year of their studies before leaving for further education in England.[13] Thus in the early years of Suankulap the English section was rather an alternative than

9. McFarland, *McFarland of Siam,* pp. 56–57; and Backus, *Siam and Laos,* p. 222. Although the school began originally with a high proportion of royal and noble pupils, there were only two *mǫm čhao* attending the school in 1882 *(Čhotmaihet sayam samai,* 4 ² 2 1244, 10 Jan. 1883) and one in 1883 *(SWA,* 22 Dec. 1883). By 1884, the school was becoming very popular among the Chinese and "common people" who lived in its neighborhood *(SWA,* 22 Dec. 1883 and 20 Dec. 1884).

10. Baboo Ramsamy, in a letter to the editor of the *Bangkok Times* (26 Sept. 1898), signed himself as "Ex-Regent of Muar and Kessang and Heir-at-Law to the Sultanate of Johore and its Dependencies."

11. Eakin, *Eakin Family,* p. 19.

12. McFarland, *McFarland of Siam,* p. 76.

13. Damrong, "Prawat čhaophraya yommarat," pp. 36–38; and Damrong, *Phraprawat čhǫmphon phračhaophiyathoe krommaluang nakhǫn chaisi suradet ratcha-ongrak* (Bangkok, 1916), pp. 2–3.

a supplement to the general Thai instruction of the school, its instruction intended primarily for those intending to study abroad, and the legacy of this internal division was to be a continuing difficulty in integrating English studies into the educational system.

Owing to the paucity of documents on the first few years of Suankulap's existence it is difficult to assess Prince Damrong's role in its development. It would appear, however, from his own recollections of those early years, that it was Damrong who was the innovator. It was Damrong who took the initiative in reviving the school in the Royal Pages' Bodyguard Corps, Damrong who decided to expand the school and broaden its scope, and Damrong who instituted its examinations; but in each case he required and obtained the full support of the king.

MASS EDUCATION AND THE EDUCATION DEPARTMENT

By 1884 Suankulap School was firmly established, offering both civil and military training to the young men of the royal and high official families. There were in addition several other government educational institutions which had been founded earlier and which by then were flourishing: the old elementary school of Phraya Si Sunthǫn Wohan; the school of the Royal Thai Survey Department, founded and run by James McCarthy, the Government Surveyor; the branch of Suankulap School that offered English instruction to the royal princes; and a religious academy located within the palace walls where young monks were instructed in Pali in preparation for the ecclesiastical examinations. There was also Dr. McFarland's Suan Anand School, conducted under a royal subsidy and under the administration of an independent committee. Each of these six schools was operated independently of the others. They were directed by no common policy, nor were any coordinated efforts made to advance the cause of education in general. Even the government schools were in a relationship of dependence upon government departments whose main business was not education, and dependent for support upon the prestige, leadership, and ability of the individuals who had founded them.

Between 1885 and 1892, modern education became a direct object of royal concern and state policy, and the first concerted attempts were made to absorb it into the secular institutional framework of Thai government. It became the distinct responsibility of a separate arm of the government and attained an independent existence in its own right. Modern secular education became a matter of some public concern. The aim of the remainder of this chapter is to examine how this happened.

The schools of 1884 catered predominantly to the upper classes, to the preparation of the children of royalty and high government officials for public office, although McFarland's school, by reason of its location and because of the egalitarian administration of its headmaster, was beginning to draw its students from its immediate neighborhood.[14] This policy is understandable when viewed in terms of the traditional social bases of Thai government, where a semi-hereditary elite monopolized the higher positions of government, positions for which a good education was becoming increasingly necessary. It was no less obvious to the king and his close associates, however, that this social stasis and educational bias could not last. The king himself, if his decree of 1875 is a reliable indication, was motivated by broader humane and religious grounds, as well as because the requirements of government demanded it, to press for the extension of better educational facilities to the general public. This is not to argue that by 1885 he was prepared to democratize Thai society fully, for his public utterances show clearly that he was not;[15] but he was sufficiently committed to the cause of administrative reform to be willing to open high office to the commonest of men if the need was sufficiently

14. *SWA,* 22 Dec. 1883, 5 Jan. 1884, and 20 Dec. 1884.
15. See above, pp. 105–06.

strong and the person properly qualified.[16] More importantly, better formal education could provide larger numbers of trained men for the lowest positions, the clerks of the bureaucracy, the telegraph operators, postmen, railway men, and policemen. Finally, the king was convinced of the inherent value of education for its own sake, for his father had shown how education made a beter monk, and he himself was certain that education could make better men.

In 1884, the king gave Prince Damrong the task of planning the extension of public education along the lines of the 1875 decree, which called for the founding of modern schools in the royal monasteries.[17] In September of that year, the king appointed a committee to prescribe the organization, textbooks, and standards for these public schools, appointing to it Prince Damrong, Phraya Si Sunthǫn Wohan, Phraya Phatsakǫrawong (Phǫn Bunnag), Phraya Samut Buranurak (Sin), Phra Sarasat Phonlakhan (Col. G. E. Gerini), Khun Owatwǫrakit (Kaen), and Dr. McFarland.[18] The committee began its work immediately, and the results of its deliberations were not slow in appearing.

The arguments in favor of establishing schools in the monasteries were so strong that no alternatives seem seriously to have been considered. Education traditionally had been carried on in the monasteries, and the physical facilities to sustain formal instruction were readily available there. The monks who acted as teachers found their pupils useful in performing the daily chores of monastery life, and by accepting them as pupils they gained an additional commitment of support from the boys' parents. In addition, subsidies long had been given the royal

16. See the "Prakat hai but kharatchakan khao rap ratchakan tam ǫpfit tangtang," 26 Aug. 1890, *RKB*, 7 (1890/91), 195–98; and in *Documents*, pp. 55–59.

17. Damrong and Ratchasena, *Thetsaphiban*, p. 3.

18. *SWA*, 6 Sept. 1884; and *Čhotmaihet sayam samai*, 4 ৩ 10 1246 (10 Sept. 1884). In the absence of an appropriate Thai term, this group was called a *"kǫmmitti."*

monasteries to promote the religious instruction of monks and novices, so that there was a useful precedent upon which support for secular schools could be based. If the government were to establish schools outside the monasteries, they would, to whatever degree they were successful in attracting pupils and local financial support, compete with the monks and monasteries, leading to duplication and waste. In his administration of Suankulap School, Prince Damrong had demonstrated, with the aid of the examination system and the instruction the school came to offer as preparation for the civil service, the attractiveness of formal modern education and its utility to considerable numbers of young men. Prince Damrong and the committee set about in 1884 transferring this utility and appeal to the monastery schools and making them effective in a world with which they were in danger of losing touch.[19]

Within six months, new schools were springing up in the monasteries of Bangkok. The first of these commonly is thought to have been at Wat Mahannapharam, within the walls of Bangkok, established in a new, four-classroom building constructed around a central hall, which opened late in 1884.[20] Several other schools followed soon thereafter. The English-educated Phraya Phatsakǫrawong (Phǫn Bunnag), then head of the Customs Department and a leading member of the Bunnag family, who had served on the Suan Anand Committee and the 1884 Education Committee, sponsored a new school at Wat Prayurawong in Thonburi which opened in November 1884. When the local response strained the school's resources, he led a public appeal for more classrooms.[21] The procedure he followed in starting this school was probably typical of the

19. Damrong and Johnson, *Prawat sangkhep,* pp. 15–20.

20. M. L. Manich Jumsai, *Prawat kansüksa khǫng thai* (Bangkok, 1959), p. 20.

21. *Čhotmaihet sayam samai,* 8 Apr. 1885. See also *SWA,* 1 Apr. 1885; and Phrakhru Phisanwinaiwat (Hem) and Phra Maha Phoem, *Prawat wat prayurawong* (Bangkok, 1928), pp. 8, 49–52.

schools of this period. As with a new school at Wat Rakhang,[22] a school building was constructed by private funds or a monastery building was renovated and furnished and a request was made to Prince Damrong for a teacher or teachers, their salaries to be paid by the government, and for the requisite textbooks, which during this period were still Phraya Si Sunthǫn's six readers. The administration of the school remained in the hands of the monks, who probably assisted in the teaching, while financial support came from the king. While it is likely that most of the student body of such schools consisted of boys who had been studying in the monastery before the schools were established, all the accounts of such schools that appeared in the newspapers of the day contained exhortations to parents to send their children to the schools, promising them education free of charge. Certainly these schools, under the circumstances, were essentially little more than the formalization of preexisting practices; but the gathering of the pupils into formal classes, where they used standardized textbooks, followed a set curriculum, and prepared for a common examination, all of this under government subsidy, was a significant innovation, and this arrangement made possible further educational development.

By August 1885, "12 or 16 vernacular schools" had recently been established in Bangkok, and Prince Damrong was being referred to in the local press as "commissioner of schools."[23] This raises the problem of when the Education Department (*krom süksathikan*) came into being. In purely legal, administrative terms one must follow the Ministry of Education's official history in tracing the foundation of the Education Department to 6 May 1887, the date on which its foundation was officially announced by royal decree.[24] In point of fact, how-

22. *Čhotmaihet sayam samai*, 29 Apr. 1885.
23. *SWA*, 29 Aug. 1885.
24. "Prakat tang krom süksathikan," *PKPS, 11,* 153–54. See Rǫng Sayamanon et al., *Prawat krasuang süksathikan 2435–2507* (Bangkok, 1964), pp. 51–52.

ever, the Department per se dates from 1885, for it was at that time that all modern education was put under Damrong's control and handled through a special bureau of his office in the Royal Pages' Bodyguard Corps. From this office it was Damrong who ran and promoted modern schools, including not only Phraya Si Sunthǫn's old school and Suankulap but also the school of the Royal Survey Department, the Pali academy, and a small but growing number of vernacular, modern-type schools in the monasteries. From this office, beginning in the summer quarter (June/July-September/October) of 1885, Damrong submitted directly to the King quarterly and annual reports on the educational activities under his direction on a letterhead marked "Office of the Education Department."[25] This explains the newspaper designation of Damrong as "commissioner of schools" at about the same time. It is thus apparent that by July or August of 1885 an Education Department had been established in the Department of the Royal Pages' Bodyguard Regiment in fact, if not by law, and it was the function of the decree of 1887 not to create the department but rather to recognize it as a separate civil department completely divorced from the military associations of the Royal Pages' Bodyguard Corps.

The military nature of Prince Damrong's office early led to a serious public misunderstanding as to the function of the new monastery schools. He found that parents were hesitant to send their sons to the new schools, fearful that the schools were but devices for recruiting boys into the army. They would have been encouraged in such thinking by Suankulap's origins as a military training school and by the fact that Damrong was

25. Unfortunately, very few of these early reports have survived. Damrong's seventh quarterly report, however, covers the period of the second through the fourth months of 1886/87 (i.e. 25 Dec. 1886–23 Mar. 1887). Counting back seven reports, one comes to the second quarter, ordinarily the eighth through tenth months of the year 1885/86. In that year, however, there were two eighth months in the old Thai lunar calendar, 12 June–11 July and 12 July–10 August. How the quarters were divided in a thirteen-month year I have no idea. Damrong's seventh quarterly report is reprinted in part in Rǫng et al., *Prawat krasuang,* pp. 54–58.

at the time an active army officer. The king acted to dispel their fears in a decree of 1 May 1885, in which he explained that the rumors to the effect that the schools were merely a disguised form of conscription were completely unfounded, and that, if he wished to conscript men into the army, he had no need to go to the trouble and expense of founding schools.[26] The rumors, however, were slow in dying, as evinced in government announcements from time to time as late as 1887. It was not until the Education Department was officially established as a separate civil agency of government in 1887 that the basis for such fears was fully removed.

Thus it was between 1884 and 1885 that the first definite steps were taken to implement what amounted to the education program of 1875, calling for the founding of government-supported, modern-style schools in the monasteries. The relationship between these late educational beginnings and the changed political circumstances of the period would, on the face of things, seem only coincidental, but there was in fact a direct relationship between the two developments. The cause of educational innovation, to be successful, required in addition to the king's support a promoter who could personally take it up and act as its advocate with its sources of funds and its potential adherents. In playing such a role, Damrong, one of the first of Chulalongkorn's generation to move into public office in the eighties, set an example that was to become increasingly common as years went by: the young prince, enamored of Western ideas and anxious to prove both to his wide circle of European friends that he was worthy of the ideas and to his compatriots that these ideas were valid for them. But there was yet another attribute of Damrong that served him well: his good political sense, his intuitive knowledge of what was possible and what was not, and his ability to use this sense to guide his advocacy of innovation. He was able to make of Suankulap a strong institution by straddling the old and the new, by heed-

26. "Prakat rongrian," *PKPS, 10,* 221–23; also in *Documents,* pp. 23–25; and translated in Manich, *Compulsory Education,* p. 21.

ing traditional sensitivities while at the same time working subtly to undermine them, by transforming the venerable institution of the Royal Pages' Corps into a training school for the modern bureaucracy. By his appointment as "Commissioner of schools" in 1885, his personal fate was linked with the progress of modern education.

EDUCATIONAL DEVELOPMENT, 1885–1892

During the first seven years of the Education Department the foundations of Thailand's modern education were laid. During this period education began to be systematized and organized so as to perform its functions better in a changing Thai society. The work of the Education Department was recorded in a series of annual reports which Prince Damrong submitted to the king.[27] Supplemented by the department's correspondence, these give an account of the growth and development of the primary and higher schools under its direction, the services for and controls over the schools that it provided, as well as an indication of the steps by which the department moved toward a comprehensive formulation of educational policy.

27. The Annual Reports of the Education Department are filed in the National Archives *(NA)*, Bangkok, as follows:

   C.S. 1248 (1886/87), NA 5 S, 18/8, 1–214.
   C.S. 1250 (1888/89), NA 5 S, 22/8, 1–39.
   R.S. 108 (1889/90), NA 5 S, 18/8, 215–32.
   R.S. 109 (1890/91), NA 5 S, 18/8, 233–335.
   R.S. 110 (1891/92), NA 5 S, 16/8, 13–38.

No reports could be found for the years 1885/86 and 1887/88, although they are known to have been submitted. The statistical supplements to the reports for R.S. 108–110 are filed separately in 6/8 and 17/8, G (Numbers of Schools and Students); 7/8 (Rosters of Government Officials); 11/8 (Inventories of Goods); 12/8 (Reports of the Department's Printing Press); and 13/8 and 17/8 E (Reports of the Textbook Bureau). Other statistical material is scattered through the department's correspondence of the period, mostly in NA 5 S, ser. 8.

After a year of rapid growth, the government monastery schools for the general public settled down to a period of slow but steady growth.[28] In the course of the seven years between 1885 and 1892 they spread over much of the country, with varying degrees of success. For the most part, however, enrollment did not keep pace with the growth in the number of schools.[29] While the number of government schools in the provinces more than doubled (from ten to twenty-four) during the period, the increase in enrollment was only 65 percent, and the total enrollment of the monastery schools of Bangkok remained almost static, at about 1,500 pupils. In both cases, independent schools *(rongrian chaloeisak)*, which registered with the Department in order to obtain free textbooks and were not under the Department's supervision, probably constituted an important source of competition for the government schools, particularly after the government schools stopped issuing free textbooks in 1890.[30] The question of the enrollment capacity of the schools does not appear to explain this stasis, as the enrollment of individual schools varied widely from year to year, as much as 100 percent in more than half the schools.

There is ample evidence that the slow pace of educational growth in the late eighties was due primarily to a lack of demand for modern education. It is indicated in the persistence of the rumors that schools were merely a disguised form of military conscription. There are, however, more concrete indications: between 1886 and 1892, eleven government schools were closed for lack of students, four in Bangkok and seven in the provinces.[31] Prince Damrong, in his reports for 1888/89 and 1889/90, noted that it was his policy to close any school

28. A general summary of educational statistics is given in Appendix A.

29. And attendance often was only 50–60 percent of enrollment. See inspection reports annexed to the annual reports for 1886/87 and 1888/89.

30. NA, 5 S, 18/8, E, Report, Education Dept., 1890/91. Independent schools in the provinces numbered 46 in 1890 and enrolled 827 pupils.

31. See NA 5 S, 6/8 and 17/8. Of the 11 cases, lack of students specifically is given as the reason for closure in 6 and has been inferred from steadily dropping enrollments in the remaining 5.

having an insufficient enrollment, and in the latter report he explained that the teachers and patrons of some schools were not sufficiently forceful to inspire in pupils and their parents a desire for modern education.

An important element in this situation must have been the inability of many families and young men to translate modern education into values meaningful in terms of their own lives. Families whose lives had not yet been seriously affected by the changing face of new Siam could hardly be expected to appreciate the ways in which improved education could prepare their young men for lives that lay beyond their imagination. Those whose vocational expectations did not reach as high as government service were still resigned to a world that was slowly passing away. Indeed, it is remarkable that the new schools gained in the provinces the response that they did; but it undoubtedly is significant that the first schools were established in the more accessible regions, often in areas where Western missionaries had been active or in areas that had prospered most heavily in the expanding export economy of the latter half of the century. The demand for modern education seems to have been strongest among those most bureaucratically oriented, among the families of government officials, and among the large, economically oriented Chinese minoriy. As they were relatively more aware of the expanding opportunities offered by government and commerce, such groups more readily could see the advantages of civil service training and the study of English, and they could perceive these in terms of their old, traditional values.[32] Given their interests, it was natural that they should have responded most readily to the special schools

32. Some pupils even took up the study of Chinese in government schools. It was taught in 1889 at the Ban Čhin Yaem School in Bangkok, founded by Baboo Ramsamy in 1888, and ten students enrolled for the course. (NA 5 S, 17/8 II, C, Quarterly Report, Educ. Dept., June 1889; and 18/8, D, Annual Report, Educ. Dept., 1889/90.) No further official mention is made of Chinese instruction in the following decade. Some of the most prominent of the Thai schools in the monasteries were at Chinese-supported monasteries, e.g. Wat Sam Čhin Tai (now Wat Traimit).

in Bangkok, in which civil service training and English instruction were concentrated.[33]

During this period there were three special schools under the control of the Education Department.[34] Preeminent among them was Prince Damrong's own Suankulap School, the enrollment of which nearly doubled during the period. It was at Suankulap that most civil service training was concentrated, with Standard II instruction being offered there to graduates of Standard I from monastery schools as well as to Suankulap's own graduates.[35] There are many possible reasons for this concentration. Quality could be better maintained by concentrating the best teachers and facilities in one place. The close proximity of Suankulap to the offices of the Education Department, a few steps away within the palace precincts, made control and supervision of the school easy, and Damrong took advantage of this to make daily visits to the school.[36] There appear also to have been social considerations involved: a continuing concern that the noble class be given every opportunity to maintain its position in the service of the king. In the 1880s, most students receiving Standard II diplomas from Suankulap were the sons of high government officials of at least the rank of *phra* and usually of *phraya*.[37] There are adequate reasons to suggest that this social bias resulted from a conscious policy.

This social question does not seem to have arisen earlier in the decade, when the king's annual speech at the school referred to it as more or less a royal preserve,[38] and the students listed by Prince Damrong for this period were mostly lineal

33. English was taught only in the special schools. Although some of the government monastery schools taught Standard II as preparation for the civil service, very few men from the monastery schools managed to pass the examinations for that standard.

34. Not including the school for the royal children at Suankulap and the Buddhist Academy, Mahathat Witthayalai.

35. See Damrong and Johnson, *Prawat sangkhep*, p. 34.

36. Prince Bidyalongkorn, "Khwamraluk khǫng nakrian suankulap doem," in Damrong, *Tamnan suankulap*, p. 41.

37. See *RKB*, 6 (1889/90), 32–35, and 7 (1890/91), 23–24.

38. See above, p. 105.

descendents of kings.[39] In April 1889, however, Suankulap instituted a twenty baht annual tuition fee for the school, in order
"to prevent common people *(khon leo)* from attending the
school, to induce students to be more regular in their attendance,
and to defray the cost of providing midday dining facilities for
the students."[40] The fee was successful on all three counts, but
it was discontinued the following year in favor of a deposit
system, by which students had to deposit twelve baht with the
school at the beginning of the year, one baht being refunded
each month if the student's attendance and conduct during the
month were satisfactory.[41] In short, although undoubtedly
there were exceptions, particularly with some wealthy young
Chinese,[42] Suankulap existed primarily as a vehicle to bring
the younger members of the nobility to face their changing
obligations to society. Nowhere is this policy toward the nobility
more clearly expressed than in a decree of King Chulalongkorn
issued on 26 August 1890.[43] In it, the king examined the
breakdown of the old apprenticeship patterns in the various
government departments, by which the sons of the nobility had
been prepared for government positions by serving with their
fathers; he noted that while these young men had ceased to be
so trained, the increased complexity and scope of government
made such education even more necessary than before. He
warned the nobility that, while he was reluctant to do so, he
would be forced to make high appointments on the basis of
knowledge and ability, taking as his standard the national
interest. Nonetheless, all else being equal, he would much
rather appoint men of noble background to high position than

39. Damrong, *Tamnan suankulap,* pp. 33–39. Of 19 pupils passing
both standards at Suankulap between 1887 and 1890, 17 were of royal
descent.

40. NA 5 S, 25/5, "Announcement, R.S. 108" (1889/90).

41. Ibid. Twelve baht at this time was equivalent to the monthly
salary of a minor government clerk.

42. Evidence on this point is more readily available from the student
lists of the early nineties, but it is highly likely that at least some began
attending Suankulap in the eighties.

43. "Prakat hai but khratchakan," *RKB,* 7 (1890/91), 195–98.

advance a commoner. In the light of this decree, the king's public utterances, and the matter of tuition fees, it was apparent that Suankulap was a primary instrument for the maintenance of the position of the nobility in public life.

The three other special schools of the 1880s reflect this concentration of civil service training at a socially restricted Suankulap. This may be seen in the results of the annual government examinations: of fifty-five students passing the Standard II examinations in the four years 1888–92, Sunanthalai, Saranrom, and the New School together supplied only one candidate, and that student received his Standard II training at Suankulap.[44] In addition, a reading of the biographies and obituaries of officials educated during this period suggests that almost none attended Saranrom, Sunanthalai, or the New School.[45] What, then, were these schools doing?

In 1885 the school of Phraya Si Sunthǫn Wohan, moved by then into the Saranrom Palace, was the oldest surviving school, having been founded in 1870. Education Department inspectors who visited it in March 1887 characterized it as being "satisfactory" in most respects. It had eighty-four pupils and twelve teachers, but most of its students were at work on the first volume of the *Munlabot* series of primers—evidently not very diligently. The description the inspectors gave of how instruction was carried on there sounds very much as if they had visited simply a large, traditional-style monastery school, and the students whose names they mentioned were all sons of government officials.[46] By the time the Education Department's report for the year 1888/89 was submitted,[47] Saranrom had been dropped from the Department's list of schools. It appears to have closed sometime during 1887. Apparently the Saranrom

44. Sources as in footnote 27, this chapter.
45. See, for example, the fifty biographies in Prince Damrong Rajanubhab, *Prawat bukkhon samkhan, chabap sombun* (Bangkok, 1962).
46. This report is appended to the Annual Report of the Education Department for 1886/87, NA 5 S, 18/8, pp. 6–16.
47. The archives contain no report for 1887/88, and the report for 1888/89 does not list Saranrom among the schools of the previous year.

Palace was taken for the use of the Ministry of Foreign Affairs
in that year, and several of its teachers were pressed into service
instructing the king's rapidly multiplying family, while its students probably contributed to the rapid growth of Suankulap
in 1887 and 1888.

Dr. McFarland's Suan Anand School and, from late 1888,
the New School founded by Baboo Ramsamy, came to serve the
interests and ambitions of the Chinese community of the capital.
In the early years of the decade, Suan Anand had begun to attract large numbers of Chinese and "common people."[48] Its
attraction for many was the lengthy course of instruction in
English that it could offer, which was imparted to all its students
concurrently with instruction in Thai, science, and the arts.
When the school, previously under the management of a lay
committee, was brought under the administration of the Education Department in 1887,[49] Prince Damrong recommended
that it be moved to a more convenient and spacious site.[50] Thus
in March 1889 it opened in the Sunanthalai estate, a splendid
new group of buildings near the Grand Palace, its "grand aim"
being "to offer to the youth of Siam the best possible advantages for acquiring an education through the medium of the
English language," "every facility" being provided "for ALL
whom [sic] may apply."[51] With the new buildings, which gave
it a new name and increased financial support through endowments, the school was able to eliminate the regulations that had
restricted its enrollment to fifty pupils, and enrollment immediately trebled, relieving the pressure on Suankulap. At the
same time, Sunanthalai instituted a course of study (in which

48. See n. 9 above.

49. Damrong and Johnson, *Prawat sangkhep*, p. 22.

50. NA 5 S, 22/8, Report, Educ. Dept., 1888/89.

51. *Bangkok Times*, 16 Mar. 1889, advertisement. The school buildings were constructed as a memorial to Queen Sunantakumarirat, who
drowned in a boating accident in 1880, with the intention of using them
for a girls' school; but a suitable headmistress could not be found, and
the buildings lay vacant until taken over for McFarland's school in 1889.
McFarland, *McFarland of Siam*, pp. 73–74.

all instruction was in English) designed to prepare students for careers in the civil service, but this program was not taught long enough to have had any significance.[52] Most of the school's graduates seem to have made their careers in commerce, where English-educated clerks were at a premium, although some undoubtedly found government employment in such departments as the Customs, the Post and Telegraphs, and, later, the Railways, where a knowledge of English was essential.

When an Englishman was appointed to replace Baboo Ramsamy Pultar at Suankulap in 1885, Baboo Ramsamy resolved to establish a school of his own.[53] By 1888 he had gained the support of Prince Damrong for such a project, and he opened the school known first as the Ban Čhin Yaem School and later as the New School, in December 1888. Like Suan Anand, the School was managed by a governing committee which included among its members one of the leading Sino-Thai officials of the day, while the school was under the general superintendence of the Education Department.[54] It offered instruction in English and Chinese to a student body that was predominantly Chinese.[55]

In Suankulap School, English instruction—with Englishmen as teachers—was until 1890 given concurrently with Thai instruction, half-days being spent on each language by those pupils who elected to take the course. Many of the students studied English in preparation for further studies abroad, while others viewed it as useful to a bureaucratic career. Prince Damrong found that the study of a second language by students who had not yet gained a thorough grounding in their own language impeded their progress in both, and in 1890 he required that students who had not yet passed Standard I of the Thai curriculum must devote all their time to their Thai studies. He allowed Standard II students to undertake part-time English study, and

52. *Bangkok Times*, 30 Mar. 1889.
53. *SWA*, 10 Jan. 1885.
54. *Bangkok Times*, 21 Nov. 1888.
55. NA 5 S, 17/8, II, C, Quarterly Report, Educ. Dept., June 1889.

graduates of Standard II could devote themselves fully to English. These regulations soon were applied to students at Sunanthalai and the New School as well.[56]

During the latter half of the decade the performance of the newly established schools was mixed. Enrollments and the examination records of individual schools varied considerably from year to year, and it appears that this fledgling educational system was, even by 1892, still on a very uncertain footing. The monastery schools had to contend with a lack of concerted and purposeful demand for their services, while the higher or special schools increasingly were overshadowed by Suankulap, which gained in the Education Department the same favored position it undoubtedly held in the affections of Prince Damrong.

Over these schools the department exerted both binding and guiding controls. Organized in a modern, functional pattern and provided with financial and administrative support by the government, it attempted to establish modern education on a firm basis and to improve its quality. As first organized by Prince Damrong in 1885, the responsibilities of the Education Department were solely those of promoting and extending modern education. The department was, however, located administratively within the military division of the Department of the Royal Pages, and Prince Damrong's primary duties were as Director of the latter. In 1887, when the Education Department was made an independent civil department of government, Damrong still could devote only a portion of his time to its work, as he held office concurrently as assistant to the commander of the army in the new Army Department *(krom yut-thanathikan)*.[57] In 1889, however, the responsibilities of the Education Department were widened to include other educational, religious, and public health services, with the grouping of the Hospital, Religious Affairs, Museum, and Royal Pundits Departments under Prince Damrong's control; the Prince final-

56. NA 5 S, 18/8 D and E, Reports, Educ. Dept., 1888/89 and 1890/91.

57. Damrong and Johnson, *Prawat sangkhep*, p. 20.

ly was relieved of his military responsibilities in 1890 and allowed to concentrate his considerable energies on the affairs of what was scheduled to become, in 1892, the Ministry of Public Instruction. The Department achieved de facto ministerial status, however, when Prince Damrong began to sit in the meetings of the Council of Ministers in 1889.[58]

Prince Damrong's organization of his department provides a good example of the way in which Thai government during this period was moving toward greater functional specialization and Western-style office procedures. In this respect, it is likely that he followed the lead of his brother, Prince Devawongse, who in 1885 began the reorganization of the Ministry of Foreign Affairs on modern lines.[59] The efficiency that such practices could offer undoubtedly was particularly important in the Education Department, where Prince Damrong was away much of the time and had to delegate considerable detailed work to others; and functional specialization was especially necessary in the department when increasingly specialized tasks, e.g. the preparation of textbooks and the provision of medical services, came under its jurisdiction. In addition, the nature of the department's work made efficient organization necessary. The department's task was not simply to keep traditional practices, organs, and institutions in operation. The essence of the department was innovation. It did not merely watch over schools as if to see that a proper tax was collected from them or a proper state of readiness maintained. It constantly had to coax the schools, urging them on to higher standards, nurturing their growth, and solving their problems. The job of the department was, while holding its policies as a guide, to examine the schools constantly, to see their strengths and weaknesses, and to devise means by which educational

58. Ibid., pp. 22–24.

59. See Damrong, "Phraprawat thewawong," pp. 122–23. See also Thailand, Ministry of Foreign Affairs, *Prawat lae rabop ngan khong krasuang kantangprathet* (Bangkok, 1963), p. 29. Similar reorganization, of course, began much earlier in the Royal Audit Office and the Ministry of Finance in the seventies.

policy might best be implemented. The work of the department required intelligence, determination, perceptiveness, imagination, and a great deal of patience and tact.

By 1890, the organization of the department as a proto-ministry was relatively complete.[60] Prince Damrong, concurrently director of the Education Department and minister-designate over the whole collection of departments entrusted to him, had two personal secretaries for English[61] and Thai[62] correspondence. Under Damrong, Phraya Wutthikanbǫdi (M.R.W. Khli Suthat na Ayudhya) served concurrently as deputy minister and as director of the Religious Affairs Department, and each of the other four departments (Central, Hospitals, Museum, and Royal Survey) had its own director. Most of the administrative functions of the larger department (ministry) were concentrated in the Education Department, which included bureaus *(wen)* for correspondence, filing, reports, accounts, stores and supplies, textbook compilation, school inspection, and publishing, each with its own clerical and specialist staff. The largest of these were the Textbook Bureau, which had on its staff five compilers of relatively high rank and two clerks and was directed by Khun Prasoet Aksǫnnit, and the Inspection Bureau, directed by Khun Prasan Aksǫnphan, with four (later five) school inspectors, each with a territory in Bangkok regularly to be covered.[63] The numbers of bureaus and divisions and the men assigned to them varied from year to year, but their functional division of labor remained basically undisturbed for several decades.

The budgets of the Education Department reveal much about its operations.[64] Administrative salaries, allowances, and ex-

60. See Bunchüa Ongkhapradit, *Khwampenma khǫng kanbǫrihan kansüksa* (Bangkok, 1962), pp. 9–11.

61. Edwin McFarland, son of Dr. S. G. McFarland.

62. Luang Phaisan Sinlapasat (M.R.W. Pia Malakul), who appears below in Chapter 7 as Phraya Wisut Suriyasak.

63. *RKB,* 7 (1890/91), 189 ff.

64. NA 5 S, 22/8, Report, Educ. Dept., 1888/89; 18/8, D, Report, 1889/90; and 18/8, E, Report, 1890/91.

penses made up more than half (53.5 percent) of the total expenditures in 1890/91, which amounted to 159,393 baht. Another 8 percent of the budget was expended on special activities placed under the department more or less for financial convenience, such as the school for royal princes in the Grand Palace and the Buddhist Academy at Wat Mahathat. Five percent of the budget went for repairs to buildings and for the printing of textbooks. The remainder, 22.8 percent for special schools and 10.7 percent for monastery schools, was used for instruction per se. These proportions seem relatively low, but it may be argued that they were reasonable. Expenditure per pupil was exceedingly low in the monastery schools, but what might otherwise have been the heaviest expenses of such instruction were eliminated by using preexisting or privately furnished buildings as schools and, in some cases, by employing teacher-monks for a nominal salary. The three special schools, which required more than twice the amount expended on forty-eight monastery schools, were made expensive by the high salaries demanded by foreign teachers (S. G. McFarland received 640 baht per month, while teachers in the monastery schools received 10 baht per month or less). In addition, a proportion of the amount expended on administrative salaries was used to support instruction in the monastery schools through the provision of textbooks, the administration of examinations, and the inspection of schools.

Originally, after the decree of 1875, each school was to be given free sets of the government textbooks, the six primers of Phraya Si Sunthon Wohan. During the first years of the Education Department these books were used almost universally in the government schools, the progress of students being measured in terms of which of the six they were engaged in studying. From the department's reports it is clear that these textbooks were unsatisfactory, as roughly two-thirds of the students each year were reported to be studying the first of the six volumes, while only a handful ever worked through to the sixth. The demand for clerks in government offices and commercial firms was so great, and the number of boys completing Standard II (and even Standard I) so small, that more than half the students left school before finishing Standard I; and this despite the fact that the department thought three years a reasonable amount of time to spend on the first standard. The solution to this problem was a new set of government textbooks, the *Rapid Readers (Baep rian reo)*, conceived by Prince Damrong and experimentally developed by him at the school of Wat Niwetthammaprawat near the king's Summer Palace at Bang Pa-in, south of Ayudhya. These readers were geared to the interests of children and could impart to them a basic knowledge of the Thai writing system in a single year, or a year and a half if the child was particularly slow.[65] They began to be put into use in 1888 but had not attained a wide circulation by 1892.

In addition to providing simple basic textbooks to the schools, the Textbook Bureau, staffed by a handful of learned men almost all of whom were former monks, made prodigious efforts to provide them with a wide range of reading, teaching, and reference materials. In 1888 they were engaged in compiling a Siamese grammar, an arithmetic textbook in Western style, an English-Siamese dictionary, an abridged version of the Royal Chronicles, a translation of a "Universal Geography" from English, and translations of several Pali works into Thai, not to mention the *Rapid Reader* series.[66] To these were added in the next few years a number of other similar books for the teaching of reading, spelling, arithmetic, poetry, history, and science.[67] The Education Department also commissioned the

65. Damrong and Johnson, *Prawat sangkhep*, p. 38; M.Č. Phunphitsamai Diskul, *Chiwit lae ngan khong somdet kromphraya damrong rachanuphap* (Bangkok, 1959), pp. 12–14; Phunphitsamai, "Somdet phračhaoborommawongthoe kromphraya damrong," pp. 9–10; and Damrong, *Prawat achan* (Bangkok, 1935), pp. (24)–(25).

66. NA 5 S, 22/8, Report, Educ. Dept. 1888/89. All but the dictionary were in print by 1891.

67. For a sample listing of books available at this time, see the frequent advertisements in the *RKB*, or the endpapers to (Sir) Robert Morant, *Ladder of Knowledge Series*, e.g. vol. 4 (Bangkok, 1891).

making and publishing of maps of Bangkok and Siam and (Sir)
Robert Morant's *Ladder of Knowledge Series* for the teaching
of English.[68] All the department's textbooks were distributed
free of charge to all schools, government and private alike,
until 1890, when the department began selling them at cost,
except in the case of private schools in the provinces, which
continued to receive them without charge.[69]

Textbooks were one of the cornerstones of government educational policy. By providing printed textbooks of good quality
free of charge to the various monasteries in Bangkok and the
provinces, the department won the interest of many monks in
educational improvement. They provided a means by which
more material might be covered in less time than had been
required when outmoded textbooks had to be laboriously copied
from fading manuscripts by each pupil, and they brought to
the monks wider information than had been available to them
hitherto. Just textbooks alone could induce a monastery to decide to establish a school on the modern lines suggested by the
department. But the department did not stop there: its intention
was to use the textbooks and the limited financial and administrative resources at its command to promote greater educational
quality and uniformity. Prince Damrong's strategy was to base
the annual examinations closely on the textbooks, so that students who had not used the government textbooks would have
difficulty in passing the examinations.[70]

Another weapon of the department's control over public
education was the examination system introduced in 1884. It
would have been easy for the department to set a minimal passing standard from the beginning, for the sake of releasing as
many trained youths as possible for openings in the bureaucracy;
but the department repeatedly raised examination standards,
and the schools and students responded to every rise in standards

68. Bernard M. Allen, *Sir Robert Morant: A Great Public Servant*
(London, 1934), p. 61; and McFarland, *McFarland of Siam*, p. 76.
69. NA 5 S, 18/8, E, Report, Educ. Dept., 1890/91.
70. NA 5 S, 17/8 I, 15, Damrong to King, 9 Feb. 1891.

with greater efforts in the examinations.[71] By passing the examinations the student gained not only a good chance of a government position but also, on completing Standard II, a lifetime release from the obligations of the military and civil corvée, without any obligation to take a government position.[72]

The possibility of a standardized curriculum had not arisen in the first days of the government schools, for each was an individual entity founded for a specific purpose. Apart from the original palace Thai school, about which very little is known, Prince Damrong's Suankulap was the first school that aimed, after about 1882, to impart a common, standardized program of instruction as a preparation for military or government service. It was the curriculum of Suankulap that was first embodied in the policies of the Education Department and eventually in the examination system. The effect of this transferral of curriculum from Suankulap to the monastery schools was to extend to the latter a course that originally had been designed as a basis for later, more specialized training. This was a curriculum which, at the basic level, concentrated on the simple mechanics of reading, writing, and arithmetic and neglected almost totally the broader areas of learning which came to be provided at Suankulap at the higher level, Standard II. Symptomatic of this concentration on Suankulap was the initial organization of the examination system, by which all the examinations were held in the same place at the same time, and all prizes and diplomas

71. NA 5 S, 17/8 I, 18, Damrong to King, 15 Feb. 1891. See also the report of the examination commissioners in *RKB*, 7 (1890/91), 23–24. Similar reports were published annually in the *RKB*.

72. "Prakat krom süksathikan," 5 Feb. 1886, *PKPS, 10*, 209–11, and in *Documents*, pp. 26–28. This decree formalized the examination system, providing that examinations be held annually, presided over by special examination commissioners, and covering specified subjects from the prescribed textbooks. In a letter to Čhaophraya Mahintharasakthamrong, 1 January 1889 (NA 5 S, 32/5, 39, also in *Documents*, pp. 36–37), the king further prescribed that any child under the age of 20 years who was still in school should be exempt from registration for the corvée, but any young man of 20 years or over who had not passed Standard II could be registered and called. The latter could, however, return to take the examinations and, if successful, be exempted from further service.

awarded in a single ceremony at Suankulap at the end of the academic year. Ideally, the best graduates of Standard I from all the schools would continue their studies in Standard II at Suankulap. In practice the system did not work this way. Not many of the boys from the provincial schools could come to Bangkok for the examinations, and when (or if) examinations began to be held in the provinces, most of the boys could not afford to come to Bangkok to continue their studies. In addition, it appears that in practice most of the boys who continued on to Standard II at Suankulap were Standard I graduates of that school, increasingly so toward the end of the decade, so that Standard II instruction (and the better government positions) effectively was not available to most Standard I graduates.

As established by the 1886 decree, the curriculum of Standard I comprised simply the subject matter of Phraya Si Sunthǫn Wohan's six primers, which must have bored and exasperated many of the students who used them.[73] The boys were taught to read and write and spell, and at a later date were given a small smattering of Western arithmetic.[74] This curriculum could hardly be called modernized or even relevant to the needs of the broad masses of the population. The students in Standard II, on the other hand, were required to study handwriting, composition, précis and letter writing, prose editing, arithmetic, and accounting by the decree of 1886, a curriculum which if not broadening was at least practical for these boys, most of whom went on to enter the bureaucracy.[75] By 1891 the overwhelmingly governmental character of the curriculum was

73. *PKPS, 10,* 209–11.

74. In most schools, however, it seems that teachers could hardly teach the old laborious traditional mathematics, not to mention Western mathematics.

75. Similar accomplishments were required of boys in the Royal Pages' Corps who were compelled by a decree of 1887 to pass a special examination which was almost identical to that for Standard II. "Prakat lai khanop thamniam mahatlek," 7 Dec. 1887, *PKPS, 11,* 123–26, and in *Documents,* pp. 29–31. This decree may have induced many young nobles to enter Suankulap. The results of the examinations were used in determining ranks and positions in the corps.

becoming yet clearer. Writing in that year to Prince Sommot, the king's secretary, Prince Damrong stated that "it is the duty of the Education Department to prepare students by curricula which will be of use in government service," and he asked Prince Sommot how he might like his clerks trained.[76] Prince Sommot's reply was not recorded, but the new curricula issued two months later reflected this bureaucratic emphasis.

With the provision of more textbooks and teaching materials in the latter half of the decade, the curriculum, as expressed in the examination requirements, was broadened accordingly. This expansion took place, however, only at the highest levels of schooling. Students in Standard I still were expected only to show an adequate knowledge of simple reading, writing, and arithmetic, while Standard II remained closely tied to the office requirements of the civil service. A new Standard III was introduced into the Thai syllabus on the level, perhaps, of secondary education, but it consisted almost entirely of an elaboration on the Standard II curriculum, adding only the refinements of literary grammar and rhetoric, logic, verse composition, expository and dialogue writing, and, in mathematics, fractions, the use of the abacus, and the making of tables and graphs. Throughout the Thai curriculum there was no formal provision for history, science, geography, hygiene, or religious instruction, although these were a part of the curriculum of a few such schools as Suankulap and Sunanthalai.[77] The response which several writers characterize as a broadening of the curriculum to include new subject matter hardly affected the Thai curriculum,[78] and the decree of 1891 had the effect of lengthening rather than widening the curriculum.

76. NA 5 S, 17/8 I, 14, Damrong to Sommot, 5 Feb. 1891.

77. The new curriculum was to go into effect with the examinations of March 1892. It was laid out in detail in a royal ordinance, "Phraratchabanyat kansǫp wicha," 17 Feb. 1891, *RKB, 8* (1891/92), 26–29, and in *Documents,* pp. 62–67. Standard III was neither taught nor examined until 1900/01, by which time it had been considerably redefined.

78. See, for example, Damrong and Johnson *(Prawat sangkhep,* p. 38), who suggest that the introduction of "Rapid Readers" left more time for "other subjects," which were incorporated into the curriculum by this decree.

The 1891 decree also added an English standard to the government curriculum and examinations. It was a six-year course, entered upon completion of Standard I of the Thai curriculum, thus formalizing Prince Damrong's earlier decision to restrict the study of English to those students who had acquired at least a minimal command of their own language. Concentration in the first four years of this standard was on the mechanics of reading, writing, and translation into and from English. Geography was added to the course in the fourth year, and foreign (but not Thai) history, commerce, astronomy, and hygiene in the sixth. Examinations were to be held at the end of each year, and not just at the end of the whole course as in the two Thai standards. The English standard thus was the only segment of the curriculum that really benefited from broadening in this period, in terms of offering to the students more than the simple mechanics of language and mathematics or the basic skills of the office. Not surprisingly, the English curriculum was the only segment of the educational system to be thoroughly modernized in its content.

Finally, the control of the Education Department over the quality of education was also exercised by a corps of school inspectors, whose duty it was regularly to inspect the schools in their districts in Bangkok. When first established in 1885, the inspectorate concerned itself solely with the academic progress of the students, but gradually its province was extended to include such things as the deportment of students, the condition of school buildings, hours of instruction, school schedules, the attendance of pupils and teachers, school finances, and teaching methods.[79] The reports of the inspectors were used to determine the awards of prizes to the best pupils in each school and to those teachers whose pupils performed best in the annual examinations. In most cases these were monetary rewards, designed to stimulate the students to hard work and to induce their teachers to follow the government standards.

79. Damrong and Johnson, *Prawat sangkhep,* pp. 34–35; and Report, Educ. Dept., 1886/87.

By these methods of control the Education Department was attempting to enforce certain minimal educational standards in the schools, while at the same time gradually raising those standards. These were set in the textbooks and the curricula and maintained through examinations, inspection, and rewards. But this much did not constitute educational policy. What were the king and the department attempting to do with the educational system?

The intentions and aspirations of Thailand's educational program are to some extent evident in the outline of the system presented above. That the desire to have an educated, trained civil service was important may readily be seen. But implicit in this program were broader objectives of political and social change which may less easily be traced in explicit statements than manifested in the actions of government. Thus, for example, the government's social biases and attempts to maintain the political position of the royalty and nobility may more meaningfully be traced in the early history of Suankulap School than constructed from the speech of Chulalongkorn mentioned above[80] or from the decree urging the sons of the nobility to enter government service, both of which could, although they might well not, be misleading if they were composed in lip service to tradition or for special audiences at specific moments. The best and most revealing glimpses of these objectives rather are contained in the educational programs drawn up at the close of the decade by Prince Damrong and his advisers.

In the formulation of educational policy and plans for its implementation, as well as in the day-to-day operations of the Education Department, Prince Damrong enjoyed the assistance of several men who were to leave lasting impressions on Siam's educational system. Dr. S. G. McFarland, who had founded Sunanthalai School and continued as its headmaster, probably enjoyed the confidence of Prince Damrong and assisted him from time to time in the affairs of the department, although

80. Page 105.

neither the fragmentary department records nor his biographer claim for him any great influence. Soon after the founding of the expanded Education Department in 1887, his son, Edwin McFarland, became Prince Damrong's English-language secretary and worked with him on plans for further educational development, traveling to the United States in 1891 "to study American educational systems and methods with the expectation of introducing them into Siam."[81]

Prince Damrong's most prominent adviser, however, was the controversial Robert Morant. Shortly after taking his degree from Oxford the young Morant came to Bangkok late in 1886 to take up a position as tutor to the young children of Prince Naret and later as tutor to Prince Phanurangsi's children. Gaining the confidence of the king, Prince Devawongse, and Prince Damrong, he was called in 1888 to the Grand Palace to serve as tutor to the Crown Prince, Prince Vajirunhis.[82] Because control over his activities fell partly to Prince Damrong, and because of the natural affinity between his work and Damrong's efforts to improve secondary education in general and English education in particular, he soon attained public recognition as the Prince's "able assistant"[83] and devoted his efforts to the improvement of the standard of English instruction through the drafting of a code of English examination standards, issued in 1891, and the writing of his *Ladder of Knowledge Series* of textbooks for teaching English to Thai schoolboys. He was given official status as "Examiner to the Government Schools" in

81. McFarland, *McFarland of Siam,* p. 76. Young McFarland seems to have undertaken this trip at least partly on his own initiative and funds, for he seems to have submitted no official report. On his return to Siam in 1892, he found that the new Ministry of Public Instruction had no position for him, and he appealed to the king for any that might be open. King to Cabinet, 17 July 1892, NA 5 S, 17/8 I, 57A.

82. Allen, *Sir Robert Morant,* pp. 46, 51–55. This biography of Morant, written from his papers and concerned primarily with his later career in England, is not wholly satisfactory on his service in Thailand, as it differs on several important points from papers concerning Morant in the archives.

83. *Bangkok Times,* 6 May 1891.

1890, and in collaboration with Prince Damrong he laid down plans for teacher training and establishing schools for the royal children. In connection with these schemes he spent his furlough in England in 1891 engaging new teachers.[84]

In addition to Edwin McFarland's study of American education, the department made two other studies of education abroad. Late in 1887, not long after the founding of the expanded Education Department, the king requested that the department make a detailed study of education in Japan. To carry out this task, Prince Damrong sent one of his officials, Khun Wǫrakan Koson (Thapthim Bunyaratthaphan), to Japan for six weeks in February-March of 1888, under very detailed instructions in the form of specific questions to be answered. Khun Wǫrakan was to investigate the entire educational system, from kindergarten to university, but he was asked to pay special attention to primary education, its organization, curriculum, statistics, the problem of coeducation, the timing of examinations, financing, and costs. He was also to heed some general questions, such as how many foreigners were employed as teachers, and how much teaching was done in the medium of Japanese as opposed to other languages, and he was asked to bring back to Bangkok samples of teaching materials, books, pictures, and translations used in the schools. Prince Damrong asked him to be free with his comments and opinions, to compare what he found with his knowledge of Thai education, to discuss problems, and to recommend steps the Thai government might take.[85] Khun Wǫrakan's three reports, dealing with primary and secondary, higher, and teacher and vocational education, were extremely detailed, straightforward accounts of what he had seen and been told, presenting a simple description of the Japanese education system of 1888 with almost none of

84. Allen, *Sir Robert Morant,* pp. 61, 65–70; and McFarland, *McFarland of Siam,* pp. 76–77.

85. NA 5 S, 4/8, 2, Damrong to Wǫrakan Koson, 20 Dec. 1887. On Khun Wǫrakan, see "Prawat [Phraya Phinitsara]," in Phraya Phinitsara, *Nangsü hitopathet kham khlong* (Bangkok, 1935), pp. i–vii.

the comment and opinion Prince Damrong had requested.[86] Because of their nature, and because of the fact that there appears to be absolutely no mention made of the reports either in the department's correspondence or in the considerable printed literature concerning this period,[87] it is difficult to assess the influence they may have had. No innovations can be traced to these reports, and they appear to have gone unnoticed.

A second survey of foreign education was made by Prince Damrong himself in 1890/91 on a visit to Burma, and again in 1891/92 when he first visited Europe, Egypt, and India for the same purpose. These personal surveys, coming as they did at the end of Damrong's period of service in the Education Department, would similarly seem to have had little influence on the course of educational development.[88]

Prince Damrong and his advisers, in their labors on educational planning and policy, had to consider the general lines of national policy as expressed by the king and felt by many of the highest government officials; the current concerns, both public and personal, of the king; and the practical limits that were imposed on possible actions. From about 1887 to 1892, the king's major public concern was the cause of administrative reform. In order to realize his objectives of rationalization and modernization of the administration and the broadening of the bases of political responsibility, it was necessary to ensure that there existed a large body of educated and competent youth among the nobility and royal family. Although the expanding government departments urgently needed trained young men for their offices, and although the new schools of the eighties provided at least a start toward meeting these requirements, the effect of these developments was felt primarily at the level of

86. NA 5 S, 4/8, 8, 34, and 63, Wǫrakan to Damrong, 18 Feb., 8 Mar., and 26 Mar. 1888.

87. E.g. Damrong and Johnson, *Prawat sangkhep;* Rǫng, *Prawat krasuang;* and Manich, *Compulsory Education.*

88. These visits are commonly spoken of as preparation for Prince Damrong's later work in the Ministry of Interior. Undoubtedly they were useful toward that end, but they were not intended as such.

Standard II education, particularly in such schools as Suankulap. Another important pressure on educational resources by 1890 stemmed from the need to educate the young princes, sons of the king and his brothers, who were reaching the ages at which they had to be prepared for further education in Europe. It was for this purpose that Morant was first brought to Bangkok and to which the English section of Suankulap began to bend an increasing proportion of its efforts. Although there had been some indications at mid-decade that the task of the Education Department might be defined in universal terms, the tone of educational policy by 1891 was unmistakably elitist in concept.

This shift from a universalist to an elitist view of education took place only gradually. It was reflected, in part, in the declining role of Dr. McFarland and in the increasing prominence of Morant on the educational scene. McFarland's Sunanthalai School had become by mid-decade a public secondary school open to all; but, probably out of the ingrained instincts for social stratification on the part of the Thai, it rapidly became merely a good school in which ordinary commoners and the Chinese commercial class might have their sons trained for minor positions in the bureaucracy and for commerce. Morant, on the other hand, having come to Bangkok specifically to prepare young princes for European education, rapidly rose to a position where he became involved in preparing the ruling class as a whole for education in Europe. In 1891 he was given permission to establish palace schools for the princes and princesses and he hired teachers in England for both. He clearly gained the favor of the king in these enterprises, and in doing so he gained a generous share of the limited resources available for education. It is more important to note, however, that Morant came to represent and express the strongest educational demands of the country at that time. While the king had to implore some elements of the nobility to put their faith in modern education, as in his decree of 1890, his own desires to have his children educated in the European fashion were at once strong, explicit, and immediate. It was natural that Prince

Damrong and the Education Department heeded Morant's advice and noted the king's support for it, especially given the lack of any concerted public demand for or appreciation of modern education.

The objective of common, universal, modern education, however inchoate, had been continually frustrated by the lack of public demand. The decree of 1875, for a variety of reasons, seems to have been almost completely ignored. Prince Damrong enjoyed some initial success with the monastery schools beginning in the mideighties, but the number of pupils served by them reached a peak in 1890 which was not to be surpassed until 1896. Toward the end of Prince Damrong's period in the department he began to plan for a major extension of monastery schools in the provinces. Having been approached by several provincial governors who wished to establish government schools in provinces as widely separated as Songkhla,[89] Chanthaburi, and Phetburi, Prince Damrong proposed to the king that government schools be established in each province *(müang)*, that the department extend them financial aid in the form of teachers' salaries and textbooks, that they be required to conform to the department's syllabus and examinations, and that the local officers responsible for religious affairs in the provinces *(krommakan tamnaeng thammakan)* be charged with supervising them. The direct cost to the department, he thought, would not exceed 320 baht annually per province for salaries, books, and supplies, and these costs might be met by local government funds from the land or dwelling taxes.[90] The king approving, Damrong met with provincial governors who had come to Bangkok for the Crown Prince's tonsure ceremony in February 1891, and, finding that "some were happy about the plan . . . but still did not understand the procedures for establishing schools,"[91] he issued, in the form of a circular

89. NA 5 S, 17/8 I, 5, Damrong to King, 24 Aug. 1890; 17/8 I, 12, Damrong to Sommot, 24 Oct. 1890; and 17/8 I, 16, Damrong to King, 11 Feb. 1891.
90. NA 5 S, 17/8 I, 13, Damrong to King, 7 Jan. 1891.
91. NA 5 S, 17/8 I, 22, Damrong to King, 18 Feb. 1891.

letter to provincial governors, a set of regulations formalizing his earlier proposals,[92] and obtained assurances from twenty müang that they would establish schools in 1891/92.[93] The schools, however, except for one in Songkhla, did not materialize, perhaps because of difficulties in obtaining funds when the budget came up for review in March and April, or perhaps because these monastery schools had to compete for funds with the expensive projects then being promoted by Morant.

When the inevitable choice came, for the state's revenues were still extremely limited, it was not a difficult one to make. There seemed every reason to opt for greater support for secondary and English education for the elite. It was a choice made easier by Morant's interests, which lay in this direction, and by the king's immediate personal concerns for his own sons and nephews; Prince Damrong was himself not wholeheartedly convinced of the necessity for great improvements in the old-style monastery schools, his view at this time being that beyond a minimal knowledge of reading and writing most boys needed only the simplest common sense education in "morality, cooking, sewing, climbing trees, swimming, building shelters, planting trees, and keeping animals," all of which could be taught by a boy's parents and relatives, except for those few boys who looked toward careers in government, commerce, or the crafts and professions.[94]

Given such views and inclinations, together with the prevailing elitist preoccupations of the government as a whole, it was clear that general primary education was not going to move ahead quickly despite a few general hopes expressed publicly on all sides. The decision to establish a teacher training college was taken in 1891, but the project was provided for on such a reduced scale that little could have been expected from it for a

92. NA 5 S, 17/8 I, 23, Damrong to Provincial Governors, Feb. 1891.
93. NA 5 S, 17/8 I, 22, Damrong to King, 18 Feb. 1891.
94. Prince Damrong Rajanubhab, "Wicha samrap tua dek," *Wachirayan wiset*, 5 (19 Oct. 1890), 625–30; reprinted in Damrong, *Prachum phraniphon bettalet*, pp. 255–66.

good many years.[95] It was for the higher schools—the Normal
School, Suankulap, and the schools for the royal children—that
funds were appropriated, teachers hired, and new standards
framed in 1891/92.

The new standards of 1891, as framed in the examination
regulations,[96] were well received in Bangkok, judging from
newspaper comment, and Prince Damrong and Mr. Morant
were complimented for establishing such clear and rigorous
guidelines for a system that would bring "education to the very
doors of [Prince Damrong's] countrymen."[97] Less than a year
later, however, the same newspaper was considerably more
reserved about "Mr. Morant's latest scheme for the education
of the youth of Siam."[98] Referring, apparently, to Morant's current activities in hiring university-trained Englishmen for the
planned schools for princes and princesses, the Normal School,
Suankulap, and private tutoring, which had been announced in
the *Bangkok Times* three days earlier,[99] the editor suggested
that the leap the country was attempting to make from monastery education in the old fashion to a modern collegiate course
was a considerable one, and very expensive. And, he added,
"Siam . . . is committing herself to a scheme which looks only
to the latter end of the curriculum, without regard to the preliminary steps, and she will learn an expensive lesson."[100] But
Damrong replied by stating that "he hoped to carry out with
complete success the programme which had already been made
public and which, he saw, had been adversely criticised."[101]
The commitment was made: as a policy decision, the government was to put its emphasis on education for the elite.

95. NA 5 S, 17/8 I, 1, Damrong to King, 10 Apr. 1891; and 17/8 II,
10, King to Ministry of Finance, 19 Apr. 1891.
96. See above, pp. 133–34.
97. "The Education Code," *Bangkok Times*, 6 May 1891.
98. "Siam's New Education," *Bangkok Times*, 23 Jan. 1892.
99. "Siam's New Education," *Bangkok Times*, 20 Jan. 1892.
100. *Bangkok Times*, 23 Jan. 1892.
101. *Bangkok Times*, 26 Mar. 1892.

DAMRONG'S DEPARTURE

Following a visit to Bangkok by the tsarevitch of Russia (later Tsar Nicholas II) in 1891, Prince Damrong was sent on his first trip to Europe as the king's special envoy to return the visit and confer Siamese decorations on European heads of state. In the course of this trip he took every opportunity that presented itself to investigate modern educational practice, and he obtained the king's permission to make special visits to Egypt and India for the purpose. He returned to Bangkok on 24 March 1892, full of enthusiasm for his educational work.[102] Seven days later, on 1 April, the long-awaited decree on the reorganization of the government was published. To Prince Damrong's surprise, the decree announced his appointment, not as Minister of Public Instruction, but as Minister of Interior *(mahatthai)*, long the most exalted civil office in the kingdom.[103]

Unable to secure an immediate audience with the king to protest what seemed to him an undue shock, Prince Damrong could only clean out his desk in his old office and move with his private secretary to the Ministry of Interior. It was not until some days later that the king called him in and ventured to explain Damrong's sudden shift in jobs. Čhaophraya Rattanabǫdin had been taken seriously ill and was unable to continue in office. Casting about for a substitute, the king found only Damrong's abilities equal to the magnitude of the tasks of the Ministry of Interior and so had moved him from his post in the Ministry of Public Instruction. When Damrong protested that he felt unequal to the job and feared that he would disgrace the king who had appointed him, that he would serve the king much more capably doing the work for which he had trained himself and with which he was familiar, the king replied, as Damrong recalled many years later, that the nation's survival

102. *Bangkok Times,* 26 Mar. 1892. On Damrong's trip to Europe, see Thailand, Fine Arts Dept., comps., *Somdet phračhao bǫrommawongthoe kromphraya damrong rachanuphap sadet thawip yurop ph.s. 2434* (Bangkok, 1968).

103. Damrong and Ratchasena, *Thetsaphiban,* pp. 5–6.

was at stake and that the task of setting the provincial administration in order was more important at that moment than education. The king was convinced that Damrong would be able to
run the Ministry of Interior quite capably and promised him
advice and every assistance. Still unsure of himself, Damrong
"asked for and obtained the King's promise that, if [he] did not
do well, [the king] would allow [him] to return to the Ministry
of Public Instruction."[104]

And so Prince Damrong, the able architect of Thailand's first
educational plans, left the Ministry of Public Instruction in
order to serve more pressing national requirements. He left
behind him unfulfilled plans and the mixed record of a decade
of experimentation, a firmly established and academically promising school in Suankulap, a small number of monastery schools,
a small body of teaching materials, a set of educational practices
and biases which were rapidly settling into place, and a new
ministry organized on modern lines, waiting to be put to work
to implement a set of ambitious but still untested educational
plans.

104. Ibid., pp. 7–8.

6

Uncertainty and Indirection, 1892–1897

The sudden and unexpected ministerial changes of April 1892 proved a serious blow to the Ministry of Public Instruction. To that point the work of the ministry in no small measure had flourished and prospered because of the ability and royal prestige of Prince Damrong. In moving him to the Ministry of Interior, King Chulalongkorn indicated the lower priority that education henceforth would enjoy in pressing its claims upon the nation's limited resources. The appointment as Minister of Public Instruction of Phraya Phatsakɔrawong (Phɔn Bunnag), who attained the rank of *čhaophraya* in December 1892, brought to the ministry a man of lesser skills and less immediate political influence than his predecessor and began a ten-year period of decline and stagnation.

Čhaophraya Phatsakɔrawong, born in 1849, was the youngest of the sixteen sons of Somdet Čhaophraya Bɔrommaha Prayurawong ("Somdet Čhaophraya Ong Yai," Dit Bunnag), who was *phrakhlang* and *kalahom* in the reign of King Rama III and died in 1855. He was raised by his eldest brother, Čhaophraya Si Suriyawong (Chuang Bunnag), and attended his family's monastery in Thonburi, Wat Prayurawong, to learn to read and write. At the age of fifteen he was sent to school in England. After three years there, during which he gained some fluency in English, he returned to Bangkok in 1867 and not long after his return was appointed King Mongkut's personal English-language secretary. He continued in that post under King Chulalongkorn and became a favorite of the young king, to whom he rendered unquestioning loyalty even when that meant defying his elder brother and guardian, the regent. He accompanied the king on his trips to Java and India and helped to frame the regulations for the Orders of the Royal Decorations, the Privy Council and Council of State, and the early palace schools. He was appointed one of the four heads of the Department of the Royal Pages (krom mahatlek) and was a member of the first Privy Council. His radical sympathies landed him in difficulties in the late seventies, although he remained in the king's favor, and he was sent to England in 1879 on a special diplomatic mission to smooth over the Phra Pricha affair.[1] On his return he was made director of the Orchards Tax Department in the Ministry of Finance. He served as Acting Minister of Foreign Affairs during Prince Devawongse's absence in 1887 and then served as director of the Customs Department before being named Minister of Agriculture in 1890. He had been prominent in educational affairs, serving on the board of governors of McFarland's Suan Anand School, the advisory committee that assisted in drawing up a program for the Education Department in 1884, and on the board of examiners for Suankulap School. In addition, he personally founded and supported the monastery school at Wat Prayurawong. By virtue of this wide experience, Phatsakɔrawong, of all the eligible senior government officials, was best qualified to assume the post left vacant by Prince Damrong; he had been instrumental in all the important educational events of the previous two decades and was one of only a handful of the men of his generation whose education had spanned the old and the new worlds.[2]

Phatsakɔrawong's first major problem on his appointment

1. See Minney, *Fanny and the Regent,* esp. p. 247.
2. Damrong, "Prawat čhaophraya phatsakɔrawong," in Čhaophraya Phatsakɔrawong, *Khamklɔn khɔng čhaophraya phatsakɔrawong* (Bangkok, 1922), pp. ii–x. See also, "Siam's New Ministry," *Bangkok Times,* 8 June 1892, which includes biographies of all the ministers in the 1892 Cabinet. Phatsakɔrawong certainly was not as unfit for his new position as Mrs.

was to replace the five key ministry officials who had followed Prince Damrong to the Ministry of Interior: the minister's private secretary, the secretary of the ministry (*samian tra,* literally "Clerk of the Seals"), the accountant, and the director and deputy director of the Education Department. Of these, undoubtedly the most important was the position of director of the Education Department. Although there were a number of men in the ministry with long experience in educational work, Phatsakǫrawong felt it necessary to have a prince of the royal blood in this position, owing to his own lack of political influence vis-à-vis a Cabinet composed predominantly of members of the royal family, on whom the ministry was forced to depend for support and funds.[3] Accordingly, the minister dismissed Edwin McFarland from his position as English-language secretary to the minister and compiler in the Textbook Bureau, and appointed his own nephew, Prince Čhantharathat Čhuthathǫn (later, Prince Wiwit Wannapricha), to hold office concurrently as director of the Education Department and compiler of textbooks in the Textbook Bureau.[4] When this appointment proved unsuitable, Prince Čhantharathat was transferred to become director of the Hospitals Department in March 1893, to be succeeded temporarily by Prince Sommot Amǫraphan, who at the same time was the king's private secretary, director of the Royal Secretariat, and, a few months later, director of the Privy Purse Department.[5]

Within the next year, however, Prince Sommot's other duties forced him to relinquish his duties in the Education Department,

McFarland (*McFarland of Siam,* p. 96) and H. Warington Smyth (*Five Years in Siam, From 1891 to 1896* [London, 1898], *1,* 34) believed.

3. Phatsakǫrawong baldly admitted to this stratagem some years later: NA 5 S, 13/5, 15, Phatsakǫrawong to Sommot, 21 June 1898.

4. NA 5 S, 3/8, Phatsakǫrawong to Sommot, 12 May 1892. Note that Prince Wiwit was Čhaophraya Phatsakǫrawong's nephew, the son of his younger sister. See Sawat Čhanthani, *Nithan chao rai* (Bangkok, 1966), 5, 9.

5. *RKB,* 9 (1892/93), 440. See also Si Wǫrawong, *Phraprawat krompbra sommot,* p. 9.

and it was not until March 1895 that Phatsakǫrawong was able
to find a worthy successor and funds to support his appointment. In that month, Dr. S. G. McFarland, who had been taken
onto the staff of the Textbook Bureau when Sunanthalai School
closed in 1892,[6] resigned after sixteen years in the educational
service; in reporting his resignation to the king, Phatsakǫrawong
asked whether Prince Kittiyakǫn, who was among the first
group of Chulalongkorn's sons to study abroad, might be
appointed to a position in the ministry on his return from
Europe. He could become director or deputy director of the
Education Department or be appointed to a new position as
"Inspector-General of Education," his responsibilities in any of
these posts to include the English translation work formerly
carried out by McFarland, and a portion of his salary could
come from McFarland's old post.[7] During the summer of that
year, the king took the measure of Prince Kittiyakǫn's fitness
for educational work by having him conduct a full-scale inspection of all government schools, which resulted in a report he
submitted to his father on 31 August 1895, suggesting measures
that might be taken to raise the standards of the schools.[8] A
week later, approving the report, the king directed that Prince
Kittiyakǫn be appointed director of the Education Department.[9]

By 1895, Phatsakǫrawong at long last had gained the assistant he had lacked for three years, but this did not bring his
ministry such an increased status as to secure for it the funds
he thought necessary for the success of its work. Among the
eleven ministries,[10] the Ministry of Public Instruction began this

6. See Wyatt, "Samuel McFarland," pp. 8–9.

7. See NA 5 S, 17/8 I, 55, McFarland to King, 16 June 1892; 28/2,
4, Phatsakǫrawong to Sommot, 31 Mar. 1895; 28/2, 8, McFarland to
Phatsakǫrawong, 1 Feb. 1895; 28/2, 7, King's memo. on 28/2, 4, early
Apr., 1895.

8. NA 5 S, 13/5, 1, Kittiyakǫn to King, 31 Aug. 1895.

9. NA 5 S, 28/2, 3, King to Kittiyakǫn, 6 Sept. 1895; and 28/2, 1,
King to Phatsakǫrawong, 6 Sept. 1895. See also *RKB, 12* (1895/96), 250.

10. The Army Ministry was included for budgetary purposes (at least
in later figures) in the *kalahom*.

period with the seventh largest budget in 1892/93.[11] It stood eighth the following year, and by 1896/97 it had fallen to tenth place. During the entire period from 1892/93 to 1897/98 the Ministry of Public Instruction never claimed more than 2.5 percent of the total national revenues (or 3 percent of total expenditures), and then only in years of high capital investment in such items as new buildings, and the Education Department's share of the total ministry budget was only one third early in the decade, rising later to one half. Over the same six-year period there was a gross surplus of 13 percent in the national budget, in monetary terms a total of almost thirteen million baht, a sum equivalent to more than forty times the ministry's budget for 1894/95. All this is to argue only that there were sufficient funds that could have been allocated to the ministry, had the king and Cabinet decided to do so. Phatsak̜rawong hoped that Prince Kittiyak̜n would help to bring the ministry the budgetary attention he thought it deserved, but in the long run he was disappointed.

The effects of budgetary starvation and of the long absence of effective direction in the Education Department are shown in the record of those years in the public primary schools, in the special and secondary schools, and in the provision of educational services.

PRIMARY EDUCATION, 1892–1895

The second of the major problems with which Phatsak̜ra-wong had to deal on joining the ministry in 1892 was the organization and development of primary education. During the ministry of Prince Damrong, primary education had undergone several reorganizations, the last in 1891 when a unitary, unilinear system was established, running straight through (at least on paper) from primary schools to university preparatory

11. See the table in Čhakkrit, *Damrong kap krasuang mahatthai*, pp. 369–70.

schools.[12] All schools at each examination-based level were bound to the same curriculum, textbooks, examinations, and inspection. This whole system, particularly where the primary schools were concerned, was posited on the assumption that the government would continue to offer substantial financial support to all schools, including those in the monasteries, and it depended upon a steadily growing supply of teachers trained to teach to the increasingly well-defined standards set by the ministry.

It must have been apparent to the ministry by 1892, as it was to the local Western community in Bangkok, that raising the standards of most monastery schools would require more than new regulations and that no really effective system of public education could develop without considerable time and effort being devoted to the training of teachers for the primary schools.[13] In May 1892, an experienced normal school teacher, G. H. Grindrod, whom Morant had hired in England on behalf of the ministry, arrived in Bangkok. It was his task to establish a school for the training of teachers, "the main object being to instill into the future teachers of the *Vernacular* schools the real principles of teaching and of education; so that there might be a sound system of teaching going on in the vernacular schools."[14] The Normal School opened on 12 October 1892, with only three of its projected ten students. Despite the fact that it awarded monthly stipends of twelve baht to its students

12. See above, pp. 133–34.
13. "Elementary Education in Siam," *Bangkok Times,* 21 May 1892, editorial.
14. NA 5 S, 17/8 I, 45A Morant to Phatsakǫrawong, 15 May 1892. See also *Bangkok Times,* 18 and 21 May 1892; and NA 5 S, 17/8 I, 45, Phatsakǫrawong to Sommot, 18 May 1892, in which the minister noted that the Normal School already was provided for in the budget of the ministry and could take ten paid students in its first year. He proposed that the school be located first at Suankulap and hoped later to expand it gradually. A month later, Phatsakǫrawong reported that he had rented a house for Grindrod near the orphanage and that the orphanage school would be used for practice teaching. NA 5 S, 17/8 I, 68, Phatsakǫrawong to Sommot, 30 June 1892.

as an inducement to enter the school and continue their studies, and in spite of continued generous financial support which provided the school with well-qualified European teachers, the school failed to attract any significant number of students, primarily because most youths could see little merit in careers as teachers when much more lucrative positions in other ministries were going begging. The school graduated only twenty teachers between 1892 and 1898, and even by 1902 it had only seventeen students in the second year of its two-year course, of whom seven were monks.[15] The Normal School in the last decade of the nineteenth century had very little impact on primary education in Thailand, however high the hopes placed in it by Damrong, Morant, and Phatsakǫrawong, if for no other reason than its inability to produce any significant numbers of trained teachers.

The ministry's difficulties in raising educational standards were further compounded in June 1892 by the cuts made in the ministry's budget by the Cabinet. In addition to paring down the funds allowed for English education, closing the ministry's printing press, deleting some positions in the Textbook Bureau, and reducing the funds available to the ministry for religious education, the Cabinet completely cut from the ministry's budget funds for all the government primary schools in the monasteries. It was only after what must have been a protracted battle with the Cabinet that Phatsakǫrawong was able to secure the restoration to the budget of funds for the four most promising monastery schools in Bangkok and an additional sum sufficient only to pay the salary of one *assistant* teacher for each of the remaining government schools in the monasteries.[16] With such a cut in its budget, the ministry found it

15. Bamrung Klatčharoen, "Prawat kanfükhat khru khǫng prathet thai," (M.A. thesis, Prasarnmitr College of Education, Bangkok, 1963), pp. 22–25. The Normal School seems to have begun offering a four-year course, but it cut its length in an attempt to make the course more attractive to students and to cut costs.

16. NA 5 S, 13/5, 15, Phatsakǫrawong to Sommot, 21 June 1898; and 17/8 II, 19, same to same, 6 June 1892. The latter sum was fixed at

impossible to maintain the policies of support and control laid down in the educational program of 1891. It could no longer pay the salaries of teaching staff, nor could it maintain educational services—textbooks, examinations, and inspection—on the scale it had anticipated. Deprived of the incentives and controls the old system provided, many of the schools simply could not continue to operate.

Phatsakǫrawong's dilemma was an unenviable one. He had been given an educational system to operate, improve, and expand, and had then been deprived of the means of doing so. There was only one reasonable choice open to him: to change the system. This was rapidly accomplished within the month of June 1892, in a process marked by the issuance of three documents: Phatsakǫrawong's first tentative proposals, of 6 June,[17] a set of three "Draft Education Laws,"[18] and a final "Royal Decree Establishing Elementary Schools," published on 14 June 1892.[19]

The minister's first proposals reiterated the three-stage system put forward in the 1891 decree, with primary, middle, and higher schools. He also proposed, however, while indicating that the Cabinet was favorable to the idea, that there be two types of primary schools, reproducing in the abstract laws the concrete situation created by the Cabinet in granting full financial support only to four of the old monastery primary schools. These two types were to be the lower primary schools *(rongrian munlasaman chan tam)*, monk-taught monastery schools following the traditional curriculum but provided with govern-

---

10 baht per school per month. The ministry, basing its estimates on requests from provincial and capital authorities for school funds, had submitted a request for 32,000 baht for government primary schools in the monasteries, but finally was granted only 10,400 baht, as compared with the sum of 16,980 baht expended in 1890/91.

17. NA 5 S, 17/8 II, 19, Phatsakǫrawong to Sommot, 6 June 1892.

18. NA 5 S, 39/5, "Draft Education Laws, R.S. 111" (1892). These are undated, but internal evidence places them between 6 and 14 June 1892.

19. "Prakat tang rongrian munlasaman," *PKPS, 13,* 113–19, and in *Documents,* pp. 68–74.

ment textbooks and preparing for examinations at a level below Standard I called "practice standard" *(prayok sǫm);* and the higher primary schools *(chan sung).*[20] These latter were to be provided with some support from local land taxes where possible, both in Bangkok and the provinces. They were to teach both the "practice standard" and Standard I, and were to keep their examinations open to students from neighboring elementary schools. Phatsakǫrawong's plan was to keep all the old government monastery schools operating as elementary schools, except for the four well-established schools at *wat* Thepsirin, Čhakkrawat, and Prayurawong in Bangkok and Wat Senatsanaram in Ayudhya, which would, in effect, *continue* as primary schools, i.e. continue teaching to the level of Standard I. He hoped that later many of the elementary schools would improve their standards and secure the funds to become primary schools. Meanwhile, the four main monastery schools, plus Suankulap and a few of the special schools, alone would continue to teach at the primary level—the level which had been intended as universal in 1891.

Regulations to formalize these changes were presented in the undated "Draft Education Laws," which in character are an expansion of and elaboration on the views expressed in Phatsakǫrawong's letter of 6 June. The first of these laws, "Education in Bangkok," described the overall educational system in broad outline. It prescribed ages of study and length of courses and added a provision that, when a primary school was established in a monastery, all children (and not specifically just boys) in the neighborhood between the ages of seven and fifteen years *must* be enrolled in it. Those children who did not attend were to be sent to a "reform school" where they would be forced to study and perform manual work. This first expression of the idea of compulsory education was dropped in the subsequent decree. "Law I," the second of this group of proposed

20. In all that follows, "lower primary schools" will be termed "elementary schools," while the "higher primary schools" will be termed "primary schools."

laws, laid down in considerable detail the curriculum proposed for elementary and primary schools in Bangkok. While both types were to offer instruction in morality, reading, writing, composition, grammar, and arithmetic, the primary schools were also to offer instruction in geography, history, science, drawing, and singing, and if qualified teachers were available they could also add to their curriculum English, arts and crafts, agriculture, and commerce. The content of this curriculum, which reflects the broadening tendencies that were beginning to appear by 1890, was explained in great detail in this proposal. Finally, in "Law II," a "simplified curriculum" was suggested for the elementary schools in the provinces, a curriculum that could include morality, reading (using any textbook), writing, composition, and arithmetic, by whatever methods, using whatever textbooks, and including such material as the teacher might alone decide. This "simplified curriculum" was little more than a formal recognition of the traditional patterns and content of monastery education, with the single exception of the provision that a monk's instruction could formally constitute a school (with modern connotations) only if he taught at least ten pupils.

The Royal Decree finally promulgated on 14 June called attention with some regret to the relatively small enrollments of the ministry's schools, which "are very small numbers, and are not commensurate with the sums of government funds which have been expended, nor with His Majesty's wish that education be extended." The law went on to describe the two levels of elementary and primary education, so divided into levels "according to the teaching abilities of the teachers and in which the knowledge of the students gradually may be increased." Omitting any reference to compulsory attendance, this decree in general followed the outline of the draft laws, but concentrated mainly upon the lower primary or elementary schools. It required that the abbots of all monasteries be responsible for arranging for regular instruction to be given to all boys in the charge of the monks of that monastery; that any group of ten or more pupils instructed by a monk be considered, ipso facto, a school; that any monk with fewer than ten pupils would have to send at least one of them to a duly constituted school; that one textbook be provided to each teacher-monk free of charge; and that all such schools be advised and inspected regularly by the ministery, if located in Bangkok, or by a member of the local government specially designated for the purpose if located in the provinces. Examinations at the "practice standard" were to be administered to them annually. The law also briefly discussed higher primary schools and independent schools at all levels, including those teaching Pali, Môn, English, Chinese, and Hindi, such special independent schools being required to register with the ministry and to submit to regular inspections.

Thus, in the month of June 1892, the Ministry of Public Instruction was forced to come to terms with its financial and staffing problems and with the low standards of most government schools then operating. The effect of these measure so taken was formally to cut the educational system into sections. The decree as much as admitted that the government simply was not getting a reasonable return on its investment in these schools, and the four schools that escaped the financial and academic axe were all schools of heavy enrollments and good examination records. For these reasons, they were maintained to serve as models for the other monastery schools.[21] Thus two sections of the bottom tier of the educational system were clearly delineated: a substantial body of public elementary schools in the monasteries, carrying on their traditional tasks on a level slightly higher than before and given some encouragement to continue raising their standards; and a growing number of elite primary schools which were fully integrated into an educational system that was to progress up to college preparatory courses and professional training.

The reasons for this reorganization and retrenchment in primary education in 1892 seem clear enough when viewed from

21. NA 5 S, 13/5, 15, Phatsakǫrawong to Sommot, 21 June 1898.

the standpoint of the ministry's situation. Faced with drastic cuts in its budget, which the minister vainly resisted, and a heretofore uneven performance by the schools, he chose to concentrate and husband his resources, awaiting better times in the future. No explanation is available as to *why* the ministry's funds were cut, but the sources allow a few tentative suggestions to be put forward

First, on the financial side, government revenues began in 1889 a steady and rapid upward climb on the order of 7–8 percent annually in the period 1889–94.[22] Although undoubtedly there were extraordinary expenses connected with the establishment of the new ministries in 1892, these ministries in fact had been building over the previous three or four years. On the other hand, the available figures on the budgets of the Education Department show a steady decline over the years 1888–91 and still further decline by 1895,[23] which might be taken as an indication either of decreasing interest in education or the growing pressure of other demands on the king and his advisers and ministers, among whom Prince Damrong is cited by Phatsakǫrawong as an eminent example of one who abruptly withdrew his support from education. Phatsakǫrawong seems also to have blamed himself, at least in part, for his own inability to command an influence within the Cabinet that could have gained sanction for his budgetary requests.[24] All these factors taken together would suggest a political situation in which Phatsakǫrawong, new to his ministry and its tasks, simply could not function quickly and effectively enough to win his case in the face of a Cabinet whose members' interests and requirements lay elsewhere.

There is a hint of another factor in this situation which is reminiscent of the difficulties the British experienced in Burma when trying to gain the cooperation of the Buddhist monkhood

22. Based on data from Wira, *Historical Patterns,* pp. 114, 121; and Čhakkrit, *Damrong kap krasuang mahatthai,* p. 369.
23. See above, pp. 127–28, and sources cited in n. 64, Chapter 5.
24. NA 5 S, 13/5, 15, Phatsakǫrawong to Sommot, 21 June 1898.

in promoting modern education.[25] There is almost no evidence whatsoever of any similar phenomenon in Thailand, partly because of the different relations between *Sangha* and state that have existed in Thailand. One would certainly expect, however, to find at least some resistance to modern education among the Thai monkhood, or at least resistance to the bureaucratization of education that was underway by 1890. A hint of such resistance is present in the decree of 14 June. Among the reasons given there for the reforms undertaken are the statement that "It is natural that monks who are teachers wish to teach their pupils themselves" and the complaint that "The monastery pupils do not attend the government schools and their teachers [in the monasteries] teach poorly." The decree required that monks with few pupils send at least one to regular school instruction, allowing them to continue to teach those who remained but without granting them the increase in alms granted to those monks in the royal monasteries teaching more than ten pupils according to the government system. In general, it would appear that there was some resistance to the new schools, for in the decree abbots were *required* to see that all the monastery boys were instructed, and each monk was *required* to send at least one of his pupils to a regular school. Yet so that he could continue to teach in the old manner, each monk was allowed to keep at least some of his boys under the old system. Because of the scattered quality of the documents from this period, one can suggest only that this factor of monastic resistance *may* have played a role, however indirect, in the retrenchment of 1892. In the balance, it would appear to have been a factor less important than the others.

This retrenchment had the effect of confirming the gulf between ordinary monastery elementary schools and the primary schools frequented by the elite. There are no available

25. See, for example, G. E. Harvey, *British Rule in Burma, 1824–1942* (London, 1946), p. 46; and U Kaung, "A Survey of the History of Education in Burma Before the British Conquest and After," *Journal of the Burma Research Society, 46*, pt. 2 (1963), 77–81.

indications that this came about as the result of a conscious choice in any quarter, although it is likely that if the Cabinet were forced by economic necessity or considerations of priorities in national expenditure to cut the budget of the Ministry of Public Instruction, it would have been less resistant to cutting the ordinary monastery schools than to cutting the funds of the schools which its members or their children attended. Under such circumstances, any choice to continue full support for the monastery schools would to some extent have required a commitment to the ideal of democratic education on the part of these twelve men, or else a far-sighted perception of the utility of these schools in providing trained men for the civil service and a judgment that the schools actually were capable of training the kinds of men they needed. But even this latter alternative would require that the ministers feel some commitment to the democratic recruitment of civil servants. It would be too much to expect such commitments from this particular Cabinet at this point in time, and although it can be argued that the king may have been more democratically inclined at least on this point than most of his brothers and ministers, the decision for educational retrenchment was taken at a time when the king was experimenting with cabinet government and trying to give his ministers a free hand in running the government. This was not the sort of issue on which he might have been tempted to override them.

The direct effect of retrenchment on the schools themselves is even more difficult to assess. Čhaophraya Phatsakǫrawong, in a later, ex parte, comment on this period, states that "their teachers were able no longer to maintain them as schools, and they were all closed."[26] He exaggerated, for a number continued to be listed annually in the official roster of the ministry.[27] Most

26. NA 5 S, 13/5, 15, Phatsakǫrawong to Sommot, 21 June 1898.
27. In the Thai archives there are no reports for the Ministry of Public Instruction for the years after 1891/92, except for the year 1898/99, although scattered statistics are available in the sources. The ministry's reports began to be published only in 1908. For a good glimpse of the

of the monastery elementary schools must have lapsed back into their old obscurity. The four higher primary schools at the prominent monasteries of Bangkok gradually were increased in number by generous private assistance from the royal Privy Purse and the queen.[28] When the impact of the 1892 budgetary cuts reached some monastery schools in Bangkok, protests were lodged with the ministry by their patrons and teachers. As a result, the king undertook to extend his patronage to additional schools at Wat Ratchabophit and Wat Ratchapradit in Bangkok and Wat Niwetthammaprawat at Bang Pa-in, enabling them to continue both religious and secular instruction which formerly he had underwritten through the ministry.[29] As for the other schools, less favored by royal patronage, the example of a monastery in Ayudhya may be indicative of the conditions they experienced. Wat Sala Pun, which flourished in the period before 1892, was aided by public subscription to continue to provide extensive Pali instruction; in writing to the ministry in 1895 to request assistance in constructing new buildings to accommodate its expanding enrollment, its abbot noted proudly that the school offered Thai instruction as well.[30] One would expect from this and similar cases that the most firmly established Thai elementary schools were located in monasteries where Pali instruction was strongest and where extensive financial support of religious education by the local officials

monastery schools in this period, as seen by the head of the Normal School (1894–96), see Ernest Young, *The Kingdom of the Yellow Robe* (London, 1898), p. 63.

28. In June 1892, Queen Saowapha founded a school for boys and girls on Kǫ Si Chang (an island in the Gulf of Siam which was a favorite resort of the royal family in this period), which she supported from her own funds. NA 5 S, 17/8 II, 26, King to Phatsakǫrawong, 20 June 1892; and subsequent correspondence in 17/8 I, 65–85, June–July, 1892.

29. NA 5 S, 3/8, 14, Phatsakǫrawong to Sommot, 12 June 1892; and further correspondence in 18/5, 2, and 19/5, 19 and 20, dated 1896 but referring back to arrangements made in 1892. For the classification of these schools, see *RKB*, 9 (1892/93), 96–99, and 10 (1893/94), 248–52.

30. NA 5 S, 84/5, 1, Phatsakǫrawong to Sommot, 18 Oct. 1895; and 84/5, 2, Phra Yantrailok to Phraya Wutthikanbǫdi, 4 Oct. 1895.

and townspeople had become customary. This appears to have been the case in the founding of new schools in the 1880s, and there are many indications of the same phenomenon in the nineties, when ministry support dwindled.

The effect of retrenchment on schools operating in 1892 was probably mainly to shake loose some insecurely founded schools, while the bulk of them continued to function, were probably registered with the ministry and received some services from it, and reentered the registers and subsidy lists when official educational activity began to accelerate toward the end of the decade. Their continued existence should not, however, detract from the significance of the period: the elementary schools in the monasteries were deemphasized and forced to the periphery of the greatly reduced sphere of the Ministry of Public Instruction's concerns.

SPECIAL AND SECONDARY SCHOOLS

In the "Draft Education Laws" of 1892 two types of schools were provided for above the primary level.[31] First there were such special schools as those for the royal children, the School of Shorthand at Suankulap (1891–93), and the Normal School —schools with special curricula for special purposes, which normally were not governed by the examination system. The law, perhaps drawing on the Japanese example, envisaged establishing such schools in the fields of the fine arts, law, medicine, agriculture, commerce, industry, and the education of the blind, but only medical and law schools were established during this decade. Next, there were the middle or secondary *(matthayom)* schools, the curricula of which could include instruction in English. These were divided into two grades, examining for Standards II and III of the examination system, and included

31. NA 5 S, 39/5, "Draft Education Law, R.S. 111." It appears that this law was promulgated as a ministerial code by the ministry. The section on elementary education, however, was issued as a decree on 14 June, 1892, "Prakat tang rongrian munlasaman," *PKPS, 13,* 113–19.

Suankulap and Suankulap English schools, Sunanthalai, and the New School.

The special schools proved to be an immediate, but not an enduring, problem to the ministry in 1892. Foremost among these was Rajakumara School, established within the palace walls in 1892 under the direction of Robert Morant. This school grew naturally as the end product of that process of development begun when King Mongkut engaged Mrs. Leonowens to instruct his children. In the late seventies and early eighties, when Mongkut's children were grown and Chulalongkorn's still infants, the need for regular Western education for the princes of the blood was met first by private tutors and then by special classes taught at Suankulap School, and the Education Department took over the responsibility for this instruction, providing teachers from its schools.[32] When Chulalongkorn's thirty-two sons and forty-five daughters, most of whom were born between 1878 and 1889, came of educable age, the strain on previous informal arrangements became too severe. Morant, who had been appointed tutor to Crown Prince Vajirunhis in 1888, took the lead in formalizing them.

Between 1888 and 1893 Morant seems to have enjoyed considerable influence in Bangkok at large and with Prince Damrong and the Education Department in particular, in the work of which he took considerable interest and to which he contributed much during a formative period. On returning to England on home leave in the summer of 1891, Morant was commissioned by Prince Damrong to hire teachers for three major educational projects: a new school for the royal princes, another for girls, and a teachers' training college, schemes which he had worked out in collaboration with Prince Damrong. For Rajakumara School for the Princes, two teachers were engaged in London and arrived in Bangkok in June 1892.[33]

32. See, e.g., NA 5 S, 21/2, 1 and 2, Wutthikanbǫdi to Sommot, 6 and 7 Aug. 1891, concerning an attempt to draft Prince Damrong's secretary into such service.

33. NA 5 S, 17/8 I, 47, Phatsakǫrawong to Sommot, 19 June 1892.

Čhaophraya Phatsakǫrawong, his ministry's educational activities already constricted by budgetary cuts, understandably was upset at the drain on his resources occasioned by their arrival and the high costs of preparations for Rajakumara School and of providing Thai teachers for it from the ministry's small staff, especially as this was a project he had taken no part in planning. He resented what he considered the continuing influence of Morant in his ministry, which in conventional Thai terms should have ceased with the transfer of Morant's patron, Prince Damrong. Finally he petitioned the king to have Morant's activities completely removed from the control of the ministry in November 1892, when Morant and Rajakumara School were transferred to the Ministry of the Palace.[34] The school, which finally opened on 7 January 1893,[35] had but a short life under Morant's direction. Morant soon found himself unable to make an impression upon the crown prince and by the latter part of 1893 was rapidly fading from favor at court. A misunderstanding and a violent outburst from Morant followed in December 1893, and the next month Morant was dismissed.[36] The school did not long outlast him, lapsing almost immediately back into little more than systematized tutorial instruction, and then, by 1896, completely collapsing, leaving behind it only tutorial

34. NA 5 S, 17/8 II, 32, Phatsakǫrawong to Sommot, 3 Nov. 1892; and 17/8 II, 33, Sommot to Phatsakǫrawong, 6 Nov. 1892. This administrative and budgetary transfer took place at the beginning of the next Thai year, April, 1893. Note that in Phatsakǫrawong's letter Morant was referred to as "*phrakhru*," "holy or reverend teacher."

35. NA 5 S, 14/8, 15, King's speech on the opening of Rajakumara School, 7 Jan. 1893. The account of the school that appeared in the *RKB*, 9 (1892/93), 381–83, contains the cryptic statement that "The opening of this school . . . was arranged by *phra-ačhan* Morant . . . as a secret from officials and ministries."

36. A considerable file of documents in the National Archives, NA R.5, no. 250, makes it quite clear that Morant's dismissal was not nearly as unjust or as politically motivated as Allen *(Sir Robert Morant,* p. 87) or *The Dictionary of National Biography 1912–1921* (London, 1927; s.v. Morant, Sir Robert Laurie) suggest. Mrs. McFarland *(McFarland of Siam,* pp. 136–37) is much nearer the truth.

arrangements for the few princes who had not yet departed for studies in Europe.[37]

Running parallel to the short history of Rajakumara School was the course of a similar institution established for the purpose of tutoring the young princesses, daughters of Chulalongkorn, although its purpose was to give the girls a broad general (and modern) education rather than to prepare them for studies in Europe. The idea for the school originated with Queen Saowapha's concern for Princess Wilaiyalongkǫn, who was attending Rajakumara School with her brothers in 1893 and was becoming too boyish and excessively indulged by the male European teachers. The queen suggested that a new, separate school be established for the younger princesses in which they could begin their Thai studies and perhaps later study with a European woman teacher. At her request, the king asked Čhaophraya Phatsakǫrawong to investigate how such a school might be established without getting Morant involved and how they might prevent any European teacher from spreading palace gossip as Mrs. Leonowens had done.[38] Phatsakǫrawong arranged for Phraya Itsaraphan Sophon (Nu) and "other elderly teachers" to provide instruction in Thai[39] and Mrs. Loftus, wife of the Government Hydrographer, to serve as instructress of

37. NA 5 S, 3/5, 1, Lewis to Sommot, 22 Dec. 1894; 3/5, 18, A-C, Sommot to James, Lewis, and Rolfe, 30 Dec. 1895; 3/5, 19, Sommot to Lewis, 1 Apr. 1896; 3/5, 21, Sommot to Phatsakǫrawong, 3 Apr. 1896; 3/5, 23, Rolfe to Sommot, 18 Aug. 1896; and 3/5, 35, Carter to Sommot, n.d. (1896). James, Lewis, and Rolfe all were teachers at Rajakumara, while Carter, tutor to Prince Phanurangsi's children, served as tutor to Crown Prince Vajirunhis from 1894 to the prince's death in 1895.

38. NA 5 S, 17/8 II, 16, King to Phatsakǫrawong, 14 Feb. 1893. The "Anna Leonowens theme" is a constant feature of all such discussions of palace education in this period, as in 17/8 II, 8, Phatsakǫrawong to Sommot, 26 Sept. 1892.

39. NA 5 S, 3/5, 29, Phatsakǫrawong to Sommot, 1 Mar. 1893. Phraya Itsaraphan Sophon (M.R.W. Nu Itsarangkun na Ayudhya, 1838–1907), a former monk who had attained Standard VII in the ecclesiastical examinations, had served as an assistant teacher in the first palace Thai school. He came to the Ministry of Public Instruction in 1892, first as accountant and then as deputy director of the Education Department

English,[40] and it opened as Rajakumari School on 11 May 1893 in the Amarin Palace building of the Grand Palace.[41] The school continued for a number of years, at insignificant cost to the Privy Purse, and captured little of the interest or attention accorded its counterpart.[42] Like Rajakumara it was a temporary measure, and it gradually closed down as it ran out of pupils in the later years of the decade.

Rajakumara and Rajakumari schools were passing phenomena on the Thai educational scene. They provided no new models, no new teaching materials, and no new influence for education as a whole. They enjoyed only brief and tenuous relationships with the Ministry of Public Instruction, being more appropriately the concern of the Ministry of the Palace in its management of the king's personal affairs. They certainly were significant as further stages in the transformation of traditional palace education and as the institutions in which the next royal generation was trained, but they hardly affected the development of public education.

A third special school, quite different in character, was the girls' school established in 1893 at the instigation of Queen Saowapha. She conceived of the idea of establishing the school "as an act of charity, to be a notable example like the building of a monastery," and she arranged with Prince Damrong for its staff and buildings.[43] On Damrong's instructions, Morant, while in Europe in 1891–92, engaged two Englishwomen as teachers

---

(1893–96). He served as a tutor to the royal children from the mid-eighties until 1896, when he retired. Praphat Trinarong, *Chiwit lae ngan khong atsawaphahu* (Bangkok, 1963), pp. 57–63.

40. NA 5 Kh, 63/8, 1, Narathip to King, 8 Feb. 1893.

41. NA 5 S, 3/5, 39, Phatsakorawong to Bidyalabh, 6 May 1893.

42. NA 5 S, 3/5, 40, "Ideas on Establishing Rajakumari School, First Stage' (1893); and 3/5, 202, Budget, Rajakumari School, 1895/96. The school's budget was 840 baht in 1893/94 and 3,000 baht in 1895/96. Its enrollment was fifteen princesses in 1893 (3/5, 40), eight princesses in March 1894 (3/5, 106), and eleven princesses in November 1894 (3/5, 140).

43. NA 5 S, 19/8, 81, King to Phatsakorawong, 12 July 1892.

for the school, and funds for their passage and salaries were provided in the ministry's budget for 1892/93.[44] No funds, however, were provided for buildings or running expenses, as these were to be provided from the estates of those of the queen's children who had died in infancy. These plans collapsed when the foreign firm with which this endowment had been deposited failed in 1892, and construction became impossible. Placed in a difficult situation in which she would lose face, especially with foreigners, if she abandoned the project, and faced with losing credit for and control of the project if she was forced to turn to her sister, Queen Sawang Watthana, to make up the deficit, she asked the king to rescue her from her predicament. The king wrote to Phatsakǫrawong in June 1892, putting the matter in his hands and warning that care should be taken to prevent palace gossip from reaching the English teachers.[45]

After more than six months of indecision, during which Suankulap and the old palace of the late "second king" were suggested as sites for the school, Sunanthalai was finally selected in December 1892, making it necessary to close the English school then located there.[46] On 1 January 1893, the new Sunanthalai Girls' School opened with an enrollment of fifteen pupils, each of whom paid a monthly tuition fee of twenty baht, which effectively limited the school's enrollment to the daughters of the upper nobility and made the school the

44. NA 5 S, 17/8 I, 83, Phatsakǫrawong to Damrong, 20 June 1892; and 17/8 I, 79, Phatsakǫrawong to Sommot, 7 July 1892. These salaries totaled 15,780 baht per annum. Morant also engaged a woman teacher for the orphanage, which was also under the queen's patronage.

45. NA 5 S, 19/8, 81, King to Phatsakǫrawong, 12 July 1892. This is a fascinating letter, not only for the personal glimpse it affords of the king's family life but also for his concern for the opinions of the foreign community and his continuing apprehensiveness at exposing foreigners to the life of the palace and its gossip. As for "slanderous rumors," he wrote, "you might think these died out years ago, but [foreigners] still believe that we worship the white elephant; and when we tell them we do not, they don't believe us. And the matter of women is the worst of all."

46. NA 5 S, 17/8 I, 79, Phatsakǫrawong to Sommot, 7 July 1892; and 17/8 I, 95, same to same, 17 Dec. 1892.

female equivalent of Suankulap. Despite continual administrative squabbles with the ministry and an incredible turnover in
staff, the school fared well. Its curriculum was brought up to
high academic standards, and its students, when they began to
sit for the government English examinations in 1896, performed quite well.[47] By 1897 the school had begun to be
favored by the royal family and enrolled thirty-two students,
among whom were some of the royal princesses. The salaries of
the school's teachers were covered by a government subsidy,
while its running expenses were met by what was, in effect,
the school's endowment: buildings on school property which
were let to government offices and commercial firms.[48] With
an additional bequest from Queen Saowapha in 1897, the school
was expanded to accommodate fifty boarding students.[49] Sunanthalai Girls' School stood in much the same financial and administrative relation to the ministry as its predecessor, McFarland's Sunanthalai; but it succeeded where McFarland had
failed, in attracting the daughters and patronage of the most
prominent families of Bangkok. By doing so its continued
financial support and existence were assured.[50]

The schools for the royal children and the Sunanthalai Girls'
School were not matters of direct and continuing concern to the
ministry. They were rather prominent sidelights to the serious
problems of promoting primary and secondary education for

47. NA 5 S, 14/5, 67, Report, Examinations, 1895/96, dated 18 July
1896. All six Sunanthalai girls who entered passed the examinations.

48. NA 5 S, 20/5, 21, Phatsakǫrawong to Sommot, 6 Mar. 1897.
The same endowment had been used until 1892 to support McFarland's
school. Among the tenants on school land were the Ministry of Public
Instruction and the offices of the *Bangkok Times*.

49. Ibid.; NA 5 S, 20/5, 29, King to Phatsakǫrawong, 13 Mar. 1897;
20/5, 31, Phatsakǫrawong to Queen Saowapha (as regent), 21 June 1897;
and 20/5, 35, Saowapha (as regent) to Phatsakǫrawong, 26 June 1897.

50. On the early years of this school, its first European headmistress,
Miss B. A. Smith, has left an interesting, if one-sided, account: "The King
of Siam," *Contemporary Review*, 71 (1897), esp. 887–89. See also Norman,
"Urgency in Siam," pp. 740–41, quoting a letter from G. H. Grindrod,
headmaster of the Normal School.

the general public; but the claims that the royal schools could make upon national resources and the influence men like Morant could exert on the direction of educational policy in general cannot be discounted. In a sense, the period from 1892 until the king's first visit to Europe in 1897 was overshadowed, as far as the ministry was concerned, both by the royal schools and by the policies laid down under the influence of Morant and Damrong. This is evident both from the course of development of secondary education and from the problems that mass primary education had to face during this period.

When Čhaophraya Phatsakǫrawong came to the ministry in 1892, middle or secondary education, which was synonymous with English education, was concentrated at three institutions in Bangkok: McFarland's Sunanthalai School, Suankulap School, and the New School. This was, however, an extremely uneven concentration, with the distribution of funds made at least partially on social class lines. The royal children, whose English education was in the hands of two Englishmen in 1892, commanded an annual educational expenditure of 13,440 baht on salaries alone,[51] giving them by far the best instruction at the greatest cost. Next came the sons of the Thai nobility, who were taught in the English division of Suankulap School at an annual cost of 416 baht per student. Far below them came the lower-ranked middle class Thai and Chinese who attended Sunanthalai, where they were taught by American teachers at an annual cost of 190 baht per pupil, and the New School, where they were taught by English-speaking Asians at an annual cost of only 21.5 baht per pupil.[52]

In their plans for the future development of secondary, English education, Prince Damrong and Morant had envisaged a competition for academic quality developing between Suan-

51. NA 5 S, 17/8 II, 17, Phatsakǫrawong to King, 18 May 1892.

52. Ibid. It should be kept in mind, however, that it was the princes and the Suankulap boys who were destined for higher education in Europe, which to some extent justified the disproportionate amount expended on their education.

kulap and Sunanthalai with their British and American teachers, while the New School, from its inability to maintain equivalent standards, would be relegated to a lesser role of serving a wider public. All English education would be confined to these three schools, and a general rise in academic standards would, it was hoped, stem naturally from this concentration.[53]

In their deliberations on the budget for 1892/93, however, the Cabinet was unwilling to approve this plan. With the impending arrival in Bangkok of the new teachers hired in Europe by Morant under orders from Prince Damrong, the department had requested a total grant of 103,440 baht for salaries, but the Cabinet would allow only 89,940 baht, and recommended that all English studies be concentrated at Sunanthalai. In June, Phatsakǫrawong, faced with the problem of a drastically cut budget and left with little room to maneuver as most of the salaries sanctioned by the Cabinet were earmarked for men under contract, could only dismiss Dr. McFarland from his position as headmaster of Sunanthalai. He gave McFarland the choice of entering the Textbook Bureau as a compiler at a salary of 4800 baht per year (formerly he had received 7680 baht) or conducting a private school under an annual subsidy of 2400 baht.[54] McFarland could only choose the certainty of the former. The English teachers at Suankulap were transferred to Sunanthalai and put under Glen Culbertson, an American and former assistant to McFarland, as headmaster. This arrangement did not last long, for in December 1892, with the foundation of the new girls' school at Sunanthalai, the English teachers returned to Suankulap and Culbertson moved across the river to the Thammasapha building on the grounds of Wat Prayura-

53. Ibid.
54. McFarland, *McFarland of Siam*, p. 110; NA 5 S, 28/2, 4, Phatsa-kǫrawong to Sommot, 31 Mar. 1895; and 17/8 II, 17, Phatsakǫrawong to King, 18 May 1892. Mrs. McFarland attributes her father-in-law's dismissal to Morant's hostility toward "that American preacher" (p. 109) and to Morant's egotism (p. 111).

wong in Thonburi.[55] In July 1893 Culbertson resigned his contract, and a year later the school again was moved, this time to an old private residence near the Customs House and put under the direction of a Thai headmaster, Kǫn Amatyakul, who had been educated in the United States.[56]

The New School, under headmaster Baboo Ramsamy, had to be moved in July 1892 because its building was required for other purposes. After some thought had been given to combining it with Sunanthalai, it was moved to new quarters at Wat Mahannapharam in Bangkok.[57] There it continued for another decade, with little notice apparently being given to it by the ministry; it seems to have been privately financed and its standards were so low that it received little attention.

It was Suankulap School that during this period became the center of English instruction in Bangkok. After the short period during which its English section was joined to Sunanthalai, it moved back to the Suankulap Palace in December 1892. It employed a steady succession of Europeans in the position of headmaster and as ordinary English teachers, who were paid salaries in the range of 400–500 baht per month. These included a Mr. Rolfe (headmaster, 1892–93), Ernest Young

55. NA 5 S, 17/8, I, 95 and 100, Phatsakǫrawong to Sommot, 17 Dec. 1892, 2 letters.

56. *Bangkok Times,* 5 July 1893, 14 July 1894, and 8 Sept. 1894. Nai Kǫn (1865–1922, later Phraya Winit Witthayakǫn, director of the Examinations Bureau in the Education Department) was the son of Phra Pricha Konlakan (Sam-ang Amatyakul), who in 1879 married Fanny Knox, daughter of the British consul-general and heroine of Minney's *Fanny and the Regent.* Phra Pricha, learning in 1876 that his former tutor, Dr. Samuel House, was returning to America, sent his son Kǫn with Dr. House to be educated. After a four-year nondegree course in mining engineering at Lafayette College in Indiana, Kǫn returned to Siam in 1889 and taught at various schools before becoming headmaster of the Ban Phraya Nana School in 1893. Feltus, *Samuel Reynolds House,* pp. 222–23; and "Prawat sangkhep ammat-ek phraya winit witthayakǫn," in *Prachum phongsawadan,* pt. 36 (Bangkok, 1927), pp. (2)–(5).

57. NA 5 S, 17/8 I, 17, Phatsakǫrawong to King, 18 May 1892; 3/8, 22, King to Phatsakǫrawong, 17 June 1892; and 17/8 I, 100, Phatsakǫrawong to Sommot, 17 Dec. 1892.

(1892–95), W. G. Johnson (1895–96), and E. S. Smith (1896–1903).[58] Given sufficient funds to employ well-qualified Englishmen on its staff, while its competitors soon had to rely on local teachers, it is not surprising that Suankulap came very soon to exercise a dominating influence on the standards of English secondary education in Thailand. By 1897 it had more than 400 students, including about eighty in its English section, and Čhaophraya Phatsakǫrawong, pointing to the crowded condition of its buildings and to the fact that foreigners frequently requested that they be shown the school, asked that new buildings be constructed for it;[59] but it was not until 1909 that it finally was able to move to new quarters at its present site near the Rama I bridge.

For the special and secondary schools this was not a particularly bright period. The three special schools were innovations, but their scope was restricted and their lives short. The secondary schools, if anything, declined over the period, only Suankulap still prospering by 1897. Sunanthalai Girls' School was perhaps the most solid step forward, the first government-aided school for girls. The record during this period for these schools taken together is undistinguished and, in comparison with the hopes, plans, and expectations of 1890–92, disappointing.

QUALITATIVE DEVELOPMENT AND EDUCATIONAL SERVICES

While the educational retrenchment of the first years of Čhaophraya Phatsakǫrawong's ministry brought about a significant quantitative decline in educational activity, there was progressing simultaneously a qualitative development which was in itself important and which had substantial effect on the subsequent course of educational reform. This was especially noticeable in the development of the curriculum, in the pro-

58. Compiled from scattered references.
59. NA 5 S, 21/5, 2, Phatsakǫrawong to Sommot, 5 Mar. 1897.

vision of textbooks, and in the examination system, three elements essentially interrelated. These had become sufficiently well established during the ministry of Prince Damrong to continue to grow and improve even on reduced resources. While the continuing development of such services did not completely or even substantially compensate for the great drop in school-centered activity, the withdrawal of the ministry into such activities—so to speak, into itself—did preserve a momentum of change and innovation through a period otherwise lean.

The general pattern of the curriculum was outlined in the Draft Education Laws and the decree of 1892 establishing elementary schools.[60] As noted already, the primary schools were divided into two types, elementary schools teaching only reading, writing, and arithmetic, and higher primary schools which also taught composition, grammar, mathematics, history, geography, and science. In essence, the curriculum policy adopted by the ministry at this time was to concentrate its efforts on the few primary schools where financial support gave it a significant measure of control, while it hoped eventually to induce the elementary schools, either by administrative pressure or by example, to raise their standards to the level of the primary schools.

The curriculum of the elementary schools was flexibly fixed, in order fully to take into account the problems raised by the lack of competent teachers.[61] Moral instruction was to be offered "if the teacher can teach it," and students were to be given practice in reading "the government textbooks or any other books the teacher may choose." Teachers were advised to instruct their pupils in counting with their fingers and hands in a crude arithmetic, and the subject was left wholly to

60. NA 5 S, 39/5, "Draft Education Laws, R.S. 111;" and "Prakat tang rongrian munlasaman," *PKPS, 13,* 113–19. On the curriculum and its historical development, see Luang Sawatsarasattraphut and Čharun Wongsayan, *Khwampenma khong laksut samansüksa* (Bangkok, 1961).

61. NA 5 S, 39/5, "Draft Education Laws, R.S. 111: Law II. Classification of the Simplified Curriculum for Ordinary Elementary Schools in the Provinces."

the teachers' preferences and abilities. This was not a great improvement on the traditional instruction offered in the monasteries, but it was a change and an opportunity for further development. If it was not constructive, it was at least realistic, given the limited resources and powers of the ministry at this time.

The laws were considerably more specific regarding the curriculum of the primary schools.[62] Specific books were recommended for teachers' use, and specified subjects were to be covered in the course of the school year. Students were required, for example, to learn arabic numerals as well as the use of the abacus in their mathematics studies, and they were to learn something of the physical and political geography of the world. Their instruction in science was to include the study of "the sun, moon, stars, weather, fire, measurement, and heat." Both types of schools were to be in session for $27\frac{1}{2}$ hours per week, but the primary schools spent ten of those hours on Thai language and literary studies, while the elementary schools spent sixteen hours. The elementary schools retained their old "four r" character, while the primary schools were in the process of broadening their curriculum to accord with more modern ideas of what education should include.

In 1895 the ministry moved to define more strictly its curricula in terms of the prescribed textbooks and to broaden further the higher levels. Standards I (primary) and II (now equivalent to a level intermediary between the contemporary primary and secondary schools) each were divided into three grades *(chan)*, each intended to cover one year's work. The contents of the curricula for Standards I and II remained roughly as they had been, although Standard I was tied more closely to the *Rapid Reader Series,* and the Royal Chronicles of the Ayudhya period were recommended for reading practice. Only in the four chan of Standard III was the curriculum fully broadened out to include the compulsory study of Pali and one

62. NA 5 S, 39/5, "Draft Education Laws, R.S. 111: Law I. Classification of the Curriculum for Ordinary Primary Schools."

other language (English or Malay), accounting, trigonometry, algebra, Euclidean geometry, geography, general science, physiology, mechanics, and physics,[63] in contrast to the simple literary definition given to that standard in 1891.[64] Standard III, however, was but of token importance at this time, for it was not to be taught for another five years. The full modernization of the curricula of the Thai schools, which first became a concern of the ministry during Prince Damrong's administration, still was limited to the untaught Standard III. The idea that education should be more broadly defined was not dismissed, but its application was confined to a limited sphere, mainly because of the continuing shortage of trained teachers and appropriate textbooks.

This curriculum was put into operation by the ministry, not so much in government schools, of which there were very few during this period, but primarily through the ministry's educational services—its textbook, examination, and inspection activities. While any judgment as to the degree to which the curricula were put into force in individual schools is necessarily difficult to make because of the absence of specific information for the period, one can trace in these activities the efforts of the ministry to shape and direct the course of educational improvement in the 1890s.

The compilation of textbooks had been an important aspect of the work of the Education Department since its foundation. A separate section *(kǫng)* was established for the purpose as early as the year 1886/87.[65] Toward the end of the Damrong administration, between fifteen and seventeen men were engaged in this work, out of a total ministry staff of 112 to 116 men.[66] A heavy proportion of their efforts prior to 1892 was

63. Rǫng, *Prawat krasuang,* pp. 107–13.
64. "Phraratchabanyat kansǫp wicha," 17 Feb. 1891, *RKB, 8* (1891/ 92), 26–29.
65. NA 5 S, 18/8, A, Report, Educ. Dept., 1886/87.
66. Exclusive of men in the Religious Affairs Department and the Hospitals Department. NA 5 S, 18/8 D and E, Reports, Educ. Dept., 1889/90 and 1890/91; and 16/8, Report, Educ. Dept., 1891/92. The

devoted to providing the monkhood with religious books. Of the thirty-six titles in print in 1891/92, six volumes were Pali grammars and another six were general religious works. There were only sixteen specifically secular educational works in print and, of these, most of the textbooks used in the teaching of Thai had been contributed from outside the Textbook Bureau, by Phraya Si Sunthǫn and Prince Damrong.[67] On the whole, these books were well suited to the level of the students who used them; they were carefully graded, some were illustrated, and they were sold at low prices. They avoided the common colonial carelessness of using the English village or city shop in their background and examples and so were relevant to the life the students led. The few textbooks available, however, did not go far toward meeting the requirements which the ministry had set itself in prescribing the curriculum which they were to serve.

In the years 1892–96, the Textbook Bureau continued to function along lines established earlier. While its staff had been cut to five men by 1892, their number gradually increased to eleven by 1897.[68] These men continued, however, to be almost entirely former monks, graduates of the ecclesiastical examinations *(parian)*, exclusively so after Dr. McFarland's retirement in 1895, and many of their efforts were devoted to the compilation of Pali works for the monasteries. In terms of published textbooks, they made virtually no advance on the accomplishments of the previous decade. In part this was due to the unwill-

----

report for 1890/91 noted that the ministry also was compiling textbooks of Malay, for use in preparing young men for service in the southern provinces.

67. See the ministry's advertisement inserted in the back of textbooks published in 1891/92, e.g. Thailand, Educ. Dept., comps., *Baep rian reo samrap rian nangsü thai, lem 2 (tǫn ton)* (Bangkok, 1891/92). See also the reports of the Textbook Bureau, 1889/90–1891/92, in NA 5 S, 13/8; and the Goods Inventory Reports of the department for the same years, in NA 5 S, 11/8, which gives figures on the numbers of copies of each title sold. As late as 1891, the *Munlabot banphakit* was outselling the *Rapid Reader* by a ratio of five to one.

68. *RKB, 9* (1892/93), 96–99; *10* (1893/94), 248–52; *12* (1895/96), 321–26; and *13* (1896/97), 482–90.

ingness of the Cabinet to grant the ministry funds for publishing the books they compiled. In refusing to grant these funds, however, the Cabinet argued that the textbooks being compiled in the ministry were "useless" or "incurable" or "foreign toys," that few were usable, and that textbooks already in existence would suffice.[69] Phatsakọrawong recognized this somewhat later, writing to the king that "textbooks are sorely needed, and the officials in the Education Department cannot write good ones, as they lack sufficient knowledge to write them."[70] Perhaps it was too much to expect the elderly parian to write geographies or science textbooks when they could call only upon a very different sort of education for their knowledge and few, if any, could read English. Finally, in the budget for 1897/98, the old Textbook Bureau was abolished and its work left to the efforts individuals might make to compile textbooks on their own time.

Despite the ministry's inability to mount a serious and sustained effort to compile the basic textbooks required by its own curricula, the few textbooks that it inherited from the previous decade and the few it managed to issue during the period did serve to bring about some improvement in educational standards. The *Rapid Reader Series* was extended to three volumes and gradually replaced the *Munlabot* series and other older primers. The arithmetic textbooks went through many printings and, perhaps because there was so little by way of traditional arithmetic textbooks with which to compete, gained an early popularity. The geography, morality, and general knowledge textbooks may have had a limited but important circulation in Bangkok. As a result both of the gradual implementation of the curricula of 1892 and 1895 and of the growing circulation of modern textbooks, the ministry began in the mid-nineties to raise its examination standards.

The ministry continued to employ the examination system borrowed from the monkhood a decade earlier. The number of

69. NA 5 S, 13/5, 15, Phatsakọrawong to Sommot, 21 June 1898.
70. NA 5 S, 4/12, 6, Phatsakọrawong to King, 18 May 1899.

students entering the examinations continually increased, and at the same time the standards of performance expected of them were raised. The examinations were held annually (semiannually beginning in 1895) at the end of the Siamese year, late in March or early in April, usually at Suankulap School. They continued for several days, a few days devoted to Standard I, a few more to Standard II, and a separate group of sessions to the English examinations. The examinations were administered by officials from the Examinations Bureau and by others preempted from other bureaus of the ministry and were marked by a group (later several groups) of honorary examination commissioners, usually consisting of one or more princes known for their scholarship, a high-ranking monk, and some such senior teacher cum royal scribe as Phraya Itsaraphan Sophon (Nu). These men themselves signed the diplomas awarded to successful candidates, a device that added prestige to the examinations and to those who passed them.[71]

In its annual reports, the Examinations Board frequently commented on the steady improvements in the candidates' performance. Reporting on the examinations for 1893 and 1894, the commissioners stated that "the standard of knowledge of students in Standard I was better than before, in both Siamese and mathematics."[72] In 1896, they indicated that this improvement was partly of their own doing: "In these examinations, a method was used for Standard I which was more comprehensive and rigorous than before. The vocabulary of the textbooks was employed, and the students were required to write two pages. Many students failed. Fine. This will give added prestige to those students who passed. And even in the face of [higher standards], the performance of the students has improved."[73] Later still, in the mid-year examinations in 1897, they reported

71. Reports of the examinations commissioners for various years, 1890–98, in NA 5 S, 14/5, 1–183; also 52/5, 9, Phatsakǫrawong to Sommot, 23 Mar. 1895, and 52/5, 15, Entries in the Thai Examinations, by School.
72. NA 5 S, 14/5, 7, Phatsakǫrawong to King, 9 Mar. 1895.
73. NA 5 S, 14/5, 67, Report, Annual Examinations, 1895/96.

that the examinations were more difficult than ever before.[74] On each occasion, the schools and students responded with better results than in the previous year.

In 1896, the ministry stepped in to strengthen the sanctions surrounding the examination system. Prior to this date, as a means of securing good attendance at the examinations and to give an incentive to good instruction, the ministry had awarded cash prizes to teachers based upon the performance of their students in the examinations. This was the old system of "payment by results," which rewarded the good schools but made it no easier for the poorer ones to improve themselves.[75] Beginning with the examinations for 1896/97, the ministry put into force a new set of regulations governing the Standard I examinations.[76] All schools were required to enter at least half their pupils in the examinations, and of those entered at least half were required to pass. If any school did not comply with these regulations for lack of adequate enrollment, the department threatened to dismiss its teacher, combine the school with another school, or move the school elsewhere. If more than half the pupils entered in the examinations from any school failed, their teacher was to be "considered as not having attended to his teaching duties, put on probation, and all future rewards [for examination results] reduced." If all the students entered from any one school failed, the teacher was to be considered unfit for teaching. At the same time the ministry made more specific the examination procedures and prescribed more nar-

74. NA 5 S, 14/5, 132, Kittiyakǫn to Wutthikanbǫdi, 27 Jan. 1898.

75. NA 5 S, 14/5, 7, Phatsakǫrawong to King, 9 Mar. 1895. For Standard I passes, four baht was awarded for each successful student from nonsupported schools and three baht for each student from government schools, while the corresponding sum for Standard II was eight baht for each student, in each case paid directly to the teachers. This system was widely used in Europe and the Asian colonies at this time. For a good treatment of its use in Malaya and a sound critique of its defects, see Chai Hon-chan, *The Development of British Malaya, 1896–1909* (Kuala Lumpur, 1964), pp. 236-37.

76. "Khǫbangkhap samrap kansǫplai prayok buraphabot khü prayok 1 rattanakosinsok 115," 1 Sept. 1896, *PKPS, 15,* 138–43.

rowly their content, tying the examinations directly to given chapters in the government textbooks.

It is doubtful whether the minister ever seriously enforced these severe sanctions. As with a regulation some years later requiring teachers to pronounce their "r's" and "l's" correctly on pain of dismissal,[77] it probably found that it would have been forced by its own regulations virtually to abolish the greater part of the educational system. In this case, however, it seems to have found a way out of its predicament that maintained standards while at the same time made them easier to attain. One of the difficulties of the old examination system was that it was administered only in terminal examinations, with single examinations at the end of the primary and middle courses and no intermediate opportunities for examination. If a school, under the new regulations, was to send half its students to the examinations each year, a good share of these simply would not be far enough advanced in its studies to pass. Beginning with the mid-year examinations in 1898/99, Standards I and II each were divided into three serial grades (chan), through which the students could pass one at a time, in this manner bringing the specifications of the 1895 curriculum into the examinations. Students could, if they were prepared, pass two or even three grades at a single examination session, or they could pass only one grade each year or half-year. From this point onward, the textbooks prescribed by the ministry became increasingly geared to this curriculum and examination framework, with separate textbooks gradually appearing for each grade.

By the year 1898/99, the curriculum for Standards I and II was in full operation, the examination system was functioning with some success, the ministry had at least sufficient textbooks compiled to teach the first two standards of the Thai curriculum,

77. NA 5 S, 85/5, 61, King to Phraya Wisut, 5 Sept. 1908; 85/5, 65, Wisut to King, 9 Sept. 1908; 85/5, 66, Wisut to King, 17 Sept. 1908; 109/5, 1, Wisut to King, 1 Dec. 1908; 109/5, 8, Wisut to King, 5 Dec. 1908; and 90/5, 5, Wisut to King, 16 Jan. 1909.

and the department's inspectorate was coming more and more to exert an influence on education in Bangkok, inspecting the schools, offering them advice on educational problems, and assisting the work of the ministry in textbook and curriculum development. Although the minister himself had some disappointments about the course of the previous six years, he could take satisfaction in the obstacles he had overcome. The budget cuts of 1892 had severely hampered the ministry's efforts in primary and elementary education and textbook development, and the ministry continually felt the serious lack of trained teachers. On the other hand, Phatsakɔrawong and his staff had managed to define the function of the ministry and the nature of education in meaningful and workable terms. If the curriculum was skeletal, with little flesh on its "four R" bones, it at least provided a solid base upon which to build. With the limited resources at its disposal the ministry gradually had won or forced acceptance of its standardized textbooks; it had given the examination system an important role in recruitment for the civil service and in opening up new avenues of social mobility; it was making progress in improving the quality of education. Phatsakɔrawong might well be satisfied with these achievements, for the ministry was fulfilling the role which he had had to define for it when faced with the limiting circumstances of the environment in which he had to work. This environment, however, had begun to change in mid-decade, and the ministry not only failed to keep pace with this change but also was being excluded from much new educational activity. The history of Thailand's educational modernization was about to take a dramatic turn for the better, and the ministry soon was to find itself excluded from participation in these new developments.

SIGNS OF CHANGE, 1895–1897

It was three years before the full implications of the ministerial changes of 1892 and the subsequent cutback of the work of the Ministry of Public Instruction began perceptibly to tell upon its position within the government. During these years, the ministry, its activities restricted and its budget in decline relative to other ministries, had at least no rivals in its own field. Beginning around 1895, however, others slowly began to realize that the ministry was not meeting the educational requirements of the society. Public criticism quickly gave way to the attempts of others outside the ministry to perform these tasks, which were so essential to the development of the nation.

For the ministry, the most important event of 1895 was the return of Prince Kittiyakọn from Europe and his appointment as director-general of the Education Department. His appointment coincided with a period during which the ministry was coming under considerable criticism from the English-language press in Bangkok. G. H. Grindrod and Ernest Young, the past and present headmasters of the Normal School, had been carrying on a public argument about the state of education in Siam between Grindrod's resignation in October 1894 and February of the following year, and their arguments were taken up editorially.[78] The most strident criticism came from the editor of the *Bangkok Times* in July, 1895. Normally sympathetic to the government (which subsidized him), the editor clearly showed in a lead editorial that he—and undoubtedly a number of his European friends in Bangkok—had lost patience with the government's educational inactivity:

> It is a matter for regret that the Siamese Government does not pursue a more decided policy with regard to some general scheme of education in this country. At present there there appears to be a continual halting between two opinions, and whilst many influential men, of whom we believe His Majesty is the chief, take great interest in educational work, there are on the other hand highly placed officials whose

78. See " 'Education in Siam'—A Reply," *Bangkok Times,* 7 Feb. 1895; and "National Schools for Siam," *Bangkok Times,* 31 Jan. 1895, editorial. Young's letter of 7 Feb. refers to one by Grindrod published on 1 October, but I could find no such issue or letter in the files of the *Bangkok Times* in Bangkok or Ithaca.

indifference acts as a wet blanket upon the fire of their more progressive compeers. . . . It seems to us that the time has now arrived when some definite declaration should be made by the authorities as to their intentions in this matter. If it is considered undesirable to carry out any broad or comprehensive scheme of education in this country, let it be announced, and let an end be made to the present expenditure of time and money in that direction. If, on the other hand, the Government having put its hand to the plough does not wish to withdraw from the good work, let it proceed at once to the very necessary task of 'putting the house in order.'[79]

The editor went on to survey the "present position of affairs," the three "Anglo-vernacular schools" (Suankulap; the Thai-English School, successor to McFarland's Sunanthalai; and the New School) with their outdated syllabi and their relative independence of each other; the Normal School's inadequate resources; and the chaos in the ordinary elementary schools in the monasteries, of which "we are unable to ascertain their number, the number of teachers, or the number of scholars." In their present state, he argued, the vernacular schools would simply waste the trained teachers the Normal School might be able to produce. What was needed was the inauguration of a sound inspection system, its work to begin with a thorough survey of public education to inform the government of where it stood and what had to be done to place these "schools on a proper footing. If however, nothing is done, the sooner the curtain falls on the present farce the better."

Within two weeks, Prince Kittiyakọn had been assigned the task of carrying out this survey to familiarize himself with the work of the department. Then only twenty-one years old, he came to this task fresh from ten years of study in England, and the contrast between his own education and what he saw in Bangkok was not lost on him. In his report,[80] he expressed

79. "Education in Siam," *Bangkok Times*, 11 July 1895, lead editorial.
80. Text in NA 5 S, 13/5, 1, Kittiyakọn to King, 31 Aug. 1895.

shock at the generally poor attendance, the lack of discipline among both teachers and pupils, the general dirtiness of school buildings, the poor facilities and equipment, and the low academic standards—and he visited only the fully-supported government schools (the five major monastery schools, the three English schools, and the Normal School). To remedy this situation, Prince Kittiyakǫn recommended that the ministry's Inspectorate be strengthened. He asked that the Standard I curriculum be made more rigorous, carrying the students further through their studies of the four "r's," and that Standard II be made more comprehensive to allow greater scope for the study of English, history, geography, composition, rhetoric, and logic. In support of these changes he urged that proper and appropriate textbooks be provided for all levels.

Prince Kittiyakǫn's report did not work directly to solve the problems raised by the *Bangkok Times* editorial of six weeks earlier. It came rather to reinforce a trend that had been growing since the late eighties: the tendency to look primarily toward the later stages of the curriculum and to pay little attention to the lowest levels of education, the vast numbers of unreformed monastery schools which continued to turn out masses of young men educated in the manner of their fathers and grandfathers. This was a natural preoccupation, for the time, with results and not with preparation, and with the elite who made decisions rather than with the general public which was required to understand them and carry them out. The two major educational projects of the next few years accordingly were elite-oriented undertakings and the ministry continued on its previous path.

The two educational projects begun in 1896 were the founding of a new English school for the elite and the first proposals for the establishment of a civil service school which ultimately was to grow into Chulalongkorn University. Both shared to a high degree the concerns of the day. Both appeared as a continuation of that trend of looking toward the later stages of the curriculum which was operating increasingly at both the practical and policy levels of Thai education since the very beginning of the reign. And both projects, although brought to some degree under the wing of the Ministry of Public Instruction, were generated outside the ministry and continued to receive the major part of their support, direction, and sustenance from outside the ministry.

The proposal for a new English school appears to have originated with A. Cecil Carter late in 1895. Carter had entered the Thai government service as a private tutor for the royal children on the departure of Morant at the beginning of 1894, serving temporarily in Rajakumara School until Morant's replacement arrived, and then returning to his previous post as tutor to the children of Prince Phanurangsi, who was the king's full brother and, during this period, minister of war.[81] After first consulting privately with several Cabinet ministers, and with the support and encouragement of Prince Phanurangsi, Carter submitted his proposal to the full Cabinet in January 1896.

Carter proposed that a boarding school on English public school lines be established at Saraburi, northeast of Ayudhya on the advancing Khorat Railway. He hoped that removing the boys from Bangkok social life and their families would solve the discipline problems that earlier had beset Morant at Rajakumara School. A four- to six-year course at the school, based on the ministry's two-standard Thai curriculum and six-year English curriculum, would be followed by a further period of two to four years of study in preparation for entrance into European universities or the Thai civil service, in a course which would include instruction in English at an advanced level, and the study of geography, geometrical drawing, advanced science, advanced mathematics, bookkeeping, shorthand, French, and Latin. He proposed that a staff of three European and

81. NA 5 B, 47/37, 1, Sommot to King, n.d. (ca. Apr. 1910); and 47/37, 3, Witchitwong to Sommot, 7 Sept. 1906.

seven to thirteen trained Thai teachers should instruct an initial
enrollment of fifty, later rising to two hundred, boys of the
upper classes. The administration of the school, as with old
Sunanthalai, would be vested in a committee of prominent Thai
officials, but all academic responsibility would be reserved to
the English headmaster, who was to be Carter himself.[82]

Carter and the school's committee were asking Cabinet support for what was, in effect, a private scheme, and the Cabinet
was not willing to accept their application without some guaran-
tees. They were skeptical about the school's proposed location
and thought it would have to be located in Bangkok if it were
to attract students. Only Prince Damrong's support for Carter's
position and Prince Phanurangsi's promise to enlist students
for the school saved the day, at least temporarily. The Cabinet
also urged that the school be made a government school and
for this reason forwarded Carter's proposals to the Ministry of
Public Instruction for consideration. Phatsakọrawong was not
pleased with the administrative arrangements, and particularly
the school's governance by a committee, and proposed instead
that the school be placed under royal patronage, leaving primary administrative responsibility in the hands of the committee but financial control in the hands of the ministry. These
proposals were accepted by the king at the end of February
1896, with the agreement that the government would provide
a total subvention of 45,760 baht for capital expenditures and
30,912 baht for the first year's salaries. Carter was to travel
to Europe for five months to engage teachers, to return in time
to open the school on 1 October 1896.[83]

The school's committee, consisting of Princes Phanurangsi,
Sommot, Damrong, Čhantharathat (Wiwit), Rabi, and Kitti-
yakọn, čhaophrayas Phatsakọrawong and Surasakmontri, and
Phraya Thewetwongwiwat, met several times in April and
May and then seems to have lost interest to the point where

82. NA 5 S, 32/5A, 12, Scheme for Saraburi School, Jan. 1896.
83. NA 5 S, 32/5A, 5, Phatsakọrawong to Sommot, 23 Jan. 1896;
and 32/5A, 33, King to Phatsakọrawong, 26 Feb. 1896.

less than a month before the scheduled arrival of the English teachers from Europe, early in September, the king had to prod them into action.[84] At this late date the committee met to decide where the school should be located. As the railway line had not yet reached Saraburi, they chose to convert for their purposes the Thonburi home of the former regent, Suriyawong, with the intention of moving the school to Saraburi when the railway line went through and then handing the Thonburi buildings over to the Ministry of Public Instruction for use as a second normal school. The Committee also agreed to delegate its administrative responsibilities for the school to the Ministry of Public Instruction during the initial period when the school was being established.[85]

After some months of trying to find sufficient students capable of paying the eighty baht admission fee,[86] of renovation and reconstruction of the school's buildings, and of indecision over a name for the school, it was finally opened on 3 May 1897, under the name "Ratchawitthayalai (Rājavidyālaya)" or "King's College."[87] The school quickly took hold at its Thonburi location, and all thoughts of moving to Saraburi soon were forgotten. By the end of the school's first year enrollment had

84. NA 5 S, 32/5A, 1, Phatsakǫrawong to Sommot, 22 Mar. 1896; 32/5A, 3, Kittiyakǫn to Phatsakǫrawong, 8 Mar.; 32/5A, 4, King to Phatsakǫrawong, 11 Apr.; and summary of King to Phatsakǫrawong in 32/5A, 36, Phatsakǫrawong to Sommot, 5 Sept. 1896. See also King to Phraya Wisut Suriyasak, 25 Feb. 1899, in King Chulalongkorn and Čhaophraya Phrasadet, *Phraratchahatlekha lae nangsü krap bangkhom thun* (Bangkok, 1961), p. 311.

85. NA 5 S, 1/2, 46, Minutes, Meeting of Committee for Saraburi School, 5 Sept. 1896, duplicated in 32/5A, 40, and communicated to the king in 32/5A, 36, Phatsakǫrawong to Sommot, 5 Sept. 1896.

86. NA 5 S, 92/5, 2, Carter to King, 20 Jan. 1898.

87. NA 5 S, 32/5A, 36, Phatsakǫrawong to Sommot, 5 Sept. 1896; 32/5A, 47, same to same, 13 Sept. 1896; 32/5A, 110, same to same, 11 Mar. 1897; and 27/2, 1, Ministry of Public Instruction report to Cabinet, 16 May 1897, which reports that the school opened with three European teachers, a European housemother, three trained Thai teachers, and a total of thirty-eight students. See also, *Prawat rongrian ratchawitthayalai* (Bangkok, 1966), pp. 1–3.

risen from thirty-nine to sixty, plans began to be made for expansion, and teaching standards reached high levels, students in the higher grades receiving "the same education as they would receive in Europe."[88] When competitive examinations for the king's scholarships for study abroad were inaugurated in 1898, King's College students dominated the awards from the beginning.

The significance of King's College lies in the high standards it attained, in its durability as an educational institution, and in its success in serving the ends for which it was founded. This success is explicable primarily in terms of the support the school obtained officially from the government and personally from many prominent men in its early years. Its governing committee was composed not of learned and powerless but rather of influential and powerful government officials, including the ministers of the most important government ministries. Such participation could ensure government support for the school and could give it the prestige it needed to attract the sons of the elite. In the student body of 1898/99, twenty-seven of the students were of royal blood, including one *phra-ong čhao* (son of the late "second king") and nineteen *mǫm čhao*. Of the remaining forty-four, no fewer than twenty-six were sons of government officials of the rank of *phraya*.[89] No school with such support and such a student body could fail.

A second important element in the school's success was its ability to maintain an identity distinct from the Ministry of Public Instruction, to the degree that funds for its support were treated separately from the general ministry budget and could be considered as a special royal charitable project, for which there were ample precedents. The ministry might well have viewed with some jealousy this rival educational project which could claim from the treasury an annual budget equivalent to one fifth the total appropriation of the entire Education De-

88. NA 5 S, 4/5, 6, Carter to Phatsakǫrawong, 24 Sept. 1898.
89. NA 5 S, 4/5, 53, Register of Students, King's College, 1898/99.

partment,[90] at a time when the ministry was still struggling for small appropriations for monastery elementary schools. It is not surprising that the ministry moved almost immediately to gain first financial and then administrative control over the school, which it henceforth never wholly relinquished to the school's committee.

Finally, a third important factor in the success of the school was Carter himself, who moved shrewdly within the context of Thai politics first to muster support for the founding of the school, and then to keep the school running without compromising its standards. By a combination of these three factors, King's College became firmly established within the space of two years, to a point where it was easily the most prominent educational institution in Bangkok. For these promising beginnings the Ministry of Public Instruction could take little credit.

The second of the two major projects of this transitional period was a series of proposals for the founding of a civil service training college, beginning late in 1896. For more than two years proposals and counterproposals were exchanged, until the school, which will be discussed in Chapter 8, was finally established in 1899. The idea of having special schools to train young men for the civil service dates from the inception of modern education in Thailand, beginning with the first Thai school within the palace walls, and repeated later in the first English school, McFarland's Suan Anand, Suankulap, and the decrees on monastery education from 1875 onward. In all these cases, however, the curriculum put forward by those who advocated these schools was little more than the old literary curriculum with the addition of what frequently was termed *Thamniam ratchakan,* the manners and practices of government, including such things as the forms employed in government correspondence and records. It was this approach that was embodied in the successive revisions of Standard II of the Thai

90. NA 5 Kh, 110/8, Budget, 1898/99, which includes detailed figures for the previous year.

curriculum and taught preeminently at Suankulap. The new proposals, beginning in 1896, marked a departure from this earlier pattern by looking more toward specialized and technical training for the bureaucracy.

Embodied in the first proposals for what became King's College was a special division of the school intended to prepare young men for the civil service,[91] but this element seems to have been dropped from consideration very early. It was at about the same time that the king began to think seriously of establishing a new sort of civil service training, the basis of which would be as much social and practical as academic. In the expansion of the government's services in the previous decade, large numbers of new men had entered the bureaucracy (and particularly the Ministry of Interior) directly from school without serving first in the Royal Pages' Corps. The king thought it unfortunate that the traditional practice of sending boys for service at court should fall into disuse, as it had allowed the king to become acquainted with his future officials and to create between them and the king close bonds of loyalty and understanding. He wished to maintain these old virtues, so on the return of Prince Rabi from Europe in 1896 he asked the prince to establish a civil service school linked closely to the Royal Pages' Corps. The prince, however, being much more interested in legal reform, asked to be excused from the task.[92] The king then gave the task to the Ministry of Public Instruction.

Prince Kittiyakǫn's "Scheme for Establishing a Special School for the Training of Civil Servants," submitted in November 1896, was the result. It is a remarkable document, and reflects

91. NA 5 S, 32/5A, 12, Scheme for Saraburi School, Jan. 1896.
92. Prince Damrong Rajanubhab, "Prawat phraya nakhǫn phra ram," reprinted in *Prawat bukkhon samkhan,* pp. 206–39. It has also been published under various other titles in other collections of the prince's writings. Prince Damrong dated this decision at 1898; but internal evidence in his account (including the return of Prince Rabi from Europe) together with documentary evidence places it two years earlier. See NA 5 S, 30/5, 2, Phatsakǫrawong to King, 30 Nov. 1896.

very well a bridging of new and old ideas.[93] The basic organization of the school set forth in his proposal was very much the same as that of Suankulap, with instruction tied to Standards I and II of the Thai curriculum. Instruction in the school, however, was to continue on into Standard III and two new standards, IV and V, were to be added to provide training in intermediate mathematics (percentages and mensuration), bookkeeping, geography and map reading, history, jurisprudence, and political, moral, and economic science in Standard IV and special training in the work of separate ministries in Standard V. In addition, progress through the five standards was to be accelerated considerably, with only one year being allotted to each standard except Standard IV, for which two years were allowed. Most importantly, the examinations at the end of each year's work were to be tied directly to the civil service, successful candidates being given the choice of leaving the school for specified grades of positions based on the standard they had attained in the examinations, or continuing on to the next standard.[94] The school was to accommodate one hundred students, each to be paid a small salary, and it was to be open to any boy between the ages of ten and twenty-five years "who has the desire, regardless of race or family or educational background, as long as he is a presentable person and suffers from no disease (such as leprosy)." Applicants would have to pass an entrance examination, but only for purposes of classifying them at their appropriate educational level, and graduates were to receive government positions, serving first, if they had not already done so, as pages at court and then moving on to the ministries and departments.

93. NA 5 S, 30/5, 8–16; and cover letter, 30/5, 6, Kittiyakǫn to Phatsakǫrawong, 18 Nov. 1896. The likelihood is strong that the general adviser, Rolin-Jaequemyns, had some part in the drafting of the proposals. See Rǫng, *Prawat krasuang,* pp. 138–39.

94. A certificate for Standard I would entitle the holder to a position as a lower grade clerk *(samian chan tam);* for Standard II as a higher grade clerk; and for Standard III as a "writer of reports or accountant." Ibid.

Prince Kittiyakon's plan was highly ambitious and open to objections on many points. Some of these were pointed out by Phatsakorawong on forwarding the proposals to the king.[95] He saw problems in teaching Standards IV and V, especially from the lack of both appropriate textbooks and teachers; but rather optimistically he suggested that he and Kittiyakon could themselves do some of the teaching, and they could persuade various princes and the king to write the necessary textbooks. Presumably he took comfort from Prince Kittiyakon's remark that "it will be a long time before students enter this Standard [IV], and perhaps in the interval we will find teachers for it."[96] As for Standard V, "when a ministry or department needs people especially trained for its work, they will request these be trained, and we will find an appropriate teacher."[97] Phatsakorawong continued to rail against "private influence" (he used the English words) being used to gain admission to the school and suggested that entrance examinations be used to counter it. He also urged that the new school's examinations, which would be conducted separately from those of the Education Department, be required generally of all applicants for the civil service.

Ignoring the radical extensions given to the initial proposals by the ministry, the king forwarded the proposals to Prince Damrong in December 1896, asking that he and Prince Rabi (who was about to become minister of justice) consider them and arrange to meet together with the king, Phatsakorawong, and Kittiyakon. After the five had met, in December or early in January, the king sanctioned the implementation of the scheme as submitted with but minor changes.[98] This might have seemed to settle the matter but when the scheme was brought before the budgetary committee of the Cabinet, first they and

95. NA 5 S, 30/5, 2, Phatsakorawong to King, 30 Nov. 1896.
96. NA 5 S, 30/5, 6, Kittiyakon to Phatsakorawong, 18 Nov. 1896.
97. NA 5 S, 30/5, 2, Phatsakorawong to King, 30 Nov. 1896.
98. NA 5 S, 30/5, 17, King to Damrong, 6 Dec. 1896; 30/5, 19, Rabi to King, 9 Dec. 1896; 30/5, 20, Sommot to King, n.d. (Dec. 1896); and 30/5, 21, King to Phatsakorawong, 16 Jan. 1897.

then the full Cabinet and the king set the proposal aside "because of its financial aspects, and asked that it be revised." Phatsakǫrawong then revised it, devising a new scheme for civil service examinations (which previously he had only suggested informally), and drafted a Royal Decree appointing special commissioners for such examinations. As the Cabinet had cut 22,600 baht from his original estimates, Phatsakǫrawong deleted the portion of the proposal calling for salaries to be paid to students in the school, and then resubmitted the proposal, asking for an appropriation of 11,330 baht for a nine-month year "because it already has been decided that the school will open on the first of July this year" (1897).[99]

But the school did not open in July. At this point the project seems simply to have died, to be resurrected more than a year later by different hands and in somewhat different form. The main stumbling blocks impeding its implementation seem to have been the Ministry of Public Instruction's inability to gain wide cooperation in the planning and organization of the school, and Kittiyakǫn's and Phatsakǫrawong's careless and unrealistic plans for the school's curriculum, which showed no evidence of consultation with other ministries. While the blame for the failure of the scheme may rest on either side, the king, at any rate, blamed the Ministry of Public Instruction.[100]

In both these projects of 1896–97, the initiative came from outside the ministry. In the case of the English school, the ministry had but limited success in its attempt to appropriate the project as its own, and the new school succeeded more from the efforts of its prominent supporters and its headmaster than from anything the ministry could do for it. In the case of the proposals for the civil service school, the initiative came

99. NA 5 S, 30/5, 22, Phatsakǫrawong to Prince Prawit Watthanodom (temporarily acting for Prince Sommot during the latter's absence on tour in Europe with the king), 21 May 1897.
100. King to Phraya Wisut, 21 Jan. 1899, in Chulalongkorn and Phrasadet, *Phraratchahatlekha*, p. 299. See also Rǫng, *Prawat krasuang*, pp. 138–39.

from the king or someone close to him, and the project was assigned to the ministry only after Prince Rabi had refused to take it on. The proposals formulated by Kittiyakǫn and Phatsakǫrawong seem to have failed, in part because of their unrealistic approach to the problems they were set to solve, and in part because of their own lack of political power to press their scheme. The ministry attempted to pull the civil service school project within its own control rather than to induce others with more influence, more immediate concern with its effects, and more political power than they to join in making it serve interests wider than those of the Ministry of Public Instruction alone. These episodes point not only to the importance of considering the ideas and abilities of Phatsakǫrawong and Kittiyakǫn and their personal power and influence, but also to the delicate position of the king, who was both in the midst of and above the political framework in and on which he had to operate.

The fundamental political factors on which hinged the fate of modernization and reform were, as much in the nineties as in the seventies, personal politics and loyalties founded on the *phak phuak* unit, the political "clientele group" or clique, a grouping of political friends bound together by some community of ideas and even greater bonds of personal loyalty and obligation. One suspects that the king's response to the gravely dangerous times in which he reigned was initially to attempt to weld the entire political elite into a single phuak, primarily through the use of his younger brothers and also through long-time friends and supporters. To some degree he was more successful with the latter than with his brothers, for fraternal jealousies were very strong, and his brothers tended to fall into competing phuak. The national phuak thus never came close to working politically. The resulting political configuration was more competitive and more chaotic than it had been at the beginning of the reign, when all the centers of power were in the hands of the Bunnags or of the royal family. By the 1890s, the king had replaced this two- or three-partied competitive arena with a multipartite political system in which power was more widely diffused. When two or more phuak could work together on a project that was to their mutual advantage, or when the king refrained from promoting projects by which one phuak might infringe on the prerogatives or power empire of another, these projects succeeded to a degree commensurate with the ability of the man or men in charge of it. The prize of a phuak's success was more power, and of failure less power. Prince Damrong's success in the Ministry of Interior gave him an increasing number of departments under his control, transferred from the ministries of others.[101] Chaophraya Phatsakǫrawong's failures to conclude mutually profitable alliances with other phuak, which he attempted to do in his search for a director of the Education Department and an opportunity for which he missed when framing proposals for a civil service school, signaled his weakness, which was accentuated by his animosity toward Prince Damrong;[102] the failures ultimately were to cost him, first, part of his ministry and then his own position.

There was no poverty of ideas in this exciting and somewhat chaotic period of the nineties. The Ministry of Public Instruction had already by 1892 been provided with a basic program which, if served with adequate funds and forcefully promoted, might have started real educational progress a decade before it actually began. The record of the period, however, is much less bright. The development of the curriculum, of examinations and textbooks was satisfactory but not outstanding, and the ability of the ministry to lead educational development, to promote the founding of modern-style schools and develop useful educational aids and services was severely hampered by the low budgets under which the ministry had to suffer. The pro-

101. A. W. Graham, *Siam: A Handbook of Practical, Commercial, and Political Information* (1st ed. London, 1912), pp. 253–58, 287; and (3d ed. London, 1924), *1*, 325.

102. See Norman, *Peoples and Politics,* p. 461; and NA 5 S, 13/5, 15, Phatsakǫrawong to Sommot, 21 June 1898.

jects that caught the attention of foreign visitors and residents during the period all were initiated outside the ministry—the schools for the royal children, the Normal School, King's College, and Sunanthalai Girls' School. And the primary reason for this situation was the political weakness of the minister and his associates and their inability to make the best of what little they had.

Why, then, if the king was sincerely interested in education, did he not replace Čhaophraya Phatsakǫrawong or put stronger men in positions subordinate to him? One explanation is that the old tradition of permanent ministers persisted down to this period.[103] But there are other possible explanations. First, it appears that there had been an especially strong personal bond between Phatsakǫrawong and the king, which grew out of the period in the seventies when Phatsakǫrawong was the king's private secretary and one of the main protagonists in the events that led up to the Front Palace crisis of 1875. By about 1890 Phatsakǫrawong was the head of the Bunnag family, an exceedingly able man and a friend of the king, and for these reasons a natural choice for a ministerial position on both political and personal grounds. Thus he served first as Acting Minister of Foreign Affairs, and then as Minister of Agriculture until 1892. On the departure of Prince Damrong for the Ministry of Interior in 1892, Phatsakǫrawong was the logical successor: his Western education, short as it was, gave him an advantage over every other person on his political level, and he had been a participant in all the important educational events of the previous decade. Second, the king undoubtedly gave little serious thought to the problems of education between 1892 and 1895: regrettably, there were more serious matters on his mind. It is quite likely that when his thoughts did turn to educational problems in 1895 he viewed the appointment of Prince Kittiyakǫn as director of the Education Department as an ideal solution to the čhaophraya's weakness as minister, one that maintained the position of Phatsakǫrawong while at the same time

103. Vella, *The Impact of the West on Government in Thailand*, p. 341.

putting someone directly in charge of education who might be expected to bring to his work a more modern viewpoint and a stronger political position. It can only have been around 1897 that the king realized that something more was needed, and on his return from Europe at the end of that year, fortified with some new ideas himself, he began to provide it.

7

An Explosion of Ideas, 1898

With the return of King Chulalongkorn from his first European tour at the end of 1897, the process of educational reform which had begun with his reign at last regained momentum, and a series of changes was set in motion which was to affect vitally the Ministry of Public Instruction and, ultimately, the entire Kingdom. Within eleven months, from January to November 1898, Čhaophraya Phatsakǫrawong's humble educational empire came tumbling at his heels as the ministry was challenged and failed to respond positively. This was preeminently a time for new ideas, generated from a variety of sources and given voice by a large number of individuals. Introduced into the tired, tepid environment of uncertainty in which the powerless ministry increasingly was being outshone by its rivals, they brought a charge, a momentum that was to propel the ministry into a new period of growth and development.

From the time of his full accession to the throne as king in his own right in 1873, Chulalongkorn harbored a strong desire to visit the great metropolitan countries of Europe whose life was only palely reflected in their colonies which he visited in 1871–72.[1] A major state visit to Europe and America was planned for 1880 but had to be deferred indefinitely because of the illness of the elderly ex-regent who had agreed to resume his former role.[2] The king traveled a great deal through his

1. Damrong, *Khwamsongčham*, pp. 175–76.
2. *SWA*, 21 Feb., 28 Feb., and 20 Mar. 1880; and King Chulalongkorn, *Čhotmaihet phraratchakit raiwan*, 9 (2d ed. Bangkok, 1935), 2–5.

own country in the 1870s and 80s and, beginning in 1890, further afield in Southeast Asia, visiting Singapore in 1890 and Java in 1896, but it was only in 1897 that he finally achieved his ambition of visiting Europe.

A number of factors coincided to make a European tour both possible and desirable in 1897. Siam's international relations had taken a significant turn for the better with the signing of the Anglo-French Agreement of January 1896, which guaranteed Thai independence in the valley of the Čhaophraya River and made it desirable for the king to garner broad European support for the strengthening of Thai sovereignty in the areas not covered by that agreement—the Malay Peninsula, the provinces of the Southeast, and the Khorat Plateau. The king appears to have acted on the assumption that his country's position could be strengthened were he to develop strong personal relationships with all the rulers of Europe, from St. Petersburg to London and Stockholm to Rome.[3] Domestic political and financial considerations were favorable, since by 1897 the Cabinet was at last showing signs of being able to carry on the business of the state without serious difficulty; and the effects of strengthened tax administration in the provinces were substantial annual surpluses in the national budget. In such circumstances, the king could justify his tour as being in the national interest.

The king was a good tourist, a keen and thoughtful observer of all that he saw, and his eight-month visit in Europe made a profound impression upon him.[4] His public statements made immediately upon his return convey not only a renewed sense of his desire to hasten the modernization of his kingdom but also a new determination to assume more effective leadership of that change. He seems to have begun to perceive the pace

3. Note Chulalongkorn to Phraya Wisut, 24 Jan. 1898, in Chulalongkorn and Phrasadet, *Phraratchahatlekha*, pp. 208–209.

4. Phraya Si Sahathep (Seng), *Raya thang sadet phraratchadamnoen praphat prathet yurop rattanakosinsok 116* (1st ed. Bangkok, n.d.; 2d ed. under title *Čhotmaihet sadet praphat yurop r.s. 116*, Bangkok, 1907), is the official record of this tour.

and pattern of his country's development with a heightened sense of perspective. He gained a much more exact sense of the technological distance between Siam and Europe and a more realistic appraisal of the amount of time required to catch up with the West. At the same time, in a speech on 1 January 1898, the king exhibited a renewed appreciation of the integrity of Thai culture and its values, of the moral and human equality of Siam and the West, which he expressed in terms of "national character" typical of a European age of nationalism.[5] His earlier expressions of support for traditional Thai culture were ambivalent, echoing with a hollow ring out of the painful dilemma which caught the king between powerful Thai opponents of reform and Western and Thai critics of Siamese traditionalism. By the time of his return from Europe at the end of 1897, Chulalongkorn had come to the realization that his earlier dilemma could be resolved: Siam could be modern and still Thai. Out of this experience, as much emotional as rational, came a new self-confidence and determination in the king's leadership.

THE REPORT OF PHRAYA WISUT, JANUARY–JUNE 1898

One area directly affected by the king's experiences in Europe was the program of educational modernization begun in the first days of the reign, which following the regime of Prince Damrong as Minister of Public Instruction had languished under the uncertainties and indirection of Čhaophraya Phatsakǫrawong's ministry after 1892. Within six months of the king's return to Bangkok his concern for educational reform had reached such a degree that it no longer could be served by the ministry, and he began to search for alternative means by which the needs he viewed as pressing could be served. In the course of this six-month process of galvanizing the king to ac-

5. Speech of King Chulalongkorn, 1 Jan. 1898, from *Bangkok Times*, 3 Jan. 1898 (in *BTWM*, vol. 2).

tion, Phraya Wisut Suriyasak, the Thai ambassador in London, played an important catalytic role.

Phraya Wisut Suriyasak (M.R.W. Pia Malakul), born in 1867, was the eldest son of Prince Prap Parapak, commander of the Thai Navy, and the grandson of Prince Chaofa Mahamala, brother of King Mongkut and senior member of the royal family during the first half of Chulalongkorn's reign. He was an outstanding student at Suankulap School, where he passed the examinations for Standards I and II of the Thai curriculum both in the same year, 1886. His unusual academic ability drew the attention of Prince Damrong, who took him into the service of the new Education Department where he rose rapidly from a position as a trainee clerk to a position as private secretary to Prince Damrong and part-time tutor to the royal children. He went with Prince Damrong to the ministry of Interior in 1892, and there he was instrumental in introducing modern office procedures and records. In 1893 he was sent to England as Thai tutor to Prince Vajiravudh (who was not yet crown prince).[6] In the Thai Embassy in London, Phraya Wisut soon was made responsible for the general supervision of the education of the royal princes, in which capacity he arranged for their admission to schools, hired their tutors, supervised their vacations, and made their living arrangements. In addition, he gradually assumed duties directly diplomatic in nature, first in an acting capacity, then as First Secretary, and, late in 1897, as Ambassador to the Court of St. James, the Netherlands, Belgium, and the United States of America, at the age of thirty years; at the same time he was put in full

6. Praphat Trinarong, *Chiwit lae ngan khong chaophraya phrasadet* (Bangkok, 1961), pp. 1–111. This is a lengthy and detailed biography of M.R.W. Pia, written by the head of the National Diary Section of the National Archives. Phraya Wisut's position must have been strengthened by the fact that his sister was Queen Saowapha's closest retainer, and he and Prince Damrong were married to sisters. See Queen Saowapha Phongsi, *Phraratchahatlekha somdet phra si phatcharinthara borommarachininat . . . phraratchathan chaophraya phrasadet surentharathibodi* (Bangkok, 1964), p. 14, n.; and Chulalongkorn and Phrasadet, *Phraratchahatlekha*, p. xiv.

charge of the education of all King Chulalongkorn's sons then studying in Europe. Because he acted, in a sense, *in loco parentis* for the king and enjoyed a position of unusual trust and responsibility, his relationship with Chulalongkorn was close and intimate, and it was natural that when the king wished advice in 1897 on the education of Thai students abroad he should turn to the man who had advised him on the education of his own sons.

Thai students had been sent to the West and particularly to Europe to study since the seventeenth century, but the practice became established only during the reign of King Mongkut. It was apparently at the beginning of Chulalongkorn's reign that the government began to take a direct interest in this mode of importing Western ideas and techniques, initially as an experiment in 1871 when a group of young princes were entered in the Raffles Institution in Singapore until their formal English education could be arranged in Bangkok. Two of this initial group, Prince Svasti and Prince Pritsadang, did, however, continue their studies in England.[7] During the seventies the government prepared to undertake a major program of sending Thai students to the United States, but discouraged at the last moment by the negative attitude of the American consul in Bangkok the students were sent instead to Germany.[8] Meanwhile, the numbers of students sent abroad under private auspices grew steadily, and in the eighties were swelled by the addition of the sons of King Chulalongkorn and his brothers. By the time Chulalongkorn visited London in the summer of 1897 there were more than fifty Thai students in Great Britain alone.[9]

7. Udom Pramuanwitthaya (pseud.), 100 *čhaofa lae senabọdi* (Bangkok, 1962), p. 473; and *RKB*, 5 (1888/89), 25, regarding Prince Pritsadang, who studied engineering.

8. Chulalongkorn, *Čhotmaihet phraratchakit raiwan* (Bangkok, 1933), *1*, 23, 26–27, 49; *2*, 21, 39; and *3*, 2.

9. Si Sahathep, *Čhotmaihet sadet praphat*, *1*, 480, lists 46 students who attended a reception for the king in London, of whom 23 were of royal blood and 19 the sons of titled officials. About ten students were absent.

Chulalongkorn's concern for these students initially was a very simple, fatherly one. The major problem they posed was their great expense, not so much to the government treasury, for few then were direct government charges, but rather to the king and his brothers. The king had to bear out of Privy Purse funds the cost of educating not only nineteen of his own sons, but also the sons of many of his brothers[10] and favorite officials. He found the expense of educating these boys in Europe considerably increased by the fact that they had to spend so long there, and he apparently felt that this heavy expenditure was not always justified. It appears to have been on these terms that he asked Phraya Wisut to undertake a survey of the general problems of educating Thai youths in Europe.[11]

Through the first three months of 1898 Phraya Wisut devoted a great deal of labor to this task, which he finally completed early in April after exhaustive study of the English educational system from kindergarten to the highest levels of university education. His final report went far beyond his original assignment to an examination of the general question of educational modernization in Thailand. He explained his deviation from his instructions by pointing out that "there is no way to change the education of Thai students in Europe other than to reform education in Bangkok so that it can attain a higher level and prepare students . . . for further education in Europe."[12]

On 8 April 1898 Phraya Wisut submitted his report directly to the Ministry of Public Instruction in Bangkok, a copy being

10. See, e.g., King to Prince Sanphasitthiprasong, 15 Feb. 1897, in NA 5 M, 5/82, 6, in which the king told his brother that although the latter's son was "clever enough," were he to be granted a government scholarship he would take the place of someone else; and the king offered to send the boy to study at his personal expense.

11. Inferred from Wisut's letters concerning the problem. The king apparently asked Wisut orally to undertake the survey. See *Bangkok Times,* 16 Apr. 1898, and the king's "advice to students on his return from Europe," 11 Jan. 1898, in Bangkok, National Library, comps., *Prachum owat* (Bangkok, 1925), pp. 1–3.

12. Wisut to King, 8 Apr. 1898, printed in Chulalongkorn and Phrasadet, *Phraratchahatlekha,* pp. 238–39.

sent also to the king.[13] Phraya Wisut viewed his problem in finite terms, born of the necessity to learn from the West. He argued that Thailand's lag behind the West was only temporary and that once his nation had mastered Western sciences and techniques and had firmly established them in Thailand the urgency (or even the necessity) of this one-sided cultural and technical exchange would diminish considerably. The key to the whole problem, he felt, was the fact that Western knowledge was encapsulated in Western languages, making it imperative that it be approached through these languages. Herein lay both the rationale behind the practice of sending Thai students abroad and the difficulties inherent in the situation, which demanded heavy expenditures in time, money, and effort.

There was, he contended, no way to diminish these expenditures other than to attack the problem at home, to shift the focus away from learning from the West in Europe and toward learning from the West in Thailand. He recommended three broad measures by which this could be accomplished. First, a primary objective should be to build up a substantial fund of textbooks, designed to introduce Thai students to the mysteries of the West through the medium of their own language. This could be done by translating English-language textbooks into Thai, either by a government agency or by commissioning or purchasing the translations of individuals. They could then be published by the government and provided cheaply to the schools, which should be encouraged to employ them in instruction. The result would be a gradual raising of Thai educational standards both in the quality of the instruction they could provide and in the breadth of the curriculum they could offer their students. Although the initial cost to the government would be high, the savings in the long run would be substantial for students would be able to cover in schools in Bangkok, through the medium of their own language, subject matter

13. Ibid. The report itself, on which the following paragraphs are based, is in the archives, NA 5 S, 31/5, 66. There is a summary in Praphat, *Čhaophraya phrasadet*, pp. 204–29.

Illustrations

King Chulalongkorn, ca. 1900 (from J. G. D. Campbell, *Siam in the Twentieth Century*, London, 1902)

Prince Damrong Rajanubhab, Director of the Education Department, 1885–1892 (from Prince Damrong Rajanubhab and W. G. Johnson, *Prawat sangkhep haeng kansüksa khọng prathet sayam*, Bangkok, 1920)

Čhaophraya Phatsakǫrawong (Phǫn Bunnag), Minister of Public Instruction, 1892–1902 (from Damrong and Johnson, *Prawat sangkhep*)

Čhaophraya Witchitwongwutthikrai (M.R.W. Khli Suthat), Minister of Public Instruction, 1902–1912 (from Damrong and Johnson, *Prawat sangkhep*)

Čhaophraya Phrasadet Surentharathibǫdi (M.R.W. Pia Malakul; 1895–1912: Phraya Wisut Suriyasak), Minister of Public Instruction, 1912–1915 (from Damrong and Johnson, *Prawat sangkhep*)

Prince Wachirayan Warorot (from Prince Sommot Amọraphan, comp., *Rüang chaloem phrayot čhaonai,* Bangkok, 1929)

that otherwise would require either study abroad or the employment of foreign teachers in Thailand at exorbitant cost.

Wisut's second recommendation was that the quality and quantity of English-language instruction in Thailand be substantially increased. He viewed this aspect of reform as a temporary measure, necessary primarily during the period when neither textbooks nor teachers were available to impart to Thai students the knowledge required in Thailand's modernization. He advocated the gradual tightening of examination standards from the lowest to the highest levels of the educational system to demand a more rigorous knowledge of English among Thai students, and he insisted that existing English schools in Bangkok concentrate more fully on English instruction per se. He based these recommendations on his somewhat inaccurate assumption that adequate teaching materials for English instruction already existed and that there were already sufficient teachers to carry out such a program.

Wisut's third and final recommendation was that the Thai educational system be made as commensurate as possible with the English system, making transfer from one system to the other more convenient. This entailed a more rigorous enforcement of standards at every level. Phraya Wisut realized, however, that the whole system should not be geared to the sending of students abroad, for the major import of his recommendations was that the necessity for this practice should in the long run be limited and even obviated. The lowest rung on the educational ladder, the common elementary education which should be offered to all children, need aim only at limited goals, the imparting of a basic fund of common knowledge of the Thai language, arithmetic, simple geography, moral instruction, civics, and the fundamentals of the roman alphabet. This segment of the educational system should be open to all, without prescription as to the ages of the students, and its content should be controlled by semi-annual government examinations. To this extent Wisut did not go far beyond existing practice, although he clearly looked toward making education at this level more truly universal and toward bringing its prescribed content up to a higher level.

With the implementation of these recommendations in the Thai educational system, Wisut envisaged a gradual lessening of the problems then plaguing the program of sending Thai students abroad. He thought that only one major restriction would have to be imposed in the future, the use of competitive examinations to select those students who should be sent abroad. If these examinations were brought to a sufficiently high level, Thai students passing Standard III of the Thai curriculum on completing their secondary education would be able to pass directly to British universities instead of having, as in the past, to return to secondary schools in England. They would arrive in Europe with a command of English equal to the educational demands put upon it and would be able to concentrate their efforts on the acquisition of the knowledge for which they had been sent, rather than being forced to spend years in gaining language fluency and in acquiring basic knowledge that they could have acquired in Thailand.

There is ample justification for ascribing to Phraya Wisut's report great significance. It is the earliest full and explicit statement of the motivation behind the sending of Thai students abroad. Its view of the process of borrowing Western knowledge and techniques as a temporary expedient, necessary until such time as the Thai could "catch up" with the modern West, is also important as an indication of the time scale in which Thai leaders were casting their plans, programs, and policies. Also important is its assessment of the qualitative problems of Thai education and its implicit criticism of the failure of the Ministry of Public Instruction's schools to attain standards commensurate with those of Europe. As will be seen, Phraya Wisut's recommendations for the solution of these varied but related problems of Thai education were very close to the solutions actually adopted in the months and years following.

An equally significant element in this episode emerges when the report of Phraya Wisut is viewed in the context of the processes of decision-making employed by King Chulalongkorn during this period. There were strong reasons in the first instance why Phraya Wisut and Phraya Suriya[14] should have been commissioned to report on the specialized problems of Thai students abroad, with which, after all, they were intimately concerned in the course of their duties as ambassadors to Great Britain and France. The subsequent fate of Wisut's report and of Wisut himself, however, reveals the operation of royal power in decision-making in a manner characteristic of Thai political patterns and instructive for the light it sheds upon the means and resources available to Thailand's rulers in their determined effort to modernize their country.

THE MINISTRY'S FAILURE, JUNE–JULY 1898

In the course of six weeks in June and July of 1898 the problem of educational reform assumed new dimensions. Faced with a new urgency in the king's concern for education and with the direct challenge to its authority and competence posed by Phraya Wisut's report, the Ministry of Public Instruction had to respond quickly. It very soon became apparent that the ministry was unequal to this challenge, and by late July the king clearly was beginning to look elsewhere for support in carrying out new educational policies then beginning to take shape.

Phraya Wisut's report reached both the ministry and the king early in May, and the king soon began to bait Čhaophraya Phatsakǫrawong for his reaction whenever they met. Exasperated after a month of hints and questions that elicited no response from the ministry, the king finally lost his patience and on 11 June directed a peremptory, brusque letter to Phatsakǫrawong asking whether he had received the report, offering to send him a copy if he had not, asking the ministry for its views on Wisut's recommendations, ordering that the report

14. Phraya Suriyanuwat (Koet Bunnag), the Thai ambassador in Paris, originally was commissioned to report jointly with Wisut on the problem, but Wisut from the beginning took the lead, with the concurrence of Suriya. See NA 5 S, 15/5, 3, Phatsakǫrawong to Sommot, 24 Sept. 1898.

should be printed for general information, and demanding that
" 'Reform' of education should begin now, in time for the R.S.
118 [1899–1900] budget, which will have to be submitted in
December. Don't waste any time."[15] At the same time, the
king confided to Phraya Wisut that he was not very hopeful
as to the scheme's success, in view of Phatsakǫrawong's inability
to argue his case effectively with the Cabinet.[16]

While Čhaophraya Phatsakǫrawong and his colleagues in
the ministry were warding off the king's nagging, they studied
Wisut's proposals with great care and temporized while attempting to formulate a response to what they could only have
regarded as an unexpected and unwarranted interference in
their affairs. When the king's letter of 11 June failed to elicit
anything more from Čhaophraya Phatsakǫrawong than an expression of the minister's pleasure at the king's interest and the
promise of an eventual counterproposal,[17] the king induced the
Cabinet as a body to put pressure on the ministry by announcing
to them his "desire to reform education in Siam so that it might
be brought up to date."[18] Čhaophraya Phatsakǫrawong could
delay no longer, and on 21 June 1898 he addressed three letters
to the king: one dealing with problems connected with the
sending of students abroad, one presenting a new national
scheme of education, and one venting a highly personal expression of his frustration.

In the first of these letters, after protesting the inability of
the ministry to provide English instruction at the lower levels
of the curriculum or to raise the standards of the curriculum
without first acquiring sufficient teachers and textbooks, Phatsakǫrawong agreed to abide by the recommendations of Wisut's
report.[19] He declared the ministry's intention "to lay down new

15. NA 5 S, 31/5, 5, King to Phatsakǫrawong, 11 June 1898.
16. King to Wisut, 11 June 1898, printed in Chulalongkorn and
Phrasadet, *Phraratchahatlekha*, p. 262.
17. NA 5 S, 31/5, 9, Phatsakǫrawong to King, 12 June 1898.
18. NA 5 S, 32/5, 1, Phatsakǫrawong to King, 21 June 1898.
19. NA 5 S, 37/5, 1, Phatsakǫrawong to King, 21 June 1898, no.
38/2035.

principles for our educational system so as to make it commensurate with the English system," to work to expand the proportion of the syllabus taught in Thai, to have students trained
abroad specifically for the purpose of preparing teaching materials, to require that Thai students sent abroad demonstrate a
good knowledge of their own language before their departure,
to institute within three years a requirement that students going
abroad have obtained first in Thailand the full equivalent of a
British secondary education, and to take measures to devise
means by which students might be directed to suitable employment on their return from Europe. One detects in this letter at
least a halfhearted acquiescence in conditions imposed upon the
ministry from outside, as well as a strong undercurrent of implication conveying the ministry's feeling that these admirable
and necessary goals could not possibly be quickly attained.

Phatsakɔrawong's second letter of the same date,[20] introducing the ministry's "Education Program" promised ten days
earlier, noted that it had been drawn up within the ministry on
the basis of Phraya Wisut's recommendations and revised after
consultations with the Cabinet. He noted, however, that if the
scheme was to serve as the basis of further educational development, its success must depend upon the provision of adequate
funds, especially for a greatly expanded program of teacher
training and for the provision of adequate textbooks. To the
latter end he requested that an advisory committee to deal with
the textbook problem he appointed at once. Other than these
three points, all of which he mentioned very briefly, he refrained completely from any comment on the scheme he enclosed.

The Education Department's "Education Program for
Siam"[21] dealt separately with education in Bangkok and the

20. NA 5 S, 32/5, 1, Phatsakɔrawong to King, 21 June 1898, no.
39/2038.
21. NA 5 S, 32/5, 4, "Khrong phaen kansüksa nai krung sayam
khɔng krom süksathikan," dated 19 June 1898; printed in Rɔng, *Prawat
krasuang,* pp. 115–47.

provinces, devoting the major share of its attention to the former. Much of what this scheme contained was no more than a reiteration of the structure and organization first explained in the report on Japanese education of 1888 and later formulated and elaborated in the ministry's code of 1891, the education laws of 1892, and the curriculum of 1895. In general, with respect to education in Bangkok, the department grouped the schools into six main categories: (1) the elementary "alphabet schools" of the monasteries[22] and the "kindergartens", i.e. unreformed traditional schools, termed *munlasüksa* (elementary education); (2) lower and higher primary schools, i.e. primary schools following the modern pattern and examining for Standards I and II, termed *prathomsüksa* (primary education); (3) secondary schools, examining for Standard III, of which there were as yet none in operation, termed *matthayomsüksa* (secondary education); (4) lower and higher Anglo-vernacular schools, examining for the Government English Code framed by Morant in 1891; (5) university education; and (6) special schools at all levels. As far as the general organization of Bangkok schools was concerned, there were no significant departures from ministry policy as previously formulated or suggested, even in the matter of their curricula, except that the general broadening of the curriculum promised since the beginning of the decade was now formally incorporated into the system at the primary level and above, subject to the provision of appropriate Thai textbooks. One other innovation was the specific suggestion that various special educational institutions such as the Law School of the Ministry of Justice (1896)[23] and the Mahamakut Buddhist Academy might be combined as faculties of a "Rattanakosin (Bangkok) University" on the fiftieth anniversary of King Chulalongkorn's accession to the throne, which would have occurred in 1918, provided that primary and secondary education be sufficiently well established by them.

22. *Rongrian k kh namo tam wat.*
23. On the Law School, see Luang Sannaiprasat (Thannya na Songkhla), *Phatthanakan kansüksa kotmai nai prathet thai* (Bangkok, 1956), pp. 2–16.

The Education Department estimated that 30,000 boys in Bangkok should be attending school,[24] but noted that government and subsidized private schools and the modernized religious schools of Prince Wachirayan together were bringing modern education to only 3,468 boys, or slightly more than 10 percent of the estimated male school-age population. The department thought that private schools might be able to teach ten thousand boys, which left the Government with almost twenty thousand boys needing school places. In order to meet this need, the department estimated that it would need 120 new primary schools, eight secondary schools, and five lower and two higher Anglo-vernacular schools.[25] To meet this need, it recommended that six new primary schools be provided each year, with places for 900 pupils. These primary schools would offer instruction free of charge, and "when there are enough of them, a Royal Ordinance should be issued compelling children of the appropriate ages to attend them." Also proposed were an expansion of the system of grants-in-aid for private schools, based on attendance instead of examination results and providing them with teachers or teaching materials; the conversion of the upper classes of Suankulap and Suankulap English schools into secondary schools, "to be followed by others in future"; and a program of scholarships to aid poor but outstanding boys to continue their education in secondary schools. In addition, the program called for the establishment of another normal school to increase the output of trained teachers to forty per year and the inauguration of new and higher salary scales for teachers at all levels. Section 6 of the Program called for a great expansion of the Inspection Bureau of the Department, in

24. Based on an estimated population of 500,000 for monthon Krungthep (Bangkok and the six surrounding provinces) and assuming that school-age boys would constitute one twelfth of this figure and that one fourth of these would be unable to attend school for one reason or another.

25. Based on the following unexplained distribution of pupils: *prathom*, 90 percent; *matthayom*, 5 percent; lower Anglo-vernacular, 3 percent; and higher Anglo-vernacular (secondary, university preparation level), 2 percent.

order to have six inspectors for each fifty schools. Section 7 dealt at great length with the establishment of a "Textbook Committee," describing in minute detail the procedures by which its business would be conducted but concentrating almost entirely on the adoption of textbooks rather than going into the question of how to get them written. After dealing briefly and superficially with special education and education for girls the department presented a rough assessment of the cost of its proposals, which it estimated would require an annual budget increase averaging 450,000 baht over the initial five-year period R.S. 118–122 (1899/1900–1903/04), which it hoped to obtain either by direct Treasury sanction or by a combination of Treasury grants and the levying of a new education tax in the Bangkok area.

This portion of the Education Department's Program dealing with education in Bangkok, although lengthy, constituting seven eighths of the whole, was generally very loosely written and poorly elaborated. Much of it was simply a rehash of old proposals, plans, and pleas, while other sections did no more than identify problems and offer categorical solutions for them. On the whole it does not seem credible, for it gave no indication of new thinking or new approaches to old problems. It said little about the problem of educational standards raised so urgently by Phraya Wisut, and its main tenor was consciously to uphold the basic soundness of previous policy and accomplishments and the ability of the ministry to achieve the desired results, given very substantial increases in funds.

The second portion of the Program, extending over less than four printed pages, dealt very briefly and on the whole rather superficially with the extension of modern education to the provinces. Using the same statistical procedures (or rules of thumb) as in the discussion of education in Bangkok, the department estimated the male school-age population at 450,000 boys, of whom about half would be unable to attend school.[26] Noting that only 1,364 boys were then attending modern-style

26. Based on a provincial population estimated at 5,500,000.

schools in the provinces and that only 28,000 were receiving traditional-style education in the monasteries,[27] the problem appeared enormous.

The department recommended that elementary instruction, the teaching of the four r's in regular classes using government textbooks, be introduced in all the monasteries of the country, with primary and secondary instruction to follow later. It suggested that the provinces be divided into six regional inspectorial districts, each with a Chief School Inspector appointed from Bangkok who would supervise the work of locally appointed inspectors at the province *(müang)* and district *(amphoe)* levels, whose task it would be to promote and supervise village and commune *(tambon)* schools. Each *monthon* or "circle" would have its own secondary and teacher-training schools. The whole system could be supported financially by the levying of education "rates" (English word), raised and spent locally. In a footnote, the department noted that it had considered appointing monthon ecclesiastical heads *(čhaokhana monthon)* "to organize education in the monasteries of the monthon, using monks as teachers to teach the alphabet as *munlasüksa* [fundamental or elementary education]." Beyond this, the Program said nothing, perhaps partly because of the sheer magnitude of the task and not least because since 1892 it had had practically no experience whatsoever with provincial education.

The Program devised by the Education Department in less than two months in mid-1898 was, on the whole, not a very remarkable document. It was consistently vague or silent on educational as distinct from administrative policy, for it avoided any direct examination of the function the educational system might be intended to serve. It made no attempts to explain why the department thought all boys of school age should receive some education or what that education should contain. It was specific and direct only where strong ministry interests, par-

27. This figure seems unduly low. Compare with the figures in Table 1, p. 335.

ticularly existing institutions or services, were at stake, where
there was an opportunity for the ministry to push its pet projects, or where the king's interests were known to lie, as with
the textbook problem. Nonetheless, there are several things
about the Program that deserve positive emphasis. It may have
been unoriginal and superficial in many of its recommendations,
but these reflected in no small measure what had long since become standard approaches to problems that had existed and
plagued the progress of educational modernization since very
early in the reign, and they sprang at least as much out of the
depths of Thai culture, custom, and conventional modes of
thought as they did from the persons of the minister and the director. Many of their ideas were reasonable and some were
excellent, as will be seen; but they lacked effective advocates
who could work to express them with conviction, argue and
fight for them, and make them work. It took little more than
the Program to convince the king of this fact.

Of the three letters addressed to the king by Čhaophraya
Phatsakǫrawong on 21 June, the most remarkable is a general
letter complaining of the treatment he and his ministry had
borne in the previous six years.[28] Reviewing his tenure in office,
the minister listed one by one the difficulties and disappointments he had been forced to endure. He complained of the
massive cuts in the ministry's services in 1892, including the
withdrawal of support from the monastery elementary schools,
the closing of the Education Department's printing press, the
loss of Edwin McFarland, and the withdrawal of support from
independent schools. He was particularly bitter at the Cabinet's
refusal to grant funds for the educational service and suggested
that Prince Damrong, once instrumental in promoting modern
education, was among his leading opponents in the Cabinet.
The minister found particularly harsh the Cabinet's judgment
of the Education Department's efforts to provide the schools
with textbooks, and particularly senseless its refusal to support

28. NA 5 S, 13/5, 15, Phatsakǫrawong to Sommot, 21 June 1898,
no. 37/2032.

extensions in English education and teacher-training. Phatsakǫrawong cited the efforts he and his staff had made to carry
on with their work through decentralization, by raising funds
from private sources, by adopting expedients, and by simple
repeated attempts to gain funds. He took pains to argue that
the department had been able to make much progress in spite
of obstacles, and he enclosed with his letter a tabulation of the
number of government schools and their enrollments as compared with the previous year, and a list of textbooks compiled by
the ministry.[29] Using these as his evidence he argued that, in
spite of repeated budget cuts,

> education at the primary level still may be considered gradu-
> ally to have progressed . . . The Director of the Education
> Department has exerted the full measure of his strength, and
> the cuts in our funds have come because our ideas have
> tended greatly not to coincide with the approach taken by
> Prince Damrong when he had the task of organizing educa-
> tion; for when he stood in the King's favor and when budgets
> did not have to be scrutinized, he was easily able to establish
> educational "centralization." But when the Education De-
> partment had to suffer such budgetary cuts as these, I could
> not help but feel that education was of absolutely no im-
> portance whatsoever, because so little government money
> was expended on it.

Then he turned to the situation newly confronting him:

> Now I learn that it is His Majesty's policy that education is
> important, as it is relevant to "administration" in every way.
> This will pose problems as well. I am a man with little in-
> fluence, and my eloquence is not equal to the task of express-
> ing my ideas: it is already exhausted. But I do have reserva-
> tions . . . Education is not like the construction of buildings,
> which can quickly be accomplished. It is rather like the

29. NA 5 S, 13/5, 23, Report on the Numbers of Schools and Students
as of 24 Apr. 1898; and 13/5, 29, Progress Report of the Textbook Bureau,
1897/98.

planting and felling of trees. Education is like the slow growth of the great tree of the forest. If it is properly nourished with funds, it will yield its fruit in due course. Thus its growth and expansion must depend upon time and the good will of His Majesty. . . . Hearing His Majesty's thoughts on education I am excited and pleased that education in the towns and provinces is to be reformed so as to yield increasing benefits. Thus I write telling you of the state of education so that His Majesty may take this into consideration in reforming education.[30]

Thus ended the Čhaophraya's lament, on a tone of reserved hopefulness; but well might he have done so. Čhaophraya Phatsakǫrawong was sufficiently a bureaucrat to know that his career was at stake, that it was necessary for him to justify himself, and he expressed quite clearly in his final paragraph his fear that the reform of education in the provinces would be carried out independently of the ministry. If this were to happen, if substantial sums were to be allocated to provincial elementary education and these funds did not pass through his ministry, it would be a clear indication of his own and Prince Kittiyakǫn's personal failure and the collective failure of the ministry to assume effective leadership of educational modernization.

Although undoubtedly some indications of the official reaction to the ministry's proposals and Čhaophraya Phatsakǫrawong's letter reached the ministry very quickly, it was not until a month later that the king's response came, in a blistering letter to Čhaophraya Phatsakǫrawong of 21 July 1898, in which two specific themes of his dissatisfaction with the ministry were expressed.[31] First, he characterized Phatsakǫrawong's complaint of repeated budgetary cuts as "disgusting and sickly" and noted that the only truth in the Čhaophraya's account was the latter's own confession that he had been unable to plead his own bud-

---

30. All words enclosed in quotation marks appear in English in the original.
31. NA 5 S, 31/5, 45.

getary case effectively with the Cabinet. But why, asked the king, had Phatsakǫrawong not elicited the aid of Prince Kitti-yakǫn in putting his case before them, a practice with prece-dent? "When one examines your budget for this year," he added, "one can see the low state of the Department." The second theme of dissatisfaction that the king took up in his letter was the nagging problem of providing textbooks for the educational system, and on this point he eschewed all delicacy. He belittled the abilities of the ministry's aging parian, the scholarly ex-monks of the Textbook Bureau. The king had a very good idea of what he could and should expect from the Bureau. From the parian he knew he could not expect truly modern textbooks. They simply had not the degree of knowl-edge required to provide the schools with real textbooks of natural science, geography, history, and modern vocational training. Yet the king knew that such textbooks were essential to the improvement of Thai education.

Once this point had been reached, once the king became firmly convinced of the inability of the ministry as it stood to deal with the problems of education in the manner he knew they demanded, change could not be long in coming. The en-suing half-year was to see the working out of that change.

NEW DIRECTIONS, JULY–NOVEMBER 1898

By mid-July 1898 the progress of educational modernization had been given a new momentum. King Chulalongkorn, in the interest he had evinced by commissioning Phraya Wisut's sur-vey and the strong reception he had given it, was beginning to show the strength of a new and vital commitment. At the same time, it was obvious that he was less than certain about the ability of the Ministry of Public Instruction to assume the task of serving that commitment. What course, however, was open to the king to achieve his goals? In the Western political con-text, the most obvious solution would have been to reorganize the ministry, appointing a new minister and a new director for the Education Department, shifting new people into the ministry from outside it or promoting forward-looking elements within it. In the Thai context at this particular point in time such drastic measures were not possible. There simply were not sufficient new men within the ministry or outside it on whom the king could depend for the firm, certain, and enlightened direction of such labors as he wished the ministry to perform. A more cogent objection to such a course, however, was the fact that in the Thai political system this would go against very strong notions of political and personal loyalty. The only alternative was to redefine the responsibilities of the ministry, taking away from it the most important of those functions that it had shown no signs of being able to perform and giving them to others. This was a pattern well established in Thai politics, employed repeatedly through the 1890s in connection with the Ministry of Interior, for example, to which were assigned at various times certain functions of the ministries of Agriculture and Finance. It was this alternative that clearly threatened the Ministry of Public Instruction in 1898.

As of mid-July, despite his serious doubts as to the capacity of the ministry to carry out what he viewed as an urgent program of educational expansion, the king nonetheless still hoped that it might prove possible for the ministry to gain the cooperation of the Cabinet and of other ministries in fulfilling this need. At the same time, however, the king took measures to bring Siam's educational problems and the solutions proposed for them to the attention of other influential men and to prepare for a major decision on the programs put forward by Phraya Wisut and the Education Department.

The king turned first to his half-brother, the prince-priest Wachirayan, who at that time was abbot of Wat Bǫwǫnniwet and patriarch of the reform Thammayut sect of the Buddhist Order. Prince Wachirayan, born to King Mongkut in 1859, had entered the Sangha for a brief period in 1873 and was ordained as a monk in 1880, residing at Wat Bǫwǫnniwet where

he acted as deputy patriarch *čhaokhana rọng)* of the Thammayut sect under Prince Pawaret Wariyakọngkọn, succeeding to
the latter's position as patriarch *(čhaokhana yai thammayutika)*
in 1893. Like his brothers Princes Phanurangsi, Devawongse,
and Damrong, Wachirayan had been educated in the palace
English school in the early seventies, and he later came under
the influence of the king's Scottish personal physician, Dr. Peter
Gowan.[32] It was natural that he should bring to the reform
sect of King Mongkut that same liberal outlook and scholarly
rigor that had so distinguished it since the Third Reign. In the
late eighties and especially in the nineties he promoted a great
improvement in the standards of religious education for the
monkhood, which took form in the Mahamakut Academy at
Wat Bọwọnniwet, and brought about in the same period great
growth in the system of ecclesiastical examinations which in
1891 became an annual affair.[33] During these years he sponsored the founding of modern-style schools in some of the
monasteries of the Thammayut sect; by 1898 there were four
schools with 450 pupils in Bangkok and three schools with 150
pupils in the provinces, administered wholly independently of
the Education Department.[34] Because he had this strong interest
in education and its quality, it was natural that the king should
turn to him for advice at this point in 1898, particularly in light
of the Education Department's recommendations concerning the
extension of modern education into the provinces, which, it will

---

32. Prince Wachirayan (Vajirañāṇa) wrote a very interesting autobiography, *Phraprawat trat lao* (Bangkok, 1961).

33. See Bangkok, National Library, comps., *Parian ratchakan thi 5*
(Bangkok, 1920), 2, 2–8.

34. NA 5 S, 32/5, 4, "Education Program for Siam," Educ. Dept.,
19 June 1898. Prince Wachirayan's first involvement in education outside
his own monastery appears to have begun in 1895, when Prince Phanurangsi decided to establish a school at Wat Thepsirin in memory of his
late wife and asked Prince Wachirayan to assume academic and administrative responsibility for it (NA 5 S, 70/5, 1, Phanurangsi to King, 20 Mar.
1896). At the end of 1896, Prince Wachirayan took charge of all secular,
Thai education in the monasteries of the Thammayut sect (NA 5 S, 19/5,
33, Phatsakọrawong to Sommot, 30 Dec. 1896).

be recalled, mentioned the fact that the department was considering working through the monkhood to achieve this end.

Three days after rebuking Čhaophraya Phatsakǫrawong for the ineffective manner in which the Ministry of Public Instruction had been performing its functions, the king sent to Prince Wachirayan a copy of Phraya Wisut's report and asked for the prince-priest's comments and counsel, explaining that he wished that further plans for educational innovation should not be decided upon without monastic participation.[35] Wachirayan replied two days later, on 26 July.[36] He approved generally of Wisut's recommendations, singling out a number of them for emphasis and adding to each his own ideas and interpretations. He saw the critical importance of education in Bangkok, but while agreeing with Wisut's plea that secondary and English instruction in Bangkok must be developed as a substitute for an excessive dependence on the sending of students for lengthy courses abroad, he argued strongly the case for raising the standards of *all* Thai schools. "It should be our cardinal principle," he stated, "to provide youth with knowledge of vocational and moral utility. If we do this, these youths will be of increasing utility to the country."[37] In order to achieve this end, however, Prince Wachirayan saw the necessity of paying particular attention to the textbook problem, and he also advocated the strengthening of religious instruction in all the schools and the establishing of several model schools under the direction of the Mahamakut Academy. The tone of Wachirayan's reply to the king's request for advice was one of reasonableness, of general agreement with Wisut's recommendations, but it also bore an element of reserve and caution, of realism and necessity. Although Prince Wachirayan concluded with a short sugges-

35. NA 5 S, 31/5, 13, King to Wachirayan, 24 July 1898, printed in Chulalongkorn and Wachirayan, *Phraratchahatlekha song mi paima*, pp. 71–73.
36. NA 5 S, 31/5, 17, Wachirayan to King, 26 July 1898, printed in Bangkok, Mahamakut Academy, comps. *Phra-aksǫn rüang čhat kanlaorian khǫng chao sayam* (Bangkok, 1949), pp. 1–9.
37. Ibid.

tion of the role his Academy might play in educational development, he did not belabor his own role and seemed content to
advise rather than to thrust his services upon the king.

Chulalongkorn especially welcomed Wachirayan's interest
in the compilation of modern textbooks and acted immediately
to procure for the prince samples of English textbooks, while
at the same time he pointedly brought Wachirayan's advice to
the attention of the Education Department.[38] He then informed
the Ministry of Public Instruction that he found their educational program of 21 June unintelligible in the language in
which it was written and asked that it be translated into English
together with Phraya Wisut's proposals.[39] It would appear that
the king was stalling for time, for his action had the effect only
of delaying the official consideration of educational policy for
seven weeks, until printed English and Thai versions of the
proposals were distributed to the monthon commissioners *(khaluang thetsaphiban)* meeting in their annual conference at the
Ministry of Interior on 17 September.[40]

On the second day of the conference, Prince Damrong
opened the morning's session by stating that the king had ordered that the commissioners discuss the question of provincial
education. The official report of the meeting simply noted that
copies of the department's and Wisut's schemes were then distributed to those attending and that discussion then passed on to
other questions. The two concluding days of the conference
passed without further mention of the subject.[41]

The proposals, however, were not dropped, for at some date
between 17 and 23 September the king requested, probably
informally, that Prince Damrong and Prince Wachirayan draw
up schemes for extending modern education into the provinces
without reference to the Ministry of Public Instruction. And in

38. NA 5 S, 31/5, 12, King to Sommot, 26 July 1898; 31/5, 22, King
to Wisut, 31 July; and 31/5, 23, Sommot to Phatsakǫrawong, 31 July.

39. NA 5 S, 31/5, 24, King to Phatsakǫrawong, 21 July 1898.

40. NA 5 S, 31/5, 29, Phatsakǫrawong to King, 16 Sept. 1898.

41. NA R.5, no. 179, 3/179 and 4/179, Reports, *Thetsaphiban* Conference, 1898.

the annual review of the year's accomplishments in his birthday speech of 21 September, the king very pointedly praised Wachirayan's educational work while completely ignoring the work of the Ministry of Public Instruction.[42]

On 24–25 September, Prince Damrong and Prince Wachirayan submitted their recommendations to the king on the subject of provincial education.[43] Their reports indicate that they had been sent copies of Wisut's and the Education Department's proposals and of Chaophraya Phatsakɔrawong's long letter of complaint, which they denigrated in no uncertain terms. Acting upon the king's expressed wish to extend modern education into the provinces on the basis of the existing system of monastery education, their reports served as the rationale on which the next decade's educational program was to be founded, and marked a dramatic shift in educational policy no less than in the composition of the group which determined that policy.

Prince Wachirayan presented his opinions in a manner which must closely have approximated his sermon style. He began, "That education which gives the best results provides knowledge, capabilities [skills], and good behavior . . . All three of these benefits should be more widespread. They are fed and nourished by the study of reading and writing, science, and the *Dhamma.*" Both traditional monastery education and the modern schools of the Education Department, he argued, had failed to achieve these ends. The old system was too diffuse, too fragmented, and too independent-minded to meet the needs of the times, while the ministry had manifestly failed to make good use of the resources, both in funds and in existing institutions, available to it. Thus "the fault for the lack of educational development lies both with the Education Department and with the monasteries." To remedy this educational deficiency, Prince

42. "A Review of Reforms in Siam: Address by the King," *Bangkok Times,* 5 Oct. 1898. The Thai text is in Chulalongkorn, *Phraratchadamrat 2417–2453,* p. 158.

43. NS 5 S, 38/12, 2, "Opinions on Education," Prince Wachirayan, 25 Sept. 1898; and 38/12, 4, "Opinions on the Organization of Provincial Education," Prince Damrong, 24 Sept. 1898.

Wachirayan argued that "we must get rid of the idea that monasteries have only a religious function, and consider all monasteries as schools, register them as such, and consider all their pupils as school students." During their general education in the monasteries, boys should learn "to use the writing system [*akkhǫrawithī*] of the country, arithmetic, to earn a living, and to know good from bad." Each of these schools should itself hold annual or semiannual examinations. He advocated that in promoting monastery education the government extend only indirect support to these schools, providing them with a full range of textbooks at minimal prices and administering examinations so as to ensure that they would meet the minimal demands of the government curriculum. Schools that performed exceptionally well could be singled out for direct support, perhaps one school in each müang. Whatever methods were adopted it was essential that the Sangha become better organized, but this would have to be accomplished in such a manner that the traditional hierarchy be maintained and given their full powers, from the Supreme Patriarch on down: "Don't let people think that the *Sangha* is under the control of the Ecclesiastical Department. This is very important." "When all this is done," he concluded,

> the world will see that Siam has many schools and pupils, that education is progressing along traditional lines and will continue to do so. All the monasteries will be of benefit to the country. The drain on government funds will be lessened. Disrepair of the monasteries will be corrected, and the people will be more faithful to their religious duties. Finally, the *Sangha* will be better administered.

Prince Damrong's "Opinions," submitted on the previous day, are very similar to those of Prince Wachirayan, and indeed each of them mentions having consulted with the other. Prince Damrong's approach to the problem was much more that of the practical man-of-the-world, the Cabinet minister and administrator:

Education . . . has two uses: to allow the common people to be better educated and behaved, and to obtain better-educated people for the use of the country in the public service. I have here considered only the first of these two functions, public education in the provinces, its improvement and expansion. I think it necessary that this be accomplished without expending large amounts of government funds, for if much money is put into it, it will not be successful. We must consider only the possible for the time being, even though it may not be the best in quality. Gradual improvement can come in the future.

His practical bias extended to his view of the monasteries:

We already have sufficient schools, dating from ancient times: the monasteries. The only reason that they are now so poor is that they have not kept up with the world. They do not lack public faith and value. These represent capital already invested, to many tens of thousands of baht which the government will not have to expend. They lack only ideas and the strength for improvement. If these can be provided, they will progress without difficulty.

Most of Prince Damrong's practical recommendations were concerned with the problem of providing the monastery schools in the provinces with textbooks. The basic primers and arithmetic textbooks already existed, compiled in the 1880s when he was Minister of Public Instruction, so that it remained only to prepare textbooks for basic vocational and moral instruction.

We do not yet have Thai textbooks to teach vocational subjects, and I have never seen one in a *farang* language which would meet our needs. It would have to be written from scratch. It should include explanations of the nature of life and the human body . . . clothing, the making of clothing and its care, foods and their preparation, etc. For moral instruction we have no textbook, nor is there any in a foreign language, so we will have to compile it from scratch, [to teach the pupils that] suffering and happiness are the lot of all life, that good behavior brings happiness and bad behavior brings suffering. [They should be taught a] knowledge of human life, of relations with others and with one's self, of one's duties to one's country, to obey the law and the *Dhamma.* They should teach the value of national independence, of being unlike other countries.[44]

Prince Damrong recommended that once the required textbooks were supplied twenty thousand copies of each title should be printed, at a cost of about 24,000 baht. These initially should be distributed free of charge through the provincial ecclesiastical authorities to win their acceptance, and later the government could begin selling them at cost or at a small profit. He also advocated having village and commune headmen "advise people to send their children to school." He thought examinations should be introduced gradually, as standards were raised by the introduction of government textbooks, and that schools performing well be converted into fully supported government schools, perhaps one to each müang, teaching fully to the government standards, to serve as examples to schools in their neighborhood. These proposals, he urged, "should be carried out. They are feasible. The only difficulty is the textbooks."

Immediately upon receipt of the princes' recommendations, the king's secretary, Prince Sommot, was instructed to convene a meeting of interested parties on the following day, 26 September, and invitations were sent to Prince Wachirayan, Prince Damrong, Prince Kittiyakǫn, and Čhaophraya Phatsakǫrawong.[45] On 26 September, at six in the evening, the meeting began, presided over by the king himself. The king opened the meeting with a lengthy statement explaining the reasons for

44. My notes on this document are defective, and the two clauses in brackets are uncertain reconstructions of the original.

45. NA 5 S, 31/5, 33–35, Sommot to Phatsakǫrawong, Kittiyakǫn, and Damrong, 25 Sept. 1898.

calling the officials together, a statement laying bare his deep
concern for education and its development which demands re-
production in full:

> We meet today to confer on how education might best be
> organized so as to be more securely established and wide-
> spread in the future. We all know that Thailand's education
> cannot compete with that of other countries, for we began
> our work much later than all of them except Japan; and
> although Japan may be considered as having begun her
> modernization at about the same time as we did, our progress
> has been very dissimilar, inasmuch as Japan was a special
> case, as its educational system had come from China, and was
> already very well developed, and the Japanese have worked
> very hard to improve it. Our late development is due to the
> fact that we have not been able to find skilled people, and
> to the fact that those skilled people that we possess have not
> had the drive to do this work. In short, we have not found
> the skilled people for the job. It is important to realize that
> an educational system cannot be established quickly, and
> takes ten or twenty years. If we do not hurry now to lay
> down the basis of one, we will still not have it in another
> "generation," and a great deal of time will have been wasted.
> The government will in the future require educated men for
> the public service. The education system established by Prince
> Damrong was very good, but it could not be taken as a basis
> for a general system for the entire kingdom. After the min-
> istry of Prince Damrong, the officials [in the Ministry of
> Public Instruction] continued to follow Prince Damrong's
> plan, but they misunderstood it and even deviated from it,
> or to their own self-deception they sought only to establish
> large numbers of schools, and by entering into their reports
> statistics as to the numbers of items of correspondence han-
> dled sought to convey the impression that these were an
> index of the respect with which their office was regarded.
> The present schools are only quantities, and as such are not

meaningful. The work that the Education Department has accomplished to the present moment is only as good as that which preceded it, and represents no advances. The flowerpot plant has grown larger and filled the pot, but it is no more beautiful or healthy. In the future, we would like to make this work more like a tree planted firmly in the earth, growing up healthy and beautiful, extending further outward. It is no wonder that people say our present education is no good. There is only the Mahamakut Academy, which Prince Wachirayan has organized and supported with all his vigor: it is good because of him. If Čhaophraya Phat has supported it, he can be credited with that, but it cannot be said that he has organized it. It is a good example of how education has been organized in conjunction with Buddhism. No education can be established which is not connected with the monastery, because to the teaching of reading and writing must be added instruction in religion. This is a goal of the first order, and if we meet without referring to it we ignore the fact that most of the Thai people do not know the Five Precepts. I have investigated in the provinces, and we have seen the great decay of a Thai people without religion, which has caused them to lose their "morals." I would like to have the educational system connected with religion. Thus I ask you to organize education in such a manner that it will be as strong and wide spreading as a banyan tree, with a firm grounding, healthy, beautiful, and splendid, and not like a potted plant.[46]

The king then asked Prince Sommot to read aloud the recommendations of Princes Wachirayan and Damrong, necessary probably because the ministry officials were unaware until this moment of their proposals or even of the fact that such a course as that put forward by the princes was even under consideration.

The discussion that ensued was turbulent and ill tempered. Prince Kittiyakọn attempted to defend the Education Depart-

46. NA 5 S, 38/12, 5, Report of Special Meeting, 26 Sept. 1898.

ment by suggesting that the princes' proposals contained nothing new and that the Education Department was already following a similar course, and his arguments only irritated all the others. The king finally interrupted the discussion to state his decision:

> In the future, I wish education to be organized as follows: all education in the monasteries, however organized, shall be handed over to Prince Wachirayan to organize completely according to his proposals, and I will grant him full authority to supervise all monastery education throughout the kingdom.

Prince Wachirayan, complaining of the manner in which the Education Department had neglected the monastery schools and agreeing that a sound system of public education spread over the kingdom could only be created with the support of the Buddhist Sangha, reluctantly agreed to assume this responsibility on the condition that Prince Damrong's Ministry of Interior lend him support and assistance,[47] to which Damrong agreed. The conferees then debated specific practical problems which might be occasioned by the new arrangement, during the course of which debate the king expressed his views on a number of important aspects of educational policy. He stated his preference, in the short run, for quantity over quality in the educational system if such a choice became necessary. Time and again he returned to the problem of providing the monastery schools with sufficient textbooks. But the critical issue immediately at hand was the question of the role the Ministry of Public Instruction should play in the program of extending provincial education. The issue was resolved by the king, who pointed out that the scheme submitted by the Education Department in June had specifically provided that elementary education in the monasteries, i.e. basic education below primary level, was of no concern to the ministry. Thereby he neatly

47. This division of labor was necessary because of disciplinary prohibitions against the handling of money by Thammayut monks.

allowed the ministry to exclude itself from the program altogether.

The king brought the meeting to a close by summarizing its decisions:

> Our discussion to this point has concluded that, as for education in the provincial monasteries, it is to be handed over to Prince Wachirayan to organize with the assistance of Prince Damrong and the monthon commissioners in disbursing funds and distributing textbooks. Examinations will be the responsibility of Prince Wachirayan and the Ministry of Interior. Thus the provinces will have nothing to do with the Education Department. As for provincial monastery schools currently receiving support, this will cease from [the beginning of] R.S. 118 [1 April 1899]. This scheme of organization is based on the scheme of the Education Department which states that the Department will not be concerned with the monastery "alphabet" schools at all, other than including them as a category [in the system]. Therefore there is no cause to think that this arrangement concerns the Education Department in the least. This is a new program. As for the education which the Education Department controls at levels above these monastery schools, this it will continue to organize in R.S. 118, but it must specify just how much it intends to do.

And on this note this stormy meeting, which must have lasted several hours, finally ended.

It would be difficult to minimize the importance of the conference of 26 September 1898. Part of its interest and significance comes from the light it sheds on the attitudes and ideas of the participants. On the ministry side of the table, Chaophraya Phatsakǫrawong uttered only three sentences during the entire course of the meeting, all in a feeble defense of his ministry's position that the educational system should be viewed as a system, with regularly graded and qualitatively controlled stages of education from bottom to top. He voiced no interest in and no ideas about the elementary monastery schools, the "alphabet" traditional schools, which he had long since dismissed from mind. It was Prince Kittyakǫn who, throughout the first half of the meeting, assumed the task of defending the ministry's prerogatives on these same lines, but he too was reduced to silence when the king pointed out the department's lack of concern for such schools in its June proposals. Both Prince Kittiyakǫn and the čhaophraya were probably quite disturbed by the tone on which the meeting had opened, and this must have neutralized much of the effectiveness they might otherwise have shown in their defense. If Čhaophraya Phatsakǫrawong showed the same persuasiveness in the Cabinet as he did in this meeting, it is not surprising that the king held the low opinion of him voiced during the summer to Wisut and Wachirayan.

The other three participants in the meeting, the king, Wachirayan, and Damrong, seem to have prepared their attack well beforehand, at least in its broad outlines. The "Opinions" of the two princes, prepared in the two days preceding the meeting, were complementary, and from the opening of the meeting the king introduced their points one by one, stating the case in favor of each and assisting from time to time in beating down the objections to them. Throughout the discussions the king showed a single-minded determination to implement their recommendations and to achieve results quickly, and he managed the meeting throughout in such a manner as to give Damrong and Wachirayan opportunities to air the details of their proposals.

The major immediate significance of the meeting, however, lies in the decisions that it reached. Since early in June the king had been hinting, both privately and publicly, that he had lost confidence in the ability of the Ministry of Public Instruction to carry out the educational reforms he deemed necessary. Until 17 September he was still showing an inclination to allow the ministry to carry out these reforms, but by 26 September he had changed his mind, and had decided to go ahead with a

major program of educational expansion in the provincial
monasteries, to be carried out without the ministry's participation. What had led him to change his mind?

One explanation of the change in policy comes from one of
the principals, Prince Damrong, who stated that although the
king at one point during the summer (probably in August)
sincerely had planned to allow the Ministry of Public Instruction to implement the new system, he changed his mind (appar-
rently in September) when, on consideration, he deemed the
ministry's proposals unworkable and liable to be defeated in
the Cabinet. Damrong suggests that he himself came up with
the alternative solution of devising a new program for provincial monastery education which lay beyond the scope of the
Ministry's program. He agreed that it was "hardly proper" for
such educational responsibilities to be entrusted to others when
a large ministry existed whose proper responsibility such matters
were; but given the king's "very strong views on this matter"
he states that there was no alternative to the solution adopted,
at least in the immediate future. However, he added in writing
to Phraya Wisut, "I still hope that in the not too distant future
someone with right ideas and the ability to carry them out will
take over the Ministry of Public Instruction, at which time I
will be happy to hand over this task to him and support him
to the full."[48]

Whatever the educational arguments for and against this
division of educational responsibilities, there can be little doubt
that it was a sound political decision. This was an era in Thai
politics when individuals and personalities were more important
than ideas and policies. The king must have been as aware as
Damrong was of the latter's susceptibility to the charge of
"empire-building," that propensity of Thai cabinet ministers
to accumulate powers and responsibilities whenever possible
and at whatever cost in efficiency and functional neatness, for

48. Damrong to Wisut, 11 Nov. 1898, printed in Chulalongkorn and
Phrasadet, *Phraratchahatlekha,* pp. 355–57.

the sake of personal prestige and simple power. King Chula-longkorn accused Čhaophraya Phatsakọrawong of just such ambitions in his speech opening the meeting of 26 September. One reaches the empirical conclusion, however, that this pro-pensity was reprehensible only when indulged in by those whose personal qualities and abilities (or merit) were not equal to the burden of the responsibilities they assumed. The operation of this principle can be seen in two types of cases. First, there were such cases as that of the Ministry of Agriculture, which for lack of adequate leadership was gradually stripped of its constituent departments beginning in the early 1890s until by 1896 it was completely abolished for a two-year period, during which its remaining functions were exercised by the Ministry of Finance. Second, there is the case of the Ministry of Interior, which began its life in 1892 under Prince Damrong as a mere skeleton of a ministry and, when Prince Damrong began to prove his outstanding qualities, gradually took over functions previously assigned to others.

Prince Damrong attempted to express in his letter to Phraya Wisut what might be termed a morally correct view of this "empire-building." He specifically disclaimed any desire to usurp "three-fourths" the functions of other ministries, which would be morally questionable, and instead justified the en-hancement of his powers on the grounds that only in this fashion could the national interest be served. Is this a credible explana-tion? In the light of subsequent events one would have to agree that it was.

Six weeks after the September meeting its decision was for-mally announced in a "Decree on the Organization of Provin-cial Education," promulgated on 11 November 1898.[49] With this decree, the provinces suddenly entered the modern educa-tional life of the nation. Much more quietly, the Ministry of Public Instruction began slowly to implement its own and

49. "Prakat čhat kanlaorian nai huamüang," *RKB, 15* (1898/99), 333; *PKPS, 16* (1899/1900), 414–17; and Praphat, *Čhaophraya phrasadet,* pp. 378–80.

Phraya Wisut's recommendations for the improvement and expansion of education in Bangkok, prodded along by a steady succession of reports, recommendations, and admonitions. These concurrent but separate developments will be treated in the following chapter.

There can be no doubt but that the year 1898 constituted a turning point in the history of Thai education and its modernization. That it was so is immediately evident upon comparing the educational stagnation of 1897 with the great vitality and activity of 1899. To what may this great change be attributed? Certainly much of the ferment of 1898 was the direct result of the king's renewed active interest in education. From what must have been an unimportant incident during his stay in London in the autumn of 1897, when he noticed that some of the Thai students had been abroad as long as twelve years, came the initial commission to Phraya Wisut to compile a report on the education of Thai students overseas. By the time the report was submitted in May, the king was already sufficiently anxious about the problem and interested enough in following through with Wisut's recommendations to press the ministry. Through the summer months one can trace his increased interest and determination in his willingness to challenge the ministry, which he had allowed to slumber for six long years. Phraya Wisut, once he had mailed his report in April, did not reenter the debate until the following year. Prince Damrong and Prince Wachirayan entered only at the request of the king, gingerly at first, and, at least on the part of Prince Damrong and by his own account, reluctantly. The ministry had to be prodded and goaded at every step of the way. From May onward it was the king who drove forward the forces of change until all concerned had to bow to them.

But was the king's strong leadership at this point an expression simply of an increased interest in education, or did its roots go much deeper? Until a great deal more research has been done into the history of the period and particularly into the process of modernization viewed as a whole no final answer will be possible. At present one has only suggestions of a change that came over the king at about this time, a change best characterized as one in his attitudes and in his approach to the problems of modernizing his country, the full implications of which will be followed and examined in subsequent chapters. One begins to see immediately upon the king's return a new firmness and confidence, a determination to lead, attributable primarily to his European tour of 1897. At the same time, one senses in his approach to problems a more wary attitude, a willingness to weigh Thai and Western values objectively in making his decisions. Late in January 1898, he declared in a public speech:

> I have convinced myself in Europe of the great benefit which Asiatic nations may derive from the acquisition of European science, [but] I am convinced also that there exists no incompatibility between such acquisition and the maintenance of our individuality as an independent Asiatic nation.[50]

Nine months later, when faced with a Ministry of Public Instruction that preferred to think in terms of a very strict definition of modern education and evidently thought little of traditional educational institutions, Chulalongkorn decided to have both: to work at least temporarily through the traditional institutions to further modern education, while at the same time strengthening the traditional moral content of education. Here was his "best of both worlds," to be brought into being not by importing the elaborate Western educational apparatus of inspectors and European standards, but rather by using traditional institutions in the pursuit of modern goals, by which both traditional and modern would be creatively transformed to create an educational system incompatible with neither.

50. *Bangkok Times*, 26 Jan. 1898.

8
Divided Labors, 1898–1902

By the end of 1898 a new momentum of change had been imparted to what had been a slow-moving process of educational change. It came as the cumulative result of the momentus developments of the preceding months: the new ideas brought forth and the concern expressed by the king and his advisers, the changes in the character of the national leadership, and the failure of the Ministry of Public Instruction to respond positively to developments potentially favorable to it. The outcome was a period of divided labors which saw a diffusion of responsibility for educational work. Under the direction of Prince Wachirayan a great expansion of public education in the provinces took place through the manipulation of such a traditional institution as the monkhood. Shorn of responsibility for provincial education, the Ministry of Public Instruction in the same period undertook a major restructuring of its modern educational system in Bangkok, while simultaneously the concern for education shown by the king and others with no direct executive powers in this field found expression in new educational experiments. Each of these developments deserves careful scrutiny in its own right; yet it is essential not to lose sight of the profound manner in which these divided labors were but interrelated aspects of a single problem and intertwined though separate attempts at its solution. It was only because these developments separately matured and prospered in the years bridging the turn of the century that their coalescence and re-integration was made possible in 1902 in a restored and revived Ministry of Public Instruction.

PRINCE WACHIRAYAN AND PROVINCIAL EDUCATION

Quite suddenly and with very little preparation Prince Wachirayan was in September 1898 given the enormous task of organizing modern education in all the provinces of Thailand,[1] a decision formalized six weeks later by royal decree. The significance of this work was understood from the beginning and indeed served as the justification for the somewhat unorthodox means taken to accomplish it; but the scope and difficulty of this undertaking could have been realized only gradually by those who were charged with it. That the decision was essentially correct, that the assumptions on which it was based were valid, and that an excellent choice had been made in selecting those who were to carry it out were fully confirmed by the results achieved by Wachirayan and his brother monks in the following three years; but they could have begun the work only with high hopes and some trepidation.

The decision to place provincial education in the hands of the monkhood and Prince Wachirayan was taken as a last resort, after other alternatives had been tried and found wanting. The 1875 decree had been virtually devoid of results, and its revival under Prince Damrong's auspices in the late 1880s had brought about the creation of only twenty-four government schools in the provinces. Although Damrong had framed more ambitious plans in 1891, these had withered under budgetary starvation after 1892, and Čhaophraya Phatsakǫrawong in 1898 could claim only to be providing partial support to some thirty-four private provincial schools with 1,214 pupils.[2] In those

1. Excepting only the Moslem provinces and dependencies of the South.
2. NA 5 S, 32/5, 4, Educational Program of the Educ. Dept., 17 June 1898. On taking these schools over, however, Prince Wachirayan claimed that there were only 15, with 555 pupils: NA 5 S, 35/12, Summary Report of Prince Wachirayan for 1898/99–1899/1900, Appendix A.

schools registered by the ministry, as well as in three provincial schools run by the Mahamakut Academy in Ayudhya province, some beginnings had been made in modernizing elementary instruction and its content in the provinces. They used the ministry's printed textbooks and were taught in formal classes by monk teachers, many of whom were Standard II graduates of the ministry's examination system.[3] There remained, however, more than twelve thousand monasteries throughout the kingdom in which boys continued to be instructed more or less as their fathers and grandfathers had been taught. A few monasteries used printed versions of such traditional textbooks as the *Prathom k ka* and even fewer had copies of Phraya Si Sunthọn's *Munlabot banphakit,* but most had neither. Arithmetic was rarely taught, and even moral instruction took no systematic form.[4] Clearly, the beginnings of modern education had not yet been felt outside Bangkok.

In initiating their educational program at the end of 1898, Prince Wachirayan and Prince Damrong had first to define clearly its objectives and to organize the means by which they might be attained. First, a "Decree on the Organization of Provincial Education," drafted jointly by the two princes, was promulgated in the government gazette in November 1898 as the official statement of the aims of the program.[5] Cast in unambiguously conservative and orthodox Buddhist terms, it proclaimed the king's intention to "support and further the progress of the entire Kingdom" and emphasized his intention to

3. NA 5 S, 27/2, 61, Report, Ministry of Public Instruction to Cabinet, n.d. (1897), reporting the registration of seven new independent schools in Bangkok, the monk-teachers in six of which were Standard II graduates. One would expect that one criterion used by the ministry in determining whether a school should be registered and supported was the educational qualifications of its teachers.

4. See the numerous reports of the monks who acted as provincial education directors in the series NA 5 S, 2/12–34/12.

5. NA 5 S, 38/12, 9, Wachirayan to Sommot, 26 Oct. 1898; 38/12, 6, Wachirayan to King, 28 Oct. 1898; and "Prakat čhat kanlaorian nai hua-müang," *RKB, 15* (1898/99), 133.

strengthen traditional institutions in the pursuance of traditional moral ends. He gave this defense of traditional moral values a modern twist, however, by announcing that he could see no better way "to extend his patronage to *all* monks"[6] than to provide them with government textbooks on moral and "other useful subjects" and to appoint Prince Wachirayan to superintend this strengthening of the religious and educational activities of the provincial monasteries. Provincial abbots could interpret this decree as meaning that the king was now to extend to every monastery the patronage that for many centuries had been reserved for a handful of royal monasteries: the tone of innovation was extremely muted, with but vague references to the teaching of modern secular subjects. The initial aims of the authorities certainly were understated, but the king, Wachirayan, and Damrong seem to have been perfectly aware of the potentialities of the institutions they were hoping to tap. They were acutely conscious as well of the fact that they had to proceed carefully, so as not to offend the traditionalist sentiments and sensitivities of monk and layman alike.[7]

In the following month, Wachirayan obtained royal approval for his "Plan for the Organization of Provincial Education,"[8] the main object of which was to embody in concrete arrangements the general intentions expressed in the proposals of Sep-

6. "Prakat čhat kanlaorian nai huamüang," *RKB, 15* (1898/99), 133. Emphasis added.

7. The *Bangkok Times* (21 Nov. 1898) quickly grasped the significance of this action. The editor stated:

It is a formal adoption by the Government of the old system, which placed the education of the people in the hands of the priests . . . but the system is to be brought more into line with modern requirements. . . . the fact that one who is himself a priest has been entrusted with the direction of the work will no doubt have a good influence in securing the co-operation of those priests who are now devoting their time to the teaching of the young.

8. NA 5 S, 20/12, 1, Wachirayan to King, 17 Nov. 1898; 38/12, 16, Sommot to King, 6 Dec. 1898; and 38/12, 15, "Plan for the Organization of Provincial Education," enclosed in 38/12, 16, Sommot to King, 6 Dec. 1898.

tember and decree of November. It announced the appointment of Prince Wachirayan as "organizer of religion and education of the Buddhist population" and delineated the respective responsibilities of the monks, the Ministry of Public Instruction, and the Ministry of Interior. Most specifically, it provided that "all monasteries will be made places of study." At least one school supported by government funds would be established in every province *(müang)* to serve as a model to other "people's schools *(rongrian ratsadǫn)*, supported by the people," which might gain government support as funds and conditions allowed. Individual instruction given in the traditional fashion in the monasteries was to be unaffected, but the program was drawn up in such a way as to give a maximum advantage to those monasteries choosing to concentrate such instruction in formal classes, which initially would be provided with free textbooks and whose teachers might be sent to the Mahamakut Academy in Bangkok for training. Funds were to be provided to the Mahamakut Academy for the compilation and publication of textbooks, for the training of teacher-monks, and for administrative expenses. Prince Wachirayan was given exclusive jurisdiction over provincial educational affairs, exerted through a corps of high-ranking monks who would serve as education and religion "directors *(phu-amnuaikan)*" in each monthon, who would travel each dry season in their provinces and meet annually in Bangkok.

On the whole, the December "Scheme" was modeled quite closely on the September proposals of the princes, with some elaboration. Its main import was quite clearly more radical than the vague assertions and suggestions of the November decree, for it specifically called for the organization of modern government and private schools in the provinces under centralized control. The essential characteristic of Wachirayan's scheme was that it came as the embodiment of his earlier warning not "to let people think that the Sangha is under the control of the Ecclesiastical Department" of the Ministry of Public

Instruction.[9] Yet, at the same time, a considerable proportion of the labors of the monks sent into the provinces under the scheme was to be devoted precisely to bringing the monkhood under government control along with the schools in which they taught, an integrative process that was to culminate three years later in a Royal Decree on the organization of the Sangha. Thus the plan of December 1898 was a double-edged revolutionary sword; but it was framed and administered in such a manner that the Sangha quite willingly wielded it.

In implementing this ambitious program, however, a great deal depended upon the quality of the monks selected to act as provincial education directors. It was Prince Wachirayan's intention to make his selections on the basis of qualifications, "because this is the first time such work has been attempted, and if it is done poorly and does not take hold, people will lose faith in it. Thus it is necessary to send out people who can be trusted completely."[10] The prince attempted, however, to nominate monks with local knowledge and family connections in the provinces to which they were sent, vital prerequisites if they were to gain the local support on which their success depended; but in doing so he did not neglect a concern for academic and ecclesiastical attainment. All twelve of his appointees were monks of high standing: all were distinguished graduates of the ecclesiastical examinations, five were *phrakhru* and four were holders of titular ecclesiastical appointments.[11] The prince apparently found no difficulty in reconciling political and qualitative criteria in his choices.

Final instructions for the provincial directors so chosen were approved by the king at the end of January 1899.[12] The direc-

9. NA 5 S, 38/12, 2, "Opinions on Education," Wachirayan, 25 Sept. 1898.

10. NA 5 S, 38/12, 6, Wachirayan to King, 28 Oct. 1898.

11. NA 5 S, 38/12, 8, List of Monks Nominated. For a listing of the main ecclesiastical offices and titles and their holders, see Prince Damrong Rajanubhab and Prince Sommot Amoraphan, *Rüang tang phrarachakhana phuyai nai krung rattanakosin* (Bangkok, 1923).

12. NA 5 S, 38/12, 31, Damrong to King, 27 Jan. 1899; and 38/12, 32, "Estimate of Provincial Work to be Accomplished in 1898/99 and 1899/1900."

tors were enjoined to travel in their provinces with local ecclesiastical dignitaries, where these had been appointed, so
as not to appear to be ignoring established hierarchical relationships. They were to inspect all monasteries for consideration
as sites for government schools, assessing the strengths and
weaknesses of each in terms of its location, relative popularity,
and ability to draw upon local support, and the availability of
monks teaching or capable of teaching to modern standards.
They were to explain the king's intentions concerning education, in the terms of the November decree, to "avert any mis-
apprehensions there may be." To monks and monasteries they
were to distribute the *Rapid Readers* and religious books, the
former "with the suggestion that they might be useful in teaching" and without the appearance of attempting to test the
knowledge of the teacher-monks, and the latter as "sources of
pleasure to monks in provincial monasteries." Implicit in this
directive was an awareness of resistance to the printed word:
while a provincial monk might be resistant to printed secular
textbooks he could hardly refuse a book of sermons composed
by Prince Wachirayan, at once one of the leading monks in the
kingdom and the king's brother. Finally, the provincial directors
were to select young monks in the provinces for training as
teachers in Bangkok, so that they might "become teachers
who will work to follow the plans which have been made to
support the extension of religion in the provinces in the future."
These instructions given the provincial directors were well-
considered and carefully set within a long-range program of
development in which as much care was taken with the preparatory groundwork as in setting ultimate goals.

Certainly one of the strongest advantages of the program em-
barked upon at the beginning of 1899 was its low cost. Prince
Damrong was able to provide for the first three months' work
out of surplus funds in the budget of the Ministry of Interior,
while putting forward a budget for the first full year's work
in 1899/1900 of only 35,800 baht; more than one fourth of
it was earmarked for the printing and distribution of textbooks
and smaller sums for the salary of a textbook compiler, travel

expenses for the provincial directors, funds to support a teacher-training program at Wat Bǫwǫnniwet, and a small sum to support government schools in the provinces.[13] Thus provided with instructions, textbooks to distribute, funds, seals of office, and credentials identifying them to provincial authorities and the Sangha, the provincial directors separately departed from Bangkok at the end of January.[14] Their work had begun.

During the absence of the provincial directors, Prince Wachirayan and Prince Damrong turned their attention to long-range problems of educational expansion and improvement. The two most important problems were the provision of adequate textbooks and the training of teachers for service in provincial monastery schools. The directors were sent to the provinces in January with only two of the four textbooks Prince Damrong viewed as essential to the success of the program: the *Rapid Reader* and a textbook of morality. Still required were textbooks for Western-style mathematics and for practical, vocational instruction. A textbook bureau was immediately established at Wat Bǫwǫnniwet, initially headed by *nai* Chu, parian, formerly a textbook compiler in the Education Department, who had been working as a curator in the National Museum since the closure of the Education Department's textbook bureau in 1897. For some reason, perhaps because nai Chu could not read English, Prince Wiwit Wanna-

13. Ibid.
14. NA 5 S, 11/12, 5, Wachirayan to Sommot, 22 Jan. 1899; 11/12, 6, Sommot to Wachirayan, 23 Jan.; 11/12, 7, Wachirayan to Sommot, 23 Jan.; 11/12, 8, "Provincial Education Directors who Attended on the King, Received Seals, and Left on 24 January 1899"; and 38/12, 37 and 38, Draft Ecclesiastical Credentials. The key phrase in the directors' credentials, which they were to present to officials—lay and religious—wherever they went, was the statement that "His Majesty could think of no better way to accomplish these ends [of educating the whole country] than by supporting the whole *Sangha* and extending to it the Royal Patronage so that it will have the strength to offer religious and academic instruction to the Buddhist population much more fully than before."

pricha, former director of the Education Department (1892–93) and then director of the Hospitals Department, was brought to the new office in May, after Damrong and the king obtained Čhaophraya Phatsakǫrawong's grudging assent to his transfer by pleading the national interest. By June, under his direction and Damrong's close guidance, the bureau had begun compiling textbooks for the study of physics and argriculture, and the textbook problem appeared to be under control.[15]

The problem of staffing the provincial schools was potentially much more difficult, for it was much easier to multiply copies of textbooks than to reproduce teachers from a standard model. In the 1880s the Education Department had shown a marked preference for lay teachers, and Prince Damrong's 1891 scheme for provincial education had been drawn up with lay teachers rather than teacher-monks primarily in mind. Even during the ministry of Čhaophraya Phatsakǫrawong in the years up to 1898, some of the provincial schools which continued to operate employed lay teachers, although they were usually located on the grounds of monasteries. The strongest arguments in favor of lay teachers were their generally stronger academic orientation and the greater interest they could bring to the secular school curriculum. The most potent argument against dependence upon them was simply their small numbers. By the mid-1890s Prince Wachirayan had found a satisfactory alternative, making use of monks educated in the government schools through Standard II to teach the Thai syllabus in the schools of the Mahamakut Academy, and at the same time using these monks to train others as teachers. In the strict sense of the word this was not teacher-training, for the education given the monks included no specifically pedagogical studies; but to the understaffed schools it was sufficient that these teacher-monks were

15. NA 5 S, 38/12, 28–30, correspondence between Damrong, the king, and Phatsakǫrawong concerning the founding of a new textbook bureau; and 4/12, 1–18, and 1/12, 47–49, correspondence between the king, Damrong, Wiwit, and Phatsakǫrawong concerning the compilation of textbooks, Jan.–Sept. 1899.

instructed in a modern curriculum, covering the same material as Standards I and II of the syllabus of the Education Department. This program was sufficiently developed by 1899 for its examination system and schools to be able to compete for students with the schools of the Education Department, and for the Ministry of Justice to send its young law students to Wat Bọwọnniwet for their Thai examinations before embarking upon their legal studies.[16] Prince Wachirayan thus had a ready-made device for providing the new provincial schools with teachers and had no occasion to consider using lay teachers.

In 1898 Prince Wachirayan had carried the Thammayut sect's educational system one step further by obtaining permission for monks to gain entrance to the Normal School, where they could have access to modern pedagogical training and where some could be trained as teachers of English. In 1899 this practice was further extended with provisions being made for large increases in the numbers of such monks brought from the provinces for the specific purpose of being trained as teachers, the first group of seven coming from monthon Chumphọn in April.[17] Čhaophraya Phatsakọrawong was not alone in judging the significance of this development: "When these monks really get spread out it will mean a great improvement in the independent [i.e. provincial] schools."[18]

The monks acting as provincial education and religion directors who had left Bangkok in January traveled over their jurisdictions through the hot and the first half of the rainy season of 1899. Accompanied by local civil and ecclesiastical authorities they called meetings of the Sangha in each locality they visited and explained the purpose of their visit, arguing the necessity for modernizing the traditional system of education and field-

16. NA 5 S, 1/12, 25, Wachirayan to King, 11 Sept. 1899.
17. NA 5 S, 12/12, 2–6, Correspondence, Damrong, King, and Phatsakọrawong, Apr. 1899; and 59/5, 2, Phatsakọrawong to Sommot, 1 Sept. 1899.
18. NA 5 S, 59/5, 2, Phatsakọrawong to Sommot, 1 Sept. 1899.

ing with varying degrees of success the objections and mis-apprehensions voiced by their audiences. In informal contacts they tried to persuade individual abbots to collect their monastery pupils into classes and to teach them using the government textbooks, which they distributed wherever they went. Their exhortations were given weight by their own religious and scholastic prestige, by their capacities as representatives of the king and Prince Wachirayan, and by their ability to assume the role of patron to provincial monasteries. The most important of their immediate tasks was through these contacts to survey the existing state of the provincial Sangha and its educational activities and to create or confirm an institutional structure in the provinces on which further educational labors might rest. Their reports of their first season's travels, drafted in August and forwarded to the king, presented for the first time to those directing the program an indication of the scope of the work that lay ahead and of the resources available for its accomplishment.

Of the eleven monthon surveyed in 1899, the directors had sufficient time to make relatively complete surveys in only three, Krungthep (the provinces surrounding Bangkok), Čhanthaburi, and Pračhinburi, all of which were relatively compact and had well-developed communications. In other monthon, such as Chumphǫn, Nakhǫn Sawan, Ratburi, and Nakhǫn Chaisi, the directors were able to visit only the main population centers, and could survey only a portion of the monasteries. Fragmentary as they were, however, the reports of the latter half of 1899 began to make clear the proportions of the problems with which the program had to deal. The directors made no attempt to investigate the large numbers of village monasteries in which no instruction whatever was offered and which later surveys were to reveal, but spoke more generally of the better-developed education of provincial towns and district centers. What they found was an improvement on the education of the seventeenth century, for they mentioned having seen

the old textbook *Čhindamani* in only one monastery. It had been
supplanted almost everywhere by the early nineteenth-century
Pathom k ka, which except in major towns must have been
available only in manuscript form. Excluding the provinces
adjacent to Bangkok, the educational developments of the
eighties and nineties had made virtually no impact, and only a
few more centrally located towns possessed even the printed
Munlabot banphakit of the seventies. Of interest is the information the directors provided concerning the distribution of more
recent teaching materials such as the *Munlabot* and the *Rapid
Readers.* Outside of monthon Krungthep, they were found in
four situations: (1) in the most important of the central provincial towns, and particularly in Phetburi, where the westernized
Bunnags long had held forth and where the monastery schools
long had had to compete with strong missionary schools; (2) in
areas where there had been government schools in the eighties,
such as Suphanburi and some areas of monthon Ratburi; (3) in
the major commercial centers, such as the tin center of Phuket
in the south and some of the teak and rice towns of the Central
Plains such as Tak and Uthaithani, areas of good communications and strong Western influences; and (4) in the monasteries
of the Thammayut sect, judging from the evidence on monthon
Ratburi, probably at least partly because of the necessarily
stronger links between these monasteries of a new sect and the
sect's headquarters in Bangkok.[19]

Intriguing are the figures given by Phra Methathammarot
on the relative satisfaction of monks and laymen alike with traditional education in monthon Nakhọn Sawan.[20] He reported
that at least one fourth of all the monks and laymen with whom
he had conversed desired a change in the educational patterns.
Who they were he does not say, nor are his figures necessarily

19. I have been able to obtain no information on the number and distribution of Thammayut sect monasteries in this period, but they probably
were very few in number. Of almost 400 monasteries in monthon Ratburi,
only 9 were Thammayut sect monasteries.

20. NA 5 S, 1/12, 38, Report, Nakhọn Sawan, 11 Sept. 1899.

representative; but other monks traveling in other provinces provided similar indications of the presence of at least a minority who desired educational changes for one reason or another, and it was at least partly on the basis of their presence in some localities that the directors in each monthon recommended the founding of new schools at specified monasteries and distributed to those monasteries the books they had brought from Bangkok.[21]

In addition to carrying out these surveys of the existing state of education and provincial attitudes toward change, the monthon directors went to the provinces as the agents of ecclesiastical change. Particularly in more remote areas where lines of contact between the provincial Sangha and Bangkok were vague or nonexistent and in which internal Sangha organization was poor, they assumed as part of their task the creation and building of local ecclesiastical hierarchies, appointing čhaokhana ("Sangha chairman") at the district and province levels and in some cases acting as čhaokhana monthon themselves. With the weakening of the tenuous ties that had bound the provincial Sangha to the Ministry of Public Instruction, the construction of such order in the provincial Sangha was indeed necessary to the success of their educational work. Inasmuch as most of the provincial directors were resident in Bangkok during most of the year, they had to leave behind them in the monthon sufficient organization to keep their work going on during the rainy and dry seasons. Their aims, however, went still deeper. They assumed the task of filling vacant ecclesiastical positions, of promoting religious instruction, and of strengthening monastic discipline and the religious life of the community in general. They would hardly have attempted less, being the men and the monks they were. In the long run, the religious activities of the directors came to assume as much significance as their educa-

21. Other factors on which they based such judgments were ease of access, availability of a suitable building for use as a school, proximity to local government offices, and the amount of local wealth that might be tapped in support of education.

tional endeavors, as a part of the general integration of the provinces into the life of the Thai nation.[22] In the short run, their efforts to create a strong and extensive religious hierarchy in the provinces contributed directly to the progress of educational development.

On a small scale, the first six months' work of the monthon directors was an unqualified success: by September 1899 they had founded 177 new schools in the provinces. Certainly no one was deluded into thinking that this many modern schools had been created almost overnight, and the directors were not equally hopeful about the prospects of each of the schools they had established. What they had done, in simplest terms, was to persuade 177 provincial abbots to have the *sitwat* of their monasteries taught in groups, using the government textbooks and submitting to regular examinations and inspection by the director and his designated local subordinates. This was, however, an enormous advance, for at a stroke they had introduced in the rural countryside a new concept of education, however subtly it may at first have been expressed. Through the textbooks and examinations they had imposed a new set of standards, common to the nation as a whole, on the traditional educational relationships between the rural population and the Sangha. They had introduced, or began soon to do so, new content into the old curriculum and, although still monks, had begun the secularization of provincial education and the centralization of government control over the provincial Sangha as an ecclesiastical institution.

With the arrival on his desk in August of the first of the provincial education reports, which he examined with great care, King Chulalongkorn immediately took steps to consolidate the results of the first season's labors as a basis upon which further work could proceed. After a lengthy correspondence

22. One of the most interesting, and one of the most easily accessible, of this first group of monthon reports is the one for Ratburi by Phra Amǫnmoli, printed in *PSSR,* pp. 73–84. Many of the others were published in *RKB.* Almost all are filed in NA 5 S, 1/12–46/12.

with Prince Wachirayan on points of detail,[23] general meetings of the directors, Prince Wachirayan, and officials of the Ministry of Public Instruction were held at the end of September 1899.[24] Discussion at the first of these sessions, on 30 September, centered on a question raised by virtually all of the directors, stated simply by Phra Methathammarot, director for monthon Nakhọn Sawan, in the following terms: "The work which I have done so far leads me to conclude that education and religious affairs are one and the same matter: each is dependent on the other. When the Sangha is in order, then may education progress."[25] The directors saw the necessity for a firm structuring of the Sangha from top to bottom, making ecclesiastical and civil jurisdictions coincide geographically as well at the subdistrict or commune (tambon) level as at the level of the monthon, thereby eliminating the older ecclesiastical hierarchy by which the Sangha was divided by sects (and even notional sects) without regard for geography. They wished to see all monks in any locality grouped under a single čhaokhana or "Sangha chairman," the čhaokhana tambon to be responsible to the čhaokhana amphoe, and so forth up to a national Sangha council. It seems clear that the absence of such clearly defined lines of authority had hindered the directors in their work, and their attempts to eliminate this problem undertaken at this time formed the basis of the Royal Ordinance on the Governance of the Sangha of 1902, which was to serve as the basis of Sangha organization for the next sixty years.[26]

The second meeting of the directors, held on 3 October, dealt

23. NA 5 S, 1/12, 3, King to Wachirayan, 20 Aug. 1899; 1/12, 5, Wachirayan to King, 22 Aug.; 1/12, 6, King to Wachirayan, 23 Aug.; 1/12, 8, Wachirayan to King, 30 Aug.; 1/12, 28, Wachirayan to King, 11 Sept. (printed in *PSSR*, pp. 67–68); 1/12, 28A, King to Wachirayan, 12 Sept.; 1/12, 29, King to Damrong, 12 Sept. (printed in ibid., pp. 68–69); and 1/12, 31, Wachirayan to Sommot, 14 Sept.

24. NA 5 S, 1/12, 58, Wachirayan to King, 18 Oct. 1899, enclosing 1/12, 59, Report of Meeting of Provincial Education Directors, 1899.

25. NA 5 S, 1/12, 38, Report, monthon Nakhọn Sawan, 1899.

26. See below, p. 304.

with specifically educational issues. The major item on the
agenda of this short meeting was to gain the directors' approval
for a revised version of the educational scheme of December,
the provisions of which called for the founding of one government school in each müang, together with public schools supported by local funds at the amphoe and tambon levels. The
directors were advised to appoint assistants in the müang and
amphoe, preferably men who would also serve as čhaokhana.
These recommendations were accepted without comment, and
the only recorded discussion of the meeting consisted of two
short exchanges at the end of the session: Prince Wachirayan
criticizing the Ministry of Public Instruction for the low state
in which he had found the provincial Sangha, a criticism pas-
sively accepted by Phatsakǫrawong; and a discussion of religious
education in the Northeastern town of Ubon, Wachirayan and
Damrong agreeing that that town should be made a special
center for Pali and religious studies.[27]

The conclusions and resolutions of the conference were by no
means either unexpected or remarkable, but its significance
should not be underestimated. The simple presence of these
ten ecclesiastical dignitaries seated around a table with government officials to discuss a common enterprise constituted an
important and, at that time, rare occurrence. In so meeting to
review the work of the past year and to plan their future common activities, to be undertaken in conjunction with official
policy and with the assistance of the Ministry of Interior, the
monkhood began its own modernization at the same time as it
began to play an active role in the modernization of the kingdom.

The problems of Prince Wachirayan's program of provincial
education after this first general meeting in 1899 were less
those of innovation than problems arising from the early reali-

27. The monthon director for monthon Isan had established a flourishing Pali school at Ubon in 1897, which had two teachers of Pali and three
of Thai. The school attracted 205 students in its first year. NA 5 S, 27/2,
Ministry of Instruction Report to Cabinet, n.d. (1897).

zation of the program's objectives. When the numbers of provincial schools and their students rose rapidly, as what had been only an idea in 1898 caught on, the demands of the program for funds and administrative skills troubled its directors and made increasingly attractive a return of their responsibilities to the Ministry of Public Instruction. At the same time, the success of the provincial program made more urgent such problems as educational integration and the formation of a national educational policy.

In the course of the year 1899/1900, education directors were sent to four additional monthon—Phuket, Isan (Ubon), Nakhǫn Ratchasima (Khorat), and Burapha (western Cambodia)[28]—thus covering all the Thai provinces of the country except monthon Phayap (Chiangmai) and Udǫn in the North and Northeast where special problems of language and ecclesiastical control prevented rapid action. This further extension into new territory, together with the expansion and consolidation of the first year's work in the rest of the kingdom, increased the program's financial requirements considerably. In January 1900, Damrong and Wachirayan submitted a budgetary request for 136,600 baht to the Ministry of Finance for anticipated expenditures in the year 1900/01.[29] The Ministry of Finance, undoubtedly due at least partly to the rationalizing and economizing zeal of the financial adviser, Rivett-Carnac, not only cut this sum but also transferred it to the budget of the Education Department. Prince Damrong, understandably, was furious, for a major objective in establishing the program was to remove provincial education from the purview of the

28. Of the monthon to which education directors were sent, only monthon Burapha specifically requested that one be appointed, in a lengthy petition presented to Chaophraya Phatsakǫrawong in November 1899. NA 5 S, 1/12, 76, Phatsakǫrawong to Sommot, 25 Nov. 1899. The director appointed, Phra Udǫnkhanarak, was apparently a Cambodian long resident in Bangkok, and he was chosen because he was "respected in the monthon." 1/12, 83, Damrong to King, 3 Dec. 1899; and 6/12, 2, Phatsakǫrawong to Sommot, 9 Dec. 1899.

29. NA 5 S, 2/12, 43, Report of Meeting of Provincial Education Directors, 9 and 16 Aug. 1900; and NA 5 Kh, 111/8, Budget, 1900/01.

Education Department.[30] In a position where appeal against
the decisions of the financial adviser was not only useless but
potentially harmful to the nation's repute, Damrong could only
acquiesce, the king advising him to take care to explain the
nature of the program carefully to the Education Department
and to try to make certain that Prince "Kittiyakǫn is given the
real responsibility, so that Čhaophraya Phat doesn't take it
over."[31] Financial responsibility for the program was thus
handed over to the Education Department while its administration remained in the hands of the monks, and the budgetary
problem continued. In August 1900 funds temporarily ran
out, causing the postponement of some directors' trips to the
provinces and holding up supplies of textbooks and support
for provincial schools.[32] Prince Wachirayan very rapidly grew
disgruntled over the bureaucratization of his program. Arguing
that the provincial education directors, as monks, "by definition" had an insufficient knowledge of government and worldly,
practical affairs, and that government was much more stable
and better organized than the Sangha, Wachirayan asked the
king whether the Ministry of Public Instruction might simply
take over the whole program, appointing education commissioners in the provinces similar to the financial and judicial commissioners then being appointed by the ministries of Finance
and Justice.[33] The king could admit the logic but not the
advisability of such a course. Replying in September, the king
admitted that "it would be appropriate for the program to be
handed over to the Ministry, but the Ministry is interested only
in mischieviously snatching it up, and once they are given charge
of it, its strength will be dissipated."[34] The possibility of transferring the program wholly to the ministry was discussed a few
days later at the provincial administration conference at the

30. NA 5 S, 1/12, 100, Damrong to King, 26 Mar. 1900, private.
31. NA 5 S, 1/12, 101, King to Damrong, 26 Mar. 1900, private.
32. NA 5 S, 2/12, 43, Report of Meeting, 9 and 16 Aug. 1900.
33. NA 5 S, 2/12, 44, Wachirayan to King, 20 Aug. 1900.
34. NA 5 S, 2/12, 48, King to Damrong, 15 Sept. 1900.

Ministry of Interior, but the idea was dropped and no such commissioners were appointed until after 1902.

Apart from the very considerable practical difficulties that engaged the provincial directors between September 1899 and April 1902, there was one notable general problem with which their success soon confronted them: the lack of strong popular support for public education in the provinces, particularly at lower social levels. The directors' first reports from the provinces in 1899 included many comments on this problem. Reporting from Chanthaburi in 1901, Phra Sukhunkhanaphon summed up the situation simply: "Apart from government officials and some Chinese, there is little faith in modern education. People think that there is no utility to be served in educating their children.[35] Two attempts at a solution to the problem were put forward in this period, first in 1900 with a specially phrased proposal for compulsory education, and then in 1901 with a suggestion that there should be greater inducements offered to generate popular enthusiasm for modern education.

In July 1900 Phra Thammatrailokachan, director for monthon Krungthep, proposed a unique form of compulsory education. He suggested that men presenting themselves for ordination as Buddhist monks must be literate and familiar with the basic precepts of their religion unless they lived in areas remote from any schools. If they were not so educated, they would not be allowed to enter the monkhood.[36] Phra Thammatrailok's suggestion was based on the simple fact that ordination as a Buddhist monk was widely regarded by Thai men as a religious, social, and cultural necessity, and that they would endure considerable sacrifice to achieve this end. Including this suggestion in his annual report, he submitted it to Prince Wachirayan, who

35. NA 5 S, 24/12, 9, Report, monthon Chanthaburi, end of R.S. 119 (Mar. 1901).

36. NA 5 S, 2/12, 55, Phra Thammatrailokachan to Phatsakǫrawong, 1 July 1900, copy. Wachirayan revealed that this idea was not a new one, having been proposed earlier by Phra Thepkrawi, director for monthon Krung Kao (Ayudhya). NA 5 S, 2/12, 54, Wachirayan to Phatsakǫrawong, 4 Sept. 1900, copy.

asked him to excise it from the report and put it forward orally, so as not to embarrass the government. Phra Thammatrailok refused to accept Prince Wachirayan's suggestion, and asked that the king rule upon it, which the king did, on the advice of Wachirayan and Phatsakǫrawong, asking that the suggestion be withdrawn. There were two strong arguments, religious and practical, against it. First, there was no sanction in the *Vinaya* for such a prescription forbidding the ordination of illiterates, and there thus could be no justification for doing so. Furthermore, the numbers of schools and teachers available simply could not begin to cope with the demand for education that such a prescription would induce, and the provinces surrounding Bangkok were far better provided in this manner than the rest of the country. The king praised Phra Thammatrailok's intentions, but agreed with the ministry and Wachirayan that this was neither the time nor an appropriate method for achieving universal primary education.[37]

A year later, another attempt was made to achieve the same end by offering an inducement to attract students to the schools and keep them there. Phra Amǫnmoli, director for monthon Ratburi and Nakhǫn Chaisi, suggested in September 1901 that students who had finished the primary syllabus (Standard I) be exempted from paying the annual head tax of six baht during their eighteenth year, and secondary graduates exempted in their eighteenth and nineteenth years.[38] Princes Damrong and Wachirayan tentatively agreed that some measure of this sort was desirable but that safeguards would have to be provided for in the examination code of 1891 which permanently exempted Standard II graduates from compulsory labor or military service or monetary payment in lieu of it. The provincial education system, however, hardly approached the level of Standard

37. NA 5 S, 2/12, 54, Wachirayan to Phatsakǫrawong, 4 Sept. 1900, copy; 2/12, 56, Kittiyakǫn to Phatsakǫrawong, 7 Sept., copy; 2/12, 53, Phatsakǫrawong to Sommot, 25 Sept.; and 2/12, 60, King to Phatsakǫrawong, 14 Oct.

38. NA 5 Q, 5/2 I, Report, *Thetsaphiban Conference,* 1901, meeting of 14 Sept.

II defined by the examination code and in practice formed a separate educational system altogether. When nothing came of the September discussions, Prince Wachirayan raised the matter again with Prince Kittiyakǫn in November, and Kittiyakǫn succeeded in having the matter discussed by the Cabinet on 9 December 1901. The ministers could agree only to continue to grant exemptions to graduates of Standard II as had hitherto been the case.[39] Popular demand and support for provincial education thus was left to develop of its own accord, without either compulsion or inducements from the government.

Three years after having assumed the task of organizing and promoting educational development and religious life in the provinces of Thailand, Prince Wachirayan submitted to the king his second and final report on the work of the program.[40] After dealing briefly with the state of the Sangha and noting that monastic reorganization in one monthon had been completed with the installation of a local, resident čhaokhana monthon in Phitsanulok, Wachirayan devoted the bulk of his report to his educational work. He pointed out that, beginning with virtually nothing, 177 new schools had been founded in the first year's operations, to which were added an additional 154 by 1901, while the number of students attending the new schools jumped from 790 in 1898 to 6,183 in 1899/1900 and 12,062 in 1900/01. For the most part, these schools were staffed by resident monks, but the directors had also chosen thirty-eight provincial monks and novices for teacher training in Bangkok during the period.[41] Generous scales of financial support for government schools in the towns and district cen-

39. NA 5 S, 98/5, 4, Wachirayan to Kittiyakǫn, 12 Nov. 1901; 98/5, 2, Kittiyakǫn to Sommot, 6 Dec.; 98/5, 1, King's minute on 98/5, 2; and 98/5, 6, Excerpts from Minutes of Cabinet Meeting, 9 Dec.

40. NA 5 S, 35/12, 1, Summary Report of Prince Wachirayan on Provincial Education and Religion for 1898/99 and 1899/1900, 20 Nov. 1901.

41. NA 5 S, 35/12, 3, Report of Prince Wachirayan, Appendix H. These monks and novices had come from monthon Chumphǫn (10), Čhanthaburi (4), Ratburi (2), Phitsanulok (8), Krung Kao (4) and Isan (4).

ters had been instituted in 1899/1900, which ranged from grants of 960 baht per year to müang schools with more than one hundred pupils down to 240 baht per year to ordinary monastery schools with enrollments between fifty and seventy-five.[42] To raise and maintain the standards of these schools, the program had arranged for the publication of textbooks for free distribution or commercial sale, depending on local policy, as a result of which action almost 13,000 copies of the first volume of the *Rapid Reader* were sent to the provinces in 1899/1900 and an additional 15,000 in the following year.[43] The fact that more than twice as many books were sent into the provinces than there were students in government schools would indicate that large numbers of these were replacing, at long last, the *Pathom k ka* in informal instruction and unrecognized schools. In addition, in 1899/1900 the annual Mahamakut Academy examinations were held in the provinces and were taken by 988 students in monthon Krungthep, Krung Kao (Ayudhya), Nakhǫn Sawan, and Čhanthaburi, as well as by an additional seventy-one students in Ubon.[44] The failure rates at each level suggest that standards were kept relatively high.[45]

Although the program directed by Prince Wachirayan and his colleagues had its origins at least partially in a disagreement with the Education Department over the question of quality in the schools, with Wachirayan and Damrong taking the view that in the initial stages quantity was more important than quality and starting more important than waiting indeterminately, Wachirayan showed that he was not willing to ignore the qualitative problems and he faced them resolutely. Naturally he had to sacrifice quality to a considerable extent in the be-

---

42. NA 5 S, 32/12, 3, Report of Prince Wachirayan, Appendix I.

43. NA 5 S, 35/12, 3, Report of Prince Wachirayan, Appendix J.

44. NA 5 S, 35/12, 3, Report of Prince Wachirayan, Appendix F; and, for Ubon, 2/12, 16, Wachirayan to Sommot, 30 May 1900, and 2/12, 20, Two-Year Comparison of Examination Results, Ubon, 1899/1900 and 1900/1901.

45. Overall failure rate was 45 percent, while it ranged from 23 percent at the lower levels to 68 percent at the highest levels.

ginning. His whole strategy was founded on the belief that
monastery schools, however low their quality, had to form
the starting point for the spread of modern education in the
provinces, and he was not given unlimited funds with which
to provide them with materials and personnel to upgrade their
standards. It may be that the end result was all the better for
this beginning. From the Sangha's viewpoint it was certainly
a wise political strategy. Once Wachirayan had introduced into
the provincial monasteries up-to-date printed textbooks, examinations, and new teachers, it was up to the town and village
monks themselves to decide whether to accept them or to resist.
Wachirayan staked the positions and prestige of his brother
monks and himself on his belief that they would respond positively, and time was to prove him right; but time also reminded
him that his was a temporary, catalytic role, and that the con-
summation of his policies ultimately must rest with professional
educators and the Ministry of Public Instruction.

THE KING AND PHRAYA WISUT, 1898–1899

If it was necessary that responsibility for provincial education should be entrusted to Prince Wachirayan until such time
as the Ministry of Public Instruction was deemed capable of
doing justice to that work, it was no less vital that steps should
be taken both to satisfy other needs beyond the resources of the
ministry and to implement such political changes as would make
a reform of the ministry possible. The Thai ambassador in
London, Phraya Wisut Suriyasak, late in 1897 had become
the king's instrument in setting this process of change in motion, and it is around him that much of the political maneuver-
ing centered and from him that a steady flow of new educational
ideas reached the king.

The central theme in the relationship of the king and Phraya
Wisut between late 1898 and the summer of 1899 was Thailand's critical shortage of skilled manpower—what the king

referred to as a "poverty of men."[46] By the late 1890s the process of administrative reform and modernization was well under
way, and the appetite of the new ministries for educated men
for new posts was ravenous. Prince Damrong required scores
of new district officers each year; the Ministry of Justice wanted
trained lawyers and judges; each ministry felt the problem.
The king found it ignominious that the Bangkok police force
was compelled to rely upon Indian men and European officers.
The practice of hiring foreign advisers, thought the king, was
dangerous and at best only an expedient. He was willing to
acknowledge their ability, their honesty and loyalty, but ultimately they had to be considered "eating friends and not dying
friends," and no more could be expected of them. The trouble
with employing foreign advisers, he explained to Phraya Wisut,
was that too often they tended to become more than advisers
and took over the departments to which they had been assigned,
because the Thai with whom they worked were capable neither
of controlling them nor of learning from them. The king was
acutely aware of the "difficulties in China concerning the hiring
of Westerners, which has almost become an 'international question' and will spread to our country."

For the dearth of good men and the dangers of employing
foreign advisers, there was, he argued, only one solution: "the
education of the Thai, who are the rulers [or owners, *chao*]
of the country." The king castigated the Ministry of Public
Instruction for failing to achieve this solution, primarily because
it persisted in blindly borrowing forms and practices from the
West, which he likened to the man who, on moving into the
jungle, decided to build a brick house and set about fashioning
mortar and bricks from the earth. What was needed, he explained, was not bricks but rather huts and wooden shelters
which could be constructed quickly and improved later; and
Čhaophraya Phatsakǫrawong was not the man for such a temporizing course. Until educational development caught up with

46. King to Wisut, 21 Jan. 1899, printed in Chulalongkorn and
Phrasadet, *Phraratchahatlekha*, pp. 292–93.

the kingdom's manpower needs, the shortage of trained men and the necessity of employing foreign advisers would continue. Meanwhile, two general lines of approach could be taken. First, Prince Wachirayan's program of provincial education could set about providing a broader base of mass elementary education, while the ministry was allowed to develop upper primary and secondary education in Bangkok, and a "civil service school" could be established to take the products of these schools and turn them into civil servants with a modicum of expertise in the shortest time possible. Second, steps had to be taken to prepare for the reform of the Ministry of Public Instruction. The king had more than a general conviction that this was needed: he had a clear idea of who was to accomplish it, and this person was none other than Phraya Wisut. Certainly, he explained, Wisut's position as a diplomatic representative of the Thai government was an important one, but "if we have domestic chaos, how can our foreign position improve?"[47]

As of January 1899, four facets of the general problem of providing the country with more effective education were perceived by the king. At bottom there was the general problem of providing the whole (male) population with a more adequate and modern education, paying special attention to training men for the new jobs and occupations of a new age. A second task was specifically to strengthen education for the civil service. The third and fourth were two faces of the same coin. The old leadership in the Ministry of Public Instruction needed to be provided temporarily with expert foreign advice in the person of a foreign adviser, while ultimately the leadership in the ministry had to be changed and Phraya Wisut and others like him substituted for the men of the "old school." For his part, Phraya Wisut directly reflected these four concerns of the king in their correspondence in 1898–99, and although each letter from each man often reflected more than one of the four themes, these progressed and ripened in logical order beginning with the general question of educational reform and ending

47. Ibid.

with the recall of Wisut from London to assume personally specialized educational tasks.

After undertaking investigations in Britain and the United States, Wisut submitted to the king in January 1899 a comprehensive scheme for establishing vocational schools in Thailand, an aspect of education that had been notably missing from his report of the previous year.[48] Strongly influenced by contemporary European social reformers, he cast his argument primarily in moral terms, arguing that the government's attitude toward popular morality could not be merely repressive and negative, devoted only to the suppression of crime and the condemnation of antisocial behavior. It was necessary that the government offer alternatives to such behavior by providing means by which young men might be prepared for honest and usefully productive lives. To this end, he recommended that vocational schools be established under the auspices of local government and ad hoc committees, perhaps under the patronage of Crown Prince Vajiravudh. He recommended that one such "industrial school" be founded immediately in Bangkok to offer instruction in the crafts, agriculture, and domestic arts, part of the expenses of the school to be met by the sale of the students' work. The importance of his proposals, the first concrete plans for vocational education in Thailand,[49] lay not so much in their immediate embodiment in any actual institutions, for none were to be founded for some years, but rather in their expression of a general line of thought, predominantly moral in its bias but containing also a strongly realistic approach to developing problems of the economy and society. His proposals initially were

48. NA 5 S, 31/5, 51, dated 19 Jan. 1899, but enclosed with 31/5, 41, Wisut to King, 1 Jan. 1899. These proposals are accurately and succinctly summarized in Praphat, *Čhaophraya phrasadet,* pp. 260–70.

49. See Čharun Wongsayan and Pramot Chaiyakit, *Khwampenma khǫng laksut achiwasüksa* (Bangkok, 1961), pp. 4–6, who date the vocational curriculum from Wisut's 1898 proposals, which called generally for some vocational education. On these grounds, an equally strong case could be made for dating the curriculum from the 1888 report on Japanese education.

well received, being given by the king for comment not to the Ministry of Public Instruction but rather to Damrong and Wachirayan, who recommended that they be implemented; but, owing to the lack of a suitable director for the project, it was shelved indefinitely by August 1899.[50]

Following his discussion with Phraya Wisut in January of that year, the king was much more immediately concerned with establishing a civil service school, and he solicited Prince Damrong's advice on the matter. Damrong recommended that the school be founded initially to train men for the service of the Ministry of Interior though it might later be expanded to train men for other ministries as well, and the king agreed to this general recommendation.[51] In February Wisut responded to the king's concern somewhat more specifically, to the extent of estimating the numbers of chairs, desks, and blackboards the school might require and sketching its curriculum and its relationship with the Education Department.[52] He envisaged an enrollment of about fifty pupils, some of whom might board at the school, and whose entrance qualifications would be minimal. He urged that all its students should be presented at court as royal pages, immediately upon enrollment if they were of good family background, or after preliminary preparation at the school if this was thought necessary. Such a provision would work to strengthen the personal relationship between the king and his officers and was strongly approved by Prince Damrong.[53] The school's curriculum would be as much practical

50. NA 5 S, 54/5, 54, King to Sommot, n.d. (May 1899?). See also 54/5, 78, Wachirayan to Sommot, 13 May 1899, requesting a copy of the scheme and its cover letter; and 54/5, 85, King to Wisut, 7 Aug. 1899, printed in Chulalongkorn and Phrasadet, *Phraratchahatlekha*, p. 344.

51. NA 5 S, 1/5, 1, Damrong to King, 20 Feb. 1899; and 1/5, 8, King to Damrong, 21 Feb. 1899.

52. NA 5 S, 54/5, 20, "Scheme for Establishing a Civil Service Training College," enclosed in 54/5, 1, Wisut to King, 16 and 22 Mar. 1899.

53. Prince Damrong Rajanubhab, "Rüang rongrian mahatlek luang," in Damrong, *Nithan borannakhadi (bang rüang)* (Bangkok, 1956), pp. 88–91. This account of the founding of the school, written many years later, differs from the documents on several significant points, but most

as academic, as much attention being given to practical instruction in the work of the various ministries as in the study of geography, history, law, economics, logic, and natural sciences. Wisut recommended that Sanan Thephatsadin na Ayutthaya (later Čhaophraya Thammasakmontri), who had just returned to Bangkok after completing a teacher-training course in England, be made director of the school while Wisut himself promised to continue to advise the project.[54]

Wisut's recommendations, sent by sea from London in February, did not reach Bangkok until early May, and in the interval Prince Damrong grew despairingly impatient. Writing to Wisut at the end of April,[55] Damrong impressed upon him the vital necessity of bringing the school quickly into operation. Thailand's precarious international position made it necessary, he explained, to "rush about making improvements in the country. If we stopped or curtailed these or were slow in our efforts at any time it would be dangerous." All his own plans for the Ministry of Interior were severely jeopardized by the lack of educated men to fill newly created positions. "As I write this letter," he added, "I am in need of two High Commissioners, not less than five governors, not less than fifteen deputy governors, and, as for district officers, who are as important nowadays as *čhaomüang* [traditional-style governors], I need about thirty. I still cannot find them." Other ministries were in difficulties no less serious. He stated that were the king to allow him to do so he would resign to return to the field of education, which was the only solution to such problems. Clearly educational reform required new and firm direction, and Prince Damrong hinted at the choice the king might make: "If His

___

markedly on the role played by Phraya Wisut in the first half of 1899. I have kept to the documents.

54. NA 5 S, 54/5, 20, "Scheme for Establishing a Civil Service Training College."

55. NA 5 S, 54/5, 49, Damrong to Wisut, 20 Apr. 1899; copy enclosed in 54/5, 47, Damrong to King, 6 June 1899.

majesty pleases to give you educational responsibilities, I would hope that you would not shun the most important work which you could do."

Damrong's anxiety was only slightly relieved by the receipt of Wisut's proposals for a civil service school two weeks later, and he was not completely satisfied with the scheme.[56] In particular, he opposed Wisut's suggestions that the school from the beginning should be designed to serve the civil service in general, that it should work closely with the Education Department, and that Nai Sanan should be appointed its director. In effect, he argued that Wisut simply was not aware of the political situation which, in the view of Damrong and the king, hindered educational reform. "On examination," he added, "it appears that Phraya Wisut does not see the urgency and importance of education in Thailand to the extent that I do." Nai Sanan and the Education Department could not be depended upon to make a success of the school, and therefore Damrong argued that the only possible course was to create the civil service school fully within the Ministry of Interior, with Damrong himself acting as director until such time as Phraya Wisut could assume the personal direction of the school in preparation for the wider educational responsibilities for which both Damrong and the king had long judged him suited.

The king appears to have mentioned the possibility of recalling Wisut from London for appointment as director of the Education Department as early as 1897, and he reminded Wisut of this conversation early in 1899.[57] Wisut long resisted this and similar suggestions, arguing that he could offer the king educational advice as well from abroad as from a post in Bangkok,[58] and he attempted to build up a reasoned argument as

56. NA 5 S, 54/5, 79, Damrong to King, 8 May 1899.

57. King to Wisut, 21 Jan. 1899, printed in Chulalongkorn and Phrasadet, *Phraratchahatlekha,* p. 299.

58. NA 5 S, 1/5, 4, Wisut to Damrong, 20 Jan. 1899; 1/5, 1, Damrong to King, 20 Feb. 1899; and King to Wisut, 11 July 1899, printed in Chulalongkorn and Phrasadet, *Phraratchahatlekha,* p. 337.

to why he should remain at his current post.[59] Damrong's despairing letter of 20 April 1899, offering to resign in order to enter the educational service, finally forced Wisut's acquiescence in their wishes; on 1 June he cabled Prince Damrong to state that if no other could be "spared for education" he would agree to return to Bangkok for that post.[60] Accordingly, a month later the king ordered his recall from London in order to organize the Civil Service School.[61] Writing privately to Wisut, however, the king indicated that the Civil Service School was not all that he had in mind for him. Although "initially it would not be generally advisable for you to get mixed up with the Education Department . . . later your responsibilities gradually can be expanded."[62] Toward the end of the year Wisut returned to Bangkok, and by the end of the Siamese year in April the Civil Service School had begun operation. By the end of 1900 it already had graduated seventeen young men for service in the Ministry of Interior and had then an enrollment of 182.[63]

Wisut's transformation from Thai ambassador in London to director of the Civil Service School was indeed radical, but it was hardly unnatural. Through most of his career, Wisut had a strong concern for education. His special responsibilities for the education of the king's sons in Europe, his unchallenged ability, and the close and candid relationship he enjoyed with the king undoubtedly marked him for an important educational post in Bangkok. His recall in 1899 for service as director of the Civil Service School was only an intermediate stopping

59. NA 5 S, 54/5, 86, Wisut to King, 7 Mar. 1899, private; printed in Praphat, *Chaophraya phrasadet*, pp. 286–98.

60. NA 5 S, 54/5, 53, Wisut to Damrong, 1 June 1899, telegram in English.

61. NA 5 S, 54/5, 111, King to Devawongse, 8 July 1899; 54/5, 114, King to Damrong, 8 July 1899; and 54/5, 118, Sommot to Wisut, n.d., telegram in English.

62. NA 5 S, 54/5, 120, King to Wisut, 10 July 1899, printed in Chulalongkorn and Phrasadet, *Phraratchahatlekha*, pp. 335–36.

63. NA 5 S, 1/5, 14, Report, Civil Service School, 25 Mar. 1901, signed by Damrong, "in charge," and Wisut, "Director."

point between the embassy and the Ministry of Public Instruction, dictated by two conditions peculiar to the times. First,
Chulalongkorn simply was not free to engage and dismiss his
Cabinet ministers at will; nor, in this particular case, was he
able to thrust aside his son, Prince Kittiyakǫn, to make room
for Wisut in the Education Department. Even if another attractive position could have been found for Kittiyakǫn in another
ministry at this moment, Chulalongkorn hardly could have expected Phatsakǫrawong and Wisut to have worked well together, especially as Wisut unmistakably had antagonized the
čhaophraya with his general recommendations on education in
June 1898. Second, the specific occasion for recalling Wisut, the
foundation of the Civil Service School, was not simply an expedient though it may appear as one. The problems which that
institution was intended to meet were of intense concern to the
Thai government. For Thailand as for China this was the
period of the "scramble for concessions," which in Thailand
took the form of attempts by foreign powers to place their
nationals in advisory positions throughout the Thai government.[64] Viewing the dangers in this situation, the king and
Damrong were agreed in arguing that it could be alleviated
only by training Thai to fill these positions so coveted by the
farang. Few could have been better qualified to assume this
task than Phraya Wisut, who during the previous six years had
been engaged in superintending the education of the next royal
generation. For him, his appointment to the Civil Service School
could be viewed as simply a change in raw materials, from which
he could be expected to produce the same end product—educated Thai capable of ruling Thailand sufficiently well to prevent the West from taking over.

In the light of these considerations it is highly ironic that
one of Phraya Wisut's last tasks in London was to accomplish
precisely what he was being returned to Bangkok to prevent:

64. See, for example, Chandran Mohandas Jeshurun, "British Policy
Towards Siam, 1893–1902" (M.A. thesis, University of Malaya, Kuala
Lumpur, 1964), ch. VI.

engaging a foreign adviser, this time for the Ministry of Public Instruction. The decision to hire an adviser for the ministry seems to have originated in the king's response to Wisut's 1898 report, when in passing he suggested that "what we need is a teacher who really knows; not someone to come and himself teach [in the schools], but rather someone to come and organize education, as an 'adviser' to the Minister or the Director of the Education Department."[65] He explained to Wisut that those Thai who had studied abroad had had only experience as students, and not as teachers or educational administrators. An adviser with administrative experience, he thought, might be able to "command more influence and respect than the Minister [Phatsakǫrawong], who as everyone knows studied only three years abroad, or the Director of the Education Department, who is just a boy out of school." The king asked Wisut to investigate whether such a person might be found, expressed the hope that he might be appointed before April 1899, and added that he would not be informing the ministry of this matter for the time being.

It was only in October 1898 that Wisut finally responded to this request, forwarding for the king's approval the name of the head of the Education Department of British Burma, John Van Someren Pope.[66] The financial adviser, Rivett-Carnac, dissuaded the king from approving Pope's appointment on the grounds that Pope was "quite elderly" and was demanding too high a salary, and the king then ordered Wisut to seek a younger man at a salary not in excess of £1,500, adding incidentally that Wisut should keep the Ministry of Public Instruction informed of his actions in the matter.[67] Wisut thus renewed his

65. King to Wisut, 11 June 1898, printed in Chulalongkorn and Phrasadet, *Phraratchahatlekha*, pp. 262–63.
66. NA 5 B, 45/37, 1, Wisut to King, 26 Oct. 1898.
67. NA 5 B, 45/37, 3, King to Sommot, 24 Dec. 1898; and 45/37, 4, Sommot to Wisut, 24 Dec. 1898, telegram. Rivett-Carnac incorrectly informed the king that Pope was demanding £2,500 per annum, while his most recent salary in Burma was only £1,300. The reason the king learned of the matter only from Rivett-Carnac was that Wisut's letter of 26 October

search for an adviser in January 1899, acting through the British Foreign Office.[68] By February he felt he had found the ideal man for the job, J. G. D. Campbell, a young man highly recommended by the British Ministry of Education who was willing to accept a salary of £1,200 on a two-year contract.[69] Instead of cabling the king this news, as instructed, however, he posted the letter by sea-mail, causing no end of confusion, embarrassment, and delay.[70] Having had no response from Bangkok by mid-May, he telegraphed requesting an immediate response,[71] only to learn that, though the king approved of Campbell, news of his appointment had not reached Bangkok in time for it to be included in the ministry's budget for the current year which began in April, and that he could not therefore be engaged before April 1900.[72] Wisut could not accept this situation, as he had demanded urgent action from the British government to obtain its recommendation, and he accordingly concluded a contract with Campbell as "Educational Adviser for the Education Department of the Siamese Government" on 17 June 1899, presenting his action to the king as a fait accompli.[73] The terms of this engagement, drawn up without reference to the Ministry of Public Instruction, vaguely required that Campbell agree

---

"arrived at a time when [he] was very busy, and [he] did not have time to read it until Mr. Carnac saw the newspapers and telegraphed." 45/37, 2, King to Wisut, 3 Feb. 1899.

68. NA 5 B, 45/37, 19, "Proposed Appointment of Educational Adviser to the Siamese Government," submitted to the British Foreign Office following their request of 9 Feb. 1899 for further details concerning the position first mentioned in Wisut to Salisbury, 10 Jan. 1899; 45/37, 10, copy.

69. NA 5 B, 45/37, 50, Wisut to King, 24 Mar. 1899.

70. NA 5 B, 45/37, 2, King to Wisut, 3 Feb. 1899, printed in Chulalongkorn and Phrasadet, *Phraratchahatlekha*, p. 306.

71. NA 5 B, 45/37, 24, Wisut to Sommot, 13 May 1899, telegram.

72. NA 5 B, 45/37, 25, Sommot to Wisut, 16 May 1899, telegram.

73. NA 5 B, 45/37, 26, Wisut to Sommot, 18 May 1899, telegram; 45/37, 27, Wisut to King, 19 May 1899, private; 45/37, 41, Sommot to Wisut, 19 May, telegram; and 45/37, 54, Agreement between J. G. D. Campbell and the Siamese Government, 17 June 1899, copy.

. . . to give his best consideration to the various matters connected with the Education Department (whether regarding
its organization or its administration) which may be brought
under his notice and will give such advice and assistance
in dealing with these matters as will to the best of his belief conduce to the successful working of the Department.
With this object he will consult with the Minister of Education for the time being and will do his utmost to see that
the instructions issued by the Minister are carried out whether
in Bangkok itself or in the provinces which he may be called
upon to visit in the performance of his duties or elsewhere.[74]

It was only in July that funds were definitely made available
for Campbell's post and Wisut accordingly notified[75] and it was
not until the last week of August that the Ministry of Public
Instruction learned that an adviser had been engaged to assist
it in its work.[76] Well might Chaophraya Phatsakǫrawong
have been incensed, as indeed he was. Wisut wisely uttered the
hope that the detailed story of the episode would not be made
public.[77]

Phraya Wisut's efforts during this year of change were not
crowned by unqualified success. He had handled the Campbell
affair badly, and for this was administered a mild rebuke by
the king.[78] His ideas on vocational education had come to
nothing. He had, however, accomplished the two things closest
to the king's heart at the time. He had been a catalyst for the
civil service school project and he had obtained for the Ministry

74. NA 5 B, 45/37, 54, Agreement between Campbell and the Siamese
Government, 17 June 1899, copy.
75. NA 5 B, 45/37, 33, Mahis to King, 13 July 1899; and 45/37, 35,
Sommot to Wisut, 15 July 1899, telegram.
76. NA 5 B, 45/37, 58, Phatsakǫrawong to Sommot, 28 Aug. 1899;
45/37, 56, Sommot to Phatsakǫrawong, 26 Aug.; and 45/37, 57, King's
minute on 45/37, 58.
77. NA 5 B, 45/37, 68, Wisut to Sommot, 7 Aug. 1899.
78. NA 5 B, 45/37, 37, King's memo. to Sommot, n.d., in which he
instructed Sommot to tell Wisut that "although his agitation worked this
time, it's not something which can be done all the time."

of Public Instruction a foreign adviser. In broader terms, his role in the educational ferment of the time was a decisive one. It had been the king's conversations with Wisut in London late in 1897 that had begun this whole process of rethinking educational policy and practice, and the two most important reports submitted by him during this period, the general report on education of April 1898, and the report on the civil service school of March 1899, both served to impart the additional momentum necessary to set in motion badly needed reforms. The importance of Wisut's role was recognized by the king on three occasions: first in London, when the king marked him for a future career in the Education Department; then in February 1899, when the king told him that "you are the spark which has set this off";[79] and finally in July 1899, when Chulalongkorn decided to recall Wisut from London, for the immediate purpose of getting the urgently required civil service school going but ultimately to take in hand the reform of the Education Department. Until the latter was possible Wisut had provided the king with two temporary solutions, the civil service school and an adviser for the seemingly moribund ministry. These were, however, only expedients, and there can have been no doubt in the minds of the king, Damrong, Wachirayan, and Wisut himself that a permanent solution for the educational crisis was not far distant and awaited only favorable circumstances and sufficient right-minded men to take the work in hand.[80]

THE MINISTRY OF PUBLIC INSTRUCTION

The Ministry of Public Instruction in the four years spanning the turn of the century left a mixed record of success and failure. It entered the period on the heels of one failure, the loss of its provincial education work which was transferred to Prince Wachirayan, and in the following year it was treated with little

79. King to Wisut, 25 Feb. 1899, printed in Chulalongkorn and Phrasadet, *Phraratchahatlekha,* p. 312.
80. See Ibid.

more than contempt by the king, who relied increasingly upon men outside the ministry for educational advice and then suddennly imposed a foreign adviser on the ministry in the summer of 1899. On the other hand, the ministry did benefit from a generally heightened interest in education, as a result of which the Cabinet became increasingly willing to grant large increases in its budgets. Signally threatened by the activities of Wachirayan, Damrong, and Wisut, Čhaophraya Phat and Kittiyakǫn unquestionably were in a position where they had to justify their own positions and policies. By deed and argument they attempted to do so.

In July of 1899, less than a year after the transfer of the ministry's responsibilities for provincial education to Prince Wachirayan, Čhaophraya Phatsakǫrawong and Prince Kittiyakǫn submitted to the king a report on their activities in the year R.S. 117 (1898/99), the only such report for the decade of the čhaophraya's ministry.[81] This report recorded a number of innovations made during the course of the year. Their administrative offices had been reorganized, six new schools were established in Bangkok, the mid-year and year-end examinations had proceeded with favorable results, the Normal School had graduated eleven new teachers, government schools were being equipped with blackboards and new furniture, a number of new textbooks were compiled and published, a major new private school had been established in Thonburi with government aid,[82] and the long-awaited Standard III syllabus had at last been issued. Despite these accomplishments, however, it is remarkable how little change in the thinking of the ministry the report actually reflects. Prince Kittiyakǫn, over whose signature the report appears, gave no indication that the growing concerns of the king in previous years—education to Western

81. NA 5 S, 95/5, 2, Report, Educ. Dept., 1898/99, dated 14 July 1899, and enclosed in 95/5, 1, Phatsakǫrawong to Sommot, 20 July 1899.

82. On this school, at Wat Anongkharam, see Phra Sakhǫnratrüangyot, comp., "Prawat kansüksa nangsü thai," in *Prawat kansatsanasüksa-kansüksa nangsü thai khǫng wat anongkharam* (Bangkok, 1957), pp. 25–40.

standards and for the civil service—had had any effect on the activities of his department, although had he chosen to do so he could at least have argued a strong case for the former, and he failed to see the significance of such real improvements as the Standard III curriculum, which he mentioned at the end of a long list of minor changes. The bulk of the report was filled with dreary statistics—the sort for which the ministry had more than once been criticized in the past—such as a detailed tabulation of the numbers of letters sent and received by the departmental office. One appendix to the report listed ten new textbooks compiled during the year, all of them precisely of the type the absence of which the king had decried in the previous year,[83] yet no attempt was made to call attention to them. Instead, the prince claimed as his major accomplishment the fact that school children at last were clean and well dressed, as "a result of the discipline of the schools." Such, however, were hardly the most urgent of the king's educational concerns, and J. G. D. Campbell was hired primarily to direct the ministry's attention to more relevant and urgent requirements.

Campbell's appointment as educational adviser caught the ministry completely unawares in August 1899. Responding to the news, Chaophraya Phatsakǫrawong could hardly conceal his hostility to the appointment.[84] He had not known the appointment would be made, had not provided funds for it in the budget, and in searching for housing for Campbell did not even know whether Campbell had a family. But even more the minister resented the implied denigration of his own work:

> Phraya Wisut's contracting for the services of Mr. Campbell without the knowledge of the Ministry of Public Instruction, without inquiring into our opinions on education and the changes and improvements which have been made by the Education Department during the past two years will cause someone coming from England considerable difficulty.

83. NA 5 S, 13/5, 45, King to Phatsakǫrawong, 21 July 1898.
84. NA 5 B, 45/37, 58, Phatsakǫrawong to Sommot, 28 Aug. 1899.

Writing to the king, he warned that Campbell would require
a considerable period of time to learn the Thai language and
familiarize himself with the state of education in Siam before
he could advise the ministry reasonably. He expressed a fear
that Campbell's presence would be resented by the small band
of Englishmen already working in the ministry, who by virtue
of long experience in Siam were better suited to advise him;
and he pointedly wondered how the adviser could be given authority over provincial education when this was no longer the
responsibility of the Education Department. In addition to being
unwanted, in the minister's view the adviser was also unneeded,
since "if we are already doing sufficiently useful work, that is
enough." "As I observe that, in his contract we have given
Mr. Campbell to understand that we have in Bangkok no system of education whatever," Phatsakǫrawong added, "I therefore take this opportunity to call our current work to your
attention."

Given the currency of such feelings as these in the ministry,
Campbell hardly could have expected a warm welcome on his
arrival in November or an easy working relationship with his
colleagues; yet there is no indication in the record of his two-
year service that his activities were prejudiced by conflict or
obstruction. To the mutual benefit of the ministry, the country,
and himself personally, Campbell assumed with some success
two roles: defender of the ministry against the budget-slashing
propensities of the Ministry of Finance and its British adviser,
and promoter of English education for Bangkok's upper classes.

Barely a month after arriving in Bangkok, Campbell was
called upon by the minister to examine the budget estimates
of the Education Department and comment upon them. He
responded vigorously, submitting through Phatsakǫrawong to
the king a reasoned argument for a substantial increase in the
department's budget, specifically for the establishment of six
new primary schools in Bangkok, an increased pay scale for
teachers, new buildings and staff for Suankulap School, and for
the inauguration of manual training and technical instruction in

the schools so that "the old industries of the country [could] be revived and Siam take its proper place among the commercial and manufacturing countries of the world.[85] He closed his remarks by arguing that the ministry's budgetary proposals formed "a connected whole & are part of one systematic scheme," and that it would therefore be a mistaken policy on the part of the government were it to accept some of these recommendations and reject others. Pointedly he added, "I should therefore be bound to consider that the government placed but little confidence in my advice, if they thought fit to reject them."

Campbell's recommendations undoubtedly pleased his immediate superiors in the ministry but they probably put the rest of the government, and particularly the Ministry of Finance, in a difficult position. The British adviser to the Ministry of Finance, Rivett-Carnac, was not regarded as a particular friend of education. Of him, Chulalongkorn some months previously had remarked:

> When Mr. Rivett-Carnac first arrived, knowing nothing of our country, he advised that we avoid having too many students at the higher levels, as there would not be sufficient employment for them, and if there were many so unemployed, they would be alienated and revolt, as in the present difficulties in India. It would be difficult for us, however, to find a single such [educated unemployed] person.[86]

Faced, however, with Campbell's reasoned arguments and his thinly veiled threat the Ministry of Finance would hardly reject the proposals, and it granted Chaophraya Phatsakǫrawong almost all that he requested in his estimates for 1900/01, a total of 935,964 baht.[87] This sum was almost 50 percent above the average of the preceding three years, and almost all of the increase had gone to the Education Department. Even granted

85. NA 5 Kh, 53/8, B, Campbell to Phatsakǫrawong, 7 Dec. 1899; copy forwarded to King, in Phatsakǫrawong to Sommot, 23 Mar. 1900, 53/8, A.

86. NA 5 B, 45/37, 2, King to Wisut, 3 Feb. 1899.

87. NA 5 Kh, 111/8, Budget, 1900/01.

that the government by 1899 was beginning to show considerably more interest in education than formerly, and that Čhaophraya Phatsakǫrawong had received almost all that he had requested the previous year,[88] it would still seem that much of the credit for the improved financial position of the ministry in 1900 must go to Campbell, who could assure the Ministry of Finance of the validity of the greatly increased claims that the Ministry of Public Instruction was making against the country's limited resources.

Inasmuch as Campbell's position was largely intramural, few of his activities in the ministry came to the notice of the king and survive in the archives. It is likely that he was consulted frequently on the ministry's internal affairs, problems, and planning, and that he may have developed a close working relationship with W. G. Johnson, inspector-general of schools. In the records, however, which concern almost exclusively matters brought to the attention of the king, Campbell's name appears in only two connections subsequent to the deliberations on the budget for R.S. 119: the expansion of King's College in 1900 and 1901, and his general recommendations on leaving Bangkok in 1901.

Late in 1900 Prince Kittiyakǫn asked Cecil Carter, headmaster of King's College, to draw up proposals for the school's expansion. Carter recommended that the school's accommodation be increased to 150 pupils and its course be lengthened from five to seven years, so that the school more effectively might provide "for the proper Education on European lines for pupils from 11–18 years of age," the cost of these changes being estimated at from 51,000 to 76,000 baht.[89] Campbell advised the adoption of these proposals, arguing, as the king had done two years earlier, that "the boys of the upper classes should receive their education in Bangkok itself and not in

88. NA 5 Kh, 111/8, Budget, 1899/1900.
89. NA 5 S, 21/5, 32, Carter to Kittiyakǫn, 9 Nov. 1900; 21/5, 25, Cost Estimate for King's College, 1901; and 21/5, 37, Estimate of Cost (Government), King's College.

Europe, and, if this is to be the case, the present provision for such education is far from adequate."[90] When Phatsakǫrawong still had failed to act on the recommendations two months later, Campbell tried flattery on the minister, suggesting that "if the enlargement takes place, much additional distinction will be added to your name as Minister and that His Majesty with his desire to advance education will appreciate the great importance of the undertaking."[91] Finally, a month later, Phatsakǫrawong forwarded the scheme to the king,[92] who overruled the minister's watered-down version of the plan and accepted the recommendations of Carter, Kittiyakǫn, and Campbell to move King's College to the Bangkok side of the river and to construct new quarters for it.[93] After some acrimonious correspondence between the king, Phatsakǫrawong, and the Cabinet, a new site finally was selected late in 1901 and funds allocated for the new buildings in 1902.[94] Although Campbell undoubtedly played an important role in bringing the ministry and government to the decision to expand and improve Thailand's preeminent educational institution, King's College,[95] he was by no means solely responsible for it.

The second major episode involving Campbell took place during his last weeks in Bangkok in August 1901. Preparing to leave for home, he addressed to Prince Kittiyakǫn a "short report on the present state of Education in Siam," in which he attempted to assess the accomplishments of his two years in

90. NA 5 S, 21/5, 26, Campbell to Kittiyakǫn, 11 Nov. 1900.
91. NA 5 S, 21/5, 23, Campbell to Phatsakǫrawong, 19 Jan. 1901.
92. NA 5 S, 50/5, 2, Phatsakǫrawong to Sommot, 9 Feb. 1901.
93. NA 5 S, 50/5, 12, Sommot to Phatsakǫrawong, 21 Feb. 1901.
94. See correspondence in NA 5 S, 91/5, nos. 4, 16, 18, 19, 20, 23, and 162, covering the period August 1901 to March 1902; and discussions on the budgets for 1901/02 and 1902/03 in NA 5 Kh, 100/8 and 101/8.
95. One good index of the academic standing of King's College is the performance of its students in the annual competitive examinations for King's Scholarships for study abroad. Of ten scholarships awarded between March 1898, and March 1902, King's College students gained six. See *Bangkok Times,* 10 Mar. 1898, 11 Apr. 1899, 12 Mar. 1901, and 13 Mar. 1902; and NA 5 S, 52/5, 20, List of Marks, King's Scholarship Examinations, 24 Mar. 1900.

Thailand and the problems remaining to his successors.[96] He concentrated his attention upon post-primary education, advocating specifically the inauguration of regular government higher primary schools, the syllabus of which would include English, in all the districts of Bangkok and all the monthon of the country. He urged that the government improve and expand Suankulap and King's College for the secondary education of the middle and upper classes respectively, and recommended that a "central technical school, with science, art, engineering & mechanic, commercial, horticultural, and other classes" be immediately established.

Two central themes recurred in Campbell's argument. First, he warned that "a ridiculously small proportion of the revenue is allotted to education compared with that given in European countries, nor can substantial progress be made until the sum is considerably increased." His second theme was more intangible and lay rather in emphasis and tone than in specific statements. His general approach and most intense concern was with the superstructure of the educational system and its function in Thai society. He expressed a conventional view of the importance of education to the economic and social development of the country, in providing it with industry and commerce and increasing the viability of its social institutions. He viewed as particularly important post-primary education for the upper classes, "for, till the rulers of the country realise what education really means, there is little hope that the foundations will be firmly laid."[97] Thus, although Campbell understood the function and importance of mass public education, both his parting report and his recommendations during his two years' service in Bangkok expressed an elitist emphasis which was as natural for an English educator of the period as for an officer

96. NA 5 S, 85/5, 25.
97. J. G. D. Campbell, *Siam in the Twentieth Century* (London, 1902), p. 246.

of Čhaophraya Phat's ministry. And the king responded to Campbell's report in much the same way as he frequently in the past had reacted to the čhaophraya's work.

I think that [Campbell's] ideas afford no basis for the strengthening of education in Thailand other than having all Thai speak English. Out of thirty million baht in the treasury, he would have us devote half of founding schools, of which 80% would be expended on hiring farang teachers, 10% on Thai teachers, and 10% on constructing schools. Children wouldn't have to learn Thai at all. He mentions nothing of which I am not aware already or which has not already been thought of but which the Ministry has not succeeded in carrying out.[98]

It was in the midst of such an atmosphere as this that Campbell left Bangkok at the termination of his contract in August 1901. Upon receiving a request from Campbell for a farewell audience the king was caught unawares, having heard nothing of Campbell's activities for many months.[99] Chulalongkorn hurriedly addressed inquiries to Phatsakǫrawong and Kittiyakǫn in order to obtain information about Campbell's work and anticipate complaints or requests the adviser might express.[100] Both replied in a similar vein.[101] Kittiyakǫn credited Campbell with having assisted in planning the expansion of King's College and in gaining budgetary support from the Ministry of Finance. Both argued that Campbell's advice merely con-

98. NA 5 S, 85/5, 30, King to Phatsakǫrawong, 18 Aug. 1901.
99. NA 5 B, 45/37, 72, Kittiyakǫn to Sommot, 5 Aug. 1901; 45/37, 73, Campbell to Sommot, 5 Aug. 1901. Campbell's report (85/5, 25) was not presented to the king until 17 August (85/5, 24), although it was dated 8 August 1901.
100. NA 5 B, 45/37, 71, King's memorandum (scribbled on envelope) on 45/37, 72, Kittiyakǫn to Sommot, 5 Aug. 1901; and 45/37, 74 and 75, Sommot to Phatsakǫrawong and Kittiyakǫn, 6 Aug. 1901.
101. NA 5 B, 45/37, 79, Kittiyakǫn to Phatsakǫrawong, 6 Aug.; and 45/37, 77, Phatsakǫrawong to Sommot, 6 Aug. 1901.

firmed the Education Department's existing policies and practices, and Phatsakǫrawong added that he and Campbell had "been well-disposed toward each other, and there were absolutely no matters on which we differed." They agreed that Campbell would not take back to England an unfavorable impression of Siam or the Ministry of Public Instruction. On 7 August, Chulalongkorn called together Phatsakǫrawong, Kittiyakǫn, Wisut, and the minister of finance, Prince Mahis, to brief him prior to Campbell's audience scheduled for the 9th.[102] The audience concluded, Campbell sailed for home on 15 August.[103] Back at work in the British Ministry of Education, Campbell published the following year an excellent general account of the Thailand of the day,[104] instructive as much for his fair-minded treatment of what he had seen and tried to do as for the glimpse it affords into the minds of the sincere and often frustrated band of men who were called upon during this period to serve both the expansion of European influence in Asia and the urgent requirements of such nations as Siam in their rush to modernize.

Prince Kittiyakǫn's and Čhaophraya Phatsakǫrawong's assessments of Campbell's record in Bangkok, understated as they undoubtedly are, are nonetheless fair comments on the state of education in Thailand in 1901 from their own point of view. Likewise, the king's reaction to Campbell's terminal report, his statement that it contained "nothing new," was just as accurate. The fact was that Campbell had arrived in Thailand in 1899

102. NA 5 B, 45/37, 76, Record of Discussion, 7 Aug. 1901. This "record" notes only that the five agreed to give audience to Campbell and to have the Ministry of Finance consult with him on his unexplained request for £600, possibly a contribution toward Campbell's pension.

103. Bangkok Times, 15 Aug. 1901.

104. Campbell, Siam in the Twentieth Century. See the reviews of this book in the Bangkok Times, 15, 20, and 21 May 1902, which includes the stated hope that "the Education Department here may see its way to publishing its experiences with and impressions of the official in question. That would certainly make an interesting companion volume" (15 May).

with preconceived ideas of the nature of education, modified by his acquaintance with the British approach to "native education" in India and Burma, but nonetheless considerably at variance with the Thai government on fundamental questions of educational policy. It was precisely on such questions and on the wider context of educational policy that Campbell leveled his most severe criticisms of the Thai government, as in his continued insistence that a larger proportion of national revenues be devoted to education and that, of these expenditures, proportionally more go to the upper levels of the system although perhaps not to the extent that the king somewhat exaggeratedly imagined. The ministry, viewing the same situation in terms of ill-defined policies or, more appropriately, approaches to education, could credit Campbell with aiding them in their battles with the Ministry of Finance and could then add, and quite sincerely believe, that Campbell had served simply to reinforce educational ideals, aims, objectives, and methods that long since had been adopted by the ministry. In doing so, justice was on their side, for Campbell was pressing on the ministry advice to do precisely the things that had been contemplated and attempted during the preceding eight years and, indeed, even during the ministry of Prince Damrong: the establishing of model schools in the provinces, increased support for higher-level schools for the upper classes and for vocational or technical instruction, and the upgrading of standards in the elementary schools. From their point of view, Campbell's single merit was that he had served to assist them in obtaining funds for these projects, and they could point with considerable pride to the results they had been able to obtain with this infusion of funds. The ministry could claim to have made progress in the field of primary education, in strengthening secondary and special schools, and in educational administration and the provision of ancillary services during the years 1898–1902.

The ministry entered this period with a roster of ninety-nine government and government-aided schools in Bangkok and the provinces. Classified in terms of the types of control the Education Department exerted over them, they fell into at least five categories. First, there were seven special schools, including King's College, the Normal School, and Suanthalai, which were formally government schools, but academic control over which was to a considerable extent left in the hands of their European headmasters and headmistresses. Second, there were four government higher primary schools which had been retained by the ministry in 1892 from the twenty-one Bangkok monastery schools left by Prince Damrong. Over these the ministry could exert considerable academic and administrative control, as it fully supported the schools financially. Third, there were forty-one partially supported higher primary and elementary monastery schools in Bangkok, which received only small subsidies from the Education Department and occasional aid in building construction and repairs, but which submitted to ministry inspection and the government examinations, the results of which determined the schools' continued eligibility for financial support. Fourth, there were the forty-two elementary schools in the provinces, fourteen of which received some financial aid from the ministry. These were not inspected by the ministry, and only those in the provinces immediately surrounding Bangkok sent their students in to the capital for the semi-annual examinations. Over this group government control can only have been minimal if it existed at all. This group of schools was turned over to Prince Wachirayan in 1898.[105] Finally, there appears to have been a small group of regularly constituted primary and secondary schools, privately established, including missionary schools, which received no government support but which occasionally entered their students in the examinations. The official records, however, took no cognizance of these.

The removal of the provincial elementary schools from the

105. Prince Wachirayan reported their number as 18, with fewer than 800 pupils, while the ministry counted 42 schools with almost 2,000 pupils. (See pp. 234–35 above.)

jurisdiction of the ministry in 1898 can have affected the ministry or the schools themselves very little. The strongest of these schools could carry on, as they had on being cast suddenly adrift in 1892, on their own resources, as did the Anglo-Siamese school at Wat Klang in Samut Prakan (Pak Nam), the municipal Thai school at Chiangmai, and a handful of schools in monthon Udǫn, the last two being left out of Prince Wachirayan's program. Others, including the schools in monthon Krungthep, Krung Kao (Ayudhya), Isan (Ubon), Phitsanulok, and Nakhǫn Chaisi, slipped neatly into Wachirayan's program, gaining additional financial support and a firmer administrative hand. The ministry was left to cope with the somewhat disorganized tangle of schools in Bangkok and was given increased funds and political support with which to do so.

A notable development of the preceding six or seven years in the schools of Bangkok was the growth of uniformity among the monastery primary schools, together with a slow but steady improvement in their standards. Of the twenty-one monastery primary schools handed over to Čhaophraya Phatsakǫrawong in 1892, sixteen managed to survive the intervening period of reduced financial support, increasing their enrollments from 1,087 pupils to 1,417. At the same time, three of the older schools expanded to the point where they split into groups of two or three schools at a single location, notably the school at Wat Ratchaburana (Wat Liap), which from a single building with forty-nine students in 1891/92 expanded to fill three schools with 246 students in 1898/99, all of whom were taught to the higher primary syllabus. By 1898/99, the earlier distinction between the higher primary and the elementary schools was meaningless. In the annual examinations of higher primary school level (Standard I), there was no appreciable difference between the performances of students from the two different types of schools, although there was a significant difference between the schools receiving full and those receiving only partial support, mainly in the variations of their performance, the government schools being much more consistent in their performance. In addition, the higher primary schools produced 57 percent of the successful candidates in the Standard II examinations, as against under 3 percent for the elementary schools.[106]

The essential difference between the two types of primary schools, then, was not the one prescribed in the ministry's definition. Indeed, some of the higher primary schools performed in the examinations even better than Suankulap, which was defined as a secondary school. The outstanding such example was the school at Wat Nuannǫradit, which had a 70 percent success rate on Standard I and 82 percent on Standard II in 1898/99. The differences lay between individual schools rather than between types of schools, between the long-established schools at the major monasteries of Bangkok (especially the royal monasteries, which could support larger monastic communities and which had stronger academic traditions) and more recent schools located in the smaller monasteries.[107] This was a natural distinction, on several grounds. First, the older schools by the late nineties were self-perpetuating in their teaching staff. This held not only for teacher-monks where mobility from one monastery to another was not great but also for lay teachers, as the older monasteries had long since begun to train their own teachers. Boys from a particular monastery passing the Standard II examinations might remain on at the same monastery to teach or be sent to teach at another monastery with which their own had a special relationship. Both lay and monk teachers could gain teaching experience alongside an older teacher and then start up separate classes on their own, either in the same school, in a separate school on the grounds of the same monastery, or at another monastery.[108] Another

106. NA 5 S, 95/5, 2, Report, Educ. Dept., 1898/99.

107. Because of Prince Wachirayan's educational activities, centering upon Wat Bǫwǫnniwet but including also several other important monasteries, the monasteries of the Thammayut sect were not included among the ministry's schools in this period.

108. It is possible that the reason why as many as five schools might be founded at a single monastery (e.g. Wat Anongkharam in Thonburi) was

factor favoring those schools with longer histories of schooling was the evident fact that resistance to modern education was something that not only took considerable time to break down but that also had to be broken down in a locality or neighborhood by its own leaders; and in this task some showed considerably more talent than others. Conspicuous examples of such men were Phra-ačhan Sayampariyat (Nuam) and Phra-ačhan Sayampariyat (Ngip), who established three schools each at Wats Prayurawong and Anongkharam in Thonburi.[109]

To raise the monastery elementary schools of Bangkok to higher primary level, create a new class of secondary schools, and bring order into a confused system, four basic requirements had to be met: the provision of adequate numbers of trained teachers, the preparation of up-to-date teaching materials and textbooks, the granting of substantial increases in school support and subsidy funds to enable the schools to employ better-qualified teachers, and the strengthening of the department's control over the activities of the schools.

The ministry's main hope for meeting the teacher shortage had for more than six years been the government Normal School whose headmaster was at this time F. G. Treyes, assisted by E. J. Wills.[110] This school prepared teachers with an English secondary curriculum to a high standard, but the school's course

---

because of the financial subsidy policy of the Education Department, which granted 10 baht *per school* per month. By founding separate schools at different buildings within the same monastery precinct, a single monastery could gain multiple subsidies instead of only one. Monasteries having multiple schools included, in addition to Wat Anongkharam, which had 3 schools, Wat Prayurawong and Wat Ratchaburana, with 3 each, and Wat Amarinthararam, Wat Chanasongkhram, Wat Sam Čhin Tai (Wat Traimit), Wat Phrachetuphon (Wat Pho), and Wat Rakhang, and possibly others, with 2 each.

109. For their biographies, see "Prawat phra-ačhan sayampariyat (ngip ketsaro)," *Prawat khru* (1957), pp. 19–25; and "Theraprawat," in *Prawat kansatsanasüksa,* pp. (1)–(10).

110. See *Bangkok Times,* 25 and 26 May 1900.

was lengthy and the output of teachers considerably delayed. In addition, the prospects of its graduates were not bright, for teachers' salaries were low and teaching positions were not yet fully established in the hierarchy of the civil service. The acceptance of Campbell's recommendations for an increase in teachers' salaries and an increase in the staff of the Normal School strengthened its position,[111] and an additional boost was given to its attractiveness when the Education Department began in 1900 to employ its graduates as school inspectors in regular-grade civil service posts.[112] These changes produced an immediate increase in the school's enrollment, from ten in 1899 to thirty-nine in 1900.[113] That Normal School graduates were not sufficient to the needs of the rapidly expanding school system in the period need hardly be said. Teachers so highly trained, and with qualifications in English, were so much in demand among the growing special and secondary schools, not to mention the ministry's administrative staff and the staffs of other ministries, that very few found their way to the ordinary vernacular primary and elementary schools. In 1902, the Inspection Department reported that of 233 teachers in seventy "ordinary Thai schools" in Bangkok with enrollments of almost seven thousand pupils, only thirty-seven were certified teachers, including four monks and novices, and the schools were then employing more lay (139) than monk (94) teachers.[114] A serious gap remained to be filled, and a number of expedient solutions were experimented with during the period, including having monks and novices trained in the secondary school at

---

111. See Campbell, *Siam in the Twentieth Century*, p. 253; and NA 5 Kh, 53/8, B, Campbell to Phatsakǫrawong, 7 Dec. 1899.

112. Bamrung, "Prawat kanfükhatkhru," p. 24.

113. See the lists of Normal School graduates in *Prawat khru* (1957), pp. 74–94; and (1958), pp. 136–37.

114. "Rai-ngan krasuang thammakan, phanaek süksathikan," *RKB, 19* (1902/03), spec. no. 6 July 1902, 1–13. This is actually W. G. Johnson's report as inspector-general for the year 1901/02.

Wat Anongkharam[115] and at Wat Mahan English School.[116] On at least one occasion the ministry expressed a desire to found a second normal school, presumably to train teachers for the monastery elementary schools,[117] but nothing was accomplished in this direction until 1903. The period thus brought no solution to the teacher shortage, but it did bring about a growing awareness of the problem and the germs of solutions which were later to be developed and brought to fruition by Phatsakọrawong's successors.

The abolition of the Education Department's Textbook Bureau in 1897 made the ministry dependent on individuals and commercial publishers for the textbooks it required. Most textbooks, however, continued to be compiled by officers of the Education Department. The inspector-general, W. G. Johnson, alone compiled five textbooks in the course of the year 1898/99, including mathematics textbooks, a geography of Siam, and an English reader, and his deputy, Sanan Thephatsadin na Ayudhya, was working on textbooks on hygiene, morals, and mathematics, and a teacher's handbook for Standard I classes.[118] The many textbooks of these years, taken together with those of the previous decade, went a considerable distance toward meeting the serious deficiences complained of by the king and his brothers in 1898. As with the teacher shortage, the textbook problem was by no means solved by 1902, but the Education Department was beginning to show considerable ability and

115. NA 5 S, 53/5, 2, Phatsakọrawong to Sommot, 10 Jan. 1899; and *Prawat kansatsanasüksa*, pp. 29, 37–38.

116. There is only one recorded indication to this effect, documents concerning the dismissal of T. Richmond Perera from the headmastership of "the normal school at Wat Mahan": NA 5 S, 25/2, 8, Sommot to Perera, 6 Sept. 1899; and 25/2, 17, W. G. Johnson to Phatsakọrawong, 14 Aug. 1899. Closure of the school was reported in the *Bangkok Times*, 19 Apr. 1900.

117. When the ministry was considering moving King's College from its Thonburi site in 1901, it proposed that the buildings be converted for use as a teacher training college. NA 5 S, 50/5, 2, Phatsakọrawong to Sommot, 9 Feb. 1901. This was in fact the plan followed in 1903.

118. NA 5 S, 95/5, 72, Textbook Activities, Educ. Dept., 1898/99, Appendix 14/117 to Report, Educ. Dept., 1898/99.

ingenuity in meeting it. The remaining flaw in their approach, however, was the continuing absence in the ministry of central direction for the attack on the problem, a deficiency not met until 1902.

The greatly increased budgets granted to the Education Department over the period made possible considerable improvement in the monastery elementary schools. The number of Bangkok school teachers whose salaries were paid by the department increased from about one hundred in April 1898, to 233 in 1902.[119] The department financed the construction of a number of new primary schools to replace monastery elementary schools and large-scale renovation of others. In 1901/02, for example, school buildings were being repaired at Wat Kanlayanamit, Wat Kaeofa Čhulamani, Wat Sang Kračhai, Wat Anongkharam, Wat Sam Čhin Tai (Wat Traimit), and Wat Sangwetwitsayaram, at a total cost of nearly ten thousand baht.[120] Financial support began to be extended to the monastery schools at rates considerably in excess of the ten baht per month subsidy which had been the limit of their support in the period 1892–97: in 1902, the subvention for teachers' salaries in the monastery primary schools averaged 921 baht per school per annum, an eightfold increase over the previous rate of support.[121] While administrative control was not a necessary consequence of such financial support, the schools' increased dependence on government funds must have heightened their receptivity to administrative direction and control, especially as there were not sufficient funds to grant each school all it needed or, indeed, to provide for all the monastery schools then operating. In addition, the increased budgets granted to the Education Department made possible a considerable strengthening of the department's most direct instruments of control, the Inspection Bureau and the examination system.

119. NA 5 S, 95/5, 42, Comparative Table of Examination Results, Appendix 7/117 to Report, Educ. Dept., 1898/99; and *RKB, 19* (1902/03), spec. no. 6 July 1902, 1–13.

120. NA 5 S, 99/5, 39, Kittiyakǫn to Wutthikanbǫdi, 22 Oct. 1901.

121. Based on *RKB, 19* (1902/03), spec. no. 6 July 1902, 1–13.

Although there had been officials in the Education Department since the eighties charged with the duties of school inspection, their functions appear to have been primarily descriptive and advisory in nature until the turn of the century. The change in the character and powers of the inspectorate dates from November 1898, when W. G. Johnson was given a six-year contract as "Chief Inspector and Organizer of all schools under the Department's control" and given the duties of assisting "in all educational matters . . . connected with the Department."[122] Johnson brought to his post as inspector-general, director of the Inspection Bureau, three years' experience as headmaster of Suankulap English School and the Normal School and an excellent knowledge of Thai, together with a great ability to get along with his Thai colleagues.[123] It became his duty to assess applications for school support, to supervise the monthly inspections of all government schools, and to develop and administer the government examinations.[124] In addition, Johnson and his staff personally took upon themselves the task of drawing up and revising the syllabi and of compiling many of the textbooks they required. These activities firmly established the inspectorate as an instrument of qualitative and administrative control. With the expansion of the ministry's funds and activities, the inspectorate became armed with effective sanctions: its reports could determine the scales on which individual teachers were paid, the sites where new school buildings could be

122. NA 7 B, 10/135, 1, Contract, W. G. Johnson and the Educ. Dept., 1 Nov. 1898; enclosed in M.Č. Piyaphakdi (Acting Minister of Finance) to Prince Phanurangsi (acting as regent), 31 May 1901.

123. Pathom Chansan (i.e. Johnson), "Nai dapliu. yi. yǫnsan," *Prawat khru* (1957), pp. 65–71. Johnson, born in 1871 in London, came to Thailand in 1895 on graduation from Borough Road Training College in Isleworth, near London. He taught at Suankulap English School for a year, then became its headmaster (1896–97), and then headmaster of the Normal School (1897–98). He remained in the Thai government service until his retirement in 1926, and on his death in 1946 received the honor of a cremation sponsored by the king. See also F. K. Exell, *Siamese Tapestry* (London, 1963), p. 77.

124. NA 5 S, 95/5, 2, Report, Educ. Dept., 1898/99.

erected, the granting or withdrawal of government support for individual schools, the curriculum schools should follow and the methods they should use in teaching it. Johnson attempted to use these powers to hasten the progress of the schools toward European academic standards.

How effective Johnson and the Inspection Bureau were during this period is difficult to assess. One index of the efficiency of the administration of the primary schools may perhaps be the increase in the average number of students per school from sixty-three in March 1899 to ninety-seven in March 1902, while even at the latter date the teacher–pupil ratio was a favorable 1:29. These figures suggest that wise inspection and administration worked to concentrate primary education in a limited number of schools which showed themselves capable of meeting the inspectorate's continually rising standards. Certainly the ministry was happy with his work. Shortly before the departure of Campbell in 1901, Phatsakǫrawong argued that there was no need to hire a replacement for the adviser, since Johnson was as well qualified as Campbell, knew the Thai language well, and was thoroughly familiar with Siam's educational system.[125] That Phatsakǫrawong's judgment was shared by the king was evinced in the decision taken in mid-1900 to place the schools of monthon Krungthep, which had been handed over to Prince Wachirayan in 1898, back under the ministry's jurisdiction, at which time school inspectors were assigned to the four müang of the monthon.[126] There could be no more certain sign that the ministry had begun to redeem itself.

The ministry's record in the wider and more diffuse field of secondary and higher education was much less promising. Although it did not lack ideas and intentions during the period, its accomplishments were overshadowed by the substantial progress made by such projects as the Civil Service School (under Phraya Wisut) of the Ministry of Interior and the semi-private King's College. While these two, together with the mili-

125. NA 7 B, 10/135, Phatsakǫrawong to Phanurangsi, 18 July 1901.
126. *Bangkok Times,* 21 Aug. 1900.

tary and naval cadet schools and the law school in the Ministry
of Justice, greatly expanded their activities during the period,
not only was the Education Department unable to mount a
program of secondary school expansion but even its single vernacular secondary school, Suankulap, entered a period of dis-
integration which was to last for a whole decade.

As organized by 1900, the Civil Service School of the Ministry of Interior was offering a three-tiered course of study to
aspiring civil servants, who flocked to the school in considerable
numbers, assured of positions in the Ministry of Interior upon
graduation. Students passed from a primary-level preparatory
course into a secondary-level training period, which combined
academic study with classroom work on subjects pertaining to
the work of the Ministry of Interior, during which they performed part-time service as pages at court, intended both to
make them known at court and to give them a firsthand acquaintance with the workings of the monarchy.[127] Having
finished their classroom work, students were sent for a period
of practical work in a branch of the school at Bang Pa-in near
Ayudhya, where they were instructed by the local head of government, Prince Mɔruphongsiriphat, and two teachers in "the
duties of provincial officials, the character of local government, land affairs, public prosecution, and revenue affairs."[128]
Drawing its students not only from the official families of Bangkok but also from provincial princely families and official-
dom,[129] the school was overcrowded by 1901, and preparations were made to construct new permanent quarters for it in
1902.[130] By then, the school clearly was a success and was

127. Damrong, "Rüang rongrian mahatlek luang," pp. 89–91.
128. NA 5 S, 1/5, 14, Report, Civil Service School, 25 Mar. 1901;
71/5, 5, Damrong to King, 5 Aug. 1901; and 71/5, 11, same to same,
20 Aug. 1901.
129. In 1901, the Prince of Chiangmai sent six of his nephews or grandsons to enter the school. NA 5 S, 71/5, 31, Damrong to Sommot, 30 Nov.
1901.
130. NA 5 S, 71/5, 22, Damrong to King, 4 Sept. 1901; and 71/5, 26,
Damrong to King, 16 Sept. 1901, private. Until 1902 the school was

beginning to infuse its graduates into the service of the Ministry of Interior to the appreciative congratulations of the king. Original intentions notwithstanding, the school was unable to serve the demands of other ministries for trained civil servants, as Prince Damrong was fully able to employ all the graduates the school could produce; thus other ministries were forced in the years to come either to press for more graduates from the Education Department's schools or to train their own men.

The other single promising work in the field of secondary education in this period was King's College, which enjoyed in common with the Civil Service School strong patronage, a factor assuring the success of both. While it was primarily Prince Damrong and the Ministry of Interior who made for the success of the Civil Service School, the sponsors of King's College were a less cohesive but no less influential group, for among the parents of young men studying at King's College were many members of the royal family and the higher nobility who wished their sons prepared for European education. With high academic standards, a highly qualified staff, and the strong support of the Education Department, including, during his tenure in Siam, J. G. D. Campbell, its place in the educational system was secure. The decision taken in 1900 to strengthen its curriculum and lengthen it from five to seven years and to move the school into new quarters augured well for its future. With these improvements, Carter argued that the school would be fully able to compete with English public schools, preparing a student for a British university at a cost equivalent to $35 per year, while even second-rate English boarding schools charged a fee of $120 per year.[131] The total cost of the school was considerable, for the salaries of its eleven teachers alone amounted to between 51,000 and 76,000 baht, a sum nearly equivalent to the total

---

quartered in the old buildings just within the Phimanchaisi Gate of the Grand Palace which, years earlier, had housed the first Thai school of Phraya Si Sunthọn Wohan.

131. NA 5 S, 21/5, 25, Cost Estimates, King's College; enclosed in 21/5, 32, Carter to Kittiyakọn, 9 Nov. 1900.

amount expended on the salaries of more than two hundred
teachers in seventy vernacular primary schools in 1901/02. Yet
the decision to move and expand the school was reached in that
year with little argument on the question of cost. The government's readiness to sanction this heavy outlay may be explained
partly by the genuine needs served by the schools, partly by the
priority the ministry assigned to the school, partly by the understanding of its function by the Ministry of Finance and its
British advisers, and certainly also in part by the social function
of the school as an exclusive preparatory school for the sons of
wealthy families, a function it had taken over from Suankulap.

In addition to King's College and the Normal School there
were five other special schools—schools teaching English—on
the roster of the Education Department in 1898. One of these,
Sunanthalai, was a boarding school for girls, which has been
dealt with elsewhere. Three others were special schools receiving partial support from the ministry: the Anglo-Siamese
School, successor to McFarland's old Sunanthalai, still carrying
on under Nai Kọn Amatyakul as headmaster; the English (or
normal) school at Wat Mahannapharam; and an evening
English school at Wat Suthat. All of these were financed in
large part by the fees of their pupils, and all entered their pupils
only in the English examinations of the Education Department.
As important as all three were, providing both government and
commerce with the English-educated young men so urgently
required at the time, unfortunately all three are hardly mentioned in the ministry's records, and they seem to have been
viewed primarily as language, rather than academic, schools,
probably justly so. Certainly no attempt was made in the case
of any of the three to integrate them into any wider system of
education, least at the secondary level. Two of them, Wat
Mahan and Wat Suthat, were closed by 1900, while the Anglo-
Siamese School was closed in 1903.[132]

132. NA 5 S, 95/5, 2, Report, Educ. Dept., 1898/99; *Bangkok Times,*
14 Dec. 1898 and 19 Apr. 1900; *RKB 19* (1902/03) spec. no. 6 July 1902,

The seventh of the special schools, Suankulap, was the key school in the vernacular system, as it had been since the eighties. In February 1898 its Thai division had an enrollment of 381 pupils, while there were 83 in the English section. At that time, the buildings of Suankulap Palace were required for the use of the Royal Pages' Bodyguard Regiment, and the school had to be moved elsewhere.[133] Čhaophraya Phatsakǫrawong obtained the promise of a site near Wat Ratchaburana, but since the site was not to become available for another two or three years, as it was thought at the time, the school had to be dispersed temporarily over the city.[134] For four years, the school was divided between buildings at Wat Mahathat and Wat Chanasongkhram, and then was reunited on another temporary site at Wat Thepsirin in 1902; it was not until 1909 that it finally settled into its permanent quarters at the Wat Ratchaburana site, where it remains to this day.[135] As a result of this period of upheaval and dispersion, Suankulap cannot have been as effective as a "model school" as the ministry would have liked. It was kept in inadequate, makeshift quarters spread over the city, and its enrollments suffered accordingly. The ministry hardly can have considered embarking upon a program of secondary school expansion when the single vernacular secondary school it possessed was being shifted about Bangkok from one foster home to another. As it turned out some years later when a program of secondary school expansion was finally agreed upon, several

---

1–13; NA 5 S, 25/2, 6, Sommot to T. Richmond Perera, 6 Sept. 1899; and 25/2, 17, Johnson to Phatsakǫrawong, 14 Aug. 1899.

133. Sa-nguan Ankhong, *Sing raek nai müang thai, 1* (Bangkok, 1959), 386.

134. NA 5 S, 21/5, 13, Report of Ministry of Public Instruction in Cabinet Meeting, 10 Feb. 1898. On this occasion, as on many others, Phatsakǫrawong referred to Suankulap as "the number one school of the Education Department, our model school."

135. *Bangkok Times,* 4 June and 15 June, 1898; and NA 5 S, 21/5, 17, Phatsakǫrawong to Sommot, 9 June 1898; 47/5, 22, same to same, 23 Mar. 1900; 50/5, 11, same to same, 20 Feb. 1901; and 99/5, nos. 21–40, July–October, 1901.

of Suankulap's former homes were ideal sites for secondary schools.

In comparison with the previous six years of inactivity, the period 1898–1902 was an active one for the Ministry of Public Instruction. For the first time it had sufficient funds to make a start on programs that long had languished for lack of funds. It began to extend substantial support, both financial and administrative, to the primary schools of Bangkok, and it finally began to make the Normal School produce. It issued, after nearly a decade of consideration, a syllabus for secondary schools and by 1900 had begun examining students on it. It had begun, somewhat informally, to make progress toward satisfying the demand for up-to-date textbooks. It had fostered the development of King's College as an excellent preparatory school. It also had established a strong Inspection Bureau which gave it a new effectiveness in enforcing its rule over the schools of Bangkok. The ministry had, however, suffered some considerable defeats. By 1902, the ministry still held jurisdiction only over the schools of Bangkok and its immediate neighborhood. Much vital educational activity was being carried on under its nose but out of its sight, in the Civil Service School of Prince Damrong and Phraya Wisut, in the schools of other ministries, and generally in the schools of the Thammayut sect of the Sangha, all of which were alternatives created to correct the ministry's failures. Most ominously, the ministry since September 1898 had been excluded from policy-making circles and rarely was consulted on educational matters by the king, who turned more frequently to Prince Damrong, Prince Wachirayan, and Phraya Wisut Suriyasak. The ministry seems to have responded to this exclusion by isolating itself. Its correspondence with the king reached a ten-year nadir, and the ministry voiced officially none of its thoughts on educational policy and planning. Its reputation among the foreign community in Bangkok was low, perhaps reflecting in part the frustrations of those Europeans who, like Campbell, had entered the service of the ministry for short periods and left it unhappily. The editor of

the *Bangkok Times,* after going several years without comment-
ing editorially on education, finally resumed criticism of the
ministry late in 1902. In September he remarked that "there are
probably more queer stories told about that department than
about any other section of the Government service," and added
that education "does not seem to get out of the slough of
despond."[136] At the same time, "a Correspondent at Bangkok"
aired in *The Times* of London his view that "probably the most
hopeless and inefficient department is the Education Department. . . . The whole department very badly wants overhaul-
ing."[137] The king long had thought so, and in 1901 he took
steps to bring this about.

THE END OF AN ERA, MARCH–APRIL 1902

The renewal of public criticism of the Education Department
in the Bangkok press late in 1901 coincided with an increasing
general frustration on the part of the king with the political
environment in which he was trying to press his program of
reform. Late in 1900 he had written his son, Prince Bọriphat
(later Prince Nakhọn Sawan), then studying in Germany, in
darkly pessimistic tones of the frustration that stemmed from
his continuing lack of trained civil servants, likening his ship
of state to a rotting hulk, manned by incompetent oarsmen,
some of whom were blind and others deaf.[138] A year later, he
had shifted his concern to the highest levels of government, the
Cabinet and the royal family, which he saw as hopelessly ridden
with factionalism, hypocrisy, subservience, and intrigue, an environment in which substantial progress toward the attainment
of modern goals was almost impossible. The problem was one

136. *Bangkok Times,* 3 Sept. 1901.
137. *The Times* (London), 7 Sept. 1901.
138. Chulalongkorn to Prince Bọriphat, 17 Nov. 1900; printed in King
Chulalongkorn, *Phraratchahatlekha phrabat somdet phra čhunlačhọmklao
čhaoyuhua lae lai phrabat somdet phra pitutčhačhao sukhuman marasi
phra akkharatchathewi* (Bangkok, 1950), p. 25.

of leadership. "The Cabinet Ministers these days are like thresh-ing-mill buffalo: if you stop goading and shouting at them, the millstones grind to a halt. I would change them, but I haven't the men."[139] One of these old, tethered, threshing-mill buffalo was Čhaophraya Phatsakǫrawong. In 1898 the king had seen no opportunity of replacing him, but by 1901 alternative leader-ship in the person of Phraya Wisut Suriyasak was ready, and grounds arose to force the čhaophraya's resignation.

In March 1901 Phatsakǫrawong and Prince Kittiyakǫn at-tended their annual meeting with officials of the Ministry of Finance to discuss the Ministry of Public Instruction's estimates for the coming year.[140] Their deliberations reverted to the pat-tern of previous years: all but three of the ministry's proposals for new projects were refused sanction and no funds were al-lowed for capital expenditures. But the Ministry of Finance officials went still further, demanding an accounting of all funds received directly by the Ministry of Public Instruction from school tuition fees and school and monastery endowments, sums which had been received and expended without reference to the Ministry of Finance. Inasmuch as the Education Depart-ment had alleged that the income from the endowments of Sunanthalai Girls' School was insufficient to cover its expenses and had applied for a supplementary grant, Phatsakǫrawong could not refuse the Ministry of Finance's demand that an auditor be allowed to audit such accounts, beginning with the endowment fund of Sunanthalai School.[141]

Early in June, an auditor of the Ministry of Finance, W. J. F. Williamson, reported to his minister that, although the Sunanthalai accounts were incomplete and not in proper order, he had found a clear case of embezzlement on the part of the managers of the school which amounted to more than 20,000 baht. With proper management, he stated, the income from the school's endowment was quite adequate to meet its expenses.

139. King to Bǫriphat, 30 July 1901, printed in ibid., p. 35.
140. NA 5 Kh, 100/8, Budget, 1901/02, Report of Budget Meetings.
141. Ibid.; and NA 5 S, 4/1, 2, Mahis to King, 24 Aug. 1901.

He recommended strongly that the director of the Education Department be given full responsibility for the school's finances.[142] Within the next two months, similar irregularities were found in the accounts of the Hospitals Department and in the accounts of the ministry itself. Told informally of the progress of these investigations, the king on 18 August ordered that the Education Department be made virtually a separate organ of government, reporting directly to the throne.[143] Immediately following the Minister of Finance's formal report on the matter,[144] the king wrote to Phatsakǫrawong and, without mentioning the findings of the audits, ordered that all endowment funds for monasteries and schools, "i.e. cash donations to monasteries, rentals accruing to monasteries, rentals accruing to schools and hospitals, funds for the support of education, funds raised by public subscription, etc.," be removed from the jurisdiction of the Ministry of Public Instruction and placed under the Ministry of Finance, further receipts and expenditures to be subjected to rigorous cross-checking.[145] Thus, in two strokes, within a single week, Čhaophraya Phatsakǫrawong found his control over both education and the ministry's finances considerably reduced.

Asked in a Cabinet meeting on 29 August to comment on the reports of the Ministry of Finance, "Čhaophraya Phat replied unclearly, generally disputing the report."[146] The Cabinet recommended that Prince Kittiyakǫn be given an opportunity to put the finances of the Education Department in order, and Phatsakǫrawong began to dig into specific cases mentioned in Williamson's report. The ministry's accountant, who confessed to the embezzlement of 927 baht from the Sunanthalai endowment funds, and another official, who had stolen a check for 500 baht, were both removed from office and jailed within three

142. NA 5 S, 4/1, 4, Williamson to Mahis, 8 June 1901.
143. NA 5 S, 11/1, 1, King to Phatsakǫrawong and Kittiyakǫn, 18 Aug. 1901, two identical letters; also in Documents, p. 96.
144. NA 5 S, 4/1, 2, Mahis to King, 24 Aug. 1901.
145. NA 5 S, 5/1, 1, King to Phatsakǫrawong, 25 Aug. 1901.
146. NA 5 S, 4/1, 19, Minutes, Cabinet Meeting, 29 Aug. 1901.

days.[147] When the ministry appeared to be dragging its feet, an auditor was assigned the enormous task of going through the accounts of the entire ministry.

After six months of careful sifting, tracing of receipts, and interrogations, the Ministry of Finance auditor finally presented the results of his audit early in March 1902. The main result of his investigation was to uncover serious shortages in the accounts of the Ecclesiastical Department, amounting to a total of 18,428 baht. Of this amount, it was found that 3,946 baht had been expended by Čhaophraya Phatsakǫrawong for unauthorized official purposes, and 11,299 baht on the minister's personal business.[148] Six weeks later, on 18 April 1902, Čhaophraya Phatsakǫrawong submitted to the king his formal resignation:

> I have served Your Majesty for more than thirty-five years; but now I am old. My memory and energy which have permitted me to serve Your Majesty in important activities have declined, and are no longer sufficient to the work which is at present expected of me, and illness has arisen in my body. I therefore ask Your Majesty's mercy in releasing me from my position as Minister of Public Instruction to give me time to restore my health.[149]

The king wrote immediately to Prince Damrong announcing the minister's resignation and the temporary appointment of Phraya Wutthikanbǫdi, director of the Ecclesiastical Affairs Department, as acting minister and asked that Damrong advise Wutthikanbǫdi on educational affairs.[150] Two days later, Wutthikanbǫdi requested that Phraya Wisut Suriyasak be appointed to serve concurrently as director of the Education Department and deputy minister, requests sanctioned by the king on 22

147. NA 5 S, 4/1, 22, Phatsakǫrawong to Sommot, 2 Sept. 1901; 4/1, 31, King to Phatsakǫrawong, 3 Sept.; and 4/1, 35, Phatsakǫrawong to King, 5 Sept.
148. NA 5 S, 5/1, 6, Mahis to King, 7 Mar. 1902.
149. NA 5 S, 1/1, 1, Phatsakǫrawong to King, 18 Apr. 1902.
150. NA 5 S, 1/1, 5, King to Damrong, 19 Apr. 1902.

April.[151] Prince Kittiyakǫn was transferred to the position of comptroller-general in the Ministry of Finance.[152] The maneuverings of the past five years at last bore their fruit.

There is almost no possibility that the čhaophraya's resignation was due either to the reasons of ill health publicly stated or to the financial irregularities that immediately preceded it, although Prince Sommot, the king's private secretary, filed the papers on the audits and the minister's resignation together in a separate file. First, the čhaophraya's health was sufficiently good to allow him to lead an active official and scholarly life in Bangkok for another twenty years. Second, if anyone had sought at any time to remove Phatsakǫrawong from office for reasons of financial irregularity, they would not have had to wait until 1902 to do so. Such irregularities connected with his pre-1892 tenure in the Customs Department were well known in Bangkok early in the nineties, [153] yet no proceedings were taken against him at the time. In 1893, Čhaophraya Surasakmontri got into serious difficulties over his unauthorized use of Ministry of Agriculture funds during the Franco-Siamese crisis, yet he was allowed to clear himself and continued on for a number of years as a Cabinet minister.[154] No attempt was made to cover up for Čhaophraya Phatsakǫrawong or to smooth over his misdeeds, although this could easily have been done, even had the čhaophraya been required to make good the deficiencies in the accounts. Clearly, the audits were undertaken and the charges against the minister made because his removal was desired.

Certainly there is no lack of evidence that the king, Prince Damrong, Prince Wachirayan, and Phraya Wisut viewed a change in the leadership of the ministry as the only solution to Siam's educational problems. Phatsakǫrawong had to be re-

151. NA 5 S, 1/1, 9, Wutthikanbǫdi to King, 21 Apr. 1902; and 1/1, 11, King to Wutthikanbǫdi, 22 Apr.
152. *Bangkok Times*, 2 Apr. 1902.
153. H. Warington Smyth, *Five Years in Siam*, 1, 34; and Norman, *Peoples and Politics*, p. 461.
154. Surasakmontri, *Prawatkan*, 4, 273–97.

moved from office as soon as Wisut was ready to fill his place.[155] The king himself, writing some years later, made it quite clear that Phatsakǫrawong's resignation was deliberately forced:

> When the time comes to draw up the budget, those who do so decide first which departments should have their funds cut. The departments whose funds are usually cut are like wells, and tend to be departments with weak ministers and directors, like the various departments of the Ministry of Public Instruction, which are worse than wells—they have been veritable lakes. If anyone is short of funds, they take it from them. I watched and guarded that Ministry with meticulous care for two years, but I was unable to bring it to life, as the head of the Ministry and the heads of the departments were unreliable. They could devise fine programs, but they could not explain them. I helped them get money, and then they did not do the work. The end result was that the head of the [Education] Department and the Minister had to be replaced.[156]

The resignation of Phatsakǫrawong came at precisely the point in time when it would have been logical to plan it, that is, at the point when Phraya Wisut had been sufficiently prepared, both personally and in the eyes of the public, to succeed him. He had worked two years on the Civil Service School, performed excellently, proven his abilities to the king and the official community, and made a name for himself, to the point where the Civil Service School was popularly known as "Phraya

155. The anomalous position of Phraya Wutthikanbǫdi will be examined in the next chapter.

156. King to Bǫriphat, 18 Mar. 1905, printed in Chulalongkorn, *Phraratchahatlekha lae lai phrahat sukhuman marasi*, p. 57. See also King to Damrong, 28 July 1907, printed in King Chulalongkorn, *Phraratchahatlekha phrabat somdet phra čhunlačhǫmklao čhaoyuhua phraratchathan somdet phračhaobǫrommawongthoe damrong rachanuphap nai wela sadet phraratchadamnoen praphat yurop khrang thi 2 nai ph.s. 2450* (Bangkok, 1948), pp. 82–88.

Wisut's School."[157] And only three weeks before Čhaophraya
Phat's resignation, the Civil Service School was reorganized,
Wisut handing over the management of the school to a new
governing committee on which he continued to serve.[158] In
April 1902 he took over the direction of the educational ac-
tivities of the Ministry of Public Instruction.

157. NA 5 S, 71/5, 33, Damrong to King, 24 Mar. 1902.
158. NA 5 S, 71/5, 35, Draft Proclamation on Establishing the Royal
Pages' School, 1 Apr. 1902.

9
Laying the Foundations, 1902–1910

The departure of Čhaophraya Phatsakọrawong brought to the Ministry of Public Instruction a new impetus to change and educational progress which stemmed as much from the effective expression of new royal interest in its work as from the character of the individuals chosen to asume the direction of its activities. No longer need the king exert pressure on the ministry from outside, for he now had his own men in the ministry. With the appointment of Phraya Wutthikanbọdi (later Čhaophraya Witchitwongwutthikrai) as minister, Phraya Wisut Suriyasak as deputy minister and director of the Education Department, and Prince Damrong as consultant to the ministry, the king could count on a sympathetic understanding of his views and efficient execution of his wishes.

The history of the Ministry of Public Instruction in the seven and one-half years from the appointment of Wutthikanbọdi in April 1902 to the death of King Chulalongkorn in October 1910 may be seen most conveniently in three aspects. The first task of the new leadership was to reorganize the work of the ministry in order to implement more effectively the educational program which had been under consideration since 1898. This process of reorganization and redirection extended over fifteen months, from April 1902 to June 1903. In the years that followed, two major problems required the ministry's attention. First, in 1906 the king and the ministry found it necessary to reexamine the policy of extending elementary education in the provinces, mainly because of the practical difficulties involved, as a result of which, in 1909, the direction of provincial education again was handed over to the Ministry of Interior. Second, during this period there was consistent and rapid development of primary and secondary education in Bangkok, as a result of which the ministry and the government as a whole by 1910 could seriously consider the possibility of introducing compulsory primary education. They reached this point, however, only after a great deal of hard work and not a little controversy, and it is with these developments that this chapter is primarily concerned.

TRANSITION AND REORGANIZATION, 1902–1903

It might seem ironic that Phraya Wutthikanbǫdi (M.R.W. Khli Suthat na Ayudhya, 1843–1913), who was raised to the dignity of čhaophraya in 1904, should be included among the "new" leaders of educational reform, for by 1902 he was nearly sixty years old and had been in the service of the ministry and its predecessors for nearly forty years. His grandfather and father had supervised the work of the ecclesiastical departments from 1829 until the late sixties, when mǫm ratchawong Khli succeeded his father. When these departments were incorporated into the proto-Ministry of Public Instruction in 1889, he became deputy minister to the twenty-seven-year-old Prince Damrong, while retaining his position as director of the Ecclesiastical Affairs Department. Despite their difference in age, Wutthikanbǫdi and Damrong worked well together, and they remained good friends until Wutthikanbǫdi's death in 1913. Neither under Damrong nor under Phatsakǫrawong after 1892 does he seem to have been given any substantial responsibility in the field of secular education, and his administrative experience was almost solely in the field of religious affairs. While this undoubtedly was a source of strength in the period after

1902, when the ministry came to place increased reliance upon the monkhood for the burden of elementary education, it was also a weakness—one further exacerbated by the fact that he knew no English and had spent only one month outside Thailand, and that in Singapore. Nonetheless, in the ordinary course of events, he was a leading candidate to succeed Phatsakǫrawong in 1902.[1]

There are a number of considerations that must have led the king to appoint Wutthikanbǫdi. His long experience in the affairs of the ministry must have been a considerable asset in his favor. Of importance, too, were the exceedingly high regard in which the king held him and the warm relationship he enjoyed with Prince Damrong.[2] He was, moreover, much better connected politically than Phatsakǫrawong. Of his four daughters, three were married to the king's nephews, including one married to a son of Prince Devawongse.[3] A more immediate factor in favor of his appointment, however, must have been the lack of alternatives. Anyone brought in from outside the ministry would have lacked the experience and special competence required to administer it well. Phraya Wisut was not yet sufficiently prepared politically to assume the post of minister. The ideal solution was to appoint Wutthikanbǫndi as minister, with the understanding that the primary responsibility for educational affairs would rest with his deputy, Phraya Wisut. This solution brought to the direction of the ministry a minister with wide experience in dealing with the monkhood and a deputy minister determined to force the monkhood to assume a greater role in modern education. The equivocal nature of this solution was emphasized further by the appoint-

1. Prince Damrong Rajanubhab, "Prawat čhaophraya witchitwong-wutthikrai," in Čhaophraya Witchitwongwutthikrai and Phraya Phritthathibǫdi, *Tamnan phra-aram luang, lae thamniap samanasak* (Bangkok, 1914), pp. (2)–(15).

2. Ibid., pp. (9)–(10).

3. Prince Phanurangsi Sawangwong, *Rachinikun ratchakan thi 3* (Bangkok, 1928), pp. 103–104.

ment of Prince Damrong as educational consultant to the ministry. To the extent that Phraya Wisut as Wutthikanbǫdi's deputy was given special responsibilities (which was a departure from usual practice in the Ministry of Public Instruction), to that extent was Wutthikanbǫdi a figurehead minister, at least where education was concerned. On the other hand, this arrangement gave Wisut the power and flexibility he needed to undertake major changes in the educational work of the ministry, while Wutthikanbǫdi's authority was enhanced by the fact that he did not need to pretend an expertise which he did not have. It was not until 1909 that even Wisut began to have second thoughts about this arrangement.

Within a week of Phraya Wutthikanǫdi's appointment as acting minister on 22 April 1902,[4] the new regime began to tackle the problems facing the ministry and to exhibit what was to be its own style in doing so. The first order of business was to clear up the financial tangle left behind by Phatsakǫrawong. The post of ministry accountant (*plat banchi*) was filled by *mǫm čhao* Tum Snidvongs (*phra-ong čhao* Sanitphong Phatthanadet), the Ministry of Finance auditor who had carried out the investigations preceding Phatsakǫrawong's resignation, and steps were taken to overhaul completely the financial administration of the ministry. Instead of having separate financial officers in each of the ministry's major divisions, the ministry accountant was given sole responsibility for all the ministry's funds and accounts, and new bookkeeping procedures were introduced.[5]

The ministry's financial reorganization heralded a process of functional rationalization which stretched over the next four months and was presented for the king's approval in September. The major feature of this reorganized administrative structure was a much higher degree of functional specialization than

4. NA 5 S, 1/1, 11, King to Wutthikanbǫdi, 22 Apr. 1902. Wisut's appointment was gazetted the same day: *PKPS, 18, 635.*

5. NA 5 S, 2/1, 1, Wutthikanbǫdi to King, 26 Apr. 1902; and 2/1, 4, King to Wutthikanbǫdi, 28 Apr.

formerly had existed in the ministry. Previously, the separate departments within the ministry dealing with education, ecclesiastical affairs, hospitals, and the museum each had had its own financial officers, its own inspectors, and its own clerical staff for correspondence and the keeping of records. Under this arrangement a considerable degree of decentralization of responsibility and control was allowed to exist. With the changes of 1902, the converse became true, and the ministry became highly centralized. A new Central Department *(krom thammakan klang)* was created under the direction of the deputy minister, and into it were collected the entire office staffs of the old departments. While the old Hospitals and Ecclesiastical Affairs departments remained substantially unchanged, the old Education Department was drastically reorganized. A new Inspection Department *(krom truat)* was created under W. G. Johnson and was given the responsibility of inspecting monasteries in addition to its old duties of inspecting schools. In addition, a new Royal Pundits Department *(krom ratchabandit)* was formed, headed by Luang Phaisan Sinlapasat (Sanan Thephatsadin na Ayudhya), with sole responsibility for the compilation, publication, and distribution of textbooks and for the supervision of two royal religious libraries (which in 1905 were to be combined with the Wachirayan Society to form the National Library) and the National Museum.[6]

In addition to the obvious benefits of financial and clerical centralization, the reorganization of 1902 served to emphasize greatly the preeminence of education in the work of the ministry. The creation of two full departments, one actively to control and supervise the work of the schools and the other to provide them with textbooks, was especially significant. So, too, was the fact that the old Textbook Bureau was revived at department level, at Prince Damrong's suggestion, and its first director was not a former monk of the type of which the king had complained in 1898, but rather a graduate of an English

6. NA 5 S, 6/1, 1, Wutthikanbǫdi to King, 13 Sept. 1902; and 6/1, 6, King to Wutthikanbǫdi, 14 Sept.

teacher-training college. Finally, the effect of all these changes was to give added importance to the position of the deputy minister in the structure of the ministry, undoubtedly to prepare Phraya Wisut to succeed Phraya Wutthikanbǫdi.

The reorganization of the ministry was but a means toward ends, and it was toward a definition of these ends that Phraya Wutthikanbǫdi and the ministry moved in drawing up what the *Bangkok Times* called "a comprehensive scheme of national education."[7] Almost immediately upon Wutthikanbǫdi's appointment, Prince Wachirayan had pressed the king for a review of provincial educational policy. Complaining, as he had a year earlier, that the continued division of educational labor between the monkhood and the ministry was inconvenient for both parties, he asked that the king reconsider the decision of 1898.[8] The course the king took, after consultation with Prince Damrong and the ministry, was to agree to the promulgation of the "Law on the Governance of the Sangha," which had been under consideration for some years. The major innovation of this law was to formalize the decision asked for in the previous year's conference of provincial education directors by requiring that the abbot of every monastery "see that boys who are pupils at the monastery follow a suitable course of study," and by making it the duty of district, müang, and monthon čhaokhana "to inspect and support religious and secular instruction in the monasteries under his jurisdiction." And it became the responsibility of the Ministry of Public Instruction, and no longer Prince Wachirayan, to support this work and enforce the execution of the provisions of this law.[9] By a further decree of 19 July, the responsibilities given Prince Wachirayan in 1898 were specifically rescinded by the formal application of the new Sangha

7. *Bangkok Times*, 1 May 1902.

8. NA 5 S, 20/12, 10, Wachirayan to King, 29 Apr. 1902.

9. NA 5 S, 20/12, 11, King to Wachirayan, 6 June 1902; and "Phraratchabanyat laksana pokkhrǫng khana song," 16 June 1902, *RKB, 19* (1902/03), 214 ff. There is a useful edition of this law in Chot Thǫngprayun, *Khambanyai phraratchabanyat khana song ph.s. 2505* (4th rev. ed. Bangkok, 1966), pp. 3.1–20.

law to fourteen of Thailand's seventeen monthon.[10] The effect of these legislative acts was to restore to the Ministry of Public Instruction the powers over provincial education that it had lost in 1898, while at the same time the organizational and operational framework created by Prince Wachirayan was maintained and given legal status. The period of "divided labors" was at an end.[11]

It remained for the ministry to define the integrated system of education made possible by its acquisition of full responsibility for provincial education. On 21 July the ministry completed the drafting of a comprehensive "National System of Education" which served through July and August as the basis for discussions between the ministry, Damrong, Wachirayan, and the provincial education directors.[12] Most notably, it began by stating that the circumstances under which further educational development would take place had changed drastically. While the ministry for some years had experienced great difficulty in persuading parents to send their children to modern schools or to see the value of modern education, such was no longer the case. By 1902 the ministry found itself unable to provide sufficient schools for all those who wished to attend, and every school was filled immediately upon opening its doors. The present problem of the ministry was to provide sufficient schools, qualified teachers, and textbooks to meet an established demand for modern education, particularly in the area around the capital. It was to meet this demand that the July draft proposed a new "National System of Education" (so titled in English). The ministry took note of the necessity to draw a clear

10. "Prakat chai phraratchabanyat laksana pokkhrǫng khana song," 19 July 1902, *RKB, 19* (1902/03), 294–96, and in Chot, *Khambanyai*, pp. 3.21–22; and "Prakat tang phrarachakhana čhaokhana monthon," 19 July 1902, *RKB, 19* (1902/03), 296.

11. The *Bangkok Times*, in a lead editorial of 25 July, rightly took these decrees to have primarily an educational significance, although the editor viewed the arrangements for provincial education as something new and untested.

12. "Khwamhen thi čha čhat kansüksa, rattanakosinsok 121," 21 July 1902, printed in *PSSR*, pp. 106–21.

distinction between general education *(samansüksa)* and special or technical education *(wisamansüksa)*, responsibility for the former to be reserved to the Education Department while the latter would be provided only on demonstrated demand and by the most appropriate authority. (Legal education, for example, was and should remain the responsibility of the Ministry of Justice.) Second, it argued the necessity for delineating the various levels of the educational system, but did so in terms of the existing divisions between primary *(prathom)*, secondary *(matthayom)*, and higher *(udom)* education, as expressed through the examination system. Similar differentiation was to be introduced into the special education system, in recognition of the fact that all special education was not at the same academic lvel. Some crafts and agricultural training, for example, could be studied adequately by students with only a primary education, while other specialized training, such as that offered by the Civil Service School (Royal Pages' School), the Normal School, or the Law School, required a secondary education as a prerequisite for entrance into a course. Although such classifications as these were basic to the structure of the educational system, they had not previously been well defined either individually or in relation to each other.

In moving on to consider the means of implementing its recommendations, the ministry stated in this July draft its intention to plan on the assumption that the government would wish to achieve universal primary education.[13] It was obvious to the ministry that it did not have the resources to provide for such an expansion of primary education if previous practices of school support were to be maintained. The solution to this problem remained the same as it had been in 1885, 1892, and 1898: to make full use of the monasteries as schools and the monks as teachers. Were education to be separated from the monasteries, the ministry argued, "we would destroy the usefulness of all the monasteries and the *Sangha,* which always have been the support and strength of our religion, and, more-

13. Ibid., p. 112.

over, we would put the government in competition with the *Sangha,* which we should not do."[14] The ministry therefore felt it should stay out of the field of "general primary *(saman-süksa chan prathom)* education," save only to establish experimental and model schools. In the field of secondary education, the ministry recommended that instruction be made more strict, geared to higher standards, and concentrated at a small number of schools, perhaps five, at central locations in Bangkok. The ministry refrained from recommending any measures in the field of higher education, as it felt that the educational system was not yet sufficiently developed to support education at this level.

In the final section of its July proposals, the ministry presented a serious and detailed discussion of the problems of upgrading and broadening the curriculum. As on similar previous occasions, the ministry recognized the degree to which such improvements depended on the provision of adequate textbooks and trained teachers, and it recommended the continuation of a concerted attack on these problems. It expressed also its awareness of the fact that provincial elementary schools presented qualitative problems quite different in nature from those of the schools of Bangkok, not least because of the higher expectations and greater demands of Bangkok parents for the education of their sons. The ministry therefore proposed to maintain officially the distinction between higher primary and lower primary (elementary) schools that already existed in fact. Primary education was to be divided into two parts: a lower level, elementary education *(munlasüksa,* literally, fundamental education) and ordinary general primary education *(prathomsüksa),* each with its own formal curriculum and examinations, the latter to follow the former. The elementary curriculum would aim only at providing the rudiments of reading, writing, arithmetic, geography, and morality, while the primary curriculum would carry the same subjects to a higher level and prepare students for secondary education. The significance of this division of pri-

14. Ibid., pp. 115–16.

mary education was that it brought together into a single system two categories of schools which Phatsakǫrawong had been forced to separate in 1892, and which thereafter had grown even further apart, particularly as a result of Prince Wachirayan's program at the turn of the century. While the perpetuation of this division allowed the ministry to continue to concentrate its efforts on the established ministry primary schools in Bangkok, the ministry at last expressed its formal intention to provide a framework within which the Bangkok primary and provincial elementary schools might eventually be brought together in a single type of primary school covering the whole range of the presecondary curriculum. The immediate choice was between creating a few relatively expensive higher primary schools to educate a small fraction of the nation's boys, or concentrating on the elementary schools in order to reach as many boys as possible in the shortest time. The ministry chose to concentrate immediately on the former, but it created a system in which, in the long run, the latter objective was attainable.

Phraya Wutthikanbǫdi elaborated on the ministry's proposals early in September, specifying the locations where secondary schools should be established and setting forth at greater length the ministry's policy on elementary and primary education, revealing for the first time the means by which he expected a great expansion in elementary education might be financed.[15] He proposed to require that the parents in any community in which elementary instruction was not yet being offered should arrange with the local monasteries for instruction to be provided in schools. Only when there were more than thirty local boys who had finished elementary schooling could they organize instruction at the primary level. Furthermore, he wished to impose

15. NA 5 S, 83/5, 2, Wutthikanbǫdi to King, 6 Sept. 1902, printed in *PSSR*, pp. 93–97, and in Rǫng, *Prawat krasuang*, pp. 158–61; and "Wa duai kansüksa," printed in *PSSR*, pp. 98–105, and in Rǫng, pp. 162–68. The *PSSR* does not indicate the source of this document nor its date; but Dean Rǫng notes that it was appended to Phraya Wutthikanbǫdi's letter of 6 September. The original copy of his letter in the archives (NA 5 S, 83/5, 2) does not include this document.

upon all monks the duty of instructing the pupils *(luksit)* committed to their charge. To finance these schools, the minister recommended that teachers' salaries in elementary schools be raised by public subscription, all such collections to be reported to the ministry so that the king could acknowledge them publicly. By the terms of this program, elementary education in the provinces was to remain in the hands of the Sangha under approximately the same arrangements as Prince Wachirayan had devised for promoting and supervising it. The ministry, however, would continue the "payment-by-results" system for rewarding monastery elementary schools sending substantial numbers of successful candidates to the examinations, while the provincial education directors—the monks who had served with Prince Wachirayan—would continue to organize and supervise the provincial schools. The only change in the arrangements, so far as the provincial schools were concerned, was that the ministry would take over the administrative functions of Prince Wachirayan's office at Wat Bǫwǫnniwet.

Some discussion of these proposals undoubtedly took place, although it went unrecorded.[16] The king finally brought the consultations to a conclusion on 10 September 1902 by asking Phraya Wisut for the final proposals for a "National System of Education," which Wisut submitted the following day with the approval of the provincial education directors and Prince Wachirayan.[17] These consisted of an abbreviated version of the drafts of the previous months from which all explanatory and argumentative passages had been deleted. Instead of a lengthy argument as to why the monkhood should assume the burdens of provincial education, there was simply a statement to the effect that it was the responsibility of the monkhood to organize provincial education. There was but one significant change: the addition of several sentences justifying the ministry's position

16. See NA 5 S, 83/5, 2, Wutthikanbǫdi to King, 6 Sept. 1902.

17. NA 5 S, 32/5, 41, Wisut to King, 11 Sept. 1902; and 32/5, 42, "Proposals for Educational Organization, 1902." The latter are printed in full in *PSSR,* pp. 122–37, and in Rǫng, *Prawat krasuang,* pp. 168–80.

that local elementary schools should be supported by public
subscription, on the ground that such education was of benefit
to the community.[18]

Out of these two months came four radical changes in educational policy. First, partly because of circumstances and partly
through its own positive effort, the ministry finally brought into
being, at least on paper, an educational system in which the
disorganized accumulated bits and pieces of educational reform
of the previous two decades could be fitted and integrated.
Second, the ministry at last abandoned the false hope of creating
a staff of lay school teachers for the elementary schools and recognized fully the necessity of using the monks as teachers and
the monasteries as schools, at least until such time as the secular
school system could provide sufficient young men willing to enter a modern teaching profession that still lacked a defined social
status. Third, the ministry recognized the necessity of relying
on local financial support for elementary schools as the only
means by which anything approaching universal elementary
education might be achieved. Fourth, a secure framework finally
was created into which the disorganized and ill-controlled secondary and special schools could be fitted, to their own profit,
and thus could begin to work toward a point where many of the
difficulties connected with the sending of Thai students abroad
could be eased. In these shifts of policy, the ministry implicitly
created for itself a role somewhat different from that which
Chaophraya Phatsakǫrawong had defined. Previously, the ministry, and especially the Education Department, had taken upon
itself something of the role of the "proprietor" of the schools it
controlled, and it had tended to neglect its service functions of
providing them with textbooks, teachers, and supervision. The
new role defined for the ministry was oriented much more
toward service for the schools and depended much more heavily
upon the initiative of individuals, whether monks, village headmen, or individual teachers. The ministry was to keep its active
involvement in the schools to a minimum, restricting it pri-

18. *PSSR*, p. 134.

marily to those areas where its presence and driving force were absolutely necessary, as in the fields of secondary and special education. It may be argued that the ministry was risking a great deal by counting so heavily upon others; but it may be that Prince Wachirayan's fruitful four years' experience with provincial education provided the ministry with a valuable example. The hallmark of the 1902 policy was realism. Phraya Wutthikanbǫdi and Phraya Wisut were promising nothing more than they could deliver. They recognized the financial limitations under which they had to operate and shaped their policies so as to accomplish as much as possible through efficient use of their resources. Their expressed policy of diverting a larger share of the Education Department's resources away from the monastery elementary schools was, in a sense, retrenchment, but it was undertaken much more hopefully than similar actions taken in 1892, as it now appeared that private and local sources could keep these schools going. By shifting a greater measure of its resources into capital expenditures in the broadest sense—textbooks, the training of teachers, and secondary education—the foundation was laid for a period of fruitful growth and development.

The seal of the king's approval of the ministry's education program was set on 7 October when he made permanent Phraya Wutthikanbǫdi's appointment as Minister of Public Instruction.[19] A few weeks later, an editorial in the *Bangkok Times* expressed satisfaction at the changes in organization and policy. The editor had reservations, however, as to the progress the Education Department might be able to make without an adequate supply of trained teachers and used W. G. Johnson's published statistics to demonstrate how poorly the schools stood in this respect.[20] Of this, and of the need for more school buildings and better textbooks, the ministry was well aware, and to solving these problems and strengthening its qualitative control over

19. "Prakat tang senabǫdi krasuang thammakan," 7 Oct. 1902, *RKB*, *19* (1902/03), 565.
20. *Bangkok Times*, 29 Oct. 1902.

the schools the ministry devoted all of its efforts as soon as its policies were approved.

The creation of a new Royal Pundits Department, headed by Luang Phaisan Sinlapasat (Sanan) and responsible for compiling textbooks was a strong and significant step toward solving the first of these problems. It was complemented by measures taken in September to establish a network of private commercial contacts through which the government textbooks might be distributed throughout the country.[21] In providing for the need for more schools buildings at minimal cost, the ministry was much more successful than it may have expected to be. The ministry's recommendation that new provincial elementary schools be built and maintained by public subscription received a good response. Reports began to flow in from the provinces of the results of public campaigns for funds to support existing schools or to found new schools. In December the Ministry of Interior forwarded a report from the town of Suwannaphum in the Northeast, stating that eighty-three officials and townspeople had contributed 76 baht to build a new school at Wat Nüa. The next day, a report from Nonthaburi, just north of Bangkok, announced a subscription of 1,073 baht for a new three-room building for the school at Wat Bǫ. Two weeks later came a report from Chaiyaphum in the Northeast stating that, as the local school had but one teacher and more than one hundred pupils, local government officials had subscribed to a fund that raised 166 baht to engage two additional teachers and buy additional benches to seat the pupils.[22] And so went the reports from all corners of the kingdom, for month after month, as new schools were founded and old schools raised funds to continue.

To increase the supply of trained teachers, the ministry applied a range of tactics. In order that the teaching service might

21. NA 5 Ǫ, 5/2 I, Report, *Thetsaphiban* Conference, meeting of 12 Sept., transcript.

22. NA 5 S, 78/5, I, 18, 27, Wutthikanbǫdi to Sommot, 4 and 5 Dec. 1902; and 78/5 I, 35, Phraya Si Sahathep (Deputy Minister of Interior), 13 Dec. There are six boxes of such reports in the archives, NA 5 S, 77/5 and 78/5, totaling some 1,200 pages, covering the period 1902–10.

compete with the civil service for bright young men, teachers' salaries were raised in August 1902, the minimum salary rising from 10 to 15 baht per month, while most teachers were put on the scales 25–40 baht and 45–60 baht per month, and certificated teachers moved up to a scale of 85–300 baht per month. At the same time, the Ministry of Finance was informed of the ministry's intention of further raising pay scales in 1903.[23] Another avenue through which the ministry attempted to improve the qualifications of teachers was the "Thai Teachers' Association *(sapha thaiyačhan),"* founded by the teachers themselves in 1900. In September 1902, the ministry virtually took over the association, providing it with a building for its meetings and evening classes, and Phraya Wisut became its president.[24] Renamed the "United Teachers' Society *(samakkhayačhan samakhom),"* it served as an institution for the in-service training of its members and as a means of two-way communication between the ministry and its teachers. The ministry's greatest need, however, was to expand its training of new teachers, and to this end two measures were taken in 1902. First, the Normal School was moved from its small buildings at the orphanage to new and larger quarters at Wat Thepsirin, which had been intended for Suankulap School, thereby giving it a more accessible location and considerably more room for expansion.[25] The school was able during the following year to institute a new course of training to prepare teachers for secondary schools.[26] The annual output of teachers from the Normal School, however, even after expansion, was only about twenty-five teachers per year.[27] This was an improvement over

23. NA 5 Kh, 87/8, 2a, Proposed Pay Scales for Ministry of Public Instruction; approved in 87/8, 3, King to Mahis, 16 Aug. 1902; and 87/8, 2, Mahis to King, 13 Aug. 1902.

24. Rǫng, *Prawat krusuang,* pp. 814–15. See also *Bangkok Times,* 3 Sept. 1902.

25. NA 5 S, 90/5, 2, Wutthikanbǫdi to King, 7 June 1902; and *Bangkok Times,* 6 June 1902.

26. Bamrung, *Prawat kanfükhatkhru,* p. 29.

27. *Prawat khru* (1957), pp. 80–82.

previous levels, but it clearly was not enough; so the ministry appointed a Committee on Teacher Education to study the matter.[28] The committee was presented with a good, if unfortunate, opportunity to expand teacher education when an outbreak of cholera early in 1903 claimed the lives of two teachers at King's College, forcing the temporary closure of the school. While the students of King's College were distributed among the secondary schools of Bangkok until such time as the school could move into its long-promised new buildings on the eastern side of Bangkok, the ministry revived the idea, first put forward by Phatsakọrawong two years earlier, of using the old King's College buildings—the former regent's palace in Thonburi—for another teacher training school. Phraya Wutthikanbọdi proposed that a new normal school be opened there to train provincial monks and novices for teaching positions in provincial primary schools, the course being open to graduates of primary schools. During their one-year course, the monks and novices could board in the numerous monasteries located nearby, while lay students might live at the school. The king gave his enthusiastic approval and the school opened on 1 May 1903, with Luang Bamnet Wọrayan (later Phraya Owatwọrakit, Hem Phonphanthin), a former teacher at the Normal School and a member of the Committee on Teacher Education, as its headmaster.[29] This combination of approaches—financial inducements, in-service training, and an increase in the opportunities for formal training—was all that reasonably could be expected of the ministry. The final solution to the problem depended upon the response of Thailand's young men.

As the ministry moved to remedy its shortages of teachers, textbooks, and school buildings, it also took immediate steps to improve the quality of existing education by restructuring the

28. Bamrung, p. 29.

29. NA 5 S, 91/5, 165, Wutthikanbọdi to Sommot, 31 Jan. 1903; 91/5, 168, Wutthikanbọdi to King, 6 Mar. 1903; 91/5, 172, King to Wutthikanbọdi, 7 Mar.; Bangkok Times, 27 Apr.; and Praphat, Čhaophraya phrasadet, p. 361.

educational system on a more integrated pattern, by strengthening the examination system and the curriculum on which it
rested, and by tightening its controls over the schools. In fitting
the old schools into a new system, the old elementary and primary schools in Bangkok presented few problems. Here the
ministry's policy was gradually to raise the standards of elementary schools to primary level, while continuing to support
them financially.[30] It was the old "special schools" that felt
most directly the impact of the new system. Prior to 1902, all
schools above primary level were "special schools." These included both those that taught English, at any level, and a few
such schools as Suankulap, which took Thai instruction beyond
Standard II of the old curriculum. At the same time, Standard II
instruction itself, which was supposed to be at secondary level,
was offered at as many as thirty schools in Bangkok, with the
result that secondary instruction was much too widely scattered
to be firmly established at any school save Suankulap; and
Suankulap, after 1897, was moving so frequently as to make
continuity of instruction and student body impossible. This
group of schools and this layer of the curriculum badly needed
reorganization and consolidation. To achieve this object, the
ministry applied two specific policies. First, it expressed its intention to create a strong vernacular secondary school system in
Bangkok which could teach to a credible secondary standard.
Second, it established a definite class of special schools from this
original group which had demonstrably "special" functions.

During the course of the year 1902/03, the ministry's
"special" schools were reorganized completely. The Normal
School, discussed above, consisted of two divisions, classed as
special primary and special secondary schools, to train primary
and secondary school teachers respectively. The syllabus of
King's College was changed to allow its students to gain a
thorough knowledge of their own language before proceeding
to the study of English. It remained a special school, as it taught
a mixed Anglo-Thai curriculum. The Anglo-Siamese School,

30. NA 5 S, 83/5, 2, Wutthikanbǫdi to King, 6 Sept. 1902.

known then as the "Ban Phraya Nana" School, successor to McFarland's old Sunanthalai Boys' School, which had offered students a mixed Thai and English primary education, was moved to Wat Samphanthawong in Sampheng, the Chinese quarter of Bangkok, and was made a special primary school. Students were required to have a primary diploma for admission to the school and were trained for positions in the Post and Telegraph Department, the Railways Department, and commerce.[31] Sunanthalai Girls' School, which covered the primary and secondary curriculum and was "special" only by reason of the sex of its students, was closed in 1902, the ministry having found it impossible to make the school flourish with European headmistresses. (It was later to be revived successfully in 1904 with Japanese teachers.)[32] While the ministry stripped the "special" schools of all their nonessential functions and prescribed their entrance qualifications in terms of general primary or secondary diplomas, it simultaneously moved to create a central core of vernacular, general secondary schools, in which Standard II instruction could be concentrated. The ministry proposed to establish five such schools, and by the end of the year four had been established, at Suankulap (then located in the building of the old Civil Service School and stripped of its elementary and primary classes), the orphanage (Sai Sawali School), Wat Benčhamabǫphit, and Wat Ratchaburana (Wat Liap).[33] No "omnibus" schools, combining special and general or primary and secondary instruction, remained. Out of a conglomeration of overlapping and disorganized schools an educational system was created in Bangkok that was rationally or-

31. NA 5 S, 85/5, 34, Wutthikanbǫdi to King, 25 Oct. 1902; and *Bangkok Times*, 20 Mar. 1903.

32. NA 5 S, 89/5, 2, Wutthikanbǫdi to King, 27 Sept. 1902; 89/5, 3, King to Wutthikanbǫdi, 28 Sept.; and *Bangkok Times*, 30 Oct. 1902.

33. A fifth secondary school opened at Wat Phichaiyatikaram early in 1903 had to be closed almost immediately when the school building was found to have been built on the condition that it be used exclusively for religious education. NA 5 S, 72/5, 1, Draft Decree on "Sukhumalai School," 25 Mar. 1898; 72/5, 5, King to Wutthikanbǫdi, 18 Feb. 1903; and 72/5, 9, Wutthikanbǫdi to King, 19 Feb. 1903.

dered and centralized, in which each school's functions and relations with other schools were defined precisely. With such an educational *system*, the ministry could begin to make changes and regulations valid for whole groups of schools rather than for individual units alone, and to work for the improvement of the system as a whole.

Changes in the curriculum and the examination system were inaugurated early in the year 1902/03. In June 1902 the administration and content of the examinations were changed.[34] The practice of holding semi-annual national examinations was modified, so that only those students sitting for their final primary or secondary diploma examinations were examined directly by the ministry. All other examinations, at intermediate stages, were held within the schools under the supervision of the local school inspector. Papers on morality were added to the primary and secondary examinations, students were expected to give evidence of a broader range of reading, and the mathematics papers on both examinations were upgraded and strengthened.[35] The ministry began to enforce a rule long since pronounced but never before implemented: it was forbidden in government schools to teach foreign languages (i.e. English) to pupils until they had completed their Thai primary education. It was this rule that was applied in closing the old Anglo-Siamese School and in reorganizing King's College.[36]

To supervise the schools under its control and assist them in meeting the ever-increasing demands placed upon them, the ministry took two steps in May and June of 1903. First, it moved to extend its direct control over provincial schools. In provinces where education was particularly well developed the monks serving as education directors had complained of the

34. NA 5 S, 85/5, 50, Announcement of the Education Department Concerning Examinations, 16 June 1902.

35. Ibid.; and Luang Sawat and Čharun, *Laksut samansüksa,* pp. 10, 22–24, 113, and 142–45.

36. *Bangkok Times,* 26 Aug. 1902, and 20 Mar. 1903; and NA 5 S, 85/5, 34, Wutthikanbǫdi to King, 25 Oct. 1902.

considerable administrative duties required of them. Accordingly, on 25 May 1903, education commissioners (khaluang thammakan), laymen with normal school certification, were appointed to monthon Phitsanulok and Krung Kao (Ayudhya), and Wutthikanbọdi and Damrong agreed that such commissioners eventually should be assigned to every monthon.[37] One month later, the ministry issued a code regulating the duties and powers of the Inspection Department in superintending education in the Bangkok area. To the inspectorate were assigned the tasks of organizing new schools, inspecting instruction and discipline, and conducting examinations. District inspectors were given the power to discipline and reward teachers with the consent of the Education Department. To the inspectorate were appointed young graduates of the Normal School, an action that both afforded the schools the benefit of informed advice and stimulated recruitment to the Normal School.[38]

By June 1903 the reorganization of the Ministry of Public Instruction had been completed. A comprehensive educational policy and guidelines for implementing it had been enunciated clearly and the ministry's administration reorganized to deal with Thailand's education as a system of interrelated schools with definable requirements and objectives to meet. The government's approval of these changes was signaled first with the confirmation of Phraya Wutthikanbọdi's appointment as minister, in September 1902, and then when the Ministry of Finance granted the ministry an appropriation of slightly more than 1,500,000 baht for the year 1903/04, including 240,000 baht for capital expenditure, which was an increase of 14 percent over the previous year and 31 percent over the appropriation for the last year of Phatsakọrawong's ministry.[39]

The effects of this reorganization and its significance will be readily apparent to any familiar with the present-day educa-

37. NA 5 S, 20/12, 14, Wutthikanbọdi to King, 23 May 1903; and 20/12, 15, King to Wutthikanbọdi, 25 May 1903.
38. Rọng et al., Prawat krasuang, pp. 154–56.
39. NA 5 Kh, 1/8, 2, Minutes, Cabinet Meeting, 7 May 1903.

tional system of Thailand, which retains many of the most prominent features of the 1902 reorganization. Its permanence is due primarily to the fact that it was at this point that an integrated, clearly interrelated educational system came into being and, as a system, began to sink its institutional roots into "traditional" Thai culture and extend its branches outward to entwine itself among other young and modern transplants. Thus firmly secured both above and below, the Thai educational tree —an analogy favored at the time—continued to grow, more firmly to enmesh itself with and adapt itself to transitional and modern Thai society. The character of the educational system created in 1902 derived in large measure from the ministry's espousal of the still-distant goal of universal education, on the one hand, and from the limited financial and academic resources available to it, on the other. Caught between these two conflicting circumstances, the ministry found it necessary to approach this goal by maximizing its limited resources, concentrating them on the more expensive and difficult areas of the system. It had to recognize clearly that it could undertake directly to control and support only special and secondary education. At the same time, while relying heavily upon private initiative and funds for primary and elementary education, especially in the provinces, it sharpened the instruments by which control could be exerted over all schools, whether government supported or not, and as time went on these instruments, particularly the inspectorate in Bangkok and the education commissioners in the provinces, proved capable of forcing the qualitative development and improvement of the whole system at a cost disproportionately low in relation to the numbers of schools and students in the system.

By mid-1903 it must have been unmistakably clear that the new directors of the Ministry of Public Instruction were no tired, plodding "threshing-mill buffalo." The king's comment when the Anglo-Siamese School was closed and English instruction restricted to primary school graduates might well have been applied generally to the whole work of their first year: "This matter was once discussed a long time ago, but nothing came of it. Now I believe it will be successful."[40]

SECOND THOUGHTS ON THE PROVINCES, 1905–1909

Much of the difficulty the Ministry of Public Instruction encountered in implementing its educational program of 1902 stemmed quite simply from the fact that the ministry was not alone in the government, nor was it the only government agency to judge its own progress essential to the modernization of the kingdom. There were limits to its powers and to the proportion of the national budget that could be allotted to educational work. The ministry began, earliest and most consistently, to run against these limits in connection with its program for provincial elementary education, and these second thoughts on provincial policy led ultimately to a radical change in policy in 1909.

The crux of the ministry's problems between 1903 and 1910 was the basic dilemma inherent in any developmental situation: the problem of priorities. In practice, this issued in a conflict between the instrumental and service functions of the bureaucracy. At the turn of the century it was the active arms of government that enjoyed budgetary preference—the military, the two administrative ministries (Interior and Capital or Local Government), and the Ministry of Finance. Of the remaining ministries, those concerned with economic development fared considerably better than the social services, though only railway construction competed successfully with the other ministries for funds.[41] Education and public health, both under the Ministry of Public Instruction, fared worst: from 1896 until the reign of King Vajiravudh they stood at the bottom of the annual budget list. Only the Ministry of Foreign Affairs re-

40. NA 5 S, 85/5, 37, King to Wutthikanbǫdi, 26 Oct. 1902.
41. See James C. Ingram, *Economic Change in Thailand*, pp. 81–83, 196–99, and 117–18.

ceived less money; and had Prince Devawongse received larger budgets, he could not easily have found ways to spend such sums. The king's, and the Cabinet's, growing awareness of the importance of education as the means by which the civil service could be provided with the educated young men it so desperately needed helped to increase the Ministry of Public Instruction's share of the national budget from 2.2 percent to 3.1 percent between 1898/99 and 1900/01, but their enthusiasm seems to have been dampened in the years that followed, as the ministry's share again steadily declined. By 1904 or 1905, the shortage of educated civil servants was growing less acute as the bulge in school enrollments of the turn of the century moved into the bureaucracy, and the level of recruitment to the service leveled off.

As if the abstract question of developmental priorities were not enough, the ministry also found itself bound by two concrete constraints. First, the great expansion in state revenues was drawing to a close by 1902. Between 1892 and 1901 the average annual increase in state revenues was nearly 14 percent, while the corresponding rate for the next period, 1901–1910, was only half that figure. This differential was due to the fact that the expansion of the 1890s had come about largely as a result of tightened financial control over the provinces, which followed closely behind the extension of Ministry of Interior administrative control. While the Ministry of Interior completed the process of intensifying the collection of the old taxes, the prospects of increasing tax revenues through rises in direct taxation were precluded by the terms of Thailand's treaties with the West. In addition, at the same time as the rate of growth in government revenues was declining after 1900, the country found itself in the midst of a foreign exchange crisis which decreased the external value of the baht. The effect of these conditions was to put a brake on the rapid growth of the previous decade.[42] The friction that resulted could not be handled by the

42. Ibid., pp. 177–80, 236, and 244.

Ministry of Finance alone, and the Cabinet was the ultimate battleground in an increasingly difficult political situation.

The political situation at the turn of the century cannot be as neatly represented as the economic situation. There are no reliable gauges of political temperatures and pressures in an absolute monarchy. Some highly conjectural readings, however, can be taken from fragmentary sources. First, it would appear that the government after the turn of the century was relatively more stable than it had been since the early eighties. There were no further wholesale shifts of ministerial posts after 1896, and the relative standings of the ministries on the annual budget lists changed little from year to year, in contrast with the first years of cabinet government. The Cabinet continued, although to a lesser extent, to be dominated by members of the royal family, who filled seven of the ten major ministerial posts in 1902 and six of the ten in 1910. Frequently bitter personal rivalries between members of the Cabinet were known to affect the government. That between Damrong and Devawongse is well known, but no less important were the feuds that kept the able Prince Svasti out of the Cabinet after 1893 or those that led to the resignation of Prince Ratburi (Rabi) in 1910.[43] Such rivalries and ill-feeling cannot but have been heightened as financial controls became more stringent.[44] As the king himself expressed it, there was a great deal of self-seeking intrigue in political circles in Bangkok, and a certain relish taken in political and personal quarrels.[45] This situation did not, however, get out of hand, and the Cabinet seems never to have repeated its fearsome paralysis of 1893 in the decades that followed. The urgent necessity of avoiding a recurrence of external crisis may have proved the most efficient check of all, and the government

43. See Norman, *Peoples and Politics,* pp. 446–47, 451–53; Phraya Satchaphirom, *Lao hai luk fang* (Bangkok, 1947), p. 125; *The Times* (London), 24 Oct. 1910; and Luang Chakkrapani Si Sinlawisut, comp., *Rüang khong čhaophraya mahithon* (Bangkok, 1956), pp. 76–78.

44. King to Bǫriphat, 18 Mar. 1905, printed in Chulalongkorn, *Phraratchahatlekha lae lai phrahat sukhuman marasi,* p. 57.

45. King to Bǫriphat, 30 July 1901, in ibid., p. 35.

put its best efforts into presenting to the world a smiling, stable political face. On occasion, the king could and did intervene to stop a particularly damaging quarrel by shuffling his ministers, packing them off abroad, or sending them into retirement. He had, however, to avoid taking a partisan position in domestic politics and acted rather as a referee in this continuous political contest, though he was less active and less effective in the later years of the decade as his health declined.[46] This was a tough political environment, in which only the strongest and cleverest could long survive. Such a government could be moved only by strong ideas, forceful leaders, and inescapable circumstances.

It was within and against this environment that Phraya Wutthikanbọdi and Phraya Wisut struggled somewhat uncertainly between 1902 and 1910. The course of their struggles was tortuously circular, as they cast and recast, again and again, the same educational programs in an attempt to break through a political and economic impasse which had little to do with the nature of their proposals.

In 1905, the Ministry of Public Instruction began to reconsider its policy and program of 1902. This policy reexamination had its origins, at least indirectly, in the increasingly difficult economic situation. After obtaining all it had asked for in the budget for 1902/03, the ministry had increasing difficulty with the Ministry of Finance, particularly with its requests for funds for provincial education. Beginning with the budget for 1904/05, the ministry's requests each year were cut back to a flat sum of 150,000 baht. It appears that this was done as a matter of policy,

46. The king was in considerable pain during much of this period. See, for example, his letters to Prince Bọriphat in ibid., pp. 61–62, 62–63, 63–64, 67, 73, and 83–84, dating from October 1906 to May 1909. The king went to Europe for medical treatment in 1907. His death in 1910 was attributed to diabetes and chronic nephritis (Bright's Disease). Malcolm Smith, *A Physician at the Court of Siam* (London, 1946), pp. 93–94. The king set forth his belief in the necessity for priorities in modernization and for his own neutral position with admirable clarity in 1903 in his *Phrabọrommarachathibai rüang samakkhi* (Bangkok, 1953).

as the Ministry of Finance was not satisfied with its plan for provincial education. The Ministry of Public Instruction was informed that no increase in the budget for provincial education could be granted until it had produced a satisfactory and "comprehensible" scheme for using such funds.[47] Phraya Wisut, confident that the 150,000 baht ceiling would be raised in the budget for 1905/06, early in 1905 ordered the construction of a school in Ayudhya to serve as a combination teacher training, secondary, and model primary school for monthon Krung Kao, at a cost of 30,000 baht. Funds for the project, however, were cut from the budget, and when the contractor involved, a European, demanded payment, Phraya Wisut was in trouble. Phraya Wutthikanbǫdi (who had been raised to the rank and style of Čhaophraya Witchitwongwutthikrai in November 1904) and Prince Damrong, still "consultant" to the ministry, investigated, and were compelled to take the case before the Cabinet. A surplus in a special ministry fund derived from the sale of textbooks was applied to the deficit, and in August 1905 Phraya Wisut temporarily entered the monkhood to "atone for his offense."[48]

Phraya Wisut made good use of his time at Wat Bǫwǫnniwet. He studied Buddhism and took "the opportunity to become better acquainted with the customs and ways of the religious community, which previously had escaped [him]."[49] Out of conversations he had with Prince Wachirayan and Prince Damrong during these four months came a new set of proposals for the "further expansion of education" which he addressed to the king in November 1905.[50] These proposals were by no means novel, for they amounted to no more than a restatement of the case for developing elementary education in the monasteries,

47. NA 5 Kh, 1/8, 2, Report, Cabinet Meeting, 7 May 1903; 2/8, Budget, 1904/05; 3/8, Budgets, 1905/06 and 1906/07.
48. NA 5 S, 84/5, 3, Report, Cabinet Meeting, 24 Aug. 1905; and Praphat, Čhaophraya phrasadet, p. 388, where the date of his ordination is given mistakenly as 1906.
49. NA 5 S, 32/5, 56, Wisut to Sommot, 22 Nov. 1905.
50. Ibid.

in terms similar to those put forward by Damrong in 1891, by Wisut, Wachirayan, and Damrong in 1898, and by the ministry in its 1902 program. The most significant inclusion in these proposals was the suggestion that help from outside the Ministry of Public Instruction was required if the objectives of the 1902 program were to be attained. Implicit in this suggestion would seem to be some disillusionment on the part of Wisut with the efficacy of his working relationship with Čhaophraya Witchitwong (which he was to express overtly two years later), as well as a feeling that the ministry's program was not sufficiently well understood in government circles, and especially in the Ministry of Finance. Wisut asked that his "opinions" be submitted for the advice of "persons with an expertise in education," that they might assist him in devising a new plan.

The king referred Wisut's opinions to Damrong and Wachirayan. Much of what they had to say on the subject of provincial elementary education was repetitive of the advice they had offered the Education Department in 1898. Neither of them took their terms of reference very seriously, for both paid only superficial attention to the specific suggestions Wisut put forward. Instead, they directed their attention to deeper questions of educational policy and basic issues to which neither the ministry nor anyone else theretofore had addressed itself.

In January 1906 Prince Wachirayan addressed to the king a carefully reasoned analysis of the current system of education and recommendations for its modification.[51] Notwithstanding a self-effacing cover letter in which he disclaimed any special knowledge of education and proclaimed himself ill informed, Wachirayan produced an analysis of the changes that had occurred in Thai education during his lifetime which displayed not only a thorough knowledge of how the educational system was functioning in practice but also a conceptual grasp of the social function of education which must have been unique among Thai men of his generation. He noted particularly the

51. NA 5 S, 32/5, 69, Wachirayan to King, 2 Jan. 1906, enclosing 32/5, 71, Prince Wachirayan's Opinions on Education.

way in which the general basic education which traditionally
had been offered in the monasteries related naturally to the
special vocational training that followed it, whether in the
monastery or, more generally, in the family, where sons were
trained to follow the vocations of their fathers. The tests of the
old system were not examinations but rather pragmatic tests: a
young man had completed his general education when he had
sufficient knowledge of reading, writing, arithmetic, and moral
conduct to derive benefit from the practical instruction that followed; and the ultimate criteria of success in this latter phase
was the ability of the young man to perform the tasks for which
he had been trained by the monks, his father, or his master.
Traditional education, the prince explained, had declined with
the substitution of manufactured goods for those traditionally
handcrafted, and with changes in social and economic conditions. The educational system had responded to these changes
only to produce clerks for the civil service, while neglecting
special education, training for the specialized tasks, the crafts,
agriculture, and the new technical vocations. These positions in
the society were increasingly being filled by foreigners, and
especially by Chinese, simply because Thai were not being
trained for them. In Wachirayan's own words, education had
become "an instrument of social mobility" (khrüang plian phün
phe, literally "an instrument for changing social status or condition"), but only within the restricted sphere of the bureaucracy.
Wachirayan strongly urged that the government consider these
social effects of education and warned that Thailand soon would
be faced with social problems similiar to those of India, where
far too many boys were being lured through the educational
system by expectations of bureaucratic careers, only to find that
their schooling fitted them for little else than perpetual clerk-
ships. Moreover, he judged that current educational policy had
the effect of weakening the traditional centers of education, the
monasteries. While boys and their parents preferred government schools, which they thought would open bureaucratic
careers to all, the monks were at a disadvantage, being able to

offer only limited instruction which was in keeping only with the old society which was passing away.

As Wachirayan saw it, the problem was one of both too much and too little education, of exclusive quality education as opposed to mass elementary education. The key to minimizing the damaging social effects of education and maximizing its virtues was, in his view, to understand the nature of education in society in both its general and special aspects, and to control the number of students admitted to the various stages of each. All boys (and he postponed any discussion of the question of education of girls) needed a basic, minimal general education, but only a very small number should receive further general education. While most would return to their homes and fields and shops, and there receive the specialized training they required to carry on their families' vocations, a few, by virtue of established family interests, wealth, or personal ability and intelligence, could go on to higher general education at the primary level or even to secondary and higher education, or to specialized vocational training. He viewed general public elementary education as the financial responsibility of the local community, although the government might extend it limited, indirect financial support. The government could concentrate on special and higher general education and could control movement into primary and secondary schools by the use of entrance examinations at all levels and tuition fees in primary, secondary, and special schools. These changes, coupled with the existing strong demand for primary education, would have the effect of putting pressure on the monks to raise the standards of elementary education, which the government might encourage by strengthening the advisory and supervisory services offered by the education commissioners in the provinces and the inspectorate in Bangkok, and by making certain that good textbooks, suited to monastery use by ill-educated monks, be readily available throughout the country. Movement of students through the educational system might be further controlled by imposing age limits for the various stages of the curriculum, which would have the effect of limiting the amount of time students might spend at any level. While many of these specific proposals were not particularly original, what is significant in this document is the way in which Wachirayan demonstrated a grasp of Thai education as a system, intimately connected with the welfare and progress of Thai society. He showed himself well acquainted with contemporary social thought, the problems of education in British India, and modern education in general. He used the English words in referring to "free education" and "entrance examinations" and translated into unmistakable Thai "the economic law of supply and demand."[52] Though Wachirayan never traveled abroad or mixed widely in Western society in Bangkok, he was remarkably well informed and possessed of an acute mind, well attuned to the world around him.[53]

It was some months before the process that Phraya Wisut had set in motion in November bore its fruit, and in the interval several significant events occurred. First, early in February 1906 the government found it necessary to consider its policy toward education in non-Siamese speaking areas, particularly Chiangmai and the North. These former dependencies had been among the last areas to be administratively incorporated into the kingdom, and certainly it was in the North that hereditary local princes (čhao) retained their prerogatives longest. As late as 1902, local resentment at the tightening of Bangkok's control had contributed to insurgency in the so-called "Shan Rebellion."[54] It may well have been with this opposition in mind that the king and Čhaophraya Witchitwong reached an agreement in February on the educational policy to be followed in the North. As the king explained it, they wished to "prepare (Lao) for government service in their own land and to be able to work

52. NA 5 S, 32/5, pp. 77, 78, 81.

53. As a young man, prior to entering the monkhood, Wachirayan was greatly influenced by the king's personal physician, Dr. Gowan, an intellectually inclined Scot. See the review of Prince Wachirayan's *Phraprawat trat lao* in *JSS, 53*, pt. 2 (1965), 205–206.

54. See Tej Bunnag, "Khabot ngiao müang phrae (The Shan Rebellion of Phrae)," *Sangkhomsat parithat, 6* (Sept. 1968), pp. 67–80.

in mutual understanding with the Thai" and to inform them "of the benefits of close association with the Thai."[55] They agreed to send an education director to monthon Phayap (Chiangmai), the king requiring that the monk sent must not be arrogant or disdainful toward the Lao. Phra Thammawarodom (Chai) was sent to the North on an initial goodwill and exploratory mission at the end of 1906, while application to the area of the Law on the Governance of the Sangha was postponed for several more years.[56]

Second, the assistance given the Ministry of Public Instruction by Prince Wachirayan and Prince Damrong at this time was not sufficient nor in time to enable the ministry to lay before the Ministry of Finance a "comprehensible" program for provincial education when the budget for 1906/07 came up for review in March, and the Ministry of Finance again imposed an arbitrary limit of 150,000 baht on this head of expenditure despite a strong request for 171,757 baht. The ministry again was reminded that no increase in the appropriation for provincial education could be expected until such a plan had been submitted and approved.[57]

Prince Damrong responded to the king's request for educational advice only on 1 April 1906. To the king he addressed his "Opinions on Education,"[58] a document similar in many respects to Wachirayan's suggestions but reflecting much more the practical concerns of the administrator than the preoccupation with ideals and ultimate goals that had moved Wachirayan. Damrong began by declaring categorically that "real security can be achieved only when most of the population is

55. NA 5 S, 87/5, 30, King to Witchitwong, 7 Feb. 1906.
56. NA 5 S, 20/12, 22, Witchitwong to King, 26 Dec. 1906; 20/12, 23, Witchitwong to Chief Commissioner, monthon Phayap, draft, Dec. 1906; and 20/12, 42, Witchitwong to Vajiravudh (as regent), 29 June 1907. The Sangha law was applied to monthon Udǫn in 1908 and to the North in 1924: see Chot, *Khambanyai*, pp. 3.23–25.
57. NA 5 Kh, 4/8, Budget, 1906/07.
58. NA 5 S, 32/5, 89, Damrong to King, 1 Apr. 1906, enclosing 32/5, 91, Opinions on Education, Damrong Rajanubhab.

educated and believes in the value of buttressing loyally the independence of their own land." The example of Japan, he added, allowed "no doubts as to the results, nor to the necessity for or potentialities of, education." He had little faith in the methods and procedures currently being employed by the Education Department, which were, in his view, ineffective. The only solution to the problem of providing for the education of "all those who are the people of the country"[59] was, as many had been arguing for more than twenty years, to turn all of the country's monasteries into schools. Prince Damrong recited all the usual arguments to this point, but the cutting edge of his argument came with a set of statistics newly gathered from the monthon commissioners, which revealed that twenty years after the foundation of the Education Department, less than 5 percent of the nation's monasteries had been turned into modern schools.[60] If the pace of educational reform was to be quickened, he argued, the Education Department must make use of the powers granted it in the 1902 Sangha law, which required that the abbot of every monastery be responsible for making certain that all boys committed to his charge be instructed. Faced with a choice between high standards and few students, or lower standards and many students, Damrong did not hesitate to choose the latter alternative: a low standard of modern instruction was preferable to none at all. He hastened to explain that this did not necessarily entail the loss of such quality as already existed in the system, as existing government monastery schools in the provinces could for the most part be maintained as primary schools. Quality in the system as a whole could be ensured by judicious use of the Education Department's powers of examination and inspection, by providing good textbooks suited to the needs of the monasteries and the abilities of the teacher-monks, and by continued efforts to train more

59. This reference reflects, as in Wachirayan's proposals, the growing concern of this period with the role of the Chinese in the Thai economy.

60. And Prince Damrong's figures were incomplete: he accounted for only 8, 226 of the country's 12,000 monasteries.

elementary school teachers. Given every incentive to raise their standards, Damrong hoped that compulsion would not be necessary. He cautioned against following a practice common in other countries of levying a special local education tax, as "people would come to think of education as a burden placed upon them by the government."

In concluding his remarks, Prince Damrong repeated Wachirayan's warnings against the dangers of overeducation while expressing the hope that educational opportunities might be kept open for those who "though of low social status have high intelligence and ability." He was concerned that the nation's educational program be carefully organized and planned, and although he was satisfied with the Education Department's ability to carry out its operational functions, he felt it to be in need of assistance in its planning. He therefore recommended that two advisory bodies be created to assist the Education Department. One, intended to deal with general questions of policy and organization, would be composed of three foreigners who were experts on the educational systems of England, Germany, and Japan, and three Thai educators, with the director of the Education Department (Phraya Wisut) serving as chairman. The other, to handle practical questions dealing with the syllabus, examinations, educational regulations, and the standardization of the Thai language, would be composed of five well-educated Thai, to whom all textbooks, syllabi, examinations, and educational regulations would have to be submitted for approval before publication.

On the whole, Prince Damrong's "Opinions on Education" reflected a strong sense of impatience with the Education Department's efforts to build quality into the educational system. He was much more interested in obtaining quick results at the least possible cost to the treasury and a minimum of compulsion and controversy. Together, Damrong and Wachirayan shared a concern that the government utilize more fully the nation's educational legacy from the past. They differed little on the procedures by which this might be accomplished, but they diverged considerably in their views of the overall role of education and the Education Department in Thai society and government. Prince Wachirayan, while naturally concerned for the central role of the monastery in Thai life, mapped out a large and significant area in which the government must be active in assuring that the educational needs of the society be fulfilled. Prince Damrong took a narrower view, paying but scant attention to that portion of the curriculum in which the Education Department had been most effective, the primary and secondary levels. He as much as stated that he was interested in basic, elementary instruction, while the Education Department was not. The import of both men's advice to the king was that the Education Department needed help in extending elementary education in community monasteries, and in educational policy and planning.

Help was slow in coming. In May 1906, when Phraya Wisut plaintively reminded the king that "Right now the Education Department is prevented from implementing such plans by a lack of intelligent men as associates and proponents" and expressed concern that some action be taken on the princes' recommendations, Chulalongkorn wrote to Chaophraya Witchitwong, ordering him to draw up a schedule for implementing their proposals.[61] His action, and the fact that Wisut implicitly called upon the king to take it, suggests that all was not well within the ministry. Whether for this reason or for some other, the king's order had no immediate effect. It was not until September, at the annual meeting of the monthon commissioners, that the proposals again were discussed. After devoting an early session to problems of recruitment into the provincial administrative service, when Damrong suggested that special training for this purpose be offered in government schools,[62] on 12 September the conferees, joined by officials of the ministries of Finance, Local Government, and Public Instruction, entered

61. NA 5 S, 32/5, 143, Wisut to King, 2 May 1906.
62. NA 5 Ǫ, 5/2 II, Report, *Thetsaphiban* Conference, meeting of 7 Sept. 1906.

upon a discussion of the means by which hospitals and schools might be provided throughout the kingdom. In a lengthy speech, Prince Damrong outlined the major points of his "Opinions on Education" on April and laid down three principles that he felt should govern educational policy:

1. All males . . . of school age must be educated; *but,*
2. They must be educated only to the extent of their ability, so that when their studies are completed they can earn a living in their home region.
3. Outstanding pupils should be given an opportunity for further study at higher levels.[63]

Damrong saw the attainment of these objectives as a simple matter, if the provisions of the 1902 Sangha law were enforced. On prompting from the floor, three further policy problems were resolved: the conference was led to agree that in areas where two languages were in use, as in the North and Northeast, th "local language may be taught, but only education in [central] Thai may be supported by the government." Similarly, they decided that mosques and Christian churches might also be eligible for government assistance, provided that they offered Thai instruction. Finally, they urged that more education commissioners be appointed for service in the provinces, to work in conjunction with and in support of the ecclesiastical authorities.

The decisions of the 1906 conference brought the discussion of provincial education policy one stage further by gaining common agreement on general policy and tactics; but two things still were lacking: willingness to examine the situation of provincial education realistically and to draw from it concrete plans for putting the principles into practice (as the Ministry of Finance had been demanding for three years), and second, sufficiently forceful leadership and determination from the Ministry of Public Instruction to carry these plans to a successful conclusion. Perhaps symptomatic of the ministry's reluc-

63. NA 5 Q, 3/2, 3, Report, *Thetsaphiban* Conference, meeting of 12 Sept.

tance to take this work seriously was its halfhearted attempts to provide the provincial schools with textbooks. Late in 1906, Čhaophraya Witchitwong reported to the king that the ministry finally had prepared textbooks for the use of the monastery elementary schools. But it had produced no new simplified grammar, no new readers designed to raise the standards of knowledge of the provincial monks or their pupils, and no new civics or moral primers. Instead, Witchitwong reported that Čhaomün Si Sanrak of the Royal Pages' School (the successor of the old Civil Service School) had taken on the task of adapting the old *Pathom k ka* for classroom use, basing his version on that published by D. B. Bradley in the 1870s.[64] The reaction of the Ministry of Finance was predictable: it again refused to increase the appropriation for provincial education in the budget for 1907/08, stating again that an increase would not be considered until a comprehensive, step-by-step program had been submitted for the expansion of provincial education.[65]

Planning at least was made easier by the completion of a survey of monastery education presented to the monthon commissioners at their annual conference in September 1907 (Table 1). This survey gathered two important sets of statistics. First, it offered precise statistics as to the number of monastery pupils of all types, including novices,[66] *sitwat* and *dekban* (these two terms distinguishing between those pupils who lived in the monastery and those who returned to their homes in the evening). Second, it presented a set of figures that attempted to measure the strength of traditional educational patterns, on the one hand, and the inroads made by modern educational practices, on the other. There were four classifications of monasteries. Class 1 monasteries were those which had been recog-

64. NA 5 S, 85/5, 48, Witchitwong to King, 11 Dec. 1906.
65. NA 5 Kh, 4/8, Budget, 1907/08; and 5/8, 2, Kittiyakǫn (now Minister of Finance) to King, 16 Mar. 1908.
66. Statistics on the novitiate are especially significant for the North and Northeast, where cultural practices frequently dictated, as they once had in Central Thailand, that boys receive their elementary instruction as novices.

TABLE 1
Survey of Provincial Education, 1907/08

Monthon	Number of Amphoe	Monasteries	Number of Monks	Novices	Number of Pupils		Total	Number of Monasteries, by Type[a]			
					Dekwat	Dekban		1	2	3	4
Krungthep	37	800	11,571	1,464	11,975	861	14,300	97	65	501	94
Krung Kao	30	1154	12,147	2,570	15,163	3,225	20,958	47	408	653	46
Nakhon Chaisi	13	341	4,062	407	2,858	1,020	4,285	9	48	183	91
Prachinburi	20	684	4,408	656	4,506	660	5,822	12	21	461	54
Nakhon Sawan	23	441	4,354	840	5,079	2,269	8,188	22	25	331	63
Ratburi	21	528	8,011	607	7,775	976	9,358	17	14	437	61
Nakhon Ratchasima	19	720	4,877	3,483	5,627	1,072	10,182	17	17	653	35
Phitsanulok	18	402	3,281	913	3,308	1,079	5,300	18	32	275	66
Phetchabun	5	152	861	744	43	548	1,335	2	1	15	115
Chumphon	17	269	1,461	416	3,053	315	3,784	10	222	37	—
Chanthaburi	11	262	2,513	67	2,542	406	3,015	10	76	116	49
Phuket	22	185	949	360	1,881	275	2,516	10	51	100	23
Nakhon Si Thammarat	20	564	4,552	704	6,147	425	7,276	18	8	474	67
Pattani	19	75[b]	657	8	1,013	67	1,088	2	—	72	1
Phayap	46	2614	12,039	24,326	7,424	695	32,445	18	13	17	2,405
Udon	30	1322	5,311	n.a.	5,962	n.a.	n.a.	9	46	55	1,207
Isan	65	2630	13,668	3,056	16,628	22	19,706	24	9	219	2,297
Saiburi (Kedah)	2	21[b]	132	17	189	—	206	—	—	21	—
Total	418	13164	94,854	40,638	101,173	13,915	155,726	338	1,060	4,720	6,774
Type of monastery as percent of total								2.6	8.0	35.6	51.5

a. For the classification of Monasteries by type, see p. 336. There are 272 unclassified monasteries.
b. Exclusive of Moslem mosques.

Source: NA 5 S, 32/12, 27, p. 10.

nized by the Education Department as regular government schools, which instructed their pupils in formal classes and taught to the Education Department's curriculum. Class 2 monasteries were those in which monks on their own initiative (though with the encouragement of the monthon director or education commissioner) had organized their pupils into classes for collective instruction, but which were not recognized as schools by the Education Department and received no government support. These two groups together, representing some degree of modern educational change, constituted 10.6 percent of the total monasteries of the kingdom in 1907/08. Class 3 monasteries were those still carrying on in the traditional manner, with monks teaching their pupils individually. Class 4 monasteries were those that offered no instruction whatsoever. The most surprising result of this survey was the high proportion of monasteries that had to be included in Class 4: 51.5 percent. That figure is so high, and the monasteries included in Class 4 so heavily concentrated in the North and Northeast, as to suggest that ability to offer instruction in central-dialect Thai may have been taken as the criteria of classification.

In discussing the preliminary results of this survey in September 1907, the conferees went over many of the points discussed the previous year, and particularly the problem of over-education. They concentrated, however, on the findings of the survey. Prince Damrong summed up the immediate objectives of provincial educational policy by asking that for the time being all efforts be devoted to raising Class 4 monasteries to Class 3 and that no further primary schools be established as long as each monthon had at least one.[67] This was a minimal approach, its objectives attainable with existing resources and within the terms of the Sangha law. The role of government in promoting provincial education, however, had yet to be worked out, and pending a final decision on this question, including the degree of financial support required, the Ministry

67. NA 5 O, 3/2, 7, Report, *Thetsaphiban* Conference, meeting of 13 Sept. 1907.

of Finance repeated its annual refusal to raise the appropriation for provincial education in the 1908/09 budget. Although
the Education Department at last did present a draft program
for provincial education in March 1908, the ministries of
Finance and Public Instruction together agreed to defer a decision on the degree to which government might support provincial elementary education until separate plans for the
strengthening of education in Bangkok,[68] then still under consideration, had been acted upon.[69] And while the Education
Department pored over statistics and various proposals for
organizing provincial schools and fretted over the relative priorities of elementary and higher education, still lacking was a
tactical and organizational device that would allow them to
accomplish both objectives and satisfy both the department's
sense of what was required of specialized education in the capital and the national need for mass education.

The key to the solution of this dilemma was provided by
Phra Phaisan Sinlapasat (Sanan Thephatsadin), director of the
Inspection Department, who went on a tour of inspection in
monthon Phuket late in 1907. The mixed population of this
rich tin-mining district of the South presented special problems
to the educational administrator. The area was prosperous
and closely linked commercially with Penang and Singapore.
In his report, submitted in April 1908,[70] Phra Phaisan called
attention to the necessity of assimilating the Chinese of Phuket
into Thai society, thereby avoiding the creation of a special
"Baba" Chinese society as in the Straits Settlements, and viewed
as potentially dangerous both the Chinese schools of Phuket,
which taught only in Chinese, and the growing tendency of local
Chinese families to send their sons to Penang or Singapore for
their education. He recommended that a government secondary
school, teaching Thai, English, Chinese, and Malay, be estab-

68. See below.
69. NA 5 Kh, 5/8, 2, Kittiyakǫn to King, 16 Mar. 1908.
70. NA 5 S, 32/12, 11, Report on Education in monthon Phuket,
enclosed in 32/12, 10, Witchitwong to King, 10 Apr. 1908.

lished in Phuket so as to compete with the educational opportunities available in Malaya and that the government generally
aid Chinese education on the condition that such schools offer
Thai instruction. He urged that each *müang* (province) in the
monthon have at least one primary school which also should
offer special instruction in such subjects as tin mining. Finally,
he insisted upon the abolition of one form of blatant social
discrimination which long had existed throughout Thailand:
the custom of prefixing the names of Chinese with the racial designation *"čhin"* (Chinese) instead of the common Thai *"nai"*
(mister).

The general problem of extending educational opportunities
in monthon Phuket was nothing less than a financial problem.
Elementary education in the monasteries depended mainly upon
the more rigorous application of the Sangha law, but a major
extension of primary and secondary education would be expensive. Both types of education needed a continuity of direction
and control and stable sources of financial support which could
not be secured under existing procedures in an area with what
amounted to a "frontier" society. Phra Phaisan recommended
that education committees be established at the monthon,
müang, and district levels, composed of high administrative
officials, the education commissioner, the head abbots (čhaokhana), schoolteachers, and influential citizens. Their duties
would be the financial support of the designated monastery and
school of their locality. In supporting these institutions they
might follow the common procedure of leading regular public
subscriptions, or they might follow the example of ad hoc
committees already operating in Phuket and Trang, which had
been given the right to collect rents on stalls in the markets of
the towns. In such cases, they might share the revenues so collected with local hospitals and dispensaries.[71]

Although Phra Phaisan's comments on the problems of

71. On the problem of Chinese education in Phuket, see also Damrong
to Naris, 9 Jan. 1936, in *Warasan sinlapakǫn*, 5 (Feb. 1952), 8–10, which
refers to the year 1912.

Chinese education and social assimilation were of immense long-term significance, particularly during his later period of service as Minister of Education from 1915 to 1926, it was his ideas on the means by which local education might be financed and directed that were most immediately important. They were commended by his minister,[72] and then by the king, who after carefully studying his report, issued a strong order to Čhaophraya Witchitwong to "Consult with the Ministry of Interior, get to work on it [the implementation of the proposals], and do not let up until it is done."[73]

It was not readily apparent at the meeting of the monthon commissioners in November 1908 that either Phra Phaisan's ideas or the king's order had had any effect.[74] With the final results of the provincial education survey in hand, Prince Damrong could expand further on the immediate priorities in provincial education work. The first objective of policy remained the upgrading of Class 4 monasteries to Class 3 status, while the number of Class 1 monasteries (with government schools) would be limited to one per district. In closing a brief discussion on these matters, Prince Damrong quietly hinted at the direction in which current discussions concerning provincial education were leading:

> The Ministry of Public Instruction wishes to hand over this task to the *monthon* [Ministry of Interior] authorities. The education commissioners sent out by the Ministry of Public Instruction would take charge of it, but they would be under the control of the *monthon* authorities.[75]

And there the matter rested, to be pursued again and finally settled the following year.

The budget for 1909/10 being adopted again without the increased appropriations for provincial education which the

72. NA 5 S, 32/12, 10, Witchitwong to King, 10 Apr. 1908.
73. NA 5 S, 32/12, 12, King to Witchitwong, 27 Apr.
74. NA 5 Q, 3/2, 11, Report, *Thetsaphiban* Conference, 26 Nov. 1908.
75. Ibid.

Education Department had been demanding for seven years,[76] it is not surprising that many of those concerned with the problem were growing impatient. Ultimately it was the king's impatience that first passed the breaking point. Crown Prince Vajiravudh, after a visit to Peninsular Siam in April and May of 1909, during which he spoke with the head abbot of monthon Phuket and the education commissioner, Khun Upakan Sinlapasoet, addressed to the king in June a blistering indictment of the Education Department's inattention to the problems of education in Phuket and forwarded with his letter a printed educational program for the monthon drawn up by Khun Upakan.[77] The king was furious. He wrote identical letters to Prince Damrong and Čhaophraya Witchitwong reminding them of Phra Phaisan's report of a year earlier and of the order he had given them at that time, and he ordered them to "look over this plan, resolve any problems, and get the program going."[78]

In replying, Damrong and Witchitwong revealed that although the Ministry of Finance had for seven years been demanding from them a comprehensive scheme for provincial education, they had only begun to draw one up after the submission of Phra Phaisan's report in April 1908.[79] Damrong tried to argue that a comprehensive plan long since had been agreed upon and its application well advanced in every monthon. Witchitwong more candidly admitted that the ministry was reluctant to commit itself to a program for the provinces until a decision had been reached on its proposals for education in Bangkok. Belittling the suggestions of Phra Phaisan and Khun Upakan as to means by which funds for education might

76. NA 5 Kh, 6/8, Budget, 1909/10.

77. NA 5 S, 32/12, 17, Vajiravudh to Chulalongkorn, 14 June 1909; and 32/12, 23, pamphlet: Khun Upakan Sinlapasoet, *Rabiap thi čha čhat kanbamrung wat lae kanlaorian khǫng monthon phuket* (Phuket, n.d.).

78. NA 5 S, 32/12, 18a and 18b, King to Damrong and Witchitwong, 15 June 1909.

79. NA 5 S, 32/12, 22, Damrong to King, 21 June 1909; and 32/12, 26, Witchitwong to King, 24 June.

be raised locally, terming them unimportant variations on the ministry's own program and probably unworkable outside Phuket, he appended to his letter the ministry's own scheme for provincial education, together with an estimate of the cost of carrying it out.[80] This program followed very closely the arguments and policies set forth in Damrong's "Opinions on Education" of 1906 and, in a few places, the ministry's own 1902 program. Only a single paragraph made the slightest concession to Phra Phaisan's proposals or the king's enthusiasm for them: the ministry agreed that education might be considered a suitable object of public philanthropy and called for the public to contribute to its support. It declined to entertain further the idea of establishing local education committees to institutionalize such sources of support. Less than half its proposals concerned elementary education in the monasteries, and it committed the government only to offer them advice, inspection, and examinations. The remainder, and all of the financial schedule, were concerned with providing schools at primary level and above, to be supported fully by government funds. The ministry proposed to establish three types of schools in the provinces: one combination secondary and teacher training school in each of the country's eighteen monthon; a model primary school in each of the eighty-six müang, which might also serve as schools for practice teaching and in-service teacher training; and one ordinary primary school in each of the country's four hundred districts *(amphoe)*. The ministry requested that two monthon, five müang, and twenty amphoe schools be started each year, which would require an annual increase in the Education Department's budget of 30,120 baht over the next twelve years until the program was complete, exclusive of capital expenditures, which the ministry suggested might be raised locally.

The king was not pleased with these suggestions. He criti-

80. NA 5 S, 32/12, 27, Proposals for Organizing Provincial Education; and 32/12, 28, Financial Schedule for Increased Budgets for the Support of Provincial Education Beginning in 1909/10.

cized the ministry for having "organized the system from the top down, so that while the roof is painted there is no floor." He was most exasperated with the ministry for having over-looked the significance of Phra Phaisan's and Khun Upakan's suggestion that local education committees be established and for ignoring similar institutions in their earlier surveys of education abroad.[81] He realized that although schools in Europe frequently were under the control of municipal authorities, Asian conditions were different, and he ordered the ministry to investigate the financing of public education in Java, the Federated Malay States, and Burma, and then to consider their findings in the light of conditions in Thailand. The ministry might, he added, learn something from the example of Khun Upakan: "He didn't disdain a small project, or decide to draw up a grandiose scheme first."[82]

Phraya Wisut spent the summer of 1909 consulting with the Ministry of Interior and preparing a revised program for the extension of provincial education. A new elementary cur-riculum was drafted in July, incorporating Wachirayan's and Damrong's suggestions on the composition of the basic, mini-mal curriculum, designed to be taught by monks with little training and few textbooks.[83] In August, Wisut apparently quarreled with Čhaophraya Witchitwong and vented his frus-tration with the elderly minister in a long letter to the king in which he complained of "the chronic illness which is eating at the Ministry of Public Instruction from within. . . . This disease arises from feebleness, t.ie weakness of the heart, which is the most important place." He decried the way in which

81. NA 5 S, 32/12, 29, King to Witchitwong, 25 June 1909. These earlier surveys of education abroad included studies of education in Ger-many, France, and Switzerland (1898), India (1899), and Japan (1903). The last two were written by Phra Phaisan. I have not mentioned these above simply because, with the king, I believe that the ministry officials most closely concerned either did not read them or did not understand their importance.

82. NA 5 S, 32/12, 29, King to Witchitwong, 25 June 1909.

83. NA 5 S, 113/5, 1, Wisut to King, 17 July 1909, enclosing 113/5, 6, Draft *Munlasüksa* Curriculum.

"men without ability and dishonest men [were] given power and rewards, causing able men in lower positions to be disinclined to continue." This "weakness of the heart," he concluded, "prevents the other members of the organism from functioning effectively."[84] And the "heart" of the ministry, of course, was the minister. The king's response to this outburst was ingenious: he simply suggested that Wisut be assiduous in attending at his office on Saturday mornings and whenever Witchitwong was away, so as to be able to take full advantage of his position as deputy minister to discipline staff, to submit plans, and to clear up any business awaiting decision in the minister's absence; and, when this course failed, he could disagree with Witchitwong and refer the matter to the king so that a favorable decision might quickly be reached.[85]

Whether because this bit of political instruction was effective, or because all possible delaying tactics had been exhausted, the long-drawn-out problem of provincial education finally was resolved at the annual meeting of the monthon commissioners at the Ministry of Interior in September 1909.[86] To the assembled representatives of the two ministries, Prince Damrong read

. . . a letter from His Majesty the King concerning provincial education which placed all elementary education in the provinces under the control of the Ministry of Interior, to be supported by the Ministry of Public Instruction. As for higher education, including primary and all higher levels, this is to [remain] under the control of the Ministry of Public Instruction. The Ministry of Interior has been given control over elementary education because it is in charge of governing the provinces, and has regular officers in every commune, and thus can much more easily and conveniently carry out this program. The Ministry of Public Instruction

84. NA 5 S, 3/1, 1, Wisut to King, 18 Aug. 1909, private.
85. NA 5 S, 3/1, 6, King to Wisut, 21 Aug. 1909.
86. NA 5 Q, 5/2 III, B, Report, *Thetsaphiban* Conference, 24 Sept. 1909; and 3/2, 15, Report, *Thetsaphiban* Conference, 25 Sept.

continues as the supporter of this education because this program involves the Royal Ordinance on the Governance of the *Sangha* ... and therefore the *čhaokhana* are involved.[87]

Prince Damrong then went on to indicate not only that he had acceded to the king's sentiments on the local financing of elementary education but also that he was beginning to look forward with less reluctance than before to compulsory education. He announced that the Ministry of Interior had decided to establish elementary education committees in each commune, composed of the commune headman (the *kamnan*), the head abbot of the commune, and the commune doctor, who as a body would be responsible for arranging for all children of the appropriate age group to receive a basic education. At an appropriate future date, he added, the curriculum would be expanded and a law promulgated compelling school attendance.

In examining this long process which led to the decision in 1909 to hand provincial education back to the Ministry of Interior, it is possible to discern several consistent themes. Two events annually punctuated this sequence: the Ministry of Finance's regular refusal, each March, to increase the appropriation for provincial education until a comprehensive scheme had been approved, and the annual meetings of the monthon commissioners, each September, at which the provincial administrators were urged to offer their cooperation in promoting the spread of modern education. In addition, the documents suggest that there was some division of opinion over the question of provincial education, increasingly toward the end of the period, as well as administrative friction which may have hindered the work of the ministry. Finally, there appears to have been a lack of unanimity within the government on broader questions of educational policy and the role and function of education in changing Thai society, as well as over the role of the Ministry of Public Instruction in directing the development of elementary education. Out of these developments, the

87. NA 5 Q, 3/2, 15.

logic of the decision grew, not least as an accommodation to compelling circumstances. The crux of the problem was the difficulty of financing mass education. The Ministry of Public Instruction was aware of the limits on the total appropriations the Ministry of Finance was willing to make for provincial education and was certainly cognizant of the difficulty in gaining substantial increases for both provincial elementary education and primary and post-primary education in the capital at the same time. Though the country needed both, the ministry found that it could gain funds for one only at the expense of the other. There was in addition a problem of administrative control and direction: the ministry simply had not the staff or the resources to attend to the needs of elementary schools in twelve thousand monasteries scattered the length and breadth of the kingdom, certainly not under such arrangements as had been in effect since 1898. The key to resolving this twofold dilemma, financial and administrative, was to open to the Ministry of Interior new sources of revenue by which provincial elementary education might be financed so that that ministry's well-developed administrative structure might organize and supervise these thousands of schools, and this key was provided by Phra Phaisan and Khun Upakan.

Since 1899, many provincial elementary schools had been organized and financed by ad hoc committees in the villages and towns, but such committees were insecurely established, dependent on the personal force of the individuals involved, on fickle sources of financial support, and on remote direction without certain authority. The virtue of the new local education committees was that they were less personal, being composed primarily of official members sitting ex officio, and their authority came from the fact that responsibility for educational leadership was vested in offices and not in individuals. These bodies initially were expected to finance educational and public health activities by raising public subscriptions, but to them were opened alternative sources of revenue, and it was not long before most such committees began to impose a "volun-

tary" annual head tax of one baht per person.[88] The creation
of this new source of finance and instrument of control made it
possible for the Ministry of Interior to assume a task of considerable magnitude, while the Ministry of Public Instruction
was left to concentrate upon a task that it knew well. The
Ministry of Public Instruction surrendered only those functions
that it had been unable fully to perform, retaining control over
primary and post-primary education in the provinces and Bangkok. The ministry handed over to Prince Damrong jurisdiction
over the provincial education commissioners and the activities
under their control, but the Education Department continued
to appoint the commissioners and to provide them with the materials and support they required. The ministry gave up the
hopeless battle of trying to finance universal elementary education out of the national budget and began to concentrate on
doing better that which it had been doing well all along.

TOWARD COMPULSORY PRIMARY EDUCATION, 1903–1911

Although much of the controversy in which the Ministry
of Public Instruction was engaged between 1903 and 1909
centered on the problems of provincial elementary education,
the ministry continued as before to concentrate the bulk of
its efforts on the schools of Bangkok. It was in Bangkok that
the greatest share of the ministry's budget was spent, its staff
concentrated, and its energies focused. Education in Bangkok
was considerably more complex than provincial education. It
was much more diverse, the ministry itself operating everything from monastery elementary schools to a medical school
and an English-style boarding school, in addition to fulfilling
its responsibilities for general administration and educational
services. The ministry's own involvement with education in
Bangkok was much more intense and its control over the schools
much stronger. Its relations with the Bangkok schools were

88. Manich, *Compulsory Education*, p. 33.

closer and more typical, in a traditional Thai sense, as personal relationships in the patron–client pattern were infinitely easier to establish and more attractive to the individuals concerned. The ministry must have hesitated when it began to consider implementing a program of universal primary education in 1902. Its correspondence and reports give the distinct impression that the ministry found it extremely difficult to think of schools as anything but fully supported government schools, with teachers on the ministry payroll and integrated into the ministry's own political clique. The ministry's annual budgets, however, were simply not sufficient to supply enough government schools to provide primary education to all boys of school age in Bangkok and, at the same time, to provide the extra concentration of post-primary education and the quality of educational services demanded by the growing, bustling, modern capital and its environs. Eventually, in 1910/11, the ministry had to make a decision on universal primary education for monthon Krungthep (Bangkok and the provinces immediately adjoining the capital) similar to that reached in 1909 on provincial education: in 1910 it decided to turn the problem over to the Ministry of Local Government, a decision implemented in 1911. The purpose of this section is to trace the course of educational development in Bangkok as it led up to this decision at the end of King Chulalongkorn's reign in 1910.

In defining its aims for metropolitan education in the educational program of 1902, the ministry committed itself to (1) preparation for universal primary education throughout the country; (2) the creation and maintenance of a comprehensive educational system in which various levels and types of instruction were formally and functionally defined in relation to each other; (3) the gradual improvement of the entire system through the constant raising of academic standards, curricular revision, the training of qualified teachers, inspection and examinations, and the provision of improved textbooks; and (4) certain specific measures designed to provide the capital with adequate numbers of post-primary schools to produce the generally and specially qualified young men required by a government and society in the process of modernization. In particular, the ministry submitted with its 1902 program recommendations for the creation of a greatly expanded program of modern vernacular secondary education. The problem of provincial education has already been discussed; it remains to examine briefly modifications in the educational structure, qualitative improvement, developments in post-primary education, and the problems of primary education in Bangkok between 1903 and 1910.

Three times during this period, in 1905, 1907, and 1909, the ministry upgraded the curriculum, thereby modifying the educational structure. In 1905 a fourth year was added to the primary course and the content of the syllabus was further broadened to include more instruction in nonliterary subjects, especially science, morality, and geography. Geometry, history, introductory English, elementary science, physical education, and "social behavior" were introduced into the secondary syllabus, bringing down into the secondary schools subjects developed for the rarely taught Standard III, the object of these changes being to prepare students as early as possible for higher specialized training to European standards.[89] These changes were emphasized by further additions to the curriculum in 1907, particularly with the addition of a further two years to the secondary course, and age limits were imposed at all levels of the curriculum.[90] Finally, in 1909, the changes of the preceding four years were incorporated in a revised "National Education Plan." The primary course was cut back to three years while retaining the same content, and the secondary course lengthened by a "higher secondary" course of general education, from which students could matriculate directly in Euro-

89. Luang Sawat and Čharun, *Laksut samansüksa,* pp. 10–11.
90. Thailand, Ministry of Public Instruction, Education Dept., *Rai-ngan krasuang thammakan, phanaek krom süksathikan, pi 127* (Bangkok, 1911), p. 4, cited hereafter as "Report, Educ. Dept., 1908/09." See also Bunčhüa, *Phaen kansüksa chat,* pp. 31–33.

TABLE 2

National Education Plan, 1909

Age (years)   7   8   9   10   11   12   13   14   15   16   17   18

Special Education
(*Wisamansüksa*)

Primary
1 — 2 — 3

Secondary
1 — 2 — 3
1 — 2

Higher
Secondary
1 — 2 — 3

General Education
(*Samamsüksa*)

Elementary
1 — 2 — 3

Ordinary
Primary
1 — 2 — 3

Ordinary
Secondary
1 — 2 — 3

Special
Primary
1 — 2 — 3

Special
Secondary
1 — 2 — 3

Source: Bunchüa Ongkhapradit, *Khwampenma khong phaen kansüksa chat* (Bangkok, 1961), p. 38.

pean universities.[91] The 1909 National Plan (Table 2) brought a distinct advance in the quality of Thai education. New subjects had been introduced at every level of the curriculum, particularly science and languages in the secondary course.[92] At its best this educational system was now approaching Western standards, and the education of boys in some Bangkok schools differed very little from that of boys in Europe and America.

This rapid improvement of education in Bangkok was due to a combination of factors. Leaving aside for the moment the importance of increasingly effective direction, which should in part be evident in an examination of the other factors and which will be discussed below, three developments contributed to the ministry's ability to deal effectively with Bangkok education and its problems: the provision of adequate funds, the increasing availability of appropriate teaching materials, and the training of substantial numbers of qualified teachers.

While the ministry experienced great difficulty in obtaining sufficient funds to develop provincial education during the period, it enjoyed considerable success in gaining increased appropriations for the work of the Education Department in Bangkok. The Education Department's expenditures grew from about 600,000 baht in 1902/03 to 1,000,000 baht in 1910/11, and its share of the total ministry budget grew from about 60 percent to about 70 percent.[93] In addition, by 1908 the Education Department was receiving considerable funds from outside sources, from tuition fees[94] and donations, which contributed to the operating costs and construction of schools in Bangkok. These funds amounted to nearly 70,000 baht in 1908 and

91. Thailand, Ministry of Public Instruction, Education Department, *Rai-ngan krasuang thammakan, chabap thi song, phanaek krom süksathikan prachamsok 2452* (Bangkok,1913), p. 2, cited hereafter as "Report, Educ. Dept., 1909/10." See also Bunchüa, *Phaen kansüksa chat,* p. 38.
92. Luang Sawat and Charun, pp. 11–13.
93. See Appendix B.
94. Tuition fees of one baht per student per month were instituted in general primary and secondary schools in 1909/10. Report, Educ. Dept., 1909/10, pp. 1–2.

115,000 baht in 1910.[95] The ministry's accounts for 1910/11
(Table 3) suggest that the schools benefited as much from these
increased funds as the administrative services of the ministry.
Clearly the ministry was by 1910 a Ministry of *Education,* for
by this time noneducational expenditures formed a minor proportion of its budget. Expenditures on the monkhood and the
upkeep of the royal monasteries remained static over the period,
and the ministry had been relieved of responsibility for medical
services and public health. The major share of its budget now
went for general administration, educational services, and,
most importantly, the schools themselves, especially the post-
primary schools.

By no means did all the schools share equally in the ministry's
prosperity. Over the period, the Education Department withdrew all financial support from elementary schools in the Bangkok area, either raising the schools to primary status and continuing their support, or turning them loose to survive as best
they could. Primary schools fared better, as they gained increasing numbers of well-paid trained teachers, who benefited from
close supervision and were given wide opportunities for in-service training and advancement within a professional educational service. It is the vernacular secondary schools, however,
that emerged as the outstanding feature of the period. The first
were established in 1902/03, and by 1909/10 they numbered
four and enrolled a total of 653 pupils, taught to a demanding
syllabus by trained teachers. There were corresponding increases
in the number and enrollment of schools teaching the special
general (English medium) and vocational syllabi. Such schools
were expensive to establish and operate, but they were certainly much less expensive than the old practice of sending
young men off to Europe for five to fifteen years of schooling.
Students continued, of course, to be sent abroad, but improvements in education in Bangkok enabled them to complete their
European education in an average stay of around three years.

Together with the improved financial position of the Edu-

95. Report, Educ. Dept., 1908/09, p. 51; and 1909/10, p. 10.

TABLE 3

Expenditures, Ministry of Public Instruction,
1910/11

Central Office		
General administration, salaries	56,400	
Ministry secretary's section, salaries	12,550	
Ministry accountant's section, salaries	19,785	
Total, Central Office		88,735 baht
Education Department		
Educational services		
Textbook Bureau, salaries	15,445	
Inspection Bureau, salaries	45,406	
Expenses	89,434	
Total, educational services	150,285	
Bangkok schools, salaries		
Foreign teachers	103,540	
General schools	309,076	
Normal School	9,481	
Medical School	30,642	
Royal Pages' School	41,002	
Total, Bangkok salaries	493,741	
Bangkok schools, expenses		
Normal School	22,951	
King's College	15,000	
Medical School	50,700	
Royal Pages' School	20,168	
Total, Bangkok expenses	157,240	
Provincial schools (primary and above)		
Administration, inspection	48,402	
Expenses	159,740	
Total, provincial expenses	208,142	
Orphanage, salaries and expenses	6,336	
Training abroad for staff	114,520	
Total, Education Department		1,081,343
National Museum, salaries and expenses		12,249
Ecclesiastical Affairs Department,		
salaries and expenses		113,956
Extraordinary and Capital Expenditures		20,000
Total, Entire Ministry		1,316,783 baht

Source: Adapted from Report, Educ. Dept., 1910/11, p. 128.

cation Department went a great increase in the number of trained teachers, which may only in part be attributed to the Normal School. Despite attempts to the contrary in 1902/03, the Normal School trained only primary school teachers, as the demand for secondary school teachers was not sufficient to justify the considerable expense of establishing a separate course of training for them during this period.[96] Similarly, the training of elementary school teachers appears to have been neglected, as the special training school for them at the ex-regent's home in Thonburi founded in 1903 had to be closed in 1906 in order that the regular Normal School might use its buildings.[97] The gap in teacher training was filled by two methods. First, teachers for the elementary schools were trained in the monthon secondary schools in Phuket, Chiangmai, and Ayudhya and in special classes attached to primary schools in Bangkok.[98] Second, teachers for the secondary schools were trained in evening and vacation courses sponsored by the United Teachers' Society under the direction of the Education Department.[99] Recruitment to the profession was encouraged by adding amendments to the Military Conscription Code of 1905 exempting from conscription monks and novices, all teachers registered with the Education Department, and all students in post-secondary schools.[100] As a result of this combination of measures, certified teachers made up nearly 70 percent of the teaching staff of Bangkok's primary schools by 1910/11—a considerable improvement over the figures for 1901/02.[101]

96. Ibid., 1908/09, p. 28; and 1910/11, p. 16.
97. Ibid., 1908/09, p. 28.
98. Ibid., 1908/09, p. 44; and 1910/11, p. 9.
99. Ibid., 1910/11, p. 16; and 1911/12, p. 211.
100. "Phraratchabanyat laksana ken thahan rattanakosinsok 124," *RKB*, 22 (1905/06), 513 ff.; and *PKPS, 10,* 302–15; "Prakat kamnot nakrian wicha chan udomsüksa tam khwam nai phraratchabanyat laksana ken thahan r.s. 124," in *Prakat phraratchabanyat lae phraratchakamnot tangtang ratchakan thi 5, pi r.s. 124* (Bangkok, 1906), p. 710; and "Kot yok wen khru chaloeisak thi pen khru sǫn nangsü čhak kanken thahan chuakhrao," *RKB, 26* (1909/10), *Kritsadika* (Legal) Section, p. 129.
101. Report, Educ. Dept., 1910/11, pp. 5, 9.

Finally, for the top positions in the educational system, as teachers in the special schools, school inspectors, monthon education commissioners, and for professional positions in the Education Department, the ministry relied to a considerable extent on foreigners and foreign-trained Thai. In 1907, for example, there were fourteen Englishmen on the teaching staff of the ministry and at least one, W. G. Johnson (then education adviser), on the administrative staff.[102] Another large group at this level consisted of graduates of the Normal School, which by 1908 had provided the ministry with five school inspectors, seventeen provincial education commissioners, and three administrative staff members.[103] Third, there were in the Education Department an increasing number of young Thai who had studied education abroad, almost all at Borough Road Training College at Isleworth, near London. By 1908 these included the acting director of the Inspection Department (Phraya Phaisan Sinlapasat, Sanan Thephatsadin), the education commissioner of monthon Phuket (Khun Upakan), the deputy director of the Inspection and Textbook Bureaus, one teacher at the Normal School, the headmaster of one special general secondary school, one school inspector, and two teachers in special secondary schools, while an additional six young men were still in teacher training in England and another seven were being prepared for such training.[104] By 1907 the ministry was regularly sending three Normal School graduates abroad each year for professional training,[105] men who in the years ahead were to provide the core of professional leadership in the schools and the educational service which would complete the task of modernization begun in the generation of their fathers.

The problem of providing the schools with adequate textbooks during this period appears to have diminished in im-

102. W. G. Johnson, "Education," in Arnold Wright, ed., *Twentieth Century Impressions of Siam* (London, 1908), p. 231. This article, pp. 226–34, is an admirable survey of the Thai education system in 1907/08.
103. Ibid., p. 230.
104. Report, Educ. Dept., 1908/09, pp. 29–30.
105. Ibid., 1910/11, p. 165.

portance, for the complaints of the previous decade are almost totally lacking in the ministry's correspondence and reports after 1903. By a combination of three methods—using English textbooks, relying on commercial publishers, and having the Textbook Bureau compile some—the schools appear to have been furnished with the textbooks they required. With these, with the provision of increased budgets for education, a rise in the number of trained teachers, and improved curricula there was a substantial rise in the quality of education available in the schools in Bangkok over the course of the first decade of this century. Some of the new problems the ministry began to face, such as the proliferation of private schools, a greater demand for trained teachers than the ministry could meet, the publication of vulgarized versions of classical Thai literature,[106] and the debasement of the Thai language, especially in its written form,[107] were as much signs of strength as of weakness. These problems stemmed at least as much from the ministry's ability, after some years of failure, to stimulate the demand for education, as from its inability to provide as much education as people desired. Similarly, the difficulties experienced by classical literature and the language were at least partially caused by a great increase in the reading and writing public. Between 1902 and 1909, the ministry had increased the enrollment of its Bangkok schools from slightly under eight thousand to more than fourteen thousand, and while most of the schools that taught at the primary level had undergone great qualitative improvement, the upper levels of the curriculum simultaneously were developed from almost nothing, to the point where they enrolled nearly two thousand students educated to European standards at great cost. In this dual process of expansion the ministry had reached a plateau by 1910, beyond which it could

106. NA 5 S, 85/5, 44, Wisut to King, 4 Feb. 1905; 109/5, 15, Wisut to King, 26 Oct. 1909; and 109/5, 16, "Considerations Concerning the Publication of Official Editions and Standard Contract between the Education Department and Publishers."

107. Correspondence between Phraya Wisut and the King, Aug. 1908 to Jan. 1909, in NA 5 S, 85/5, 51, 53, 61, 65, 66; 90/5, 5; and 109/5, 1, 8.

TABLE 4

Education in Bangkok, March 1910

	Number of Schools[a]	Enrollment Male	Female	Total Enrollment
Higher education *(Udomsüksa)*				
Education Department schools[b]	4	213	31	244
Schools of other ministries (1908)[c]	7	1,361	—	1,361
	11	1,574	31	1,605
Secondary education *(Matthayomsüksa)*				
Special schools *(phiset)*				
Fully supported[d]	5	218	47	285
Missionary schools[e] (est.)	2	120	—	120
General schools *(saman)*[f]	5	653	21	674
	12	991	68	1,059
Primary education *(Prathomsüksa)*				
Special schools				
Fully supported[g]	3	292	—	292
Partially supported[h]	2	409	—	409
Private schools[i]	3	79	91	170
Missionary schools[j]	2	550	—	550
General schools				
Fully supported[k]	69	8,651	429	9,080
Partially supported	4	398	—	398
	83	10,379	520	10,899
Elementary education *(Munlasüksa)*				
Schools registered				
Fully supported	12	459	—	459
Partially supported	10	414	73	487
Private schools	24	859	146	1,005
Private schools not registered[m]	50	1,750	750	2,500
Monastery schools[n]	420	22,300	—	22,300
	516	25,782	969	26,751
Total	622	38,726	1,588	40,314

a. The number of Educ. Dept. schools is inflated by nine schools, owing to multiple counting of some mixed schools.

b. Normal School, Medical School, King's College Sixth Form, and Midwives' School.

c. From W. G. Johnson, "Education," p. 230. These included the Royal Military College, Royal Naval College, Royal Survey College, College of Agriculture, Civil Service College (Royal Pages' School), Post and Telegraph School, and Gendarmerie School.

d. Wat Pathumkhongkharam Commercial School, King's College, Wang

not easily pass. The ministry had reached its financial limits, but it had also reached the point where the government could begin to consider concrete plans for introducing compulsory elementary education. Here was the turning point in the history of Thai education at which traditional education was finally left behind and the long march toward a fully modern system of state education commenced.

Surveying the state of education in Bangkok early in 1910, one is struck by the statistical progress of the Ministry of Public Instruction since 1902 (Table 4). Simply in quantitative terms, without considering the qualitative improvements of the period, the ministry was providing instruction to thousands of children in its own schools and it shared, and to some extent participated in, a great expansion in private schools, missionary schools, the schools of other ministries, and monastery education. It was, however, very weak in the field of elementary education for

---

Lang Girls' School, Rachini Girls' School, and Thepsirin (formerly Suankulap English).

e. Based on figures for 1910/11, which listed two missionary secondary schools, Assumption, and Christian Boys' High School. Report, Educ. Dept., 1910/11, p. 158.

f. Wats Ratchaburana, Nuannoradit, Anongkharam, and Benchamabophit; and Satri Witthaya Girls' School.

g. King's College, Thepsirin, and Wat Mahaphrittharam.

h. The evening English and crafts schools sponsored by the United Teachers' Society.

i. Rachini Girls' School, Wang Lang Girls' School, and the school of traditional Thai medicine (Wetchasamoson).

j. Estimate based on figures for 1910/11, which listed two missionary primary schools, Assumption, and Christian Boys' High School. Report, p. 158.

k. Includes primary departments in the secondary and special schools.

m. Estimated on the basis of figures for 1910/11, which listed 73 private schools with 3,641 students.

n. The number of schools was obtained by subtracting the number of regular government schools in the monasteries (112) from the total number of monasteries offering instruction (533). The number of pupils, all of whom were boys, is from the 1909/10 report.

Source: Report, Educ. Dept., 1909/10, unless otherwise noted.

boys between the ages of seven and nine years. Of a total of approximately 27,000 boys in elementary schools, the ministry itself took official cognizance of fewer than 2,000, while there were an estimated 89,000 boys of this age group in monthon Krungthep.[108] By 1909 the education of these boys could no longer be delayed.

Early in 1909, the ministry was informed that the Ministry of Finance wished to reserve judgment on its proposals for provincial education until its program for Bangkok had been drafted, and accordingly the Ministry of Public Instruction drew up a scheme of education for Bangkok and, with the approval of the Ministry of Finance, submitted it for royal approval early in March 1910.[109] This "Procedure for the Organization of Bangkok Education," which was much more an appropriations request than a serious statement of educational policy, provides clear indications of the framework within which the ministry was prepared to consider its tasks in the months after its withdrawal from provincial education. The most striking characteristic of this document is its unreality. The ministry opened its argument by stating in categorical terms that, of six thousand boys in elementary schools, four thousand would continue on to primary schools, one thousand to secondary schools and one hundred to higher education, of which only five eventually would obtain positions as departmental heads (*chaokrom*) in the government service. This argument was intended to justify expansion at the lower end of the educational ladder; but the authors of the program made no attempt to indicate that those who left the system at any intermediate point were of any value to the society. A second assumption on which the proposals were based was the false assertion that, assuming the population of the monthon to be about 860,000—which was approximately correct—the number of boys between the ages of seven

108. Estimated on the basis of census figures for 1909, taking into account male-female imbalance in monthon Krungthep.

109. NA 5 S, 32/5, 152, Witchitwong to King, 9 Mar. 1910; enclosing 32/5, 154, Procedure for the Organization of Bangkok Education.

and fifteen would be "not less than 40,000," of whom 45 percent (18,000) should receive an elementary education, 35 percent (14,000) a primary education, and 20 percent (8,000) a secondary education, while only 13,540 boys in this age group currently were in school. To provide schooling for all these boys, the ministry estimated that it would require "twice as many schools as we now have," 1,158 teachers, an additional 842,940 baht for teachers' salaries, forty additional teachers for special and higher education, forty-four additional school inspectors and education commissioners, and considerable sums for operating expenses. Combined with the costs of implementing the ministry's program for post-elementary education in the provinces and for secondary education, the total bill would amount to an increase of 1,364,750 baht in the annual budget of the Education Department (a sum equivalent to the total budget for the entire ministry in 1910), which the Education Department suggested be granted in annual increments of 100,000 baht over the next thirteen years.

Leaving aside the obvious difficulty that the ministry had failed to take into account the natural increase of Bangkok's population, which would raise the number of school-age children by nearly 50 percent in thirteen years,[110] even the initial figure of 40,000 boys in the age group 7–15 years is open to serious question. On the basis of the total population figures for 1911/12 and the number of boys in the age group 6–14 years in that year, a more plausible estimate of the number of boys aged seven to fifteen years in monthon Krungthep in 1909/10 would be about 89,000.[111] The most likely explanation of the

110. Assuming an annual growth rate of 3 percent, which, judging from the census reports for 1909 and 1911, would be on the conservative side.

111. This estimate and those that follow are based on the 1909/10 census, which gives a population for monthon Krungthep of 513,692 males and 371,031 females, a total of 884,723. The estimate of the number of boys aged 7–15 years is based on the ratio of boys aged 6–14 years to the total numbers of *women* in fourteen monthon. *Thetsaphiban, 10*, spec. no. (Nov. 1910), p. 139. The 1911/12 figures (in Report, Education Dept., 1911/12) come out the same, ca. 89,000.

source of this gross underestimate is that the ministry based its calculations on its own 1898 proposals, which were in turn based on a population estimate of about 500,000 for monthon Krungthep and gave the same total of 40,000 boys of school age. In short, the 1910 proposals ignored a 75 percent increase in the *known* population of greater Bangkok since 1898. Furthermore, in distributing its estimated 40,000 pupils through the schools, the ministry expected to have more boys attending elementary schools than fell into the appropriate age group. In short, the statistical side of the ministry's proposals was grossly inaccurate, shortsighted, and inconsistent. As a result, these statistics made little sense except as a framework on which to hang a budgetary request.

A final point to note in the 1910 proposals is that almost no mention was made of the possibility of raising funds for educational purposes from nonofficial sources or of the possibility of creating local education committees. The ministry clearly did not envisage any further diminution of its powers and responsibilities. The king thought otherwise, and after sending the ministry's proposals to Prince Čhanthaburi at the Ministry of Finance to examine, he administered to the Ministry of Public Instruction what was more than a mild scolding.[112] While admitting that the ministry certainly was entitled to larger budgets and that there was much in the proposals to commend, he asked why the Ministry of Local Government had not been invited to assist with the development of elementary education in Bangkok, just as the Ministry of Interior had taken over similar functions in the provinces. In other countries, such as Japan, he explained, "elementary education does not use government funds, which are employed only in the later stages." He continued,

> On all matters pertaining to the financing and regulation of education, those in charge in the Education Department pro-

112. NA 5 S, 32/5, 185, King to Witchitwong, 13 Mar. 1910; and 32/5, 190, Sommot to Čhanthaburi (formerly Prince Kittiyakǫn), 13 Mar. 1910.

ceed on the assumption that if the Ministry of Finance grants you large sums of money you can accomplish much, and if they grant you little you can accomplish little. Your basic objectives are to obtain government funds and to instruct students so that they can all rise from positions as clerks to become ministers of state, all entering the government service. Such ideas are not consistent with an intention to afford a good education to the general populace.

The king advised the ministry to work on a program of truly national education, which could be more than just training for the bureaucratic service, and which the people could themselves pay for. He asked that a commission of three men be appointed to study education in such countries as Japan and Burma and that the ministries of Public Instruction, Interior, and Local Government together study their recommendations and put them into practice.

Despite the king's assurances to the contrary, the ministry did not obtain the increases requested in the budget for 1910/11, as the year was a bad one and all ministries had to accept a 3 percent cut in their budgets.[113] Nevertheless, the ministry did follow through on the king's recommendations. Toward the end of May 1910, Čhaophraya Witchitwong presented to the king the results of discussions between the ministries of Public Instruction, Interior, and Local Government.[114] Their deliberations resulted in four recommendations: (1) that the appointment of a commission to study education abroad be postponed until such time as alternative measures for school financing and universal education, then under consideration, had received a fair trial; (2) that the procedures for extending education in the provinces, including the establishment of commune education committees, be further strengthened and that it be made clear to parents that it was their duty to send their children to school; (3) that the Ministry of Public Instruction,

113. NA 5 Kh, 7/8, Budget, 1910/11, Minutes of Cabinet Meeting, 6 May 1910.
114. NA 5 S, 32/5, 192, Witchitwong to King, 25 May 1910.

in order to support its primary and secondary schools, be allowed to impose higher tuition fees for such schools both in Bangkok and in the provinces, and that it should require all new schools to provide their own buildings; and, most important of all, (4) that universal elementary education be introduced in Bangkok from 1911/12. It was the Ministry of Local Government, and not the Education Department, that put forward this recommendation, in the following terms:

> Čhaophraya Yommarat [Pan Sukhum, Minister of Local Government] thinks that any province or commune may organize its education in the manner of the Ministry of Interior; but in Krungthep it is necessary that a Royal Ordinance be issued requiring that the parents or guardians of all boys between the ages of eight and fourteen must arrange for their education. Čhaophraya Yommarat will draft such an ordinance, and forward it to Your Majesty. Initially this law should only be issued for the information of the public [i.e. not be compulsory], while its issuance should . . . [be postponed] until 1911/12, because this year is the first year of military conscription [in Bangkok] and the first year of government fees. Both these are innovations newly enacted, and there already are many things the people must do for their country. If another imposition were added, it would be too many for a single year, so we ask that it be held off until the beginning of next year.

Given the informal approval of the king, Witchitwong's letter containing the four recommendations was read the following day to the Cabinet, which approved it without discussion, and on 27 May, in letters to each of the ministries concerned, Chulalongkorn ordered the adoption of the Cabinet's decision.[115] Im-

---

115. NA 5 S, 32/5, 191, King's minute on Witchitwong to King, 25 May; 32/5, 196, Minutes, Cabinet Meeting, 26 May; 32/5, 203, King to Damrong, 27 May, no. 42/336; 32/5, 201, King to Witchitwong, 27 May, no. 6/338; and 32/5, 205, King to Yommarat, 27 May, no. 17/337.

plementing this decision, however, was to prove quite another matter.

The king's order of 27 May was not the end of the affair. Almost immediately, Prince Damrong raised objections to the text of the proposed decree on compulsory education drafted by the Education Department and Čhaophraya Yommarat, as a result of which discussions concerning the decree dragged through the summer months.[116] The king, apparently disappointed with the lack of enthusiasm for his advanced ideas on the part of Witchitwong and Wisut, began a private correspondence with the head of the Inspection Department in the Ministry of Public Instruction, Phraya Phaisan Sinlapasat (Sanan Thephatsadin na Ayudhya), in much the same manner as, twelve years earlier, he had turned to Phraya Wisut when he was unable to stimulate Čhaophraya Phatsakǫrawong to action.[117]

116. NA 5 S, 32/5, 222, Sommot to King, 27 May 1910; 32/5, 223, (King to Sommot), n.d.; 32/5, 224, Sommot to Wisut, 30 Aug.; 32/5, 225, Wisut to Sommot, 2 Sept.; and 32/5, 236, Sommot to King, n.d. (ca. 30 Sept.).

117. Most of the letters in this short-lived correspondence have been published in *Warasan sinlapakǫn,* 3 (Oct. 1949), 1–18, and some are translated in Prachoom, *Chulalongkorn the Great,* pp. 87–95. Phra Phaisan (Sanan) was the eighteenth child of Phraya Chaisurin (Čhiam), and was born in Bangkok in 1877. His father died when he was eight years old, and his mother earned a living as a seamstress in order to educate her sons. He began his education under the traditional system at Wat Bǫphitphimuk, then attended Suankulap, Sunanthalai, and the Normal School, graduating from the last at the top of the first class in 1894. He served as assistant to the headmaster of the Normal School from 1894 to 1896, and then was sent for further training in England, returning to teach at the Normal School in 1898. He became deputy director of the Inspection Department in 1900, director of the new Royal Pundits' Department in 1902, director of the Inspection Department in 1906, Deputy Minister of Public Instruction in 1912, and was Minister of Public Instruction from 1915 to 1926 and from 1932 to 1933. Under the title "Phaisan Sinlapasat" he was appointed to the rank of *luang* in 1899, *phra* in 1903, and *phraya* in 1909, and became Čhaophraya Thammasakmontri in 1917. He died in 1943. For his biography, see Thawin Thephatsadin "Chiwaprawat," in Čhaophraya Thammasakmontri, *Bot praphan bang rüang khǫng khru thep* (Bangkok, 1943), pp. i–xviii.

The opening of this correspondence seems to have been brought about by Princess Phunphitsamai Diskul, one of Prince Damrong's daughters, who early in 1910 drew the king's attention to a printed copy of Phraya Phaisan's 1903 report on education in Japan. Late in June the king wrote to Phaisan about his report, gently criticizing his excessive concern with educational administration and lack of attention to such fundamentals as the influence of Japan's special historical circumstances on her educational development and the ingredients that had gone into Japan's success, and particularly the means and devices by which Japanese education was financed. "This," he explained, "is not only important; it is the very basis of educational progress, or, more directly, the basis of all progress."[118] Phraya Phaisan's response must have been favorable, for in the next few months the king wrote to him regularly, raising questions of educational policy which formerly he had been accustomed to address to Phraya Wisut and Damrong. In particular, the king sought Phraya Phaisan's assistance in conveying to the Bangkok press and public the government's case for introducing and raising tuition fees in the government schools.[119] When Phaisan suggested that a royal decree might best allay popular misconceptions,[120] the king suggested that such a decree might take a form similar to that of the Japanese "Imperial Rescript on Education" of 1890 and asked that Phaisan revise it to suit conditions in Thailand, writing at the same time to Phraya Wisut to inform him of the matter.[121]

On the day Wisut received the king's new order, he had just completed a set of proposals for establishing a vocational crafts school in Bangkok and was about to begin work on proposals

118. King to Phaisan, 21 June 1910, in *Warasan sinlapakǫn, 3* (Oct. 1949), 1–2.
119. NA 5 S, 83/5, 37, King to Phaisan, 6 Aug. 1910, in ibid., pp. 6–8.
120. Phaisan to King, 7 Aug. 1910, in ibid., pp. 8–9.
121. King to Phaisan, 7 Aug. 1910, in ibid., p. 10; NA 5 S, 83/5, 44, King to Wisut, 8 Aug. For the Japanese decree, see Ryusaku Tsunoda, William Theodore de Bary, and Donald Keene, comps., *Sources of Japanese Tradition* (New York, 1958), pp. 646–47.

for a school of commerce.[122] He laid down these tasks and set to work with Phaisan drafting the decree the king had requested. As they began their work, the king wrote privately to Phraya Phaisan, subtly suggesting that a large donation might be made available for some educational project and asking how Phraya Phaisan might like it spent.[123] Phaisan advised the king of the desirability of building a new secondary school at Wat Thepsirin, which would cost in the vicinity of 90,000 baht, to set a notable example for private philanthropy.[124] Accordingly, the king wrote Wisut the next day to offer him the sum of 80,000 baht for the construction of a new school building at Wat Thepsirin as a memorial to his eldest surviving *čhaofa* daughter, Princess Sawankhalok, who had died in 1909, with the request that his donation be handled as conspicuously as possible, so as to provide an example that others might follow.[125] The significance of this episode lies not so much in the specific project decided upon, although it marked a distinct step forward in the development of secondary education in Bangkok, but rather in the manner in which it took place, the project having been worked out informally rather than through official channels. The king's favorite in the Education Department was no longer Phraya Wisut, but rather the young, English-trained professional educator, Phraya Phaisan, who not many years later was to succeed Wisut as Minister of Education.

It was not until 23 August that Wisut was able to forward to the king the decree on education requested two weeks earlier. In the name of the king, Wisut and Phaisan drew attention to the way in which the growth of international trade had brought Thailand into close economic and intellectual contact with the rest of the world, and the educational change that this intensive contact made necessary, in order both to preserve that which

122. NA 5 S, 83/5, 48, Wisut to King, 8 Aug. 1910; 83/5, 49, Report on Industrial Arts School, 8 Aug.; and 83/5, 65, King to Wisut, 10 Aug.
123. King to Phaisan, 10 Aug. 1910, in *Warasan sinlapakǫn, 3* (Oct. 1949), 12.
124. NA 5 S, 32/5, 208, Phaisan to King, 11 Aug., in ibid., pp. 13–15.
125. NA 5 S, 99/5, 43, King to Wisut, 11 Aug., in ibid., pp. 15–16.

was excellent in Thai tradition and to enable Thailand to compete with the West on equal terms. They specifically attacked the popular misconception of the nature of education and the government's responsibility for providing it, explaining that education was a means of inculcating correct behavior and encouraging economically useful knowledge of the arts and sciences, and that it was the duty of all parents to educate their children for the sake of their moral, physical, and economic welfare. It was the responsibility of the Ministry of Public Instruction to lay down the principles upon which such education should be based, namely, that in their studies His Majesty's subjects should (following the Japanese Imperial Rescript)

> pursue learning and cultivate arts and thereby develop intellectual faculties and perfect moral powers; maintain the good name of your family; be affectionate toward your brothers and sisters, as husbands and wives be harmonious in sharing both sorrow and joy, be honest as friends, be thrifty, show benevolence toward all others; support the common good, which is the good of all together; obey the laws; and, when the time comes when the nation and country need your help, give your bodies and your loyalty with bravery, with loyalty to His Majesty the King and gratitude for his great mercy, and be you always loyal to the King.[126]

Chulalongkorn apparently was greatly pleased with the decree, as he evinced great impatience during the month of September while awaiting Prince Damrong's comments on the draft.

Damrong, however, was busy with the annual conference of monthon commissioners, at which were reported the actions taken to implement the previous year's decision to transfer provincial elementary schools to the Ministry of Interior. The com-

126. NA 5 S, 32/5, 228, Draft Decree on the Education of Siam, presented to the king on 23 Aug. 1910; printed in *Warasan sinlapakọn, 3* (Oct. 1949), pp. 10–12. Also translated in Prachoom, *Chulalongkorn the Great,* pp. 87–89. As this decree was in part a translation into Thai of the English version of the Japanese Imperial Rescript, I have followed the Japanese Rescript here.

missioner for monthon Nakhǫn Ratchasima (Khorat) reported that commune education committees had been organized in 127 of the monthon's 209 communes and emphasized the great difficulties occasioned by the region's severe shortage of qualified teachers. The participants were informed of the decision to hand over elementary schools in monthon Krungthep to the Ministry of Local Government beginning in April 1911, under arrangements analogous to those made with respect to provincial schools. Two further conferences with officials of the Ministry of Local Government were held in May and June 1911, to complete the transfer of elementary education to local authorities.[127]

Still, at the end of September 1910, Damrong had not returned the decree to the king. Inquiries revealed that Damrong had asked Wisut to rewrite the decree, evidently without reference to Phaisan, and that he had not yet had time to examine the finished result.[128] Whatever the delay, it was sufficiently extended to kill the decree. No one could have realized how little time they had, least of all the king, who busily kept up his ordinary, staggering load of correspondence through the first two weeks of October. Then, suddenly, on 16 October, his health began to decline rapidly, and on 23 October 1910 he died at the age of fifty-seven, to the profound shock and undisguised grief of the kingdom he had ruled for forty-two years.[129]

To say that Chulalongkorn left behind him a mass of unfinished work is only to emphasize the obvious, for the very character of his reign was the setting in motion of an ancient nation toward the achievement of modernity. He lived to see

127. The proceedings of the conferences are summarized in Report, Educ. Dept., 1910/11, pp. 1–3. See also Report, Educ. Dept., 1911/12, pp. 15–18.

128. NA 5 S, 32/5, 231, Phaisan to King, 28 Sept. 1910; 32/5, 234, King to Sommot, 28 Sept.; 32/5, 235, Wisut to Sommot, 29 Sept.; and 32/5, 236, Sommot to King, n.d. (ca. 30 Sept.).

129. Čhotmaihet phrabat somdet phra čhunlačhǫmklao čhaoyuhua song phraprachuan čhon thüng sawannakhot," in *Burutrat* (Bangkok, 1958), pp. (147)–(157).

the first steps taken toward compulsory education, but he would
have had to live more than ten years longer to see his hopes embodied in law. In April 1911 elementary education in Bangkok
was handed over to the Ministry of Local Government, but that
ministry and the Ministry of Public Instruction together decided to postpone for some years the issuance of a decree of compulsory education,[130] and it was not until 1921 that the first
compulsory education law was enacted. Similarly, the decree
of educational policy drafted by Wisut and Phaisan was issued
only in emasculated form in April 1911, and then as a ministerial and not a royal decree.[131] Both the goals of the suspended
decrees and the man who was to bring them to fruition, however, worked on in the Ministry of Public Instruction, and
neither in the long run could be denied.

THE FINAL DECADE, 1902–1911

In many ways this period of the ministry of Čhaophraya
Witchitwong was a puzzling period in the history of the Ministry of Public Instruction. It was marked by two striking
themes. The most obvious was the reluctance of the ministry to
commit itself fully to a policy of universal elementary education and to its implementation. The second was the ambiguous
role of the king as both patron of education and silent partner
of Phraya Wisut, on the one hand, and the slow deterioration of
relations between the king and the ministry, on the other. It
was only in the year immediately preceding the king's death
that both these themes seemed on the point of resolution.

There were strong and insistent pressures in the direction of
universal elementary education very early, most noticeably
around 1898, when the king's relationship with Phraya Wisut
seemed to promise a great upsurge of interest in public education. The sense of urgency and concern expressed by Wisut,

130. Report, Educ. Dept., 1911/12, p. 17.
131. Ibid., p. 19.

Damrong, Wachirayan, and the king, however, was dissipated after the ministry was reorganized in 1902/03, since the ministry seemed to concentrate upon narrow empire-building, as the king came to see it. Certainly the ministry was inhibited by the annual reductions of its budget for provincial education, but these financial restrictions were due mainly to the ministry's own unwillingness to commit itself to a concrete program of educational expansion in the provinces even in the face of the Ministry of Finance's promises that such a program would be given a sympathetic hearing. Neither was the ministry held back by a lack of demand for modern education, for the contrary was the case. The ministry was interested in universal elementary education, but it was little interested in the sort of mass education advocated by the king, Damrong, and Wachirayan, which amounted to little more than a dressing up of traditional educational patterns in new terms and a minimum of new content. One might not expect of the ministry the same enthusiasm for the old monastery schools evinced by Wachirayan and Damrong, for to expect this of them would be like expecting the Hospitals Department to make more use of the traditional Thai doctors.[132] Among other things, the Education Department was the agent of relatively major social change, and to ask it to serve, in effect, as temporary caretaker of the old monastery schools was to ask it to deny its own ideals, ideals that were constantly being strengthened by foreign advice and example and by the return of young Thai educators from abroad. The generation of Phatsakorawong, Witchitwong, and Wisut was a transitional group, forced to uphold modern ideals, the nature of which they too imperfectly understood. They seem to have felt their role to be an inflexible one: they lacked the self-confidence to compromise between idealized modern

132. This is a poor analogy, as the curriculum of the Medical School included the study of Thai traditional medicine and the old pharmacopoeia. These studies were, however, in a distinctly subordinate position; and advocates of the traditional medicine finally resorted to founding a private school of traditional medicine, the "Wetchasamoson (Vejasamosara)." Report, Educ. Dept., 1909/10, p. 15.

education and the practical requirements and restraints imposed upon them by Thailand's situation at the turn of the
century. They found it difficult to conceive of schools without
ministry-paid teachers, professionally trained, and integrated
into the sociopolitical hierarchy of the ministry. Although when
pressed during periods of heightened royal interest in education
to do something with monastery elementary education they
responded with appropriate words and actions, they were consistently unenthusiastic about this role which was thrust upon
them.

It seems clear that King Chulalongkorn, whose thinking on
such problems was far in advance of his contemporaries, gradually became aware of this lack of enthusiasm on the part of
the Education Department and disappointed with Phraya Wisut.
His disappointment undoubtedly was shared by Prince Wachirayan and Prince Damrong. As Prince Wachirayan seems to
have washed his hands of educational affairs in 1902, the king
was left with only Damrong; and once the king reached the
judgment that the Education Department was incapable of
building the sort of mass elementary education system that he
deemed necessary—a judgment that can be dated between April
1908 and June 1909[133]—it was to Damrong that he turned,
and to him that provincial elementary education was transferred
in 1909. At the same time, after Phraya Phaisan's close involvement with the events of 1908–09, it was natural that the king
should eventually turn to Phaisan for advice and to encourage
him to take up the ideals that his superiors had failed to realize.
The king had a delicate part to play, constrained by a degree of
dependence on others that few have understood. However
much power the king enjoyed in making decisions, his power to
implement them was dependent on those who served him. As
his most effective decisions inevitably were the appointments
he made, and as demotions were nearly impossible to accom-

133. See NA 5 S, 32/12, 12, King to Witchitwong, 27 Apr. 1908;
32/12, 18, King to Damrong and to Witchitwong, 15 June 1909; and
pp. 339–40 above.

plish, once the king was disappointed with Witchitwong and Wisut he had no choice but to make the best of an imperfect situation, allowing the ministry to continue doing what it did well, assigning to others the tasks the ministry was incapable of performing to his satisfaction, and cultivating the men whom he ultimately would appoint to high positions in the Ministry of Public Instruction.

Despite the king's disappointments with the ministry, and despite the ministry's lack of enthusiasm for some of the tasks assigned it, the king, Damrong, and Wachirayan consistently challenged the ministry with a line of policy which, however feebly followed and belatedly adopted, ultimately was efficacious in just the manner it was expected to be. This, coupled with the ministry's genuine adherence to its own policies for post-elementary education, and qualitative improvement made the decade one of real and substantial educational progress. The ministry entered the period in 1902 with only seventy-nine schools under its control, of which only five taught above a rudimentary primary level. Most of the 7,560 students in the schools were studying the old Standard I curriculum, which as yet included very little of modern content. The ministry had only recently begun its program of school inspection and carried on no activities outside metropolitan Bangkok. With the transfer to the ministry of about 350 provincial schools and perhaps 12,000 pupils in 1902, the ministry's responsibilities became very heavy. The Bangkok schools were in urgent need of improvement, the provincial schools taken over from Prince Wachirayan had to be maintained and the foundations of a good educational system laid in the provinces, and the work of extending education to every village had to be continued.

In two of these three tasks the ministry enjoyed considerable success. By 1910/11, all of the older government elementary schools in Bangkok proper had been upgraded to primary status and provided with trained teachers, professional supervision, and improved teaching materials. Special and secondary education were greatly expanded and brought to higher standards by insistent pressure from the ministry and assistance from the United Teachers' Association. In addition, vocational education by 1910 was beginning to receive the attention that would give it a deservedly important place in the educational system in the following decade. A similar transformation was worked on the provincial schools taken over from Prince Wachirayan in 1902. Designated centers of modern primary and secondary education were established throughout most of the kingdom, and the standards of these schools were the standards of Bangkok. The 350 schools and 12,000 provincial elementary school students of 1902 had grown by 1901/11 to 2,732 elementary, 197 primary, and 6 secondary schools in the provinces with a total of nearly 70,000 students, and further expansion to nearly double this number of students in government-supported schools was to be reached by 1916/17.[134] These schools too were provided with professional supervision by qualified education commissioners trained and appointed by the ministry in Bangkok, and all the primary and secondary schools remained under the control of the ministry even after the elementary schools were transferred to the Ministry of Interior. The effect of these developments in post-elementary education was to create an integrated system of education which was truly national.

The elementary schools, however, presented problems radically different in nature. While the ministry might realistically consider establishing, financing, and staffing several hundred primary schools in Bangkok and provincial capitals, a system comprising eight or ten thousand government schools was clearly beyond the capacities of the ministry or the national budget. The ministry was able to take only limited steps toward the realization of the goal of universal elementary education. The most important initiatives it took in this direction owe at least as much to Damrong and Wachirayan as to the ministry itself; the appointment of monthon, and later *müang,* educa-

134. In 1916/17, there were 3,115 schools and 130,278 pupils. Report, Educ. Dept., 1916/17.

tion commissioners, which amounted to the secularization of responsibilities earlier carried out by monks under the direction of Prince Wachirayan, and the classification of monasteries in terms of the instruction they offered appears to have been undertaken at the initiative of Prince Damrong. These measures were vital instruments of educational development in the provinces after 1909. The number of monasteries in Classes 1 and 2 rose from 10 percent of the total in 1907–09 to 36.6 percent of the total in 1911/12, declining thereafter only as government, nonmonastery, and private schools began to provide large numbers of provincial boys with a modern education with which the monasteries as such could not compete. Even with the combined efforts of the ministries of Public Instruction, Interior, and Local Government, however, less than half the 5,050 communes in the kingdom were provided with schools by 1921, and it was only in 1935 that the extension of modern education to every commune in the kingdom was finally accomplished.[135] Even so, judging from the literacy statistics of the 1960 census, it is only those generations educated since 1940 that have benefited from virtually universal elementary education.[136]

To say this much is not to slight the undeniable advances in modern education in Thailand in the first twenty-five years of the Ministry of Public Instruction, and especially in the years after 1898. The literacy statistics of the 1910 census revealed a noticeable bulge in the literacy rate beginning with those young men between the ages of 21 and 25 years (i.e. those whose schooling began between 1892 and 1896) as well as for subsequent age groups.[137] Similarly, the annual report of the Education Department for that same year revealed that, of nearly 1,000,000 boys between the ages of 6 and 14 years, 85,000 were

135. Manich, *Compulsory Education,* pp. 37, 42.
136. Thailand, National Economic Development Board, Central Statistical Office, *Thailand Population Census 1960: Whole Kingdom* (Bangkok, 1962), p. 20, Table 10.
137. *Thetsaphiban,* 10, spec. no. (Nov. 1910), pp. 152–207.

TABLE 5
Education in Thailand, March 1911

Monthon	Age Group, Boys 6–14[a]	Attending School[b]		Monastery Pupils[c]	Total Studying	Percent of Age Group
		Elementary	Primary			
Krung Kao	64,203	7,266	546	24,048	31,820	50
Chanthaburi	15,310	4,957	464	5,383	10,804	71
Chumphon	20,063	2,465	850	5,815	9,130	45
Nakhon Chaisi	35,270	3,358	1,187	7,930	12,475	36
Nakhon Ratchasima	63,720	6,630	263	17,408	24,301	38
Nakhon Sawan	37,454	4,145	1,608	9,411	15,164	41
Nakhon Si Thammarat	57,061	357	603	11,186	12,146	21
Pattani	30,288	183	460	2,055	2,698	9
Prachinburi	42,128	3,852	1,194	8,716	13,762	33
Phitsanulok	30,364	859	243	8,373	9,475	31
Phayap	143,589	7,561	1,991	36,563	46,115	32
Phetchabun	8,936	1,865	219	3,015	5,999	57
Phuket	23,925	3,460	297	4,511	8,268	35
Ratburi	55,515	1,575	706	8,868	11,149	20
Isan	189,557	7,143	1,845	27,876	36,864	19
Udon	82,903	1,025	535	9,463	11,023	13
Total, Provinces	898,543	53,538	16,174	190,621	260,333	29
Krungthep (estimate)	92,000	7,842[d]	7,510	18,638	33,990	34
National Total	990,543	61,380	23,684	209,259	294,323	29

a. From Report, Educ. Dept., 1911/12, age group 7–15. b. Secondary schools omitted, as their pupils out of age group. c. Including novices, *sitwat*, and *dekban*. d. Includes about 3,000 pupils in private schools and about 4,000 in the new municipal schools transferred to the Ministry of Local Government in April 1911. *Source:* Report, Educ. Dept., 1910/11, unless otherwise noted.

attending elementary and primary schools, while another 210,000 still received some form of instruction in the monasteries. This amounted to a total of 29 percent of the school-age population (Table 5).

The ministry had accomplished a great deal. By 1910 the government had arrived at a definition of educational policy and of responsibilities for its implementation that ultimately would enable it to meet the heavy burdens it had assumed. The limitations of the Education Department were recognized and its duties limited to education at primary level and above, the provision of educational services, and lending qualitative leadership to the system as a whole. To the ministries of Interior and Local Government were given the task of mobilizing the popular support upon which the extension of elementary education to every village and commune depended. Upon the patient and virtually silent monkhood fell the heavy burden of a task for which it was but poorly prepared. A thirty-year war on ignorance, isolation, and illiteracy had just begun in earnest when the commander in chief died in 1910, but the objectives, the strategy, and the guiding spirit which were to bring about ultimate victory were indelibly his.

10

The Beginnings of Modern Education in Thailand

During the forty-two years of King Chulalongkorn's reign came the definitive break between the old Siam and the new Thailand. Whether this marked the passage to modernity in any strict definition of the word is at once a more specific question and a considerably more complex one. The course of educational modernization, which has been treated in the preceding chapters, provides a number of insights that may illuminate the broader questions. The most important of these is the question of the respective roles of ideas and men in this profoundly important period in Thai history.

Thailand is one of only a handful of Asian countries to have survived the most dangerous epoch of Western colonial expansion, between the middle of the nineteenth century and World War I. The reasons for their respective survivals are dissimilar, as are the characteristics of each in transition. A feature of great significance for Thailand's survival, however, was the fact that the transformation of her society and government was accomplished largely through action from above, by leaders who were more than leaders; visionaries who were sensitive to the needs of the age and who forced change upon their nation and themselves directed and ordered its economic, social, and political development.

In the Thai case, as in Japan's, it is necessary in assessing the transformations that these leaders engineered to distinguish between the men, in their social, cultural, and political environment at home, on the one hand, and the modern, Western ideas, techniques, and political circumstances with which they were confronted, on the other. This is not a neat distinction, nor necessarily a valid one, for men are not easily distinguished from the ideas and values that enlighten and guide them. It can, however, be a meaningful distinction in a context such as this, where the rulers of old Siam were confronted with a whole universe of ideas, values, and attitudes which were not their own, in a situation in which they were under strong pressure to adopt the ways of others. Many Westerners who visited and worked in Thailand during Chulalongkorn's reign desired, indeed, even more: implicit in many of their recommendations and criticisms was a demand that the Thai cease being Thai and become "civilized" like themselves. Had the Thai done so, this study would have been an examination of Thailand's "Westernization." Needless to say, they did not. The Thai interacted with these new ideas, choosing from among them those aspects of the modern world that they deemed necessary, desirable, digestible, and workable; and by attempting—consciously or not—to distinguish the "modern" from the "Western" elements, they fused these *modern* elements with the enduring values of their heritage to create a modern nation. It is with this serial process of choice that we must here be concerned: the major choices that had to be made, the circumstances in which they were made, the degree to which these choices were freely taken, and the nature of the result. The application of this line of questioning to Thailand's educational development suggests hypotheses which, if valid, contribute to a better understanding of all of Chulalongkorn's reign.

A singular feature of this series of decisions is the degree to which each was governed by political circumstances and thus, frequently, was not truly free. This is especially noticeable in the first half of the reign, when domestic political circumstances held reform to ransom for nearly ten years. In general, seen from the schools and the Ministry of Public Instruction, the central rhythm in the events of the reign is a political one, to which the course of educational modernization had to conform. The fortunes of education and the ministry hung, not on any rarified currents of intellectual change and choice, but on the web of Thai politics. The ideas of individuals, although in the long run profoundly important, were not allowed to interfere with their actions. Men could be swayed by their convictions and commitments or attitudes, but their environment was so strongly constrained by convention and current economic and political conditions as to render stillborn any idea whose time had not come. The king's task was, first, to seize power from his father's generation, and then so to use it as to bring the nation to a point at which it could accept his dreams and make them its own.

Chulalongkorn and "Young Siam" were, it is true, held together as a group in the early years of the reign by common attitudes and shared ideas. They shared a receptivity to and admiration of the West and the modern elements of the culture which it bore. They shared also a sincere reverence for their cultural heritage and the ties of continuity that bound them to their own past and assured their identity as Thai. Chulalongkorn's generation, however, was even more directly shaped by the difficult times through which they lived, as boys during the regency, as avid reformers in 1874, and as heartbroken young rulers in 1893. They struggled for their power, first against the generation of their fathers and grandfathers, and then against France and the West. In both crucial battles they came too close to losing not only their personal power but also their nation. In the early years of the reign they were identified with modernity and "civilized" standards and maintained their commitment to change even when change was impossible in any fundamental manner. By the nineties, when finally able to begin to refashion the kingdom, they were suddenly the object of Western criticism and abuse for proceeding too slowly with the work of modernization. It is hardly surprising that they became adept at the techniques of traditional Thai politics, for only through the exercise of every device practiced by their opponents and of everything of utility they could borrow from the West could they even begin to rule on their own. Similarly, it is not surprising that after 1875 and 1893 they could view the "civilized" West with a healthy detachment.

Throughout his reign, Chulalongkorn and his brothers and friends were the objects of great pressure, first to fit into the comfortable but weak neotraditional[1] mode of King Mongkut's reign, and later to modernize. In the first half of the reign they could not modernize; and in the latter half of the reign they were forced to modernize if they were to maintain their independence. By inclination they were willing and even anxious to modernize for a great many reasons; yet foreign attitudes generally were much more of a threatening than of an encouraging nature. If the Thai did not reform and innovate, they knew that they stood little chance of maintaining their independence and their identity. Reform and power were inextricably entwined: Chulalongkorn had to gain power in order to modernize, which would allow him to retain power; and the power of the West stood behind European demands that he modernize. Much more strongly than its Western advisers and critics, Chulalongkorn's generation saw the ambiguity in its predicament and suffered from it. Forced to modernize to protect their independence, they found that modernity threatened their identity as Thai. Some found that modern techniques and ideas threatened their personal and political prerogatives, but Chulalongkorn and his brothers were pained as they saw their Western borrowings eating away at the foundations of Thai culture. Almost as a cry of relief came the king's speech on his return from Europe in 1898, at his discovery that "there exists no incompatibility between [the acquisition of European science] and the maintenance of our individuality as an independent Asiatic nation."[2] Like his Japanese contemporaries, Chulalongkorn learned only slowly the difference between

1. Fred W. Riggs, *Thailand: The Modernization of a Bureaucratic Polity* (Honolulu, 1966), pp. 370–71.
2. *Bangkok Times,* 26 Jan. 1898.

Westernization and modernization.[3] Only modernization could permit the survival of a Thai national identity.

The whole of Thailand's confrontation with the West in Chulalongkorn's reign was fraught with contradictions, dilemmas, and ambiguities. Her rulers both admired and feared the West; they wanted to be both Thai and modern; they were asked to move closer to "civilized" standards yet wished to maintain the continuity that bound them to the values and traditions of their own civilization, and they wished to be accepted by the West as equals, yet were reluctant to pay the high cost of such acceptance. They learned only slowly that compromise was possible, that they could modernize without Westernizing, and that they could recast their old society, cultural traditions, and institutions in new, modern modes without destroying the values that made them uniquely Thai.

The history of the beginnings of modern education in Thailand provides ample illustrations of these general phenomena, and particularly of the necessity of distinguishing between instruments and functions. By the middle of the nineteenth century, Thailand had a long record of social health. Its educational institutions had on numerous occasions in the past adapted foreign instruments—knowledge, practices, and techniques—to serve the requirements of a changing society without any loss of essential continuity. The functions of these institutions remained the socialization of the individual so as to prepare him for a life in harmony with the basic moral, social, and economic ends of the society. The Third and Fourth reigns of the Bangkok period saw a quickening of foreign contacts and the introduction of discrete blocks of foreign knowledge which were integrated into Thai life without any momentous effects upon the life of the society. This phase of borrowing served both social values and national needs: the social and economic utility of technical knowledge, and the need for greater understanding of the West, which still was dimly perceived as a threat to the na-

3. See Hideo Kishimoto, "Modernization *versus* Westernization in the East," *Journal of World History*, 7 (1963), 871–74.

tion. Mongkut and his contemporaries, however, saw and felt no threat to their own identity as Thai and easily integrated these limited instruments of control over and knowledge of the physical world into traditional institutions. Mongkut's hiring of Mrs. Leonowens as tutor to his children stands as an example of the integration of new fields of knowledge into the traditional tutorial regime provided for young princes, without any significant change in the institution itself. Here was a case of traditional educational institutions being modified to function in the service of changing social and political needs as defined by the ruling class.

The two educational innovations of the regency period, the palace Thai and English schools, represent a further development of the same process of response to changing requirements, in this case, the king's (and probably a few others') perception of the need for a better-educated official class. These institutions were not very successful, as they exceeded the felt needs of the ruling classes. Patterson's English school was notably unsuccessful, if one excepts the great influence it had on three or four of Mongkut's sons, who in their thinking and attitudes were a generation ahead of their contemporaries, as was the king. The continued existence of the Thai school of Phraya Si Sunthǫn Wohan may be attributed not to its success in performing the functions defined for it by the king, but rather to its success in fulfilling functions sanctified by tradition, providing a social (and not specifically academic) avenue through which young men might attain official positions—a further embellishment on the Royal Pages' Corps. The values embodied in this school were not the academic and intellectual ones advocated by the king, but rather traditional social values, and particularly the value placed upon the service of the king as such. The students of this school undoubtedly gained from regularized and standardized instruction imparted in Western-style classes, but the school was overwhelmingly a Thai institution, infused with Thai values, serving traditional though broadened functions, and inculcating traditionally desirable knowledge. The trace of borrowed Western instruments—printed textbooks and common classes—only marginally defined its character.

The founding of McFarland's Suan Anand School a few years later provides a curious example of the differing degrees to which various elements of the society perceived the changing requirements of the society for Western or modern instruments of progress. Although initially founded by and for members of the ruling classes, it was rather the mercantile classes of the capital, predominantly Chinese, who responded to it. The school did fulfill a new social function, but this was a function most readily perceived and appreciated by Bangkok's Chinese minority and marginal elements in the society of the capital. They could see the advantages of English instruction as an avenue either to commercial success in the increasingly outward-looking economic activities of the capital, or to partly traditional and partly modern opportunities in those specialized new branches of the bureaucracy which required men with a working knowledge of English or such modern skills as accounting, surveying, or telegraphy. The basic values of the society and its basic institutions were not yet deeply affected.[4]

The quality of these enduring values and institutions became evident when Prince Damrong began his educational activities early in the 1880s. First in founding Suankulap School and then in promoting the development of modern-style monastery education, Prince Damrong clearly indicated that it was his intention to turn these modern educational instruments to the service of traditional, culturally acceptable functions. Suankulap's origins thus tied it to the social and political functions formerly served by the Royal Pages' Corps and the monastery schools sincerely were made to appear as further refinements of monastery education. Initially there was only a slight distortion of the traditional institutions and more a reaffirmation

4. I have examined the problem of Thai popular response to modern educational opportunities in "Education and the Modernization of Thai Society," in *Change and Persistence in Thai Society*, ed. G. William Skinner (*Homage to Lauriston Sharp*, vol. 2 Ithaca: Cornell University Press, forthcoming).

of traditional values of government service and Buddhist lay-manship than an introduction of new values. The guiding theme in these developments was the elevation of Thai society to a new plane, with a heightened degree of competence in dealing with its own changing world; but at this point in time, com-petence still enjoyed a general definition, the "liberal educa-tion" of Thai tradition.

It was during the last few years of Damrong's period, from 1887 or 1889, that the modernization–Westernization dilemma first began to present itself as the Thai government began con-sciously to import Western institutions on a grand scale, at the same time as Western political pressure was reaching its height. The pressure to conform must have been intense: one need only read a few of Morant's letters to see how heavy it must have been; and Prince Damrong was one who was more noticeably successful than most of his contemporaries at pleasing the *farang*. Not the least of the legacies of this period was the creation of a department and soon a ministry, the functions of which were officially defined in borrowed terms. Their creation was itself an imitation of Western practice. The difficulties of most of the remainder of the reign stemmed from the inability of successive ministers to relate the instruments they had bor-rowed to the functions these were to serve.

Those officials charged with the administration of these new organs of government, from Chaophraya Phatsakǫrawong to Phraya Wisut, were men whose experience of the West was limited and who had a strong tendency to grasp the West intact. They were too insecure in their roles as educational innovators to know how much real innovation and how much com-promise was expected of them. Out of their insecurity came a preoccupation with secondary and special education in Bangkok and a lack of serious concern for elementary and provincial edu-cation. The 1898–1902 interlude in the ministry's history illustrates some of these themes. Though the concern of Dam-rong and Wachirayan for general public elementary education was voiced in terms of a blend of Western and Thai values and practices, the ministry concentrated on the imitative aspects of its activities, leaving Wachirayan to develop provincial education and lay the groundwork for solid educational progress a decade thence.

The year 1898 marks the dawn of the king's realization that educational modernization could be accomplished without damage to the Thai national identity, and, on the contrary, that it could shape and brighten that ideal in a form acceptable both to traditional sensitivities and to the West. The implications of this discovery grew slowly on the king, but even more slowly on the Ministry of Public Instruction. Chaophraya Witchitwong and Phraya Wisut made a promising gesture in their educational program of 1902, but by 1905 it was clear that it was only a gesture. The ministry so conceived of its role in Western terms that it was unable to see the validity of the modern Thai alternative. It was to Damrong and Wachirayan that the king turned on this occasion, as on others, for modern educational advice. The strength of these two men was the unique fact that both were involved in running—and running successfully—deeply traditional Thai institutions on modern lines. More completely than any of their contemporaries they had taken institutions and remolded them with no damage to their traditional nature: paradoxically, both the monkhood and the provincial administration became, once reformed, closer to the traditional ideals that nourished them. These were and are two of the most fundamental institutions in the society, sources and instruments of social cohesion, social order, and cultural identity. The king demanded no more of the Ministry of Public Instruction than he had obtained from the Ministry of Interior and the Sangha.

Over twenty years, the Ministry of Public Instruction did make substantial advances toward the creation of a truly modern educational system. Unlike the Ministry of Interior, it could not begin with a ready-made structure to contain the essentially secular educational system the nation required. It had to begin as a ministry from nothing. The administration it created and the services it provided took over a decade to find their proper functions and to begin to fulfill them. In the end, its functions sought the ministry, and it accepted them only gradually and somewhat reluctantly. It took the ministry a decade to shake off the purely imitative patterns established in the eighties and nineties, a decade to shift the character of its secondary education away from the excessively English and civil service orientations of Suankulap. It took a decade to create effective educational services and meaningful syllabi in the schools. But by the end of Chulalongkorn's reign the crisis had passed. A professional class of educators which was both modern and Thai in its commitments had grown up in the Ministry's service, men like Chaophraya Thammasakmontri (Sanan) who clearly were of a new generation. With the passing of the king, Prince Damrong, Phraya Wisut, and most of their generation from public office in the second decade of the century, it was these men, products of early modern Thai education, men securely modern in their minds and Thai at heart, who would complete and consolidate the great revolution begun by Chulalongkorn the Great.

If there is a single thread running consistently through this long period, it is the insistent presence of the king, who was his country's most devastating critic, its gadfly prophet, its guiding spirit through a revolutionary epoch in world history. He was, in Sidney Hook's phrase, an "event-making man,"[5] who took his generation and his country by the ear and flung them outward into the world. His rare understanding of both what it meant to be modern and what it meant to be Thai and the skill with which he manipulated the power at his command meant for his country the preservation of its independence and the creative shaping of its modern identity. Many kings have been remembered for less: few could be thanked by their country for more.

5. Sidney Hook, *The Hero in History: A Study in Limitation and Possibility* (Boston, 1955), p. 154.

Appendixes

SUMMARY EDUCATIONAL STATISTICS,
1885–1912

Year	Bangkok Schools	Bangkok Students	Provinces Schools	Provinces Students	Total Schools	Total Students
1885/86	19	1,504	10	510	29	2,014
1886/87	21	1,500	13	488	34	1,988
1887/88	21	1,476	16	602	37	2,078
1888/89	22	1,474	17	568	39	2,042
1889/90	25	1,595	20	730	45	2,325
1890/91	24	1,800	27	915	51	2,715
1891/92	24	1,584	24	841	48	2,425
1892/93					98[a]	2,515
1893/94		Not Available			94	2,640
1894/95					75	2,565
1895/96					61	2,336
1896/97	34	1,634	26	986	60	2,620
1897/98	49	2,364	43	1,825	92	4,189
1898/99	56	3,430	43	1,990	99	5,420
1899/00	(55)[b]	(4,000)[b]	202[c]	6,147	257	10,147
1900/01	55	4,956	348	12,258	403	17,214
1901/02	79	7,560	350	14,106	429	21,666
1902/03	(76)	(7,200)	300	14,917	376	22,117
1903/04	(75)	(7,900)	306	16,817	381	24,717
1904/05	(74)	(8,700)	336	19,082	410	27,782
1905/06	81	8,175	330	19,881	411	28,056
1906/07	90	8,660	328	19,997	418	28,657
1907/08	91	9,894	340	20,244	431	30,138
1908/09	137[d]	13,359[d]	307[d]	16,603[d]	444	29,962
1909/10	131	14,174	1,347	29,899	1,478	44,073
1910/11	179	13,933	2,936	70,033	3,115	83,966
1911/12	437	18,006	3,235	115,438	3,672	133,444

a. These figures for the years 1892–96, provided retrospectively by Čhao-phraya Phatsakǫrawong in 1897, would appear to include private schools registered with the Education Department, but without including their students in the enrollment figures.

b. The figures in parentheses in these columns are estimates based on the bar graph in the Report, Educ. Dept., 1908/09.

c. At this point in the column of figures for provincial education the results of Prince Wachirayan's provincial work have been incorporated. Note that all statistics for provincial education here are estimates. Inasmuch as the monthon directors often submitted reports irregularly, I have used for each province the most recent available figures, which in a few cases were as much as seven years out of date. Beginning in 1908/09, there are good statistics for the provinces in the Annual Reports of the Education Department.

d. In 1908/09, 41 schools and 4,801 pupils in monthon Krungthep (the provinces surrounding the capital) were transferred from the class of "provincial education" to "Bangkok education," and I have moved them accordingly.

Sources: Annual Reports, Educ. Dept.; and NA 5 S, Series 12, reports of monthon Education Directors.

APPENDIX B

THE MINISTRY OF PUBLIC INSTRUCTION
AND THAILAND'S NATIONAL BUDGETS,
1888/89–1911/12

Year	Total National Budget (in thousands of baht)	Education Department Budget (in thousands of baht)	(as percent of national budget)	Ministry of Public Instruction Budget (in thousands of baht)	(as percent of national budget)
1888/89	13,647	191	1.4		
1889/90	12,020	164	1.4		
1890/91	n.a.	159			
1891/92	n.a.	n.a.			
1892/93	14,919			297	2.0
1893/94	18,175			407	2.2
1894/95	12,487			301	2.4
1895/96	12,686	98	0.7	342	2.7
1896/97	18,483			295	1.6
1897/98	23,997	196	0.8	710	3.0
1898/99	23,788	286	1.2	518	2.2
1899/00	27,053	294	1.1	507	1.9
1900/01	31,841	732	2.3	1,006	3.2
1901/02	36,647	728	2.0	1,000	2.7
1902/03	39,028			1,138	2.9
1903/04	43,909	684	1.6	1,218	2.8
1904/05	46,635	767	1.6	1,373	2.9
1905/06	50,036	804	1.6	1,349	2.7
1906/07	56,837	851	1.5	1,427	2.5
1907/08	56,503	881	1.6	1,422	2.5
1908/09	58,379	932	1.6	1,464	2.5
1909/10	58,845	938	1.6	1,281	2.2
1910/11	59,077	898	1.5	1,252	2.1
1911/12	64,017	879	1.4	1,364	2.1

Note: All figures given are for actual expenditures.
Sources: Wira, *Historical Patterns,* p. 114; Annual Reports, Educ. Dept.; NA 5 Kh, Series 8, Budgets, Ministry of Finance; Čhakkrit, *Damrong kap krasuang mahatthai,* pp. 369–70; and Thailand, Ministry of Finance, Dept. of General Statistics. *Statistical Yearbook of the Kingdom of Siam,* vol. VI (Bangkok, 1921), pp. 48–49, 35.

Glossary

Ačhan—Teacher, from Sanskrit *ācāriya*.

Amphoe—District, primary subdivision of the province.

Athibǫdi—Director-general of a *krom*, of higher status than a *čhao-krom*.

Čhao—(1) Ruler, proprietor, owner; (2) Member of the hereditary ruling class in the North.

Čhaofa—Child of a king by a queen.

Čhaokhana—Head of a geographical or sect division of the *Sangha*, e.g. the *čhaokhana monthon* is the chief monk or head abbot of a *monthon*. Wells translates this term as "*Sangha* Chairman."

Čhaokrom—Director of a *krom*, of lower status than an *athibǫdi*.

Čhaomüang—The hereditary governor of a *müang* or province under the traditional system of government.

Čhaophraya—The highest rank in civil government, generally conferred upon those who were ministers *(senabǫdi)* of one of the six major traditional *krom* or one of the twelve ministries (after 1889).

Dekban—A monastery pupil who lived at home.

Dekwat—A monastery pupil who lived in the monastery *(wat)*.

Farang—A Westerner.

Kalahom—(1) By the fifteenth century, the department *(krom)* of military affairs; (2) in the eighteenth and nineteenth centuries, the department having primary responsibility for the administration of the Southern and Western provinces; (3) after 1894, the Ministry of War; and (4) the name by which the head of the *krom kalahom* was known.

Kamnan—The headman of the commune *(tambon)*, elected from among the headmen of the villages included within his jurisdiction.

Khaluang—A commissioner, usually a royal commissioner, appointed from the capital to undertake responsibilities in the provinces.

Khaluang thammakan—A commissioner attached to the *monthon* or *müang* administration with responsibility for religious and educational affairs.

Khaluang thetsaphiban—A commissioner appointed by the Ministry of Interior to superintend the administration of a *monthon*.

Khun—Rank in the civil administrative hierarchy, between *mün* and *luang*.

Kong—Section, major subdivision of a *krom*.

Krasuang—Ministry of State, one of the twelve created in 1889–1892.

Krom—Department of State. Before 1889–1892, most offices of State were termed *krom,* but after that date this term was reserved for the primary divisions of ministries; e.g. the *krom süksathikan* (Education Department) was one of the major constituents of the *krasuang thammakan* (Ministry of Public Instruction), and included within itself various *kong* or sections.

Luang—Rank in the civil administrative hierarchy, between *khun* and *phra*.

Luksit—Pupil or disciple, generally of a monk.

Mahatlek—Royal Page.

Mahatthai—(1) By the fifteenth century, the department *(krom)* charged with the general superintendence of civil administration; (2) in the eighteenth and nineteenth centuries, the department having primary responsibility for the administration of the Northern and Eastern provinces; and (3) after 1894, the Ministry of Interior, in charge of provincial administration in general.

Matthayom—Secondary (of education), as in *rongrian matthayom* (secondary school) and *matthayomsüksa* (secondary education).

Mom čhao—The child of a prince of the rank of *phra-ong čhao. Mom čhao ying* is used to designate daughters.

Mom ratchawong—The child of a prince of the rank of *mom čhao*.

Monthon—A group of provinces *(müang* or *čhangwat)* headed by a commissioner, under the form of administration inaugurated in the 1880s and formalized by the Ministry of Interior in the 1890s.

Müang—(1) In this study, this word generally has been used to denote the province headed by a governor, the primary subdivision of the *monthon*. The term also may be applied (2) narrowly to a town or city, or (3) widely to denote the entire nation.

Munlasüksa—Elementary or basic education for children aged seven through nine years, at times also termed "lower primary education" *(prathomsüksa chan tam)*.

Nai—Common polite prefix for male names.

Parian—A monk or novice who passed the grade of Standard III or higher in the ecclesiastical examinations. Used as a suffix to the monk's name and honorific, e.g. Phra Satsanasophon, *Parian* VI.

Phak phuak—Clique, faction, "clientele group," conspiracy. A social group bound together by personal ties.

Phayaban—To nurse or care for the sick. *Krom phayaban* I have generally translated as "Hospitals Department," although late in the Fifth Reign it functioned more in the manner of a "Public Health Department."

Phra—(1) Rank in the civil administrative hierarchy between *phraya* and *luang;* (2) honorific for monks; (3) general honorific term for persons and objects having religious associations, as *phra traipidok,* "Holy Tripitaka."

Phra-ačhan—Reverend Teacher.

Phra-ong čhao—(1) Children of a king by a concubine; or (2) children of a prince of the rank of *čhaofa* and a princess of high royal rank.

Phrakhlang—(1) Early in the Ayudhya period, that *krom* (and its minister) which served as a ministry of finance; (2) later, the omnibus ministry exercising general treasury functions and the administration of the coastal provinces and foreign affairs; (3) after 1875, the Ministry of Finance; and (4) the name by which the head of the *krom phrakhlang* was known.

Phrakhru—(1) Reverend Teacher, title conferred upon scholarly monks, usually in the royal monasteries; and (2) an honorific applied to such men as Sir Robert Morant. See also *phra-ačhan.*

Phraya—Rank in the civil administrative hierarchy between *čhaophraya* and *phra.* It was held by men generally at subministerial rank.

Phu-amnuaikan—Director.

Plat banchi—Designation for the accountant of a ministry or department of government.

Prathom—Primary (of education), as in *rongrian prathom* (primary school) and *prathomsüksa* (primary education).

Ratchabandit—Royal Pundit, an officer of the government appointed to assist in the education of monks and novices.

Ratchakan—Government.

Rongrian—Literally, a building *(rong)* for study *(rian);* school.

Saman—General or ordinary, as in *samansüksa* (general education), as opposed to *wisamansüksa* (special education, e.g. vocational education).

Samian tra—Literally, clerk *(samian)* of the seals *(tra);* designation for the chief secretary of a department or ministry.

Sangha—The Buddhist monkhood.

Senabọdi—Minister of state, head of a ministry.

Sitwat—Monastery pupil.

Süksa—Education (in compounds).

Süksathikan—Literally, the business of education; designation for the Education Department *(krom süksathikan)*.

Tambon—A commune, group of villages. (Sometimes spelled *tambol.)*

Thammakan—(1) Literally, the business of *Dhamma;* (2) one of the traditional *krom* of government, charged with the superintendence of religious affairs; (3) as a *krom* (1889) and then a *krasuang,* the Ministry of Public Instruction, having charge of religious and educational affairs.

Thetsaphiban—The system of provincial administration formalized by the Ministry of Interior after 1894, the chief administrative unit of which was the *monthon.*

Udom—Higher (of education), as in *rongrian udom* (higher school, i.e. one requiring secondary school diplomas for admission) and *udomsüksa* (higher education).

Uparāja—Deputy or "second" king, sometimes heir-apparent.

Wat—Monastery, monastic institution, including all the buildings within the monastery compound.

Wen—Sometimes used to designate a subdivision within a *krom,* superseded by *kọng.*

Wisaman—Special, as in *wisamansüksa* (special education) and *matthayomwisamansüksa* (special secondary education).

Selected Bibliography

A. MANUSCRIPT SOURCES

The major source for this study has been the National Archives, a division of Thailand's Fine Arts Department housed in a wing of the old National Library in Bangkok. The archives consist almost entirely of the files accumulated in the Royal Secretariat *(krom ratchalekhathikan)*, which were handed over to the Cabinet Secretariat *(krom lekhathikan khana ratthamontri)* after the Revolution of 1932 and passed into the custody of the Fine Arts Department between 1936 and 1956.

The Royal Secretariat's records of the reign of King Chulalongkorn fall into two major groups. Those in the first, the product of the period prior to the introduction of Western-style office procedures and filing systems, were written in traditional style on heavy, accordian-folded black books or on loose sheets of rice paper. These were stored in the Wachirayan Pavilion at the National Museum. About half of these, including all the documents relating to education, were destroyed by fire in 1960. Records dating from the creation of modern ministries in the years 1885–92 were handwritten, and later typewritten, on imported paper, and all such records that passed through the Royal Secretariat were kept and grouped by the kings' private staff. Although some documents have been reclassified since entering the National Archives, most are still grouped in the manner in which Prince Sommot Amoraphan left them.

In citing Thai archive materials, I have followed the National Archives' classification scheme, prefacing each citation with the initials "NA." The succeeding set of two indices indicates the reign and the ministry, e.g. "5 S" in a citation indicates that the document in question comes from the Fifth Reign (King Chulalongkorn, Rama V) and the files dealing with the Ministry of Education *(süksathikan)*. The next number, expressed as a fraction, e.g. 31/5, refers to a file number in a series, in this example, to the thirty-first file in the fifth series. The final number in the citation refers to the page number of the particular document within the file, except in series 12, where it refers to the order in which the document falls within the file. There is but one exception to this general scheme of classification: there are a few Fifth Reign files that have not yet been reclassified by the archives staff and assigned to a ministry series. These are cited as "NA, R.5 (Fifth Reign), no. 179" or "no. 250," followed by file number (e.g. "3/179") and page number.

Listed below are the series consulted in the course of research.*

*As of early 1969 the files in the National Archives had been reclassified as follows:

S   Series 1, 2, and 8 combined in new series 1. Series 5 and 12 remain

S　　Ministry of Public Instruction
　　　　Series 1: "Education," 12 files (a miscellaneous collection).
　　　　Series 2: "Education," 29 files (incomplete, 1892–98).
　　　　Series 5: "Schools," 114 files (1892–1910).
　　　　Series 8: "Correspondence, Ministry of Public Instruction,"
　　　　22 files (1886–92).
　　　　Series 12: "Organization of Religion and Education," 46
　　　　files.
Kh　Ministry of Finance
　　　　Series 8: "Budgets," 111 files.
M　　Ministry of Interior
　　　　Series 11: "Education," 13 files.
　　　　Series 82: "Correspondence, Royal Commissioner, monthon
　　　　Lao Kao."
O　　Royal Scribes' Department
　　　　Series 1. "Legislative Council," 10 files.
　　　　Series 2. "Cabinet," (also includes records of the *Thetsa-
　　　　phiban* Conferences).
B　　Miscellaneous
　　　　Series 37: "Hiring of Foreigners."
　　　　Series 7 B 135: "Hiring of Foreigners" (Seventh Reign).
Unclassified, Fifth Reign (R.5)
　　　　Series 179: "Reports, *Thetsaphiban* Conferences."
　　　　Series 250: "Concerning Mr. Morant," 1 file.

B. NEWSPAPERS AND PERIODICALS

Bangkok Times, Bangkok: weekly, 1887–90; semi-weekly, 1891–94:
　　　thrice weekly, 1894–95; daily, 1896–1941.
Bangkok Times Weekly Mail, Bangkok: weekly, 1897–1941.
Čhantharakasem, Bangkok: Educational Information Division, Office
　　　of the Undersecretary, Ministry of Education, 1962, 1963.
　　　B-444.*

---

　　　　as before.
Kh　Series 8 renumbered series 5.
M　　Series 82 renumbered series 57.
O　　Series are in the process of reclassification.
B　　Series are being renumbered.
Unclassified series 179 classified as M, series 2.
Unclassified series 250 classified as T (Ministry of Foreign Affairs),
series 2. I am indebted to Craig Reynolds for providing this information.
　　　*Thai titles have been given their reference number from Bernath,
Catalogue of Thai Language Holdings, whenever applicable.

Chao krung (Bangkokian), Bangkok: monthly. B-452.

Chotmaihet sayam samai (Siam Times), Bangkok: monthly, fortnightly, weekly, 1882–86.

Darunowat, Bangkok: weekly, 1874–75.

Miusiam rü rattanakot, Bangkok: monthly, 1877–78.

Nangsü 'Court' khao ratchakan, Bangkok: daily, 1875–76. B-1756.

Prawat khru (Teachers' Lives), Bangkok: Teachers' Institute of Thailand, annual, 1937–63, 1963 . B-3571.

Ratchakitčhanubeksa (Royal Thai Government Gazette), Bangkok: weekly, 1858–59, 1874–79, 1888–. B-3541.

Siam Directory, Bangkok: annual, 1878, 1890, 1891, 1910.

Siam Repository, Bangkok: quarterly, 1869–74.

Siam Weekly Advertiser, Bangkok: weekly, 1869–86.

Sinlapakǫn, Bangkok: Fine Arts Department, bi-monthly, 1957–. B-3183.

Thetsaphiban, Bangkok: Ministry of Interior, monthly, 1906–. B-4313.

Wachirayan, Bangkok: monthly, 1894–1905. B-4515.

Wachirayan wiset, Bangkok: weekly, 1884–94. B-4575.

Warasan sinlapakǫn, Bangkok: Fine Arts Department, bi-monthly, 1947–55. B-4641.

Witthayačhan. Bangkok: United Teachers' Society, monthly, 1900–.

C. BIBLIOGRAPHIES

Bernath, Frances A., comp., *Catalogue of Thai Language Holdings in the Cornell University Libraries Through 1964*, Data Paper No. 54, Ithaca, N.Y., Southeast Asia Program, Dept. of Asian Studies, Cornell University, 1964.

Bibliography of Material About Thailand in Western Languages, comp. Central Library, Chulalongkorn University, Bangkok, 1960.

Education of Thailand: A Bibliography, comp. Library, Prasarnmitr College of Education, Bangkok, 2506 (1963).

Mason, John Brown, and H. Carroll Parish, *Thailand Bibliography*, Bibliographic Series, No. 4, Gainesville, Fla., University of Florida Libraries, Dept. of Reference and Bibliography, 1958.

Thailand, Fine Arts Department, comps., *Raichü nangsü phraniphon somdet phračhaobǫrommawongthoe kromphraya damrong racha-nuphap (Bibliography of the Writings of Prince Damrong Raja-nubhab)*, Bangkok, Fine Arts Dept., 2505 (1962).

————, Royal Institute, comps., *Rainam nangsüphim khao süng ǫk pen raya nai prathet sayam (List of Periodicals Which Have Been Issued in Siam)*, Bangkok, 2474 (1931).* B-4073.

Yim Panthayangkun, comp., "Banchi nangsü phim čhak tonchabap hǫsamut haeng chat (List of Books Published from Manuscripts in the National Library)," *Warasan sinlapakǫn*, 2, nos. 1–6 (1948–49), supplements.

————, "Banchi nangsü phim čhak tonchabap hǫsamut haeng chat (List of Books Published from Manuscripts in the National Library)," unpublished typescript (covers years 1949–1963).

————, *Saraban khon rüang, lem 1, nai nangsü phim čhak tonchabap hǫsamut haeng chat, ph.s. 2444 thüng ph.s. 2470 (Index, Vol. 1: Books Published from Manuscripts in the National Library, 1901–1927)*, Bangkok, Fine Arts Dept., 2484 (1941). B-138.

D. BOOKS AND ARTICLES

1. In Thai Language

Anuman Rajadhon, *Phraya* (Yong Sathiankoset), "Phraprawat phra-wǫrawongthoe phra-ong čhao phrǫmphong athirat (Biography of Prince Phrǫmphong)," in *Tamnan sunlakakǫn (History of the Customs Department)*, Bangkok, 2482 (1939), pp. i-xv. B-53.

————, *Rüang loek that nai ratchakan thi 5 (On the Abolition of Slavery in the Fifth Reign)*, Bangkok, 2499 (1956). B-43.

Anusǫn 25 phutthasattawat, see Bangkok, Wat Mahathat.

Bamrung Klatčharoen, "Prawat kanfükhatkhru khǫng prathet thai (History of Teacher-Training in Thailand)," M.A. thesis, Pra-sarnmitr College of Education, Bangkok, 2506 (1963).

Bangkok, Mahamakut Academy, comp., *Phra-aksǫn rüang čhat kan-laorian khǫng chao sayam (Letters of Prince Wachirayan on the Education of the Thai People)*, Bangkok, 2492 (1949).

————, National Library, comp., *Čhotmaihet sadet praphat tang prathet nai ratchakan thi 5, sadet müang singkhapo lae müang betawia khrang raek, lae sadet praphat prathet india (Documents on the Royal Travels Abroad in the Fifth Reign, to Singapore, the First Trip to Batavia, and to India),* Bangkok, 2460 (1917). B-639.

————, *Parian ratchakan thi 5 (Ecclesiastical Degree-Holders of the Fifth Reign),* 2 vols. Bangkok, 2463 (1920). B-115.

————, *Prachum owat (Moral and Religious Instructions),* Bangkok, 2468 (1925).

Bangkok, Wat Mahathat, *Anusǫn 25 phutthasattawat wat mahathat yuwaratcharangsarit (Commemorating the Twenty-fifth Buddhist Century),* Bangkok, 2500 (1957). B-189.

Bradley, Dan Beach, ed., *Nangsü prathom k ka čhaek luk aksǫn lae čhindamuni kap prathom mala lae pathanukrom: Elementary Tables & Lessons in the Siamese Language,* 8th ed. Bangkok, 1875.

Bunčhüa Ongkhapradit, *Khwampenma khǫng phaen kansüksa chat (The History of the National Plan of Education),* Publications of the Department of Educational Techniques, Ministry of Education, General Education Development Project Series, No. 1, Bangkok, Ministry of Education, 2504 (1961).

Chakkrit Nǫranittiphadungkan, *Somdet phračhaobǫrommawongthoe kromphraya damrong rachanuphap kap krasuang mahatthai (Prince Damrong Rajanubhab and the Ministry of Interior),* Bangkok, Institute of Public Administration, Thammasat University, 2506 (1963). B-374.

Chakkrapani Si Sinlawisut, Luang, comp., *Rüang khǫng čhaophraya mahithǫn (The Story of Čhaophraya Mahithǫn),* Bangkok, 2499 (1956). B-383.

Charun Wongsayan and Pramot Chaiyakit, *Khwampenma khǫng laksut achiwasüksa (History of the Curriculum in Vocational Education),* Publications of the Department of Educational Techniques, Ministry of Education, General Education Development Project Series, No. 3, Bangkok, Ministry of Education, 2504 (1961).

Chot Thǫngprayun, *Khambanyai phraratchabanyat khana song ph.s. 2505 (Lectures on the 1962 Royal Ordinance for the Buddhist Monkhood),* 4th rev. ed. Bangkok. Religious Affairs Department, 2509 (1966).

"Čhotmaihet phrabat somdet phra chunlachǫmklao chaoyuhua song phraprachuan chon thung sawannakhot (A Record of the Illness and Death of King Chulalongkorn)," in *Burutrat,* Cremation volume for Phraya Burutrat Ratchaphanlop (Nop Krairoek), Bangkok, 2501 (1958), pp. (147)–(57). B-325.

Čhotmaihet sadet praphat tang prathet nai ratchakan thi 5, sadet müang singkhapo lae müang betawia khrang raek, lae sadet praphat prathet india, see Bangkok, National Library.

Chula Chakrabongse, Prince, *Čhao chiwit (Lords of Life),* 2d ed. Bangkok, Khlang Witthaya, 2505 (1962).

Chulalongkorn, King, *Čhotmaihet phraratchakit raiwan (Royal Diary).* 24 vols. Bangkok, 2476–2508 (1933–65). B-629.

————, "Čhotmaihet phraratchakit raiwan nai ratchakan thi 5 (Royal Diary of the Fifth Reign)," *Warasan sinlapakǫn, 2:3* (Oct. 2491/1948), 63–77, and 2 (Dec. 2491), 52–59.

————, *Phrabǫrommarachathibai rüang samakkhi (Royal Discourse on Unity),* Bangkok, 2496 (1953). B-706.

————, *Phrabǫrommarachowat nai ratchakan thi 5 (Royal Advices of the Fifth Reign),* Bangkok, 2503 (1960).

————, *Phraratchadamrat nai phrabat somdet phra čhunlačhǫmklao čhaoyuhua (tangtae ph.s. 2417 thüng ph.s. 2453) (Speeches of King Chulalongkorn, 1874–1910),* Bangkok, 2458 (1915). B-658.

————, *Phraratchahatlekha phrabat somdet phra čhunlačhǫmklao čhaoyuhua song thalaeng phrabǫrommarachathibai kaekhai kanpokkhrǫng phaendin (Speech of King Chulalongkorn Explaining the Changes in the Government),* Bangkok, 2470 (1927). B-659.

————, *Phraratchahatlekha phrabat somdet phra čhunlačhǫmklao čhaoyuhua lae lai phrabat somdet phra pitutčhačhao sukhuman marasi phra akkharatchathewi (Letters of King Chulalongkorn and of Queen Sukhuman Marasi),* Bangkok, 2493 (1950). B-670.

————, *Phraratchahatlekha phrabat somdet phra čhunlačhǫmklao čhaoyuhua phraratchathan somdet phračhaobǫrommawongthoe kromphraya damrong rachanuphap nai wela sadet phraratchadamnoen phraphat yurop khrang thi 2 nai ph.s. 2450 (Letters of King Chulalongkorn to Prince Damrong Rajanubhab During the Second Royal Tour of Europe, in 1907),* Bangkok, 2491 (1948). B-674.

————, *Samnao phraratchahatlekha suan phra-ong phrabat somdet phra čhunlačhǫmklao čhaoyuhua thüng čhaophraya yommarat (pan sukhum) kap prawat čhaophraya yommarat (Copies of King Chulalongkorn's Personal Letters to Čhaophraya Yommarat, Pan Sukhum, Together with a Biography of Čhaophraya Yommarat),* Bangkok, 2482 (1939). B-716.

————, *Thamniam ratchatrakun nai krung sayam (Customs of the Royal Family of Siam),* Bangkok, 1958.

————, and *Čhaophraya* Phrasadet Surentharathibǫdi (M.R.W. Pia

Malakul), *Phraratchahatlekha lae nangsü krap bangkhom thun khong čhaophraya phrasadet surentharathibodi (Royal Letters, and the Letters of Čhaophraya Phrasadet)*, Bangkok, 2504 (1961). B-666.

————, and *Čhaophraya* Thammasakmontri (Sanan Thephatsadin na Ayudhya), "Phraratchahatlekha nai phrabat somdet phra čhunlačhomklao čhaoyuhua waduai phrarachobai kiaokap kansüksa khong chat song mi thüng čhaophraya thammasakmontri . . . ph.s. 2453 (Letters of King Chulalongkorn Concerning the Royal Policy on National Education, Written to Čhaophraya Thammasakmontri . . . in 1910)," *Warasan sinlapakon, 3* (Oct. 2492/ 1949), 1–18.

————, and King Vajiravudh, *Phraratchahatlekha song sang ratchakan nai ratchakan thi 5 lae 6 kap rüang prakop (Royal Letters of the Fifth and Sixth Reigns on Official Matters, with Supplementary Documents)*, Bangkok, 2507 (1964). B-679.

————, and Prince Wachirayan Warorot, *Phraratchahatlekha phrabat somdet phra čhunlačhomklao čhaoyuhua song mi paima kap somdet phra mahā samanačhao kromphraya wachirayan warorot (The Correspondence Between King Chulalongkorn and Prince Wachirayan Warorot)*, Bangkok, 2472 (1929). B-676.

Damratdamrong Devakul, *Mom čhao, Phraprawat somdet phraratchapitula borommaphongsaphimuk čhaofa kromphraya phanuphanthuwong woradet (Biography of Prince Phanurangsi Sawangwong)*, Bangkok, 2472 (1929). B-764.

Damrong Rajanubhab, Prince, "Athibai rüang ratchathut thai pai yurop (Explanation of the Sending of Thai Embassies to Europe)," *Prachum phongsawadan,* pt. 29; new ed. vol. 7, Bangkok, 2507/ 1964, 310–45.

————, *Khwamsongčham (Memoirs)*, Bangkok, Social Science Association of Thailand, 2506 (1963). B-785.

————, "Laksana kansüksa khong čhaonai tae boran (Characteristics of the Education of Royalty in Former Days)," in Damrong, *Prachum phraniphon bettalet,* pp. 117–20.

————, *Phraprawat čhomphon phračhaophiyathoe krommaluang nakhon chaisi suradet ratcha-ongrak (Biography of Marshal Prince Nakhon Chaisi)*, Bangkok, 2459 (1916). B-800.

————, "Phraprawat somdet phračhao borommawongthoe kromphraya thewawong waropakan (Biography of Prince Devawongse)," in Damrong et al., *Phraratchaprawat ratchakan thi 5 kon sawoei rat,* pp. 100–69. B-816.

————, *Phraratchaphongsawadan krung rattanakosin ratchakan thi 5*

(Royal Chronicles of the Fifth Reign of the Bangkok Period), 2d ed. Bangkok, 2494 (1951). B-813.

————, *Prachum phraniphon bettalet (Collected Miscellaneous Writings)*, Bangkok, Teachers' Institute Press, 2504 (1961). B-820.

————, *Prawat ačhan (A Teacher's Life)*, Bangkok, 2478 (1935). B-823.

————, *Prawat bukkhon samkhan, chabap sombun (Biographies of Important People, Complete Edition)*, Bangkok, Khlang Witthaya, 2505 (1962). B-821.

————, *Rüang phrarachanukit (On Royal Duties)*, Bangkok, 2489 (1946). B-3893.

————, "Rüang rongrian mahatlek luang (On the Royal Pages' School)," in Damrong, *Nithan borannakhadi (bang rüang) (Tales of the Past, Selections)*, Bangkok, 2499 (1956), pp. 88–100.

————, *Tamnan suankulap (History of Suankulap)*, Bangkok, 2506 (1963).

————, and W. G. Johnson, *Prawat sangkhep haeng kansüksa khǫng prathet sayam (Short History of Education in Siam)*, Bangkok, 2463 (1920).

————, and *Phraya* Ratchasena (Siri Thephatsadin na Ayudhya), *Thetsaphiban*, Bangkok, 2503 (1960). B-896.

————, and Prince Sommot Amǫraphan, *Rüang tang phrarachakhana phuyai nai krung rattanakosin (On Appointments of High Ecclesiastical Dignitaries in the Bangkok Period)*, Bangkok, 2466 (1923). B-3284.

————, et al., *Phraratchaprawat phrabat somdet phra čhunlačhǫmklao čhaoyuhua müa kǫn sawoei rat (Biography of King Chulalongkorn Before His Accession to the Throne)*, Bangkok, Teachers' Institute Press, 2504 (1961). B-816.

Dhanit Yupho, ed., *Chaloem phrakiat somdet phra si phatcharinthara bǫrommarachininat phrabǫrommaratchonni nai ratchakan thi 6 lae ratchakan thi 7 (In Honor of Queen Saowapha, Mother of Kings Rama VI and Rama VII)*, Bangkok, 2507 (1964). B-914.

————, *Somdet čhaophraya bǫrommaha si suriyawong müa pen phusamretratchakan phaendin nai tǫn ton ratchakan thi 5 (Suriyawong as Regent at the Beginning of the Fifth Reign)*, Bangkok, 2511 (1968).

————, *Somdet phra narai maharat lae nakprat ratchakawi nai ratchasamai (King Narai the Great and the Poets and Savants of His Reign)*, Bangkok, 2499 (1956). B-922.

Duangčhit Čhittraphong, *Mǫm čhao ying*, "Phraprawat somdet čhaofa kromphraya naritsaranuwattiwong (Biography of Prince Naris)," *Čhantharakasem*, no. 51 (Mar.-Apr. 2506/1963), 4–20.

Kachorn Sukhabanij, *Kao raek khǫng nangsüphim nai prathet thai (The Beginnings of Journalism in Thailand)*, Bangkok, 2508 (1965).

Kong Sin, *Čhamün* (Run), "Čhotmaihet hon (Astrologer's Record)," *Prachum phongsawadan*, pt. 8; new ed. vol. 4 (Bangkok, 2507/ 1964), 116–62.

Lingat, Robert, ed., *Kotmai tra sam duang (Laws of the Three Seals)*, 5 vols. Bangkok, Teachers' Institute Press, 2504–05 (1961–62).

Mahintharasakthamrong, *Čhaophraya* (Pheng Phengkun), *Čhotmaihet rüang phrabat somdet phra čhǫmklao čhaoyuhua song prachuan (Record of the Illness of King Mongkut)*, Bangkok, 2490 (1947).

Manich Jumsai, *Mǫm luang*, *Prawat kansüksa khǫng thai (History of Thai Education)*, Bangkok, 2502 (1959).

Mongkut, King, *Prachum prakat ratchakan thi 4 (Collected Decrees of the Fourth Reign)*, 4 vols. Bangkok, Teachers' Institute Press, 2503–04 (1960–61). B-1465.

Nai Honhuai, pseud., "Rongrian matthayom wat benčhamabǫphit (Wat Benčhamabǫphit Secondary School)," in *Benčhamabǫphit-anusǫn*, Bangkok, 2495 (1952), pp. 35–45. B-200.

Naritsaranuwattiwong, Prince, and Prince Damrong Rajanubhab, *San somdet (Princes' Letters)*, 26 vols. Bangkok, Teachers' Institute Press, 2504 (1961). B-1581.

Natthawutthi Sutthisongkhram, *Somdet čhaophraya bǫrommaha si suriyawong*, 2 vols. Bangkok, Si Tham, 2504–05 (1961–62). B-1594.

————, *Somdet phra nang rüa lom (The Queen Who Fell from the Boat)*, Bangkok, Si Tham, 2503 (1960). B-1595.

Parian ratchakan thi 5, see Bangkok, National Library.

Phanurangsi Sawangwong, Prince, *Tamnan thahan mahatlek (History of the Royal Pages' Bodyguard Regiment)*, Bangkok, 2496 (1953). B-1761.

Phatsakǫrawong, *Čhaophraya* (Phǫn Bunnag), *Khamklǫn khǫng čhao-phraya phatsakǫrawong (phǫn bunnak) (The Klǫn Verse of Čhaophraya Phatsakǫrawong)*, Bangkok, 2465 (1922).

Phinitsara, *Phraya* (Thapthim Bunyarattaphan), *Nangsü hitopathet kham khlong*, Bangkok, 2478 (1935). B-1821.

Ph'sanwinaiwat, *Phrakhru* (Hem), and *Phra Maha* Phoem. *Prawat wat prayurawongsawat, čhangwat thonburi (History of Wat Prayura-wong, Thonburi)*, Bangkok, 2471 (1928). B-2436.

Phra-aksǫn rüang čhat kanlaorian khǫng chao sayam, see Bangkok, Mahamakut Academy.

Phunphitsamai Diskul, *Mǫm čhao ying, Chiwit lae ngan khǫng somdet kromphraya damrong rachanuphap (The Life and Work of Prince Damrong Rajanubhab),* Bangkok, Ruam San, 2502 (1959). B-2148.

————, "Somdet phračhaobǫrommawongthoe kromphraya damrong rachanuphap (Prince Damrong Rajanubhab)," *Čhantharakasem,* no. 46 (May-June, 2505/1962), 6–33.

Prachum owat, see Bangkok, National Library.

Praphat Trinarong, *Chiwit lae ngan khǫng atsawaphahu (The Life and Work of Aśvabhahu, King Rama VI),* Bangkok, Thai Watthana Phanit, 2506 (1963). B-2377.

————, *Chiwit lae ngan khǫng čhaophraya phrasadet (The Life and Work of Čhaophraya Phrasadet),* Bangkok, Udomsüksa, 2504 (1961). B-2375.

Prasoet Aksǫnnit, *Luang* (Phae), and *Phraya* Si Sunthǫn Wohan (Nǫi), *Borannasüksa lae withi sǫn nangsü thai (Ancient Education, and Methods of Teaching Thai),* Bangkok, 2502 (1959).

Prawat kansatsanasüksa-kansüksa nangsü thai khǫng wat anongkharam lae tarunanusat, see Thonburi, Wat Anongkharam.

Prawat phraya owatwǫrakit (kaen), Bangkok, R.S. 126 (1907). B-2433.

Prawat rongrian ratchawitthayalai (History of King's College), Bangkok, 2509 (1966).

"Prawat sangkhep ammat-ek phraya winit witthayakǫn (kǫn ammattayakun) (Short Biography of Phraya Winit Witthayakǫn, Kǫn Amatyakul)," in *Prachum phongsawadan,* pt. 36 Bangkok, 2470 (1927), pp. (2)–(5).

"Prawat yǫ rongrian matthayom wat ratchabǫphit (Short History of Wat Ratchabǫphit Secondary School)," in *Ratchabǫphitthaksina,* Bangkok, 2499 (1956), pp. 1–13.

Prayut Sitthiphan, *Phaendin phraphutthačhao luang (King Chulalongkorn),* Bangkok, Thammasewi, 2501 (1958). B-2450.

Ratchasakunwong (Royal Genealogy), 7th rev. ed. Bangkok, 2507 (1964).

Ratchawǫrin, pseud., "Nakrian thai nai tangprathet khon raek (The First Thai Students Abroad)," *Chao krung, 12* (Jan. 2506/1963), 35–39.

Rǫng Sayamanon, et al., *Prawat krasuang süksathikan 2435–2507 (History of the Ministry of Education, 1892–1964),* Bangkok, Teachers' Institute Press, 2507 (1964).

Salao Lekharutčhi and Udom Pramuanwitthaya, *Piyamaharat čhula-*

longkǫn (Chulalongkorn the Great), Bangkok, Odeon Store, 2504 (1961). B-3535.

Sa-nguan Ankhong, *Sing raek nai müang thai (First Things in Thailand)*, vol. 1, Bangkok, Phrae Phitthaya, 2502 (1959). B-2981.

Sa-nguan Leksakun, *Rüang ngan patirup nai ratchakan thi 5 (On the Reforms of the Fifth Reign)*, Bangkok, 2497 (1954). B-2978.

Sannaiprasat, *Luang* (Thannya na Songkhla), *Phatthanakan kansüksa kotmai nai prathet thai (The Development of Legal Education in Thailand)*, Bangkok, 2499 (1956).

Saowapha Phǫngsi, Queen, *Phraratchahatlekha somdet phra si phatcharinthara bǫrommarachininat phrabǫrommaratchonni nai ratchakan thi 6 lae ratchakan thi 7 phraratchathan čhaophraya phrasadet surentharathibǫdi (Letters of Queen Saowapha, Mother of Kings Rama VI and VII, to Čhaophraya Phrasadet)*, Bangkok, 2507 (1964). B-3022.

Sathian Laiyalak et al., comps., *Prachum kotmai pračham sok (Collected Laws, Arranged Chronologically)*, 69 vols. Bangkok, 1935–53. B-4022.

Sawat Chanthani, *Nithan chao rai (A Farmer's Tales)*, 5 vols. Bangkok, Teachers' Institute Press, 2509 (1966).

Sawatsarasattraphut, *Luang,* and Čharun Wongsayan, *Khwampenma khǫng laksut samansüksa (History of the Curriculum in General Education)*, Publications of the Department of Educational Techniques, General Education Development Project Series, No. 2, Bangkok, Ministry of Education, 2504 (1961).

Si Sahathep, *Phraya* (Seng Wiriyasiri), *Raya thang sadet phraratchadamnoen praphat prathet yurop rattanakosinsok 116 (The Royal Tour of Europe in 1897)*, Bangkok, Bamrungnukunkit, n.d.; 2d ed. titled *Čhotmaihet sadet praphat yurop r.s. 116*, 2 vols. Bangkok, R.S. 126 (1907). B-3225.

Si Sunthǫn Wohan, *Phraya* (Nǫi Ačhanyangkun), *Munlabot banphakit*, Bangkok, Sinlapabannaklan, 2501 (1958). B-3229.

Si Wǫrawong, *Phraya* (M.R.W. Čhit Suthat na Ayudhya), *Phraprawat phračhaobǫrommawongthoe kromphra sommot amǫraphan (Biography of Prince Sommot Amǫraphan)*, Bangkok, 2459 (1916). B-3250.

Sommot Amǫraphan, Prince, comp., *Rüang chaloem phrayot čhaonai, chabap mi phra rup (On Promotions in the Ranks of Royalty, Illustrated Edition)*, Bangkok, 2472 (1929).

Surasakmontri, *Čhaophraya* (Čhoem Saeng-Xuto), *Prawatkan khǫng čhaophraya surasakmontri (The Life of Čhaophraya Surasak-*

montri), 4 vols. Bangkok, Teachers' Institute Press, 2504 (1961). B-3439.

Sutčharit Thawǫnsuk, *Phraprawat lae ngan khǫng somdet phrǎčhao-bǫrommawongthoe kromphraya damrong rachanuphap (The Life and Work of Prince Damrong Rajanubhab)*, 3 vols. Bangkok, Teachers' Institute Press, 2508 (1965).

Tej Bunnag, "Khabot ngiao müang phrae (The Shan Rebellion of Phrae)," *Sangkhomsat parithat*, 6 (Sept. 1968), 67–80.

Thailand, Fine Arts Dept., comp., *Čhaonai lae kharatchakan krap bangkhom thun khwamhen čhat kanplianplaeng ratchakan phaendin r.s. 103 lae phraratchadamrat nai phrabat somdet phra čhunlačhǫmklao čhaoyuhua song thalaeng phrabǫrommarachathabai kaekhai kanpokkhrǫng phaen din (Opinions on the Reorganization of the Government Presented to the King in 1885, and Royal Speech of King Chulalongkorn Explaining the Changes in the Government)*, Bangkok, 2510 (1967).

———, *Čhindamani lem 1–2 kap banthük rüang nangsü čhindamani lae čhindamani chabap phrǎčhao bǫrommakot (Čhindamani, Volumes 1–2, Together With Notes on the Book "Čhindamani" and a Version of Čhindamani from the Reign of King Bǫrommakot)*, Bangkok, Sinlapabannakhan, 2504 (1961). B-1003.

———, *Čhotmaihet phraratchakit raiwan ph.s. 2411 (plai ratchakan thi 4–ton ratchakan thi 5) (Royal Diary for 1868/69, End of the Fourth Reign–Beginning of the Fifth Reign)*, Bangkok, 2508 (1965).

———, *Lamdap rachinikun bang chang (Genealogy of the Royal Maternal Line "Bang Chang")*, 3d rev. ed. Bangkok, 2501 (1958). B-110.

———, *Phasa thai khǫng phraya si sunthǫn wohan (The Thai Language of Phraya Si Sunthǫn Wohan)*, 2 vols. Bangkok, Khlang Witthaya, 2504 (1961). B-3237.

———, *Phrabǫrommarachowat phrabat somdet phra čhunlačhǫmklao čhaoyuhua phraratchathan phrǎčhaolukyathoe, phraratchaprarop nai phrabat somdet phra čhunlačhǫmklao čhaoyuhua waduai rüang that lae kasian ayu, kap samnao krasae phrabǫrommaratchaongkan phraratchabanyat phraratchadamrat phraratchahatlekha lae prakat kansüksa nai samai phrabat somdet phra čhunlačhǫmklao čhaoyuhua (Royal Advice of King Chulalongkorn Given to His Sons, Royal Considerations of King Chulalongkorn Concerning Slavery and Emancipation, and Copies of Royal Decrees and Orders, Royal Ordinances, Royal Speeches, and Royal Letters*

Concerning Education in the Time of King Chulalongkorn), Bangkok, 2509 (1966).

———, *Prachum phongsawadan (Collected Chronicles),* 81 pts. Bangkok, privately published, 1914–67. Commercial edition, Bangkok, Progress Bookstore, 1964–.

———, *Prathom k ka, prathom k ka hat an, pathom mala, aksǫranitti baeprian nangsü thai, chabap hǫsamut haeng chat (First ABC's . . . Thai Textbooks, National Library Edition),* Bangkok, Sinlapabannakhan, 2506 (1963). B-3878.

———, *Somdet phrǎčhao bǫrommawongthoe kromphraya damrong rachanuphap sadet thawip yurop ph.s. 2434 (Prince Damrong Rajanubhab's Trip to Europe in 1891),* Bangkok, 2511 (1968).

Thailand, Ministry of Foreign Affairs, *Prawat lae rabop ngan khǫng krasuang kantangprathet (History and Organization of the Ministry of Foreign Affairs),* Bangkok, 2506 (1963).

Thailand, Ministry of Public Instruction, Education Department, *Raingan (Report),* Annual (title varies), Bangkok, Ministry of Public Instruction, R.S. 127 (1908/09)–B.E. 2475 (1932/33). B-3700.

———, *Baep rian reo samrap rian nangsü thai (Rapid Readers for the Study of Thai),* 2d ed. Bangkok, Education Department, R.S. 109 (1890/91).

Thailand, Office of the Prime Minister, Commission for the Publication of Historical, Cultural, and Archeological Documents, comp., *Prachum sila čharük phak thi 3 (Collected Inscriptions, Part 3),* Bangkok, Government House Printing Office, 2508 (1965).

Thailand, Post and Telegraph Department, *Sarabanchi suan thi 1, khü tamnaeng ratchakan samrap čhaophanakngan krom praisani krungthep mahanakhǫn, tangtae čhamnuan pi mamae benčha sok čhunlasakkarat 1245, lem thi 1 (Directory, Part 1, Government Officials, for Officials of the Post Office Department in Bangkok, for the Year of the Goat, Fifth of the Decade, C.S. 1245, Vol. 1),* Bangkok, Post and Telegraph Department, 1883.

Thailand, Secretariat to the Cabinet, comp., "Phubǫrihan ratchakan phaendin samai adit (Government Administrators of the Past)," in Prince Damrong Rajanubhab et al., *Rüang thiao thi tangtang phak 2 (Concerning Various Travels, Part 2),* Bangkok, 2505 (1962), pp. 65–118. B-4111.

Thawin Thephatsadin na Ayudhya, "Chiwaprawat (Biography of Čhaophraya Thammasakmontri)," in Čhaophraya Thammasakmontri, *Bot praphan bang rüang khǫng khru thep (Miscellaneous*

Articles by "Khru Thep"), Bangkok, 2486 (1943), pp. i-xviii.

Thiphakǫrawong, *Čhaophraya* (Kham Bunnag), *Phraratchaphongsawadan krung rattanakosin ratchakan thi 3 lae phraratchaphongsawadan krung rattanakosin ratchakan thi 4 (Royal Chronicles of
the Third and Fouth Reigns of the Bangkok Period),* Combined
ed. Bangkok, Khlang Witthaya, 2506 (1963). B-4330.

――――, and Prince Damrong Rajanubhab, *Phraratchaphongsawadan
krung rattanakosin ratchakan thi 1 lae phraratchaphongsawadan
krung rattanakosin ratchakan thi 2 (Royal Chronicles of the First
and Second Reigns of the Bangkok Period),* Combined ed. Bangkok, Khlang Witthaya, 2505 (1962). B-4328.

Thonburi, Wat Anongkharam, *Prawat kansatsanasüksa-kansüksa nangsü thai khǫng wat anongkharam lae tarunanusat (History of Religious and Thai Education at Wat Anongkharam, and "Tarunanusat"),* Bangkok, 2500 (1957). B-4352.

Udom Pramuanwitthaya, pseud., *100 čhaofa lae senabodi (One Hundred Princes and Ministers),* Bangkok, Khlang Witthaya, 2505
(1962).

Wachirayan Warorot, Prince, *Phraprawat trat lao (Autobiography),*
Bangkok, Teachers' Institute Press, 2504 (1961).

Wibun Sawatwong, *Mǫm čhao, Khwamsongčham (Memoirs),* Bangkok, 2485 (1942).

Witchitwongwutthikrai, *Čhaophraya* (M.R.W. Khli Suthat na Ayudhya), and *Phraya* Phritthathibǫdi (Ǫn Komalawanthana), *Tamnan phra-aram luang, lae thamniap samanasak (History of the
Royal Monasteries, and Directory of Ecclesiastical Officials),*
Bangkok, 2457 (1914). B-4729.

Wyatt, David K., "Khana song pen khrüang yok thana khün nai sang-
khom thai boran (The Buddhist Monkhood as an Avenue of
Social Mobility in Traditional Thai Society)," *Sinlapakǫn, 10*
(May 2509/1966), 41–52.

2. In Western Languages

Allen, Bernard M., *Sir Robert Morant: A Great Public Servant,* London, Macmillan, 1934.

Ambhorn (Jayapani) Meesook, "The Educational System of Siam: A
Study in the Light of Comparative Education," Ph.D. diss., Rad-
cliffe College, 1946.

Anuman Rajadhon, *Phraya, The Nature and Development of the Thai
Language,* Thai Culture, New Series, No. 10, 2d ed. Bangkok,
Fine Arts Dept., 1963.

Backus, Mary, ed., *Siam and Laos as Seen by our American Missionaries,* Philadelphia, Presbyterian Board of Publication, 1884.

Bastian, Adolf, *Reisen in Siam im Jahre 1863,* Die Voelker des Oestlichen Asien, Studien und Reisen, III, Jena, Hermann Costenoble, 1867.

Bode, Mabel Haynes, *The Pali Literature of Burma,* Prize Publication Fund, vol. 2, London, Royal Asiatic Society, 1909.

Boonsom Arawarop, "A Study of the Development of Childhood Education in Thailand," M.A. thesis, University of Georgia, 1955.

Campbell, J. G. D., *Siam in the Twentieth Century: Being the Experiences and Impressions of a British Official,* London, Edward Arnold, 1902.

Carter, A. Cecil, *The Kingdom of Siam,* New York, G. P. Putnam's Sons, 1904.

Chandran Mohandas Jeshurun, "British Policy Towards Siam, 1893–1902," M.A. thesis, University of Malaya, Kuala Lumpur, 1964.

Chula Chakrabongse, Prince, *Lords of Life,* New York, Taplinger, 1960.

Clarke, Sir Andrew, "My First Visit to Siam," *Contemporary Review, 81* (1902), 221–30.

Detchard Vongkomolshet, "The Administrative, Judicial and Financial Reforms of King Chulalongkorn, 1868–1910, M.A. thesis, Cornell University, 1958.

Dhani Nivat, Prince, "The Reconstruction of Rama I of the Chakri Dynasty," *Journal of the Siam Society, 43,* pt. 1 (1955); reprinted in *Selected Articles from the Siam Society Journal, 4* (Bangkok, 1959), 238–65.

———, "The Reign of King Chulalongkorn," *Journal of World History, 2* (1954), 446–66.

Eakin, Paul A., *The Eakin Family in Thailand,* Bangkok, Prachandra Press, 1955.

Exell, F. K., *Siamese Tapestry,* London, Robert Hale, 1963.

Feltus, George Haws, *Samuel Reynolds House of Siam: Pioneer Medical Missionary, 1847–1876,* New York, Fleming H. Revell, 1924.

Graham, A. W., *Siam: A Handbook of Practical, Commercial, and Political Information,* 1st ed. London, Alexander Moring, 1912; 3d ed. 2 vols. London, Alexander Moring, 1924.

Griswold, Alexander B., *King Mongkut of Siam,* New York, Asia Society, 1961.

Hanks, Lucien M., Jr., "Merit and Power in the Thai Social Order," *American Anthropologist, 54* (Dec. 1962), 1247–61.

Hutchinson, E. W., *Adventurers in Siam in the Seventeenth Century,* London, Royal Asiatic Society, 1940.

Ingram, James C., *Economic Change in Thailand Since 1850*, Stanford, Stanford University Press, 1955.

Johnson, W. G., "Education," in Arnold Wright, ed., *Twentieth Century Impressions of Siam*, London, Lloyd's, 1908, pp. 226–34.

Kaung, U., "A Survey of the History of Education in Burma Before the British Conquest and After," *Journal of the Burma Research Society*, 46 (Dec. 1963), 1–124.

Kirsch, A. Thomas., "Phu Thai Religious Syncretism: A Case Study of Thai Religion and Society," Ph.D. diss., Harvard University, 1967.

Leonowens, Anna Harriette, *Siam and the Siamese: Six Years' Recollections of an English Governess at the Siamese Court*, Philadelphia, Henry T. Coates, 1897.

Lingat, Robert, "La Vie religieuse du roi Mongkut," *Journal of the Siam Society*, 20, pt. 2 (1926), 129–48.

Loubere, Simon de la, *A New Historical Relation of the Kingdom of Siam*, tr. A. P. 2 vols. London, 1693.

McFarland, Bertha Blount, *McFarland of Siam*, New York, Vantage Press, 1958.

McFarland, Mrs. S. G. (Jane Hays McFarland), "The Schools of Siam," in Mary Backus, ed., *Siam and Laos as Seen by Our American Missionaries*, Philadelphia, 1884, pp. 206–22.

Manich Jumsai, *Mọm luang, Compulsory Education in Thailand*, 1st ed. Paris, UNESCO, 1955; 2d ed. Bangkok, Police Press, 1958.

Minney, R. J., *Fanny and the Regent of Siam*, London, Collins, 1962.

Moffat, Abbot Low, *Mongkut, the King of Siam*, Ithaca, N.Y., Cornell University Press, 1961.

Mookerji, Radha Kumud, *Ancient Indian Education*, London, Macmillan, 1947.

Morant, Sir Robert L., *Ladder of Knowledge Series. Volume IV. Fifty Steps Towards English Composition, with Special Reference to the Difficulties of the English Verbs*, Bangkok, Government Education Office, 1891.

Mosel, James N., "A Poetic Translation from the Siamese: Prince Damrong's Reply in Verse to Rama V," *Journal of the Siam Society*, 47, pt. 1 (June, 1959), 103–11.

Norman, Sir Henry, *The Peoples and Politics of the Far East*, New York, Charles Scribner's Sons, 1895.

———, "Urgency in Siam," *Contemporary Review*, 64 (1893), 737–48.

Pallegoix, Jean Baptiste, *Description du royaume thai ou siam*, 2 vols. Paris, 1854.

Pensri (Suvanij) Duke, *Les Relations entre la France et la Thaïlande (Siam) au XIXe siècle, d'après les archives des affaires étrangeres,* Bangkok, Chalermnit, 1862.

Prachoom Chomchai, ed. and tr., *Chulalongkorn the Great: A Volume of Readings Edited and Translated from Thai Texts,* Tokyo, The Centre for East Asian Cultural Studies, 1965.

Schouten, Joost, *Siam 250 Years Ago: A Description of the Kingdom of Siam,* Bangkok, Bangk'olem Press, 1889.

Schweisguth, P., *Étude sur la littérature siamoise,* Paris, Imprimerie Nationale, 1951.

Senn van Basel, W. H., *Schetsen uit Siam,* Amsterdam, J. H. de Bussy, 1880.

Smith, B. A., "The King of Siam," *Contemporary Review,* 71, (1897), 884–91.

Smith, Malcolm, *A Physician at the Court of Siam,* London, Country Life, 1946.

Smith, Samuel J., tr., *Siamese Domestic Institutions: Old and New Laws on Slavery,* Bangkok, 1880.

Smyth, H. Warington, *Five Years in Siam, From 1891 to 1896,* 2 vols. London, John Murray, 1898.

Swat Sukonterangsi, "The Development of Governmental Control of Public Education in Thailand," Ph.D. diss., Indiana University, 1961.

Tasniya Isarasena, "The Development of Elementary Education in Thailand," Ph.D. diss., University of Wisconsin, 1953.

Thamsook (Ratanapun) Numnonda, "The Anglo-Siamese Negotiations 1900–1909," Ph.D. diss., University of London, 1966.

Thiphakǫrawong, Čhaophraya (Kham Bunnag), *The Dynastic Chronicles, Bangkok Era, The Fourth Reign,* 3 vols. Tokyo, Centre for East Asian Cultural Studies, 1965–67.

United States, Consulate, Thailand, *Despatches from United States Consuls in Bangkok, 1856–1906,* File Microcopies of Records in the National Archives, No. T–134, 11 reels of microfilm, Washington, D.C., National Archives, 1959.

United States, Department of the Interior, Bureau of Education, *Progress of Western Education in China and Siam,* Washington, D.C., Government Printing Office, 1880.

Vella, Walter F., *The Impact of the West on Government in Thailand,* Berkeley and Los Angeles, University of California Press, 1955.

———, *Siam Under Rama III,* Locust Valley, N.Y., J. J. Augustin, 1957.

Vincent, Frank, Jr., *The Land of the White Elephant,* London, Sampson, Low and Searle, 1873.

Vliet, Jeremias van, "Translation of Jeremias van Vliet's Description of the Kingdom of Siam," tr. L. F. van Ravenswaay, *Journal of the Siam Society, 7, pt. 1* (1910), 1–108.

Wales, H. G. Quaritch, *Ancient Siamese Government and Administration,* London, Bernard Quaritch, 1934.

Wells, Kenneth E., *Thai Buddhism: Its Rites and Activities,* 2d ed. Bangkok, 1960.

Wira Wimoniti, *Historical Patterns of Tax Administration in Thailand,* Bangkok, Institute of Public Administration, Thammasat University, 1961.

Wyatt, David K., "The Beginnings of Modern Education in Thailand, 1868–1910." Ph.D. diss., Cornell University, 1966.

———, "The Diaries of King Chulalongkorn," *Bulletin of the School of Oriental and African Studies, 31* (June 1968), pp. 382–85.

———, "Education and the Modernization of Thai Society," in *Persistence and Change in Thai Society,* ed. G. William Skinner (Homage to Lauriston Sharp, vol. 2, Ithaca, Cornell University Press, forthcoming).

———, "Family Politics in Nineteenth Century Thailand," *Journal of Southeast Asian History, 9* (Sept. 1968), pp. 208–28.

———, "Samuel McFarland and Early Educational Modernization in Thailand, 1877–1895," in *Felicitation Volumes of Southeast-Asian Studies Presented to His Highness Prince Dhaninivat,* Bangkok, Siam Society, 1965, *1,* 1–16.

———, and Constance M. Wilson, "Thai Historical Materials in Bangkok," *Journal of Asian Studies, 25* (Nov. 1965), 105–18.

Yen Lavangkura, "The Administration of Religious Affairs: A Study of the Relationship between the Government and the Sangha in Thailand," M.A. thesis, Thammasat University, 1962.

Young, Ernest, *The Kingdom of the Yellow Robe,* London, Archibald Constable, 1898.

Index